1986

University of St. Francis
GEN 891.73 S180g
Saltykov, Mikhail Evgrafo
The Golovlevs /

W9-CLF-761

THE WO[R]

THE G[

M. E. SALTYKOV (pen-name 'Shchedrin') was born in 1826 of landed gentry stock. As a young civil servant in St Petersburg in the 1840s he moved in intellectual and literary circles, and published his first story in 1847. In 1848 he was exiled to Vyatka for the 'subversive' tone of another story and spent seven years there working as an official in the provincial administration. After returning to St Petersburg in 1855 he continued his official career, at the same time becoming a regular contributor to major journals in the capital, especially the radical *Contemporary*. In 1868 he retired from government service and devoted himself entirely to literary and journalistic work. From 1868 to 1884 he was one of the editors (from 1877 chief editor) of the leading radical monthly *Notes of the Fatherland*, in which the bulk of his writings were published. After *Notes of the Fatherland* was suppressed in 1884, he continued writing for other journals until his death in 1889. Saltykov is best known as Russia's greatest satirist: for more than thirty years in his pungent and amusing monthly articles and sketches he maintained an unflagging attack on the backwardness of Russia's social institutions, the tyranny and ineptitude of officialdom, the predatoriness of the new bourgeois capitalist, and the political pusillanimity of the educated classes. Though much of his work was high-quality journalism concerned with the issues of the day, Saltykov showed himself to be a major literary talent in works such as the *Fables*, *The History of a Town*, and *The Golovlevs*, which is acknowledged to be his masterpiece.

I. P. FOOTE teaches Russian at Oxford, where he is a Fellow of The Queen's College. His publications include articles on Saltykov, an edition of his satirical writings, and the first English translation of *The History of a Town*. He has also published translations of Lermontov and Tolstoy.

THE WORLD'S CLASSICS

M. E. SALTYKOV-SHCHEDRIN

The Golovlevs

Translated by
I. P. FOOTE

Oxford   New York
OXFORD UNIVERSITY PRESS
1986

LIBRARY
College of St. Francis
JOLIET, ILLINOIS

Oxford University Press, Walton Street, Oxford OX2 6DP

Oxford New York Toronto
Delhi Bombay Calcutta Madras Karachi
Kuala Lumpur Singapore Hong Kong Tokyo
Nairobi Dar es Salaam Cape Town
Melbourne Auckland
and associated companies in
Beirut Berlin Ibadan Nicosia

Oxford is a trade mark of Oxford University Press

The Golovlevs first published in book form 1880
This translation first published 1986
Introduction, Further reading, Chronology, Translation
and Notes © I. P. Foote 1986

All rights reserved. No part of this publication may be reproduced,
stored in a retrieval system, or transmitted, in any form or by any means,
electronic, mechanical, photocopying, recording, or otherwise, without
the prior permission of Oxford University Press

This book is sold subject to the condition that it shall not, by way
of trade or otherwise, be lent, re-sold, hired out or otherwise circulated
without the publisher's prior consent in any form of binding or cover
other than that in which it is published and without a similar condition
including this condition being imposed on the subsequent purchaser

British Library Cataloguing in Publication Data
Saltykov-Shchedrin, M. E.
The Golovlevs.—(World's classics)
I. Title II. Foote, I. P. III. Gospoda
Golovlevy. English
891.73'3 [F] PG3361.S3G6
ISBN 0-19-281616-0

Library of Congress Cataloging in Publication Data
Saltykov, Mikhail Evgrafovich, 1826–1889.
The Golovlevs.
(The world's classics)
Translation of: Gospoda Golovlevy.
I. Foote, I. P. (Irwin Paul) II. Title.
ISBN 0-19-281616-0 (pbk.)
PG3361.S3G613 1986 891.73'3 85–21629

Set by Grove Graphics
Printed in Great Britain by
Hazell Watson & Viney Limited
Aylesbury, Bucks

891.73
5180g

CONTENTS

120, 161

ACKNOWLEDGEMENTS

I should like to acknowledge with gratitude the help and advice generously given to me in the preparation of this translation by Marina Fennell, the late Iosif Gilinsky, Irina Nikolaeva, Dmitry Nikolaev, Emma Shotton, and Virginia Llewellyn Smith.

INTRODUCTION

MIKHAIL EVGRAFOVICH SALTYKOV (1826–89), who wrote under the pseudonym of Shchedrin, was a leading figure in Russian letters from the 1850s to the 1880s. With the exception of *The Golovlevs*, however, what he wrote is little known abroad. His work as a writer was chiefly devoted to comment on the events and movements taking place in Russian society in his own day and this specific, now historical, interest makes his writings largely unexportable in translation. He was a major contributor to the leading radical journals of the time *The Contemporary* and *Notes of the Fatherland* (both suppressed by government order) and enjoyed wide popularity and prestige for his sharply observed and pungently written essays and satirical sketches on the state of contemporary Russia. Born of a landowning family (partly the inspiration of the Golovlevs), educated in St Petersburg, condemned as a young civil servant to seven years of exile for the too-liberal tone of an early story, later a high-ranking official in the provincial administration, he had, when he came to be a full-time writer, a wealth of experience and a profound understanding of his country which qualified him admirably as a chronicler and commentator of his times. It was Turgenev's opinion that Saltykov 'knew Russia better than any living man'. His knowledge of Russia gave him a deeply negative view of its society and institutions, which he characterized as being ruled by 'arbitrariness, hypocrisy, lying, rapacity, treachery, and vacuity', and he saw it as his task as a writer to denounce and destroy this rule. The major themes of his work were official Russia and the social condition of the country in the period of change and reform that came with the accession of Alexander II after the long winter of Nicholas I's reign. Saltykov found little fundamental difference between Russia reformed and Russia unreformed: in political, economic, and social life he noted the persistence of the same features as before. The unchanging nature of the Russian state system, characterized by tyranny, subservience, and folly, was the subject of his most celebrated satirical work *The History of a Town*, published in 1870.

Saltykov's standard literary product was the monthly narrative or discursive sketch, usually one of a series, on some topic or trend of the day. It was in such a group of sketches that *The Golovlevs* had its origin. In 1872 Saltykov had begun a sketch-cycle entitled *Well-Intentioned Speeches*. It was intended, as he later explained in a letter to E. I. Utin, to expose the falseness of those principles which the contemporary 'establishment' declared to be the 'bases of society'—the principles of *family, property,* and *state*. 'Family Court', the opening chapter of *The Golovlevs*, first appeared as a part of this cycle in October 1875 and was soon followed by 'Kith and Kin'. The success of these early parts (they were especially praised by Turgenev) encouraged Saltykov to expand the 'Golovlev' theme into a full-length novel. Within a fifteen-month period he had written six instalments, then after an interval of over three years he completed the last chapter 'The Reckoning', which was published in 1880. In the same year *The Golovlevs* appeared as a separate volume.

'It was to attack the family principle that I wrote *The Golovlevs*,' Saltykov declared in his letter to Utin. That it certainly did, but, in fact, the novel took on a much wider scope, in that Saltykov chose to illustrate his theme of the instability of the family as a fundament of society by the example of a gentry landowning family, with the result that the novel acted not only as a rejection of the 'family' principle, but also as an indictment of a whole social class. Both the family theme and that of the landowner were already familiar in Russian literature. The family theme had been popularized in the 1850s, especially by Tolstoy (*Childhood, Adolescence, Youth*, later *War and Peace*) and Sergey Aksakov (*Family Chronicle, Childhood Years*). The theme of the provincial landowner (serf-owner, too, until 1861) had been widely explored in the works of Gogol, Turgenev, Goncharov, Tolstoy, and others. These works had in general taken a sympathetic, even sentimental, view of the family and had peopled the 'gentry nests' they described with generally amiable, cultivated individuals with higher, if frustrated, aspirations. Saltykov, writing in the 1870s, took a more sombre view of both matters. He saw the family as denatured and unstable (a feature of the age reflected also in *Anna Karénina* and *The Brothers Karamazov*, written about the same time as *The Golovlevs*) and he saw the landowning class from its obverse, uncouth side which earlier gentry writers—Gogol apart—had largely ignored. In its treatment of the landowner theme *The Golovlevs* was also apt to its time—the picture of decline it presents fitted well with the period of the novel's action (from *c*.1855 to the late 1870s), which for the landowning class was a time of crisis and change: the emancipation of the serfs in 1861 not only removed from the landowners the age-long prop of a free and tributary labour-force, it also created a new economic situation with which many gentry landowners found it impossible to cope.

Saltykov presents his gentry family, the Golovlevs, in three generations: Arina Petrovna and her husband Vladimir Mikhailych; their sons Stepan, Porfiry, and Pavel (a daughter, Anna, is dead); and their grandchildren Petya and Volodya (sons of Porfiry) and Anninka and Lyubinka (orphaned daughters of Anna). It is on family relationships that the noval concentrates. The Golovlevs (with the exception of Anninka and Lyubinka) are seen only within the confines of the family nest, Golovlevo, and the neighbouring Dubrovino and Pogorelka. There is no contact with characters outside the family circle; external events make no impingement on their lives. The moral corruption of the family is an internal process unattributable to malign influences beyond the family itself. The vitality of the Golovlevs has been sapped by generations of idleness and social irrelevance. 'Idleness, incapacity for any activity whatsoever, and hard drinking' are the symptoms and causes of the *malaise* which afflicts them. As individuals, the Golovlevs are all in some way corrupted or inadequate, vicious or inept. None lives to any positive purpose. Arina Petrovna amasses wealth which is not used, Vladimir Mikhailych is a tippling old *roué*, Stepan follows his frivolous example, Porfiry is a 'bloodsucking' pettifogger, Pavel a man 'bereft of deeds'; the third generation produces two suicides, a convict, and a ruined alcoholic actress. As members of the family, there is between them no moral bond, no common interest, no affection. The 'family feelings' are hatred, contempt, envy, fear. 'Witch', 'devil', 'bloodsucker', 'Judas', 'murderer', 'scoundrel', 'dolt' are among the Golovlev terms of reference for their kith and kin. The novel's conflicts are between parent and child, brother and brother, and Golovlev falls victim to Golovlev as the stronger bully, torment, and exploit the weak—proclaiming *ad nauseam* as they do so their dedication to the 'family'.

The dominant characters in the family are Arina Petrovna and Porfiry. Arina Petrovna—significantly, not of Golovlev blood—is a forceful, energetic woman who devotes her life to the enlargement of the estate and the accumulation of wealth. She does this 'for the sake of the family', yet so possessed is she by the acquisitive urge that the pursuit of property becomes the sole object of her life. Her family she regards as an encumbrance, a threat to the property *she* has acquired, she prefers to hoard rather than use the produce of the estate, and physically and morally so neglects her children that when they enter life on their own account they are already broken or corrupted in spirit. With her limited perspective, she fails to see the irony that she destroys the family she claims to have toiled to maintain and is aware only of their unworthiness to come into *her* heritage—'Who have I provided for?' is the plaintive refrain of her last years. She is a hard character who has made her way in a hard world, but all for nothing. There is a tragic irony in the skilfully depicted decline of Arina Petrovna from domestic despot to helpless old woman, isolated, dependent, and aware at last of the futility of all her endeavours. In the end her life proves to have been no more than an empty ritual of activity that brought benefit to no one.

'Emptiness' is the principal characteristic of the life of the Golovlevs. Repeatedly Saltykov refers to 'empty' talk, 'empty' minds, 'empty' hearts. This emptiness of the Golovlevs reaches its apogee in Porfiry, who from the third chapter becomes the central character of the novel. Unlike Arina Petrovna's ritual existence, which had at least some relation to practical life, Porfiry is concerned only with form. He has no faith, but is piously devotional, ruins his family but is all for 'kith and kin', litigates regardless of failure or success, delights in business schemes executed solely on paper. Form without substance is the essential characteristic of hypocrisy, and Porfiry ('Judas' and 'Bloodsucker' to his family) is rightly renowned as a classic figure of the humbug. But his hypocrisy is only an aspect of his condition. He is a pathological case of human futility. For him life is a grotesque game in which he systematically performs acts of meanness, petty and gross, accompanied always by some justifying aphorism, text, or proverbial saw. He nauseates by his incessant moralizing and endless drivelling cant. Words too are for him a mere form, their content irrelevant. A peasant remarks of Porfiry that with his talk he could 'fester a man's soul'. This empty talk is a symptom of the emptiness of his life. Porfiry's personality is a vacuum around which he erects a barrier of homiletic talk and pious pretence. He is devoid of all natural affection. He has no inner life: 'For him there exists neither sorrow nor joy, neither hatred nor love. The whole world in his eyes is a tomb fit only to serve as pretext for his endless prattling.' In 'Family Scores' Saltykov pauses to discuss Porfiry's hypocrisy and characterizes it as a specifically Russian phenomenon. Porfiry is no Tartuffe, he says, because in Western Europe the hypocrite is a hypocrite for a cause: in the West there are acknowledged standards to which the hypocrite feels obliged outwardly to conform; in Russia, however, such standards do not exist and so there are no 'principled' hypocrites, but only 'liars, humbugs, and prattlers'. Saltykov is here making a tendentious point in support of the thesis of *Well-Intentioned Speeches*—that there are *no* bases of principle underlying Russian life. He takes a too narrow view of his own creation. Porfiry, well though he fits into Saltykov's perception of contemporary Russia, is more than a national type. This image of spiritual barrenness and ritual living has a significance that transcends the national context and earns Porfiry a place among the 'great' characters of world literature.

The question of how to resolve the character of Porfiry and end the novel caused Saltykov some difficulty. This explains in part why the final chapter was delayed for over three years. In December 1876 the novelist Ivan Goncharov (author of *Oblomov*) expressed the view to Saltykov that a character such as Porfiry was incapable of attaining the clarity of conscience which might cause him to lay hands on himself. Saltykov seems, in the end, to have taken a different view, for in the final chapter this is effectively how he does develop him. Porfiry shows recognition of his guilt and seeks to make amends, even, it seems, to destroy himself. The key to this 'redemption' (if such it can be called) is that, though long suppressed, Porfiry's humanity is not extinct. Some clues to this have been laid by Saltykov in passing references to a flickering of conscience or feeling which Porfiry has promptly extinguished. In the last scene of the novel, however, under the pressure of his mental and physical decline and the taunts of Anninka, the mask of the humbug cracks. For the first time he shows some human feeling to another when to Anninka who has repeated again the story of her degradation and her sister's suicide he responds: 'Poor girl! My poor girl!' Porfiry belongs still, after all, to the human fold.

The reader may, like Goncharov, consider such a twist unlikely and unconvincing. It is, though, not out of keeping with Saltykov's general view of life. His work as a whole was concerned with human shortcomings in public and private life and on the basis of his writings, which reveal such an uncommon percipience of the fallibility of man, it would not be unreasonable to conclude that Saltykov was a pessimist. Yet he was *not* a pessimist. Despite his awareness of human imperfection, there is no cynicism in Saltykov's attitude towards it. The indignity and wretchedness of man appals him because he is concerned for his dignity and well-being, which he believes to be attainable. Bleak though his view of the world was, Saltykov throughout his life retained a faith in the eventual triumph of decent human values. How precisely society was to achieve the leap from its present dire condition to the better future he believed in is never explained. For him the first task was to stir men's consciences to an awareness of the disparity between what they are and what they might be, and it was to this task that he devoted his own energy and talent.

The faint note of hope on which *The Golovlevs* ends does little to detract from its reputation as 'the gloomiest novel in Russian literature' (D. S. Mirsky). The history of the Golovlevs is an unrelieved catalogue of misdeed and misery. No wholesome character, no act of decency finds any place in the family chronicle (significantly, the few charitable deeds recorded are done by peasants who, for all their backwardness, are the moral betters of the Golovlevs). In the course of the novel's twenty-year span all but one of the Golovlevs die—Anninka alone barely survives at the end, doomed to an early death by drink and consumption. Chapter by chapter the deaths are recorded: Stepan, Pavel, Vladimir Mikhailych, Volodya, Arina Petrovna, Petenka, Lyubinka, Porfiry—the novel is, as a critic has described it, 'one long obituary'. As they approach their end, the principal characters (Arina Petrovna, her sons, Anninka) are overtaken by a consciousness of the sterility of their lives and seek refuge from this truth in mental fantasies, drink, or both. There is a cyclic pattern in the descriptions of the death agony of these characters: days spent in aimless gazing from windows and vindictive daydreaming, nights spent in drinking, raking up the past, mentally paying off old scores, and then oblivion as they sink into the void of drunkenness.

The setting is in harmony with the grim life of the Golovlevs. They live in still, stuffy houses set in the midst of bleak, empty fields. The weather is almost always inclement, with snow, sleet, rain, and seas of black mud. The dull, clouded landscapes are matched by the dimly lit interiors of the Golovlev dwellings. The Golovlevs live in a perpetual dusk which is linked symbolically with the moral dusk of their lives. They shun the daylight and, when evening comes, they welcome the onset of the darkness which will obscure for them the reality of their condition. Confined to their manor-houses, they are remote even from the life that goes on around them: they look outside from their windows at peasants toiling in far-away fields, and inside their own homes they are cut off from the daily activities of the household, which they hear as distant sounds in other parts of the house. Golovlevo itself stands as a symbol of the moribundity of the family: 'Coffin! Coffin! Coffin!' echoes in Stepan's ears as he returns, spent, to die in his old home, while for Anninka 'Golovlevo—that was death itself, malign, empty-hearted; it was death, ever watchful for some fresh victim'.

This sombre intensity is characteristic of Saltykov's manner of writing. He was not one for delicate tones, but for strong effects. In *The Golovlevs* he transferred his publicistic manner to the literary genre. He does not write detachedly, his language is neither neutral nor restrained. He applies to Porfiry the nick-names 'Judas' and 'Bloodsucker' as if he himself were a Golovlev, mimics Porfiry's constant references to Arina Petrovna as 'Mother dear', and shows the cutting sarcasm which he so effectively employed in his satires—for instance, when he speaks of Porfiry's customary benignant manner 'from which it was impossible to tell whether he was going to be nice to you or suck your blood'. Saltykov's powerful descriptions and analytical digressions may sometimes strike the gentler reader as being over-strong, but for these dense passages there is compensation in the uninhibited verve of the dialogue. The essence of the novel and its characters is contained in the series of conversational duels that takes place between the main protagonists, and it is in these that Saltykov shows his greatest stylistic mastery. What Turgenev said about his unrivalled knowledge of Russia could as well be said of his knowledge of the different modes of the Russian language. The speech of the characters is admirably observed and authentically presented—the richly expressive colloquial language of Arina Petrovna, the footling baby-talk of Porfiry, the modish jargon of Stepan and Petya, the vulgarly pretentious locutions of Kukishev. These features are, alas, those which inevitably suffer most from the hand of a translator, and the English reader must take on trust the varied richness of the original language.

The thematic and stylistic power of *The Golovlevs* makes it one of the most notable works of nineteenth-century Russian fiction. Saltykov's robust literary talent and his deep concern for the cause of humanity are to be found in all he wrote, but because of their generally fragmented form and restricted topical reference none of his other works can make the same telling impression on the general reader as *The Golovlevs*. It is fitting that Saltykov wrote at least one work by which foreign readers, unattuned to the issues and polemics of his day, can discover something of his merits as a writer. If, outside Russia, Saltykov's literary reputation must rest more or less entirely on *The Golovlevs*, it can fairly be said that it rests on a firm foundation.

I. P. FOOTE

FURTHER READING

TRANSLATIONS OF OTHER WORKS
BY SALTYKOV-SHCHEDRIN

Fables, tr. Vera Volkhovsky (London, 1931 and 1941, repr. Westport, Conn., 1977).

Tales from M. Saltykov-Shchedrin, tr. D. Rothenberg (Moscow, 1956).

The History of a Town, tr. I. P. Foote (Oxford, 1980).

The History of a Town, tr. Susan Brownsberger (Ann Arbor, 1982).

The Pompadours, tr. D. Magarshack (Ann Arbor, 1985).

A number of translations of shorter pieces, chiefly his prose fables, have appeared in various collections of Russian short stories.

WORKS ON SALTYKOV-SHCHEDRIN

N. Strelsky, *Saltykov and the Russian Squire* (New York, 1940, repr. 1966).

K. Sanine, *Saltykov-Chtchédrine, sa vie et ses œuvres* (Paris, 1953). See also:

H. Gifford, *The Russian Novel* (London, 1964).

V. S. Pritchett, *The Living Novel* (London, 1946) ('The Hypocrite', pp. 226–32, on Porfiry Golovlev).

ARTICLES ON *THE GOLOVLEVS*

I. P. Foote, 'M. E. Saltykov-Shchedrin: *The Golovlyov Family*', *Forum for Modern Language Studies*, iv(1), 1968.

Karl D. Kramer, 'Satiric Form in Saltykov's *Gospoda Golovlevy*', *Slavic and East European Review*, xiv(4), 1970.

William Mills Todd III, 'The Anti-Hero with a Thousand Faces: Saltykov-Shchedrin's Porfiry Golovlev', *Studies in Literary Imagination*, ix (1), 1976.

M. Ehre, 'A Classic of Russian Realism: Form and Meaning in *The Golovlyovs*', *Studies in the Novel*, ix, 1977.

CHRONOLOGY OF
M. E. SALTYKOV-SHCHEDRIN

1826   Born on family estate in Spas-Ugol, province of Tver (modern Kalinin).

1836–44   Educated in Moscow and at the Tsarskoe Selo *lycée*.

1844   Entered civil service.

1847   First story ('Contradictions') published in *Notes of the Fatherland*.

1848   His story 'A Tangled Affair' deemed subversive: Saltykov exiled to Vyatka, works there in the provincial administration.

1855   Accession of Alexander II. Saltykov permitted to return to St Petersburg.

1856   Continues in government service; resumes writing. First satirical work, *Provincial Sketches*, published 1856–7. Contributes to various journals, principally *The Contemporary*.

1858–62   Vice-Governor of Ryazan province (1858–60) and of Tver province (1860–2).

1862   Leaves government service. Joins editorial staff of *The Contemporary*.

1864   Resumes official career. Senior postings in Penza (1865–6), Tula (1866–7), and Ryazan (1867–8).

1868   Retires from government service. Becomes joint-editor (with N. A. Nekrasov and G. Z. Eliseev) of *Notes of the Fatherland*, to which he is a principal contributor.

1875   Serious illness. Prolonged stay in France and Germany (until summer 1876) for health reasons.

1877   After Nekrasov's death, becomes chief editor of *Notes of the Fatherland*.

1881   Assassination of Alexander II.

1884   *Notes of the Fatherland* closed by government order.

1884–   Saltykov's works published in *Herald of Europe* and *Russian News*.

1889   Dies in St Petersburg.

Principal writings (sketch-cycles, larger works): *Provincial Sketches* (1856–7); *Satires in Prose* (1857–63); *Signs of the Times* (1863–71); *Pompadours and Pompadouresses* (1863–74); *The History of a Town* (1869–70); *Fables* (1869–86); *Diary of a Provincial in St Petersburg* (1872); *Well-Intentioned Speeches* (1872–6); *The Golovlevs* (1875–80); *A Contemporary Idyll* (1877–83); *The Sanctuary of Mon Repos* (1878–9); *In Foreign Parts* (1880–1); *Letters to Auntie* (1881–2); *The Petty Things of Life* (1886–7); *Old Times of Poshekhonie* (1887–9).

PRINCIPAL CHARACTERS
AND NOTE ON NAMES

THE GOLOVLEV PARENTS

ARINA PETROVNA
VLADIMIR MIKHAILYCH

THEIR CHILDREN

STEPAN VLADIMIRYCH (STEPKA)
PORFIRY VLADIMIRYCH (PORFISHA, PORFISHKA,
'JUDAS')
PAVEL VLADIMIRYCH (PAVLUSHA, PAVLUSHKA,
PASHKA)
ANNA VLADIMIROVNA (ANNUSHKA, ANYUTKA)

PORFIRY'S SONS

VLADIMIR (VOLODYA, VOLODKA, VOLODENKA)
PETR (PETKA, PETENKA)
VLADIMIR (EVPRAKSEYUSHKA'S BABY) (VOLODKA,
VOLODENKA, VOLODYUSHKA)

ANNA'S DAUGHTERS

ANNA SEMENOVNA (ANNINKA, ANYUTKA)
LYUBOV (LYUBINKA)

The name Golovlev (spelt thus in Russian) is pronounced Golovlyov, a fact registered in some transliteration systems, but not in the one used by me. The stress is on the last syllable.

To the non-Russian reader Russian names can be perplexing. The use of forename and patronymic, which may sometimes cause confusion, does not in *The Golovlevs* present any difficulty. There is, though, a fair amount of name modification by which the emotion felt (basically, affection or scorn) by the namer for the named is indicated--thus, Stepka for Stepan, Porfisha for Porfiry, Anninka for Anna, etc. Though these mutations may seem confusing to the uninitiated, the different forms are an important means of expression in Russian and the substitution of the standard name for its derived form detracts something from the tone of the original. In this translation I have chosen to retain the names in the form in which they occur in the Russian text, hoping the reader will find it possible to guess the tone of the form from the context. To avoid confusion I offer here an identification table for the major characters (names of the lower orders are consistently mutated, usually by the demeaning suffix -*ka*). One Golovlev name I have not treated in the way mentioned is 'Judas', Porfiry Golovlev's family nickname. In Russian this appears as 'Iudushka' (standard 'Iuda'), which suggests 'petty Judas': the use of the English form of the name seems necessary to make the point of the nickname clear, and unfortunately the twist provided by the suffix can hardly be rendered in English without distortion (the solution of 'Little Judas' favoured by some translators is not, I think, a happy one).

This translation is dedicated to
SERGEY ALEKSANDROVICH MAKASHIN
editor and biographer of Saltykov,
doyen of Saltykov scholars
on his eightieth birthday

THE GOLOVLEVS

*

FAMILY COURT

ONE day Anton Vasiliev, the bailiff of a distant patrimonial estate, had concluded his report to his mistress, Arina Petrovna Golovleva, concerning his journey to Moscow to collect the quit-rent due from her peasants living there on permit,* and had already received her permission to take himself off to the servants' quarters, when he suddenly began shifting from foot to foot in a mysterious way that suggested that he still had information to lay before her which he could not make up his mind to declare.

Arina Petrovna, who thoroughly comprehended not only the slightest gesture but also the innermost thoughts of her retainers, was immediately concerned.

'What else is there?' she asked, glaring at the bailiff.

'That's all, ma'am,' replied Anton Vasiliev in an attempt at evasion.

'Don't give me that! There is something else; I can see it in your eyes!'

But Anton Vasiliev could not bring himself to answer and continued to shift from one foot to the other.

'Come on, tell me—what have you go to say?' Arina Petrovna demanded sharply, raising her voice. 'Out with it! Don't shilly-shally with me, turncoat!'

Arina Petrovna was fond of bestowing nicknames on members of her administrative and domestic staff. She called Anton Vasiliev 'turncoat' not because he had ever actually been caught in any act of treachery, but because he had a long tongue. The estate of which he was manager had as its centre a considerable market village where there were a great many taverns. Anton Vasiliev liked to take a glass of tea in a tavern and brag of the omnipotence of his mistress, and in the course of this bragging he would inadvertently say more than he should. And since Arina Petrovna constantly had law-suits of various kinds in train, it often happened that the agent, by his garrulity, revealed his mistress's stratagems before they could be put into effect.

'True, there is something else . . .' Anton Vasiliev muttered at last.

'What? What is it?' said Arina Petrovna, perturbed.

As a woman with authority and endowed besides with a fertile imagination, she had in a moment conjured up in her mind visions of every possible contradiction and contrariness to her will and was at once so seized by this prospect that she actually turned pale and sprang from her chair.

'It's Stepan Vladimirych, he's sold the Moscow house . . .' pronounced the bailiff.

'Well?'

'He's sold it, ma'am.'

'Why? How? Don't shilly-shally! Tell me!'

'To pay off his debts . . . It must be that. You don't go selling up for any good cause !'

'It was sold by the police, I suppose? By court order?'

'I suppose so. They say the house was auctioned and went for eight thousand.'

Arina Petrovna sank heavily into her chair and stared at the window. For the first few minutes the news evidently deprived her of her senses. If she had been told that Stepan Vladimirych had murdered somebody, or that the peasants at Golovlevo had risen in revolt and refused to work the master's land, or that the institution of serfdom had collapsed*—she could not have been more thunderstruck. Her lips quivered, her eyes gazed blankly into the distance. She did not even spot Dunyashka the servant-girl, who was about to dash across in front of the window with something hidden under her apron, but on seeing the mistress abruptly stopped, turned, and walked slowly back (such an event at any other time would have been the subject of a thorough investigation). However, at last she recovered and declared:

'A fine caper!'

There ensued a further few minutes' ominous silence.

'So the house, you say, was sold off by the police for eight thousand?' she asked again.

'Yes, ma'am.'

'That was his heritage, his parents' blessing! A fine one he is—the scoundrel!'

Arina Petrovna felt that in view of the news she had received she should at once take some decision, but she could think of nothing, for her mind was in a turmoil of conflicting thoughts. On the one hand, she was thinking: 'Sold off by the police! But they wouldn't do that right off, would they? There must have been an inventory, a valuation, a notice of sale? They sold it for eight thousand and only two years ago I paid out a full twelve thousand for the self-same house. Had I but known, I could have got it for eight thousand myself at the auction!' On the other hand, the thought also occurred to her: 'Sold off by the police for eight thousand! And that was his parents' blessing! The scoundrel! Parting with his parents' blessing for eight thousand roubles!'

'Who did you hear it from?' she asked at last, having finally registered that the house was now already sold and any hope of acquiring it cheaply was thus lost to her for ever.

'Ivan Mikhailov, the tavern-keeper, told me.'

'And why did he not tell me in advance?'

'I suppose he was afeared to.'

'Afeared! I'll give him "afeared"! Have him called from Moscow and when he comes, pack him straight off to the recruiting station* and get him an army haircut! "Afeared", indeed!'

Although serfdom was already coming to an end, it was still in existence. Anton Vasiliev had many times received very peculiar orders from his mistress, but even he was disconcerted by the unexpectedness of her decision in the present case. At the same time he could not help recalling his nickname of 'turncoat'. The peasant Ivan Mikhailov was a sound man, not one you would ever think any disaster might befall. Besides which, he was a close friend, his children's godfather—and now suddenly he was to go for a soldier, and all because he, Anton Vasiliev, like the 'turncoat' he was, had failed to hold his tongue!

'Forgive him . . . forgive Ivan Mikhailych!' he began, attempting to intercede for him.

'Off with you, you . . . conniver!' shouted Arina Petrovna, in such a tone that left him with no thought of persisting in his defence of Ivan Mikhailov.

Before continuing my story, however, let me invite the reader to make closer acquaintance with Arina Petrovna Golovleva and her family situation.

Arina Petrovna is a woman of some sixty years, though still brisk and accustomed to having her own way. She has an awesome bearing; she is in sole and absolute control of the extensive Golovlevo estate, leads a sequestered, thrifty, almost niggardly life, cultivates no friendship with her neighbours, is on good terms with the local authorities, and demands of her children obedience such that, whatever step they take, they should ask themselves: 'What will Mother say?' In general, she has an independent, inflexible, and to a degree fractious disposition— which is considerably fostered by the fact that in the whole Golovlevo estate there is no person from whom she might encounter opposition. Her husband is a frivolous man and a tippler (Arina Petrovna likes to say she is 'neither widow nor wife'); her children either have government posts in Petersburg or have taken after their father and, as 'outcasts', are granted no part in family affairs. In these circumstances Arina Petrovna soon found herself an isolated figure and, if the truth be told, actually got out of the ways of family life—although the word 'family' is constantly on her lips and, ostensibly, her activities are dictated solely by a constant concern to order the affairs of the family.

The head of the family, Vladimir Mikhailych Golovlev, was known from his early years for his shiftless and mischievous character, and in Arina Petrovna, who was always serious and practical by nature, he never evoked any kindred feeling. He led an empty, idle life, most often shutting himself up in his study, where he spent his time doing bird imitations—starlings, cocks, etc.—and composing so-called 'free verse'. In his more effusive moments he would boast of having been a friend of Barkov,* who, he claimed, had even blessed him on his death-bed. Arina Petrovna took an instant dislike to her husband's poems, which she referred to as filth and buffoonery, and since Vladimir Mikhailych had in fact taken a wife for the express purpose of having an audience for his poems ever ready to hand, it was quite clear that before long there would be quarrels. The result of these quarrels, which gradually increased in frequency and bitterness, was that Arina Petrovna came to have a total, contemptuous indifference to her buffoon of a husband, and he a heartfelt hatred for his wife, a hatred which had in it, though, a good measure of rank fear. The husband called his wife 'the witch' and 'the devil', and the wife called her husband 'the windmill' and 'the stringless *balalaika*'. On these terms they had lived together for over forty years without it ever occurring to either that there was anything unnatural in such a way of life. As time went on the mischievous ways of Vladimir Mikhailych not only failed to diminish but actually took a more vicious turn. Apart from his poetic exercises in the manner of Barkov, he began drinking and took pleasure in waylaying the maids in the passage. To begin with, Arina Petrovna regarded this latest pursuit of her husband with distaste and even with disquiet (which, however, stemmed more from the challenge to her authority than actual jealousy), but she then disregarded it and merely took care to see that the hussies did not bring the master any liquor. From then on, having told herself once and for all that her husband was no helpmate to her, she directed her entire attention to one single object—the consolidation of the Golovlevo estate; and indeed, in the forty years of her married life she increased her property tenfold. With astonishing patience and perspicacity she had kept a wary eye open for villages near and far, made confidential enquiries about their owners' relationship with the Board of Guardians,* and never failed to turn up out of the blue when they were auctioned. In the vortex of this fanatical drive to acquire property, Vladimir Mikhailych retreated further and further into the background and in the end became a total recluse. At the moment when our story begins he was already a decrepit old man who hardly ever got out of bed and if on occasion he did leave his bedroom, it was only in order to poke his head through the half-open door of his wife's room and shout 'Devil!', before once more disappearing.

Nor was Arina Petrovna much more fortunate in her children. She was altogether too independent, too much of a 'bachelor', one might say, to see in her children anything but a superfluous burden. The only time she felt at ease was when she was alone with her accounts and estate affairs, when there was nobody to disturb her business discussions with bailiffs, village elders, housekeepers, and so on. In her view, children constituted one of those fated circumstances of life against which, in sum, she felt she had no right to protest, but which none the less touched no chord of her inner being, devoted as it was entirely to the countless practical details of daily life. There were four children—three sons and a daughter. Of the eldest son and the daughter she was reluctant to speak; to her youngest son she was more or less indifferent, and only her middle son, Porfisha, evoked any feeling in her—and that was a feeling of fear rather than affection.

Stepan Vladimirych, the eldest son, who will be the main subject of the present narrative, was known in the family as 'Booby Stepka' or 'Scallywag Stepka'. Very early in life he was numbered among the outcasts and from childhood his household role had been part that of pariah and part that of jester. By ill fortune, he was a gifted lad who only too readily and quickly absorbed the impressions created by the milieu in which he lived. From his father he acquired an inexhaustible capacity for mischief-making, from his mother a quick perception of people's weaker sides. The first quality soon made him his father's darling —which only increased his mother's dislike of him. Often when Arina Petrovna was absent from home on business, the father and adolescent son would retire to the study (which was adorned with a portrait of Barkov), read scurrilous poems, and engage in tittle-tattle—directed in particular against the 'witch', i.e. Arina Petrovna. But the 'witch', as if by instinct, guessed how they spent their time; she would drive unheard up to the front steps, tiptoe to the study door, and listen to their merry talk. For Booby Stepka the consequence was a prompt and cruel thrashing. But Stepka did not give up: he was insensitive to beatings and admonitions alike and half an hour later he was up to his tricks again —cutting up the kerchief of Anyutka the maid, popping flies into the mouth of the sleeping Vasyutka, sneaking into the kitchen to steal a pie (for the sake of economy Arina Petrovna half-starved her children)—which, though, he would straightway share with his brothers.

'Killing's what you need!' was Arina Petrovna's constant refrain. 'I'll kill you—and not answer for it! And the tsar won't punish me either!'

This continual disparagement was not without effect on its soft-natured, heedless recipient. It did not lead to animosity or protest; it created instead a servile character with a taste for buffoonery, lacking all sense of moderation and totally without prudence. Such persons succumb readily to any influence and may become anything—drunkards, spongers, jesters, criminals even . . .

At the age of twenty Stepan Golovlev had completed his schooling in one of the Moscow *gymnasiums* and entered the university. His life as a student was, however, wretched. First, the money provided by his mother was exactly the amount required to keep him from starving; secondly, he proved to have not the slightest vocation for work, but instead was bedevilled by a brilliance which found its chief expression in a facility for mimicry; thirdly, he was afflicted with a constant need for company and could not for a minute bear to be alone. As a result, he cast himself in the undemanding role of hanger-on and *pique-assiette*, and because of his readiness to engage in any escapade he soon became a favourite among the moneyed students. These moneyed students, however, while admitting him to their circle, still clearly understood that he was not one of themselves, but simply a jester, and as such his reputation was established. Having once set himself in this role, he naturally drifted lower and lower and by the end of his fourth year he was good for nothing else. None the less, his ability to follow and memorize anything once heard enabled him to pass the examinations and he received his bachelor's degree.

When he appeared before his mother with his diploma, Arina Petrovna merely shrugged her shoulders and said: 'That's a wonder!' After keeping him a month or so in the country she sent him off to Petersburg with a monthly allowance of one hundred roubles in assignats* to live on. He there began a drifting progress through various government departments and offices; he had no patronage and not the least inclination to make his way in the world by any exertions of his own. The young man's idle mind was so little accustomed to concentration that even such bureaucratic ordeals as preparing a report or the summary of a case proved too much for him. Golovlev's endeavours in Petersburg lasted for four years until in the end he had to admit that there was no prospect of ever establishing himself as anything more than a government clerk. In reply to his complaints Arina Petrovna wrote him a menacing letter which began 'I knew from the start . . .' and ended with an order to present himself in Moscow. There it was resolved by a council of the most regarded Golovlevo peasants that the Booby should be put to serve in the law court under the supervision of an attorney who had for years represented the Golovlev interest there. What Stepan Vladimirych did and how he conducted himself in the court is not known, but three years later he was no longer there. At that point Arina Petrovna decided to take extreme action: she 'tossed a morsel' to her son—a morsel which, incidentally, was also to serve as his 'parents' blessing'. This morsel consisted of the house in Moscow, bought by Arina Petrovna for twelve thousand roubles.

For the first time in his life Stepan Golovlev breathed freely. The house promised to bring in a thousand silver roubles a year, an amount which, compared with what he had had before, seemed a real fortune. He ecstatically kissed his mother's hand ('See you here, though, Booby—don't go expecting any more!' said Arina Petrovna as he did so) and he promised to justify the boon he had been granted. But, alas, he was so little accustomed to handling money and had such an inept understanding of real life that his fabulous thousand a year sufficed for a very short time indeed. Within four or five years he was completely broke and only too happy to stand in for a conscript in the militia then being levied.* The militia, though, had got only as far as Kharkov when the peace was concluded, and Golovlev returned once more to Moscow. His house had by now been sold. He wore his militia uniform, shabby as it was, with trousers untucked over his knee-boots, and he had a hundred roubles in cash in his pocket. With this capital he ventured into speculation—that is, gambling at cards—and before long had lost the lot. He then took to dropping in on the more prosperous peasants of his mother who were working on their own account in Moscow, having dinner with one, cadging a quarter of tobacco or borrowing a copper or two from another. But finally the moment came when he was, so to speak, confronted by a blank wall. He was by now nearly forty and he was forced to recognize that he could no longer keep up this roving life. There was only one road left—the road to Golovlevo ...

The eldest of the Golovlevs after Stepan Vladimirych was the daughter, Anna Vladimirovna, of whom Arina Petrovna also did not care to speak.

The fact was that Arina Petrovna had had intentions for Annushka, and Annushka had not only failed to live up to these aspirations, but instead caused a scandal which reverberated round the whole district. When her daughter left the institute, Arina Petrovna had her to live in the country in the expectation of making of her an unpaid domestic secretary and book-keeper, but, instead of this, one fine night Annushka ran off with Cornet Ulanov and married him.

'Marrying without her parents' blessing, just like a pair of dogs!' Arina Petrovna bemoaned the event. 'It's something at least that he took her to the altar! Anybody else might have used her and flitted off and left you to whistle in the wind for him!'

Arina Petrovna treated her daughter with the same resolution as she had her outcast son—she 'tossed her a morsel'. She settled on her a capital sum of five thousand roubles, a wretched village of thirty souls,* and a tumbledown manor-house where draughts blew through every window and there was scarcely a floorboard that was sound. In a year or two the young couple had spent all the capital and the Cornet had run off, leaving Anna Vladimirovna with a pair of twin daughters, Anninka and Lyubinka. Three months later Anna Vladimirovna herself passed away and Arina Petrovna had no option but to take the orphans under her care. This she did, putting the infants in a wing in the grounds and setting a one-eyed crone called Palashka to look after them.

'God has many mercies,' she said. 'The little orphans won't eat all that much and they'll be a comfort in my old age! The Lord's taken one daughter from me—but given me two in return!'

At the same time she wrote and told her son Porfiry Vladimirych that 'your sister died as wayward as she lived, saddling me with her two whelps ...'

In general, however cynical the observation may appear, it must in all fairness be said that these two events which had occasioned the 'tossing of morsels' did nothing to impair the state of

Arina Petrovna's finances—on the contrary, they even contributed indirectly to the consolidation of the Golovlev estate by
reducing the number of those who would share it. For Arina
Petrovna was a woman of strict principles and once she had
'tossed a morsel', she reckoned that all obligations in respect of
the outcast child to be at an end. It never even entered her calculations that she might one day make some provision for her
orphaned granddaughters. She merely did her utmost to extract
all she could from the small estate she had allotted to Anna
Vladimirovna and deposited the proceeds with the Board of
Guardians. In so doing, she would say:

'I'm putting the money by for the little orphans and take
nothing for what it costs to feed and look after them. For my
bread and salt God, no doubt, will repay me.'

Finally, the two younger children, Porfiry and Pavel Vladimirych, were in government service in Petersburg: the first in the
civil branch, the other in the military. Porfiry was married, Pavel
was a bachelor.

Porfiry Vladimirych was known in the family by three names:
'Judas', 'Bloodsucker', and 'Candid Lad'—nicknames which had
been given him by Booby Stepka when he was still a child. From
his earliest years he had liked to snuggle up to his 'dear mother',
to kiss her slyly on the shoulder, and sometimes, too, to tell her
the odd sneaking tale. Without making a sound, he used to open
the door of her room, creep silently into the corner, and sit and
stare at his mother as if entranced as she busied herself with her
writing or accounts. But even then Arina Petrovna already
regarded the ingratiating ways of her son with some suspicion.
Even then she sensed something enigmatic in the gaze with which
he fixed her, and even then she could not precisely determine
what it exuded: venom or filial piety.

'What's in his eyes I just can't tell,' she reflected sometimes.
'When he looks at you, it's like he was laying a snare—oozing
poison, leading you on!'

And on these occasions she would recall the portentous indica-
tions at the time when she was still carrying Porfisha. There lived
then in the house a certain pious and prescient old man: they
called him 'Holy Porfisha' and Arina Petrovna always consulted

him when she wanted to have foreknowledge of anything in the future. And it was this same old soothsayer who, when asked by her if her time would soon come and if God would present her with a son or a daughter, had made no direct reply but crowed three times like a cock and then mumbled:

'The cock, the cock, sharp in the claw! When the cock crows, look out, the hen! Cluck-cluck goes the hen—but it's too late then!'

And that was all. But three days later (there you are—three times it was he crowed!) she gave birth to a son (there you are again—the cock! the cock!), who was named Porfiry in honour of the ancient seer . . .

The first half of the prophecy was fulfilled; but what could be the meaning of those mysterious words 'Cluck-cluck goes the hen—but it's too late then!'?—it was to this that Arina Petrovna's thoughts kept turning as she surreptitiously looked at him sitting in his corner and eyeing her with that enigmatic look of his.

But Porfisha continued to sit there meekly, without a sound, staring at her so intently that tears came into his fixed, gaping eyes. It was as if he could see the doubts which stirred in his mother's heart and acted on the calculation that even the keenest instinct to distrust would acknowledge itself disarmed when confronted by his meekness. Even at the risk of irritating his mother he hung around her all the time, as if to say 'Look at me! I hide nothing from you! I am all obedience and devotion, and obedience not out of fear but for conscience' sake.' And despite an inner certainty that told her that Porfishka, the villain, was just sucking up to her while his eyes showed clearly that he was laying a snare, nevertheless in the face of such selfless devotion her heart gave way. And her hand automatically picked out the best morsel in the dish to give to her attentive son, even though the very sight of this same son instilled in her a vague dread of something enigmatic and evil.

The complete opposite of Porfiry Vladimirych was represented by his brother Pavel. He was the very embodiment of a man bereft of deeds of any kind. As a boy he had never shown the least inclination for study, games, or company, preferring to exist apart, shunning other people. He would hide sulking in his corner and let his fancy wander. He would imagine that he had eaten oatmeal which made his legs go thin, so that he did not have any lessons. Or that he was not Pavel, the son of gentryfolk, but Davydka the shepherd, that like Davydka he had a lump on his forehead, and that he cracked his whip and did not have any lessons. Arina Petrovna would keep looking at him, and her mother's heart would boil.

'What are you sulking like that for?' she would snap, losing patience with him. 'Or is there some venom at work in you already? Why is it you never come to your mother and say, like, "Give me a kiss, Mother darling"?'

Pavlushka would abandon his corner and come to his mother, stepping slowly as if being pushed from behind.

'Like, give me a kiss, Mother darling,' he repeated in a deep voice unnatural for a child.

'Out of my sight, you slyboots! You think if you hide in your corner that I can't tell what you're up to? I know you inside out, my sweetheart! All your plots and schemes, I can see them clear as day!'

And Pavel, with the same slow steps, went back and hid once more in his corner.

The years went by and gradually Pavel Vladimirych developed into that apathetic, curiously glum kind of personality who will end up as a man bereft of deeds. He may have been good, but to no one did he ever do good; he may even have been quite sensible, but never in all his life did he do a sensible thing. He was hospitable, but no one ever sought to enjoy his hospitality; he liked to spend money, but no one ever had profit or pleasure from his spending; he never gave offence, but no one saw this in him as a virtue; he was an honourable man, but no one was ever heard to say how honourably Pavel Golovlev had behaved on any particular occasion. To crown it all, he quite often snapped back at his mother, though he feared her like the plague. He was, I repeat, a glum man, but beneath the glumness there lay—a lack of deeds and nothing else.

In their mature years the difference in character between the two brothers was most pointedly revealed in their relations with their mother. Judas every week without fail dispatched a lengthy missive to his dear mother, in which he apprised her at length and in detail of life in Petersburg and assured her in the most elaborate terms of his totally selfless filial devotion. Pavel wrote rarely and briefly, even cryptically on occasion, as though every word he wrote had been dragged out of him by pincers. Porfiry Vladimirych, for instance, would write to her:

The money amounting to so much for such and such a period I have received, dear precious Mother, from your agent, the peasant Erofeev, and for the dispatch of the same for my maintenance, according, dear Mother, to your kind indulgence, I express my heartfelt gratitude and with unfeigning filial devotion kiss your hands. What grieves me and torments me with doubt is whether you do not overtax your precious health by your constant concern not only for our needs, but for our fancies?! As for my brother, I do not know, but I . . .

—and so on. On the other hand, Pavel, in the same connection, expressed himself thus:

The money amounting to so much for such and such a period I have, dearest Parent, received and by my reckoning there are still six-and-a-half roubles to come. for requesting which I respectfully beg your pardon.

When Arina Petrovna wrote to admonish her children for extravagance (which she did often enough, though there were no serious grounds for it), Porfisha always meekly submitted to her rebukes and wrote:

I know well, Mother dear, the intolerable burdens you bear on behalf of us, your unworthy children; I know that we all too often fail to justify your maternal solicitude for us and that—worst of all—erring, as man is wont to do—we actually cease to remember this your care, and for this I offer my sincere filial apologies, hoping in time to be rid of this vice and to be prudent in the disbursement of the money remitted to us by you, dear precious Mother, for our maintenance and other expenses.

While Pavel replied: 'Dearest Parent, although you have not yet paid off any debts of mine, your rebuke, in which you refer to me as a "wastrel", I fully accept, and of this I beg you to accept my sincere assurances.' Even Arina Petrovna's letter announcing the death of their sister received from the two brothers quite different responses. Porfiry Vladimirych wrote:

The news that my dear sister and companion of my childhood, Anna Vladimirovna, has passed away filled my heart with grief, a grief made all the greater by the thought that to you, Mother dear, has been sent yet one more cross to bear in the person of her two orphaned infants. Does it not suffice that you, the benefactress of us all, deny yourself everything and devote all your energies, not sparing your health, to provide for your family sufficient and more than sufficient to meet their needs? True, at times, sinful though it is, you cannot help but repine. For you, dearest Mother, I feel the sole resource in the present circumstances is to recall as often as you may the sufferings which Christ himself endured.

Pavel, on the other hand, wrote:

I have received the news of the death of my sister, who has died a victim of circumstances. I hope, though, the Almighty will give her repose in his heavenly mansions, though there is no knowing about that.

Arina Petrovna read over these letters from her sons and tried to tell which of them would be her downfall. She would read Porfiry Vladimirych's letter and it would seem that he would be the evil one.

'Just look at the way he writes! Look at all that claptrap!' she exclaimed. 'Booby Stepka didn't call him Judas for nothing! Why, there's not a word of truth in it! It's all lies! "Mother dear", and my burdens, and my cross—he doesn't feel a thing of it!'

She would then take up a letter of Pavel Vladimirych and again fancy that it was he who would be her evil one.

'He's a dolt, but see the sly way he gets at me. "Of this I beg you to accept my sincere assurances . . ." Really! I'll show you what "accept my sincere assurances" means! I'll toss you a morsel, the same as I did to Booby Stepka—you'll know then what I think of your "assurances"!'

And at the end, there burst from her mother's heart a truly tragic cry of anguish:

'And who am I doing it for, all this hoarding and storing? Going short of sleep, going short of food . . . Who is it for?'

Such was the family situation of the Golovlevs at the time when Anton Vasiliev, the bailiff, informed Arina Petrovna that Booby Stepka had squandered away the 'morsel' he had been tossed, which (because of the low price it had fetched) was now doubly significant as having been his 'parents' blessing'.

Arina Petrovna sat in her bedroom, unable to regain her composure. Something stirred within her and she could not clearly understand what it was. Whether some miraculous access of pity towards the outcast (who was, after all, her son) was involved, or whether it was simply her sense of outraged authority, only the most practised psychologist could tell—so confused and so rapidly shifting were the feelings and sentiments within her. Finally, from the general accumulation of her thoughts one stood out with greater clarity than all others: the fear that the outcast would make himself once more an encumbrance to her.

'Anyutka burdened me with her whelps, and now there'll be the Booby too,' she reckoned.

She sat thus for a long time, never uttering a word and staring blankly through the window. They brought her dinner and she scarcely touched it; they came to ask if the master could have his vodka and, without looking, she tossed them the key to the pantry. After dinner she ordered all the icon-lamps to be lit in the oratory and went and closeted herself there, having first given instructions to stoke up the bath-house. These were all sure signs that the mistress was 'in a temper', and as a result the whole house fell into a death-like silence. The chambermaids went on tiptoe; Akulina, the housekeeper, scurried about like one distracted because it had been arranged to do the jam-making after dinner and now the time had come and the fruit was all washed and ready, but the mistress gave no orders to start or to stop it; Matvey, the gardener, came to ask if it was not time to be picking the peaches, but so vigorously was he told to hush in the maids' room that he beat an immediate retreat.

After saying her prayers and making her ablutions in the

bath-house Arina Petrovna felt somewhat calmed and again summoned Anton Vasiliev to answer for himself.

'Well, what's the Booby up to, then?' she asked.

'Moscow's a big place—you could walk for a year and not cover it all.'

'He's got to eat and drink, though, hasn't he?'

'He gets his keep from our peasants there. He takes his dinner with one and gets a copper or two from another for his baccy.'

'And who said they could give it to him?'

'Come now, ma'am! How could the peasants take offence! If they give to the poor what are strangers to them, would they refuse their own masters?'

'I'll teach them charity! I'll pack the Booby off to your village and the lot of you can keep him at your own expense.'

'It's for you to say, ma'am.'

'What? What's that?'

'I said, ma'am, it's for you to say. If you so order, we'll provide for him.'

' "We'll provide for him"—a fine thing that is! Don't bandy words when you talk to me!'

There is silence. But not for nothing was Anton Vasiliev nicknamed 'turncoat' by his mistress. He cannot contain himself and again starts shifting from foot to foot, burning to tell her something.

'He really is a rascal!' he declares at last. 'They say that when he came back after the campaign he brought a hundred roubles with him. It's not that much, a hundred roubles, but it's enough to live on for a bit.'

'And?'

'Well, you see, he reckoned on making good, so he speculated . . .'

'Come on, out with it! Don't shilly-shally!'

'Well, you see, he took it down to the German Club,* thinking as how he'd find some stupid chap there he could pluck at cards, but instead he fetched up against a sharp one. He made a dash for it, but they say as they caught him in the hallway. Took all his money they did!'

'And gave him a beating too, no doubt?'

'Yes, and that. Next day he comes round to Ivan Mikhailych and tells him about it himself. And the funny thing was—he laughed . . . very cheery he was, as if he'd been given a pat on the head!'

'Serves him right! As long as he never shows his face here!'

'But I reckon that's what'll happen.'

'What's that! I won't let him inside the house!'

'That's what'll happen though, there's no other way,' repeats Anton Vasiliev. 'Ivan Mikhailych said he let it slip himself. "I quit!" said he, "I'll go back to the old woman and live with her on bread and water!" And truth to tell, ma'am, he's got nowhere else to go except here. He can't keep on for long living off the peasants in Moscow. He'll need clothes, too, and a bit of peace . . .'

This was the very thing Arina Petrovna had feared, it was the very essence of that vague presentiment which had subconsciously troubled her. Yes, he would come, there was nowhere else for him to go—it was inescapable. He would be there, for ever in her sight, contrary, outcast, forgotten! Why had she tossed him that 'morsel'? She thought that once he had had 'his due' he would be gone for good—and here he was now coming to life again! He would arrive and make demands and plague everybody with his beggarly look. And his demands would have to be met, for he was a brazen fellow, fit to cause all kinds of trouble. You couldn't keep *him* locked up out of the way; *he* was capable of appearing in his ragamuffin garb even before strangers, capable of causing a scandal, or running to the neighbours with tales of all the closest secrets of the Golovlev affairs. Should she perhaps have him sent off to the Suzdal monastery?*—but who knew if this Suzdal monastery still existed, or if it really did exist for the purpose of removing refractory offspring from the sight of their aggrieved parents. There was a 'house of correction' too, so they said . . . but then, how would you get a great lout forty years old delivered to such a place? In short, Arina Petrovna was completely put out by the very thought of all the ills that threatened to disturb the peace of her existence with the arrival of Booby Stepka.

'I'll send him to your village! You can feed him at your own cost!' she threatened the bailiff. 'Not at the village cost either, but your own!'

'What should you do that for, ma'am?'

'To put a stop to your crowing. Craw! craw! "That's what will happen, there's no other way!" Out of my sight, you . . . crow, you!'

As Anton Vasiliev turned on his left foot to go, Arina Petrovna halted him again.

'Hold now! Wait a minute! So it's true he's making for Golovlevo?' she asked him.

'Why would I tell you lies, ma'am? It's true—he said: "I'll go back to the old woman and live with her on bread and water!" '

'I'll show him what sort of bread the old woman's got in store for him!'

'But why bother, ma'am? He'll not that long abide with you.'

'What do you mean?'

'He's coughing something terrible, keeps catching hold to his left side . . . He'll not last long!'

'The likes of him, my friend, live longer than anybody else! He'll outlive the lot of us! Coughs and coughs, does he—what's it to him, the great lanky lout! Well, we'll see. Go now: I must take steps.'

Arina Petrovna spent the whole evening thinking and finally decided on summoning a family council to determine the Booby's fate. Making such constitutional gestures was not in her nature, but on this occasion she resolved to depart from the traditions of autocratic rule in order to have a decision made by the whole family to protect herself from the censure of well-meaning people. She had, however, no doubts about the outcome of the impending family council, and it was with an easy mind that she sat down to write the letters instructing Porfiry and Pavel Vladimirych to come at once to Golovlevo.

While all this was happening, the party responsible for all this commotion, Booby Stepka himself, was already making his way from Moscow in the direction of Golovlevo. In Moscow at Rogozhskaya Bar* he had taken a seat in one of the 'diligences' in which small dealers and peasant traders used to travel in times past (and still today in a few places) when setting off on a visit to their home parts. The diligence was bound for Vladimir and that same tender-hearted tavern-keeper, Ivan Mikhailych, was taking Stepan Vladimirych at his own expense, having secured him a seat and providing his food during the whole journey.

'Yes, you do that then, Stepan Vladimirych: you get off at the turn and walk the rest of the way: go in to your mother dressed as you are,' said Ivan Mikhailych as they discussed what he should do.

'Oh, yes, yes,' agreed Stepan Vladimirych. 'Not all that far to walk is it—only fifteen versts!* I'll be there in no time! And turn up all covered in dust and dung!'

'When your mother sees you in that rig-out, she'll maybe have pity on you.'

'Have pity on me? Oh, yes, she's sure to—a very kind old lady, my mother!'

Stepan Golovlev is not yet forty, but from his appearance you would take him to be fifty at least. Life has so jaded him that there is no sign now of his gentry birth, not the faintest indication that he once attended the university and had addressed to him the improving word of science. He is an extremely lanky fellow, uncombed, practically unwashed, lean from undernourishment, with a sunken chest and long, grasping arms. His face is bloated, his hair and beard dishevelled and heavily streaked with grey; his voice is loud, but hoarse and croupy; his eyes are bulging and inflamed—the result partly of excessive indulgence in vodka and partly of constant exposure to the wind. He is dressed in an ancient grey militia jacket, quite threadbare and stripped of the braid, which has been sold for melting; beneath his trousers he wears knee-boots which are worn, rusted, and patched. The militia jacket is undone and reveals underneath a shirt so black it might have been rubbed with soot—which, with true militia cynicism, he calls his 'flea-bag'. He looks sullen and grim; the grimness is not, though, the expression of some inner discontent, but comes from a certain vague apprehension that at any moment he might, like a worm, perish from hunger.

He talks incessantly, rambling from one topic to another; he talks when Ivan Mikhailych is listening and he talks when Ivan

Mikhailych has been lulled to sleep by the music of his discourse. He is fearfully uncomfortable in the diligence. There are four people in it and it is therefore necessary to sit with one's legs bent double, which after three or four versts causes the knees to ache excruciatingly. However, despite the pain, he talks incessantly. Clouds of dust pour through the window of the conveyance; from time to time the slanting rays of the sun creep in and the inside of the diligence seems suddenly seared by fire—but still he talks on and on.

'Yes, old boy, I've had my troubles in life,' he told Ivan Mikhailych. 'It's time now I put my feet up! I shan't eat her out of house and home, after all, and there's bound to be the odd crust going! What do you think, Ivan Mikhailych?'

'Your mother's got crusts aplenty!'

'Only not for me—is that what you mean? Yes, my friend, she's got piles of cash, but to me she'd grudge giving a copper of it. She's always hated me she has, the old witch! Why should she? Well, she won't have it her way now, old boy. I've nothing to lose and I'll choke something out of her all right: if she tries to kick me out, I shan't go, and if she won't feed me, I'll help myself. I did service for my country, old boy, and everybody's got a duty to help me. All I'm afraid of is that she won't let me have any tobacco—a bad business that'd be!'

'You'll be kissing goodbye to your baccy, that's for sure!'

'Then I'll get on to the bailiff. That bald-pated devil can give some to his master!'

'He can give you some right enough—but what if your mother tells him not to?'

'Well, then I'm sunk. Tobacco's the last luxury left from my old days of glory! Time was, old boy, when I was flush, I'd get through a quarter of Zhukov's* a day!'

'You'll be kissing goodbye to vodka as well.'

'A bad business that'll be too. Why, vodka is even good for my health—it cuts the phlegm. When we were on the march to Sevastopol, old boy, why, we'd put away a couple of gallons a head before we even got to Serpukhov!'*

'Plastered, were you?'

'I can't recall. Something of the sort. I went all the way to

Kharkov, old boy, and stone me if I remember a thing about it! I can just remember going on and on through villages and towns, and then in Tula the liquor-contractor made us a speech. Shed tears he did, the scoundrel! Yes, those were hard times for dear old Mother Holy Russia! Those liquor-contractors, those suppliers and receivers of stores!* It's a marvel she survived!'

'But your mother made a nice little profit out of it, too. Half the men who went to fight from our village never came back and now they say as there's to be an exemption warrant* for every one such of them. And a warrant costs more than four hundred roubles if you buy one official.'

'Oh, yes, old boy, our mother's a smart woman! She ought to be a minister instead of skimming jam at Golovlevo. Do you know what? She's not been fair to me, treated me badly she has —but still I respect her! Clever as the deuce she is, and that's the main thing! But for her, where would we be now? We'd have nothing but Golovlevo—and a hundred and one and a half serfs! But she—just look at all the property she's bought up—it's a devilish lot!'

'Your brothers will be well-off!'

'That they will. And I'll end up with nothing, that's for sure! I'm down the drain, old boy. My brothers will be rich, though— especially the Bloodsucker. He'd worm his way in anywhere. And the time will come when he'll do for the old witch herself: he'll suck her dry—property and capital. I've got a prophetic eye for these things! Brother Pavel, though, he's a good fellow; he'll send me tobacco on the sly—you'll see. Soon as I get to Golovlevo, I'll drop him a line: "My dear brother, blah-blah-blah, console and comfort me!" Oh dear, oh dear! If only I was rich!'

'And if you were, what would you do?'

'First, I'd shower you with gold . . .'

'Me? What for? You should think of yourself—I'm well content, by your mother's mercy.'

'No, just a minute, *attendez*, old boy! I'd make you commander-in-chief and put you in charge of all the estates! Yes, dear fellow, you've fed and warmed an old soldier—and thanks be to you for that! If it weren't for you, I'd be hoofing it now to the ancestral home on Shanks's pony! And I'd give you your freedom too, like a shot, and put all my treasures at your disposal—so you could eat, drink, and be merry! And what did you think I'd do, old friend?'

'Oh, don't you have concern for me, sir. What else would you do, though, if you were rich?'

'The second thing I'd do would be to get myself a nice piece of skirt! When I was in Kursk I went to make my devotions at our Virgin Lady's, and there was one there—a real peach! A lively piece she was, couldn't keep still a minute!'

'But she'd maybe not have been keen to take you on?'

'What's money for! What's the purpose of filthy lucre! If a hundred thousand's not enough, take two hundred! When I'm flush, old boy, I'll go the whole hog to have a good time! As a matter of fact, I did make her a bid of three roubles through the corporal—but the little minx said she wanted five!'

'And you were short of five at the time?'

'I really can't say, old boy. I tell you the whole thing was like a dream. She might even have come along with me and I've forgotten. The whole way, two whole months—I've forgotten everything. That's never happened to you, I suppose?'

But Ivan Mikhailych is silent. Stepan Vladimirych looks closely at him and sees that his companion is rhythmically nodding his head and from time to time, when his nose almost touches his knees, gives an awkward start before proceeding to nod once more in time with the motion.

'Ah me!' he says. 'Rocked you to sleep, has it? Want to get your head down! You've got too fat, old boy, on all that tavern tea and victuals! And I can't sleep at all, just can't, and that's that! Still, what about a bit of jollification? Perhaps some fruit of the vine . . .'

Golovlev looks round and establishes that all the other passengers are asleep too. The merchant sitting next to him keeps bumping his head against the cross-member, but he sleeps on. His face is shiny as if coated with varnish, and flies are swarming around his mouth.

'Now if I were to assist the passage of all those flies into his maw, that'd really shake him!' With this bright idea in mind, he is already advancing a stealthy hand towards the merchant to execute his plan, when he recalls something and stops short.

'No, no more pranks—that's all done with! Sleep, my friends, enjoy your repose! And in the meantime I'll . . . now, where did he stow that bottle? Ah, there it is, the darling! Come on, come on, this way! Oh L-o-ord, save thy p-e-eople!' he sings under his breath, as he extracts the vessel from the canvas bag fixed to the side of the vehicle and places its mouth to his lips. 'There now, that's fine! That's warmed me up! What about another? No, that's fine . . . it'll be twenty versts yet to the post-station, time enough to get pickled . . . Still, what about another? Ah, devil take this vodka! The very sight of the bottle and you're tempted! Drinking's a beast, but you can't do without a drink—that's why I don't sleep. Damn it, if I could only get to sleep!'

After a few more gulps from the bottle he pushes it back in its place and starts filling his pipe.

'Fine thing!' he says. 'A drop to drink, now for a pipe! The witch won't give me tobacco, not she—he was right about that. Will she give me anything to eat? Send me scraps from the table, I expect. Ah, me! once I had money, now I have none! Once I was man alive, and now no more! That's the way with everything in this world! One day you're full of meat and drink, living like a lord, smoking your pipe,

> "And comes the morn—where art thou, man?"*

But I should have a bite to eat. You go on drinking like a leaky barrel, but never take a bite to go with it. And the doctors all say that drink only does you good when "accompanied by wholesome sustenance", as Archbishop Smaragd* said as we passed through Oboyan. Was it Oboyan? Devil knows, it could have been Kromy! But that's beside the point—question is, how to get hold of a bite now? I remember him putting a sausage and three French loaves in the bag. I bet he grudged buying any caviare! Goodness, how he sleeps, and what tuneful snoring! No doubt, he's tucked the food away beneath him, too!'

He feels about with his hands, but finds nothing.

'Ivan Mikhailych, hey, Ivan Mikhailych!' he calls.

Ivan Mikhailych wakes up and for a moment seems unable to understand how he comes to be sitting facing the master.

'I was just dropping off to sleep,' he says at length.

'That's all right, old boy, you sleep. I only wanted to ask where you had stowed the food bag.'

'You'd like something to eat? You should have a drink first, though.'

'Good idea! Where's the bottle?'

After having a drink, Stepan Vladimirych tackles the sausage, which turns out to be as hard as rock and as salty as salt and encased in a skin so tough it needs the point of a knife to pierce it.

'A bit of white salmon would be nice,' he says.

'Very sorry, sir, it quite slipped my mind. I remembered it all morning. I even said to the wife she should be sure to remind me about the salmon—but then I go and let you down.'

'No matter, we can eat the sausage. Ate worse things than that when we were on the march. There was a story Father told about two Englishmen: one bet the other he would eat a dead cat—and he did!'

'Ha! Ate it, did he?'

'Yes, he did. Though it made him sick afterwards. He cured himself with rum. Drank two bottles straight down and was right as rain. Then there was another Englishman who bet he would live just on sugar for a whole year!'

'And did he win?'

'No, two days before the year was up he snuffed it. What about you, though? Like a tot of vodka?'

'I never touch it.'

'You just fill yourself with tea? No good, old boy! That's why you're getting such a paunch on you. You've got to watch out with tea, too: after a cup of tea you need a nip to settle it. Tea builds up the phlegm, vodka clears it. That's right, isn't it?'

'I wouldn't know. You've got education—you'll know best.'

'Quite right. When we were on the march, there was no time for your teas and coffees. Vodka, that was the thing—unscrew your canteen, pour it in, drink it down, and done with! They pushed us along mighty fast then, that fast I didn't get a wash for ten days!'

'You've had a hard time of it, sir!'

'Maybe, maybe not—but you just try hoofing it along the highway! True, it wasn't all that bad going out—people gave you things, fed you dinners, and there was drink ad lib. But on the way back there was no more fêting!'

Golovlev strenuously gnaws at the sausage and finally after much chewing succeeds in swallowing a piece.

'This sausage is on the salty side, old boy!' he says. But then, I'm not fussy. My mother, after all, won't be feeding me fancy food either; a plate of soup, a bowl of kasha*—and that'll be it!'

'God is merciful. Maybe on feast-days she'll let you have some pie.'

'No tea, no tobacco, no vodka—you were right on that. I hear she's fond of a game of "donkey" these days: might there be a chance there? Perhaps she'll have me in to play and give me a drink of tea. But as for the rest—not a hope, old boy!'

They had a stop of three or four hours at the post-station to fodder the horses. Golovlev had by now finished off the bottle of vodka and was acutely hungry. The passengers went off into the post-house and took their places for dinner.

Stepan Vladimirych wanders about the post-station, takes a look at the back-yard and at the horses feeding at the manger, shoos off some pigeons, and attempts even to go to sleep, but in the end decides that the best thing is to follow the other passengers into the post-house. There is already steaming cabbage soup on the table and to one side on a wooden trencher lies a large joint of beef which Ivan Mikhailych is cutting into slices. Golovlev sits down a little way off, lights his pipe, and for a long time is at a loss about how he might satisfy his hunger.

'Enjoy your meal, gentlemen!' he says at last. 'Nice and rich that soup, by the look of it?'

'It's not bad soup,' replies Ivan Mikhailych. 'You should order some, sir.'

'No, it was just by the way. I'm not hungry.'

'Not hungry? Why, you've had nothing but a morsel of sausage and that darned stuff don't but swell your belly more. Have something to eat—I'll get them to lay a table for you separate—then you tuck in! Hey, mistress, lay a separate table for the master!'

The passengers set about their food in silence, exchanging only enigmatic glances. Golovlev guesses they have 'rumbled' him,

120, 161

LIBRARY
College of St. Francis
JOLIET, ILLINOIS

even though during the journey he has with some brashness cast himself in the role of master and referred to Ivan Mikhailych as his cashier. His brow is knitted, clouds of tobacco-smoke pour from his mouth. He is ready to refuse the food, but so insistent are the demands of hunger that he falls voraciously on the bowl of cabbage soup set before him and empties it in a trice. With his hunger satisfied, he regains his self-confidence and, turning to Ivan Mikhailych, says nonchalantly:

'Cashier, just settle up for me, will you, while I go for a snooze in the hay-loft?'

Swaggeringly he sets off for the hay-loft and now, with his stomach replete, he falls asleep and sleeps like a lord. At five o'clock he is already on his feet again. Seeing the horses standing by, rubbing their muzzles against the sides of the now empty manger, he sets about waking the driver.

'Dead to the world, the dog!' he shouts. 'We must get on and there he is dreaming sweet dreams!'

In this fashion the journey continues until they come to the post-station where the road turns off to Golovlevo. Only now does Stepan Vladimirych become a measure more serious. He is clearly dispirited and falls silent. At this point Ivan Mikhailych tries to hearten him and suggests in particular that he should throw away his pipe.

'As you get to the house, sir, you throw your pipe in the nettles. You can always find it again afterwards.'

At last, the horses which are to take Ivan Mikhailych on his way are ready. The moment of parting arrives.

'Goodbye, old chap!' says Golovlev, his voice quavering, as he kisses Ivan Mikhailych. 'She'll do for me!'

'God is merciful. Don't you be too frightened!'

'She'll do for me!' repeats Stepan Vladimirych with such certainty in his voice that Ivan Mikhailych instinctively lowers his eyes.

With these words, Golovlev turns sharply and sets off down the lane, supporting himself on a knotted stick he has cut previously from a tree.

For some time Ivan Mikhailych watches him go, then quickly runs to catch him up.

'Here, master!' he says on reaching him. 'When I cleaned your jacket the other day there were these three silver roubles in the side pocket—now see you don't accidentally lose them!'

Stepan Vladimirych can be seen to hesitate, uncertain how to act in the circumstances. At length he stretches out his hand to Ivan Mikhailych and, with tears in his eyes, says:

'I see—you'd help an old soldier to buy his baccy. Thanks! As for the other . . . she'll do for me, good friend! You mark my words—she'll do for me!'

Golovlev finally heads off down the lane before him; five minutes later his grey militia cap can be glimpsed in the distance, disappearing, then suddenly coming back into view behind the thicket of saplings. It is still early, a little after five o'clock; a golden morning mist hangs over the lane, barely penetrated by the rays of the sun which has just appeared over the horizon; the grass glistens; the air is full of the smell of spruce, mushrooms, and berries; the road winds through low-lying land which swarms with countless flocks of birds. But Stepan Vladimirych notices none of this. All his levity has suddenly departed and he walks as if going to meet his doom. His whole being is filled with the single thought—that in three or four hours from now it will be the end of the road for him. He recalls his old life at Golovlevo and has the feeling that the doors of a dank cellar are opening up before him and that as soon as he crosses the threshold the doors will at once slam shut—and all will be over. Other details come to mind which, though of no direct concern to him, are undoubtedly characteristic of the ways of Golovlevo. There was his uncle, Mikhail Petrovich (commonly known as 'Rowdy Mishka'); he too was one of the 'outcasts' and grandfather Petr Ivanych had sent him to Arina Petrovna to be confined in Golovlevo, where he had lived in the servants' quarters and eaten out of the same bowl as Trezorka the dog. Then there was his aunt, Vera Mikhailovna, who had lived with her brother Vladimir out of charity and had died 'of moderation', because every morsel she ate at dinner and every billet of wood used to heat her room was an object of reproach from Arina Petrovna. Something similar is now in store for him. In his imagination there is the vision of an interminable succession of dawnless days vanishing into some yawning grey abyss—and instinctively he shuts his eyes, from now on he will be all alone with this evil old woman, who is, though, not evil in fact, but simply lost to feeling in the apathy of power. This old woman will do for him—not, though, by torment but by oblivion. There will be nobody to speak to, no refuge to run to—*she* will be everywhere, domineering, deadening, disdaining. The thought of this inescapable future so dejects him that he stops by a tree and for some moments beats his head against it. The whole of his life with all its affectation, idleness, and buffoonery suddenly in his mind's eye stands revealed to the light. He is going now to Golovlevo, knowing what awaits him there—yet still he goes, because he cannot not go. There is no other road for him, none! The least of men can do something for himself, can earn his bread—he alone can do *nothing*. For the first time, it seems, the thought dawns on him. He has on occasion before thought about the future and envisaged all kinds of prospects, but they were always prospects of a free-and-easy life— never of toil. And now he is to pay the price for that mindless bliss in which his past has sunk without trace. It is a bitter price, expressed in the one dread phrase: 'She'll do for me!'

It was about ten in the morning when the white bell-tower of Golovlevo came into sight over the trees.

Stepan Vladimirych's face paled, his hands shook; he took off his cap and crossed himself. He recalled the Gospel parable of the return of the prodigal son, but at once realized that to have any such thoughts in relation to himself was mere delusion. Finally, he spotted the boundary-post set by the roadside and found himself on Golovlevo land, that unloved land which had borne him unloved, raised him unloved, sent him unloved into the world and now received him again unloved into its bosom. The sun was already high and blazed mercilessly down on the endless Golovlevo fields. But Stepan Vladimirych turned paler and paler and felt himself begin to shiver.

At last he reached the graveyard and there his spirits forsook him completely. The manor-house looked out peacefully through the trees as if nothing out of the ordinary took place within; but it had the effect on him of a Medusa's head. He sensed it to be his coffin. Coffin! coffin! coffin! he repeated unconsciously to himself.

And he could not bring himself to go straight to the house, but called first on the priest, sending him to announce his arrival and discover if his mother would receive him.

The priest's wife was grieved at the sight of him and busied herself making scrambled eggs; village boys gathered round and goggled in astonishment at the master; peasants silently pulled off their caps as they passed, regarding him somewhat dubiously; an old man, one of the house-serfs,* even ran up and asked to kiss the master's hand. They all understood that before them was an outcast who had returned to this unloved place, had returned for good, and that there was for him no way out but feet-first to the graveyard. And they all had the same feeling of pity and dread.

At last the priest came and said that his mother was ready to receive Stepan Vladimirych. Ten minutes later he was already *there*. Arina Petrovna met him with solemn severity and icily looked him up and down; but she engaged in no futile reproaches. She did not not allow him inside the house, but met him simply on the back steps and left him, after ordering that the young master should be conducted through the other entrance to see his father. The old man was dozing in his bed in a white night-cap with a white blanket over him, and he was all white, like a dead man. Seeing Stepan, he came to and gave a half-witted chortle.

'So the witch has got you in her clutches, my boy!' he cried, as Stepan Vladimirych kissed his hand. He then crowed like a cock, laughed again, and several times repeated: 'She'll do for you! She'll do for you!'

'She'll do for me!' Stepan Vladimirych, like an echo, repeated inwardly.

His expectations were fulfilled. He was put into a separate room in the outbuilding where the estate office was. There they brought him homespun calico underwear and an old dressing-gown belonging to his father, in which he at once robed himself. The doors of this vault were opened, admitted him—and slammed shut.

There followed a succession of blank, listless days, which vanished one by one into the yawning grey abyss of time. Arina Petrovna would not receive him, nor was he allowed to visit his father.

After two or three days Finogey Ipatych, the bailiff, announced to him the 'conditions' set by his mother; these were that he would be provided with board and clothing and also, once a month, a pound of Faler's† tobacco. He listened to his mother's decree and merely noted:

'You've got to hand it to the old woman! She's nosed it out that Zhukov's costs two roubles and Faler's only one ninety—so she'll be making ten kopeks a month out of me! No doubt, she intends tipping it to some beggar to pray for my soul!'

The signs of greater moral sobriety which had manifested themselves in him on the road to Golovlevo had again disappeared. Levity once more came into its own and this led also to his coming to terms with his mother's 'conditions'. The future, hopeless and inescapable, that had once flashed in his mind and filled him with trepidation, now became daily ever more shrouded in mist and ceased in the end to exist at all. For him the stage was now occupied by the passing day in all its cynical starkness and this it did with such brazen impudence that it entirely dominated his every thought and all his being. And besides, what function can there be for any thought of the future, when the whole course of life has been decided already, irrevocably and in every detail, in the mind of Arina Petrovna?

For days on end he paced up and down in his allotted room, never removing his pipe from his mouth and singing snatches of songs, church hymns unexpectedly alternating with songs of the utmost ribaldry. When the estate clerk was in the office, he would go in to him and reckon up the income received by Arina Petrovna.

'What on earth does she do with a pile of money like that!' he wondered when he had totted up a figure of over eighty thousand roubles in assignats. 'She doesn't send that much to my brothers, that's a fact, she leads a niggardly life herself and feeds Father on salt meat . . . Does she put it out to interest? There's nothing else she can do with it!'

Occasionally, Finogey Ipatych himself would come to the office bringing in the quit-rent, and then on the office table would be

† A well-known tobacco-manufacturer of the time, a competitor of Zhukov [Saltykov's note].

laid out in bundles that very money which Stepan Vladimirych so hankered after.

'Just look at that pile of money!' he would exclaim. 'And she bags the lot! Never thinks of sparing a wad for her son! "Here, my son, you've fallen on hard times, take this for a drink and a smoke!" '

And then Stepan Vladimirych and Yakov, the clerk, would have endless and highly cynical conversations on how Arina Petrovna might be mollified and made to dote on him.

'There was a tradesman fellow I knew in Moscow,' Golovlev would recount, 'and he knew a "word" . . . And any time his mother refused him money, he'd just say this "word" . . . And straightaway she'd get the shakes—arms, legs, the lot!'

'He must have put a powerful strong spell on her,' surmised Yakov the clerk.

'Make of it what you will, but it's the honest truth that such a "word" does exist. Then there was a man who told me you should take a live frog and stick it in an ant-heap at dead of night; by morning the ants will have eaten the frog and all that'll be left is one little bone; well, you put this bone in your pocket and as long as it's there you can ask what you like of any woman and she won't say no!'

'Why that's something you could do straightaway!'

'Ah, but the point is you've first got to put yourself under a curse, old boy! But for that, I'd have the old witch eating out of my hand!'

Whole hours were passed in such conversations, but they could never hit on any practical resource. It was always a matter of putting yourself under a curse or selling your soul to the Devil. As a result, there was no alternative but to live according to his mother's 'conditions'—with certain adjustments in the form of arbitrary exactions from the village headmen, from each of whom Stepan Vladimirych claimed tribute in tobacco, tea, and sugar. He was fed extremely badly. Usually he was sent what remained of his mother's dinner, and since Arina Petrovna was abstemious to the point of meanness, there was naturally little left for him. This caused him particular anguish, because since vodka had become forbidden fruit for him his appetite had rapidly increased. From morning to night he was hungry and his only thoughts were how he could fill his stomach. He deliberately waited for the times when his mother was resting, then slipped into the kitchen or even dropped into the servants' quarters, laying hands on anything there was. Sometimes he would sit by the open window and lie in wait for a passing cart. If a Golovlevo peasant drove by, he would make him stop and pay tribute—in the form of an egg, a curd tart, or such like.

Already at their first meeting Arina Petrovna had set out in brief the full intended scheme for his daily life. 'Stay then, for the time being!' she said. 'There's a corner for you in the office, and food and drink you'll have from my table—as for anything else, it's just too bad, my sweetheart! Delicacies I've never had in my life and I won't be providing them for the likes of you. Your brothers will be here any time and whatever they recommend for you, that's how I'll act. I won't burden my soul with sin, so what your brothers decide—that's how it will be!'

So now Stepan Vladimirych was impatiently awaiting the arrival of his brothers. But his expectations were not at all concerned with what effect their visit might have on his subsequent fate (he had evidently decided it was not worth considering), he only wondered whether Pavel would bring him any tobacco and, if so, just how much.

'He might shell out a bit of cash, too,' he added to himself. 'Bloodsucker Porfisha won't, that's for sure, but Pavel . . . If I ask him to give an old soldier the price of a drink—he'll do it! How could he refuse!'

Time passed; he did not notice it. His life was one of total idleness, but he found it scarcely irksome. Only the evenings were tedious, because the clerk went home around eight o'clock and Arina Petrovna allowed him no candles—on the grounds that pacing up and down the room could be done perfectly well without them. But he soon grew accustomed to this as well and acquired a liking for the dark, since it gave freer rein to his imagination, which transported him away from hateful Golovlevo. Only one thing troubled him: his heart was playing up and there was a strange fluttering sensation in his chest, particularly when he went to bed. Sometimes he would leap out of bed in a terrible state and run about the room, clutching the left side of his chest.

'Ah! If only I could snuff it!' he thought at these times. 'No, but I shan't! Still, maybe...'

But when one morning the clerk reported with a mysterious air that his brothers had arrived overnight, he instinctively shuddered and changed countenance. He suddenly felt a childish urge to rush to the house and see what they were wearing, and what beds had been made up for them, and if they had travelling-cases like the one he had once seen that belonged to a captain in the militia; he wanted to hear them and Mother talking together and sneak a glance at what they had for dinner. In short, he felt an urge to be reunited with that life by which he was so adamantly rejected, to throw himself at his mother's feet and win her forgiveness, after which perhaps he might in celebration get his teeth into a fatted calf. In the house all was still quiet, but he had already slipped in to the see the cook and find out what had been ordered for dinner: to start, a small tureen of fresh cabbage soup and yesterday's soup warmed up; for the second course, cold salt fowl and, separately, two pairs of cutlets; for the third, mutton and, separately, two brace of snipe; for pudding, raspberry pie and cream.

'Yesterday's soup, salt fowl, and mutton—that's for the outcast, old boy!' he said to the cook. 'And I don't suppose there'll be any pie for me either!'

'That's for your mother to say, sir.'

'Ah, me! And time was when I too ate great snipe! Oh yes, I ate them all right, old boy! I once even had a bet with Gremykin—he was a lieutenant—that I'd eat fifteen of them at a sitting—and I won! Only for a month after I couldn't bear to look one in the face!'

'But you would eat them again now?'

'She'll not give me any! But why should she begrudge me? Snipe—it's a wild bird, it don't need feeding or looking after, it lives on its own account. She doesn't buy snipe and she doesn't buy mutton, but then, you've got to hand it to her, the old witch knows very well that snipe's tastier than mutton, and that's why she won't give me any. She won't, she'd rather see it rot! And what's being put on for breakfast?'

'There's liver, mushrooms in sour cream, pastries . . .'

'You might at least send me over a pastry . . . Do your best, old boy!'

'I'll do my best. I tell you what, sir—as soon as your brothers sit down to breakfast, send the clerk round, and he can take you a couple under his coat.'

The whole morning Stepan Vladimirych waited, wondering if his brothers might come, but they never did. Finally, about eleven o'clock, the clerk brought him the two promised pastries and reported that his brothers had just ended their breakfast and were now closeted with their mother in her bedroom.

Arina Petrovna greeted her sons solemnly, weighed down with grief. Two maids supported her by the arms; strands of grey hair poked from under her white cap, her head drooped and swayed from side to side, her feet barely dragged themselves along. She was, in general, fond of presenting herself to her children as the venerable, afflicted mother, and on such occasions she would laboriously shuffle about and require the maids to support her. Booby Stepka called this solemn pantomime the 'bishop ritual', with his mother in the role of 'bishopess' and Polka and Yulka, the maids, as her crozier-bearers. But since it was after one in the morning when the meeting took place, no words were exchanged. In silence she proffered her hand for her children to kiss, in silence she kissed them and made the sign of the cross over them, and when Porfiry Vladimirych declared himself ready to spend the rest of the night, if need be, confabulating with his dear mother, she made a gesture of refusal and said:

'Go now. Rest after your journey. This is no time for talk; we will talk tomorrow.'

In the morning both sons went to kiss the hand of their father, but he did not give them his hand to kiss. He lay on his bed with his eyes closed, and as his sons came in he cried out:

'Come to judge the publican, have you? Get out, you pharisees . . . get out!'

None the less, Porfiry Vladimirych emerged from his father's study agitated and in tears—while Pavel Vladimirych, like the 'senseless dummy' that he was, simply picked his nose.

'He's very poorly, Mother dear! Oh, very poorly indeed!' declared Porfiry Vladimirych, falling on his mother's breast.

'Is he that bad today?'

'Oh, he's bad, very bad. He'll not much longer be with you.'

'Oh, he'll last out yet awhile!'

'No, Mother dear, no! You've had no special joys in life, I know, but when I think of all these blows coming on you at once—it really is a marvel where you get the strength to bear such trials!'

'Ah well, my dear, you can bear them, if so the good Lord wills. You know what it says in the Scripture: Bear ye one another's burdens—well, it's me Our Lord has chosen to bear the burdens of my family!'

Arina Petrovna even screwed up her eyes: so fine did it seem to her that while for them everything was found and provided, she toiled the whole day alone and bore the burdens of them all.

'Yes, my dear,' she said after a minute's silence. 'It's not at all easy for me now I'm old! I've laid in store for you children to my cost—and now I should rest. It's no joke having four thousand souls and running a great concern like this when you are my age! Watch everybody, check everybody, and all the time hither and thither! Just look at these bailiffs and overseers we've got: never believe them when they look you in the eye! They pretend to serve you, but they're really only out to do you down. Untrustworthy they are! Well, and what about you?' she suddenly broke off, turning to Pavel. 'Picking your nose, are you?'

'What should I care!' snapped Pavel Vladimirych, disturbed just as he was most deeply engrossed in his pursuit.

'What should you care, indeed! He's your father, isn't he? You might feel sorry for him!'

'All right, he's my father. The same old father! Ten years he's been like this! Why are you always keeping on at me?'

'Why I keep on at you, my boy, is because I am your mother! Look at Porfisha—he's shown his affection and pity the way a good son should, but you won't even look your mother in the face—the sulky, sly way you look at me, I might be your worst enemy, not your mother at all! Kindly don't snap at me!'

'But what have I . . .'

'Hold now! Wait a minute! Let your mother speak! Do you remember what the commandment says?—Honour thy father and mother that it may go well with thee . . . I suppose you don't want it, then, to "go well" with you?'

Pavel Vladimirych said nothing and gazed at his mother in perplexity.

'There you are, you've nothing to say!' Arina Petrovna went on. 'You must know you're in the wrong! Ah well, God be with you! For the sake of a happy reunion, we'll say no more about it. God, my sons, sees everything, and I . . . ah, how long I've known you inside out! Ah, my sons! my sons! You'll remember your mother when she's in her grave, you'll remember—but it will be too late then!'

'Mother dear!' interposed Porfiry Vladimirych. 'Don't think these dismal thoughts! Don't think them!'

'Die we all must, my son,' declared Arina Petrovna sententiously. 'These are not dismal thoughts, but very . . . godly thoughts, I'd say. I'm ailing, my sons, ah, I'm ailing for sure! I'm not what I used to be—weak and sick is all I am now! Even those servant hussies can see it—they never take a scrap of notice of me! Whatever I say, they answer back. All I can do is threaten I'll complain to the young masters. Sometimes then they'll hold their tongues a bit.'

Tea was served, then breakfast, during which Arina Petrovna went on complaining and waxing emotional about her life. After breakfast she asked her sons to come into her bedroom.

When the door was locked, Arina Petrovna at once broached the matter for which the family council had been convened.

'It's the Booby. He's back,' she began.

'So we have heard, Mother dear, so we have heard!' replied Porfiry Vladimirych with what might have been irony or else the good-humour of a man who has just eaten a decent breakfast.

'He came back as if it was the right and proper thing to do: as if to say—however fast and loose I've lived, there'll always be a crust for me at Mother's. What malice I've had from him in my lifetime! What torments I've suffered from his antics and tricks! The trouble I went to to get him a post—it was all like water off a duck's back! In the end I fretted myself and thought: Lord above, if he won't make an effort for himself, why on earth should I make my life a misery on account of him, the lanky Booby? I'll toss him a morsel, I thought, and maybe with money of his own he'll settle down a bit. So that's what I did—I found him a house myself, with my own hands paid out a full twelve thousand silver roubles for it. And what happened? It's not three years since and now he's hanging round my neck again. How long am I to put up with these affronts?'

Porfisha cast his eyes upwards to the ceiling and sadly shook his head as if to say: 'Ah, me! What a business! There was no need to upset dear Mother so! We might all now be sitting quietly in peace and harmony, and there would be none of all this, and dear Mother would not be vexed . . . ah! what a business!' But Arina Petrovna, being a person who could not suffer any interruption to her train of thought, did not take kindly to Porfisha's gesture.

'Don't you go wagging your head just yet,' she said. 'You hear me out first! What was it like for me to find out that he had thrown away his parents' blessing, tossed it down the drain like a gnawed bone? How do you think I felt at his doing such a thing after all my efforts—going short of food and sleep, I might say! But what does he do? It was as if he'd just bought a spillikin in the market and tossed it out the window because he had no use for it! He did that with his parents' blessing!'

'Ah, Mother dear, how could he do such a thing! How could he!' Porfiry Vladimirych began, but again Arina Petrovna cut him short.

'Hold now! Wait a minute! You can have your say when I tell you! The villain, if only he had told me in advance—"Mother," he might have said, "it was wrong of me—and so forth—but I gave way." Why, I might have got the house for a penny-price myself, had I but known betimes. If the worthless son can't make good use of it, then let the worthy ones have the benefit! That house, why it would easily bring in fifteen per cent annual! And I might have thrown in another thousand for him to keep the wolf from the door. But, oh no!—here am I without ever an inkling and he's already gone and done it! Twelve thousand for that house I paid out, and he let it be sold off for eight!'

'But, Mother dear, worst of all is that he should have dealt so basely with his parents' blessing!' Porfiry Vladimirych added hastily, as if fearing to be again cut short by his mother.

'It's both the one and the other, my son. Any money I've got was not come by easily; it wasn't got by cheating and swindling, but by toil and sweat. How was it I came by my wealth? When I married your father, all he had was Golovlevo, a hundred and one souls, and another twenty here and thirty there in the distant parts—a hundred and fifty souls all told, maybe. And as for me, I had nothing, nothing at all! Then just you see what a great concern I've built up from that! Four thousand souls—a tidy lot that is! I'd happily take them to the grave with me, but that I can't do. And do you think I came by them easily, these four thousand souls? No, deary, it wasn't easy, it wasn't easy at all. I would stay awake at night and keep wondering how I could clinch a deal before anybody else got wind of it. How to make sure nobody put in a higher bid and you didn't spend a kopek more than you need! And what I've not been through! Roads under slush and mud and ice—I've travelled them all. It's only lately I've come to go jaunting about in carriages—in the early days they would get me a peasant cart, fix on a cover of sorts, hitch up a pair of nags, and clip-clop, off I'd go to Moscow! I'd jog along and all the time be thinking somebody else would buy up the property from under my nose. Then when I got to Moscow, I'd put up at the inn at Rogozhskaya Bar;* stink and filth—I've suffered it all, my dears! Time was, I'd grudge the ten kopeks for a cab and walk all the way from Rogozhskaya to the Solyanka.* Even the doormen wondered at me: "A young lady like you, with money," they would say, "Why put yourself to such exertions?" But I suffered on in silence. The first time, all the money I had was thirty thousand in assignats—I had sold off the outlying bits of land Father had, a hundred souls, maybe—and, would you believe it, with that amount I set out to buy a thousand souls! I had intercessions said at the Iverskaya chapel,* then off I went to try my luck on the Solyanka! And what do you think! It was as though our Lady

Intercessor had seen the bitter tears I shed—for she let the property go to me! It was like a miracle: when I bid thirty thousand, the mortgage apart, it was like I had put a stop to the whole sale! Before it had been all noise and commotion, but then even the bidding came to a stop, and it suddenly went all quiet. It was the auctioneer—he'd got up and was congratulating me and I couldn't take it in! There was an attorney there, Ivan Nikolaich, and he came up to me, "Good luck to you, ma'am, with your purchase!" he said, and I just stood there like a wooden post! But how great is the mercy of God! Just think of it: if anybody, seeing the state I was in, had had the mischief to say thirty-five thousand, I was that carried away I might have gone and bid forty! And where would I have got it from?'

Arina Petrovna had many times before told her children the saga of her first steps in the sphere of property acquisition, but evidently in their eyes it had still lost none of its novelty. Porfiry Vladimirych listened to his mother, now smiling, now sighing, first rolling his eyes upwards, then casting them downwards, as befitted the varying fortunes she had experienced. And Pavel Vladimirych listened wide-eyed, like a child who is told a familiar fairy-tale, which he is yet never tired of hearing.

'And you think your mother came by her property for nothing!' Arina Petrovna continued. 'Oh no, my dears, you don't get a pimple on your nose for nothing: six weeks I lay in a fever after that first purchase! So you can just imagine what it's like for me, after all the torments I've endured, to see my hard-earned money being tossed down the drain!'

There was a minute of silence. Porfiry Vladimirych was ready to rend his garments, but feared that here in the country there might be nobody to mend them. Pavel Vladimirych, once the 'fairy-tale' was over, drooped again into listlessness and his face resumed its former look of apathy.

'So that was why I sent for you,' Arina Petrovna began afresh. 'You be the judges between me and him, the villain! It shall be as you say. If you find him guilty, then he's to blame; if you find me guilty, I am. Only I'm not going to let that villain put on me!' she added, unexpectedly.

Porfiry Vladimirych felt that now his time had come and gave forth, full-throated as a nightingale. But, like the true bloodsucker that he was, he did not come straight to the point, but began in a roundabout way.

'If you will permit me, dearest Mother, to voice my opinion,' he said, 'it can be put in two words: it is the duty of children to obey their parents, to comfort them in their old age—and that is all. What are children, dear Mother? Children are loving creatures in whom everything—from their own person to the last rags they wear—everything belongs to their parents. Parents may, therefore, be judges of their children, but children never judges of their parents. The duty of children is to honour, not to judge. You say we should be judges between you and our brother. That, Mother dear, is magnanimous, it is mag-nif-icent! But how can we, without fear, even think of such a thing, we who from the day we were born have been blessed by you from top to toe! Do as you will, but it won't be judgement, it will be sacrilege! Oh, such a sacrilege! . . .'

'Hold now! Wait a minute! If you say you can't be judge of me, then find me right and him wrong!' broke in Arina Petrovna, who was listening carefully and could not fathom what trickery it was Bloodsucker Porfishka had in mind.

'No, Mother dearest, that I cannot do either! Or rather, I dare not, I haven't the right to. I cannot find you right or wrong—I cannot be judge of you at all. You are the mother—you alone know how to deal with us, your children. You reward us for our merits and punish us for our faults. It is our part to obey, not to criticize. Even if you should, in a moment of parental anger, go so far as to be unfair—even then we dare not complain, for the ways of Providence are not revealed to us. Who knows? Perhaps that is how it should be! Exactly as in the present case: our brother Stepan has done a base, you might say even, a black deed, but you alone can decide what retribution he deserves!'

'You refuse then? You're telling your dearest mother she can get out of it as best she may!'

'Oh, Mother, Mother! To have such a sinful thought! Oh dear, oh dear! All I am saying is that brother Stepan's fate should be whatever you think fit—and you . . . oh, the black thoughts you think me to have!'

'Well, and what about you?' said Arina Petrovna, turning to Pavel Vladimirych.

'What do I care! You're not likely to do anything I say,' Pavel Vladimirych began, as if half-asleep, but then unexpectedly rallied and went on: 'Of course, he's in the wrong . . . tear him to shreds . . . grind him to dust . . . goes without saying . . . What do I care!'

Having muttered these disjointed words, he stopped and gaped at his mother, as if unable to believe his own ears.

'I'll speak to you later, my sweetheart!' Arina Petrovna cut him short icily. 'I can see you're keen to follow after Stepka . . . Don't make that mistake, my son! You'll be sorry for it, and it will be too late then.'

'What did I say? I didn't say anything! All I said was: do what you like. What's . . . disrespectful about that?' said Pavel Vladimirych, capitulating.

'Later, my son, I'll speak to you later! You think because you're an officer there's no way to master you! But we'll find a way all right, we'll find a way. So, the both of you refuse to give judgement?'

'Yes, I do, Mother dear . . .'

'I do too. What do I care! As far as I'm concerned, go ahead, tear him to shreds . . .'

'Be silent, now, for mercy's sake . . . you bad son! (Arina Petrovna realized that she was entitled to call him 'scoundrel', but for the sake of the happy reunion restrained herself.) 'Very well, then, if you refuse, I'll have to judge on my own. Here's my decision then: I'll try once more to deal kindly with him: I'll make over to him that bit of property of Father's in Vologda, put up a little house for him, and there he can live like a pauper and be kept by the peasants.'

Although Porfiry Vladimirych had indeed refused to act as judge of his brother's case, he was, however, so taken aback by his mother's magnanimity that he simply could not conceal from her the dangerous consequences likely to ensue from the measure she now proposed.

'Mother!' he exclaimed. 'You are more than magnanimous! Here you are, faced with a deed—a deed as base and black as ever was . . . and suddenly, all is forgotten and forgiven! It is mag-nif-icent! But you must pardon me . . . I am afraid for you, Mother dearest! Judge me as you will, but in your place . . . I would act otherwise.'

'Why so?'

'I can't say . . . Perhaps I'm lacking that magnanimity, that—shall we say—maternal feeling . . . But still it occurs to me—what if our brother Stepan (depraved as he is) should do the same with this second parental blessing as he did with the first?'

It emerged, however, that Arina Petrovna had this consideration already in mind and was harbouring another idea as well, which it was now for her to disclose.

'The Vologda land is anyway family property, on Father's side,' she grated. 'And sooner or later he'll have to have a share of Father's estate.'

'That I understand, Mother dear . . .'

'If you understand that, then I suppose you can also understand that, if he's given the Vologda land, he can be got to sign an undertaking that he's had his share from Father and is content with it.'

'That I understand too. But, dearest Mother, in the goodness of your heart you made a great mistake: when you bought him the house—that was the time to get an undertaking from him that he had no more claim on Father's estate!'

'It can't be helped! I never thought of it.'

'He was so pleased then he would have signed anything! But you in the goodness of your heart . . . ah, what a mistake that was! Oh, such a mistake, such a mistake!'

' "Ah!" and "Oh!"—you should have "ah-ed" and "oh-ed" then when there was still time! You're ready enough now to lay it all at my door, but when it comes down to business, you keep well clear! Anyway, his signing a paper doesn't come into it—though I might yet get a paper from him. It will be a while yet, no doubt, before your father dies, and till he does the Booby's got to eat and drink. So if he won't sign, I can show him the door and tell him to wait till Father's gone. But what I want to know is: what is wrong with my giving him the Vologda property?'

'He'll squander it away, Mother dear! He squandered away the house, he'll squander away the estate.'

'If he does, he'll have only himself to blame!'

'But then he'll come back to you again!'

'Oh no, not on your life he won't! I'll not have him in the house! I wouldn't give him water, the hateful lout, much less bread. And people wouldn't blame me, nor God punish me for it. Look at him! Squandered away a house, squandered away an estate—am I one of his serfs that I should spend my life just providing for him? I've other children too, haven't I?'

'He will still come back to you, Mother dearest. He's a brazen fellow.'

'I tell you I won't have him in the house! Why do you keep on like a chattering magpie with your "he'll come back", "he'll come back"—I won't have him here!'

Arina Petrovna was silent and stared out of the window. She too vaguely realized that the Vologda property would give her only temporary respite from the outcast, that in the end he would indeed squander it away and then come back to her again, and that *as his mother* she would be *unable* to refuse him shelter—but when she thought that her bugbear would remain with her for ever, that, even incarcerated in the office, he would still every moment haunt her imagination like a ghost, the thought so oppressed her that she shuddered all over.

'No, never!' she finally cried aloud, banging her fist on the table and springing up from her chair.

And Porfiry Vladimirych looked at his dear mother and rhythmically shook his head in sorrow.

'There now, Mother, you are angry!' he said at last, his voice so sugary that he might have been about to tickle her in the ribs.

'By your reckoning, I should be dancing a jig, then, should I?'

'A-a-h! What does the Scripture say about patience? "In patience possess ye your souls," it says. "In patience"—just that. Do you suppose *God* does not see? No, no, Mother dear, he sees everything! We may have no inkling, as we sit here thinking this way and that, while God has already made up his mind: "I'll send him as a trial to test her"! A-a-h, Mother dear! And here was I thinking you were a good girl!'

But Arina Petrovna knew very well that Bloodsucker Porfisha
was only laying a snare, and was now really angry.

'Are you trying to make a fool of me!' she snapped at him.
'Here's your mother talking serious, and you act the clown! It's
no good your trying to wheedle me! Say straight out what you're
thinking! You want him left to live off his mother in Golovlevo
—is that it?'

'Yes, indeed, Mother dear, if you should so please. To leave him
just so placed as he is at present—and have him sign a paper about
the inheritance, too!'

'I knew it . . . I knew that's what you would suggest! Well, all
right. Suppose we do as you say. It will be more than I can stand
to see my bugbear round me all the time—but so be it, I've nobody
to look to for pity, that's clear. I bore a cross when I was young,
and it's not for me to refuse to bear one now in my old age!
Suppose we do that, there's another thing to think of. As long
as your father and me are alive, he'll live on too in Golovlevo and
won't starve to death. But—what then?'

'Mother, dear Mother! Why have such black thoughts?'

'Black they may be or white, but it's still got to be thought of.
We're not young any more, and when we're both dead and gone,
what's to become of him then?'

'Mother! Do you really have no trust in us, in your children?
Is that the way you brought us up?'

And Porfiry Vladimirych gave her one of those enigmatic looks
which always caused her consternation.

'It's a snare,' said a voice within her.

'The greater the joy it is for me, Mother dear, to help a poor
man! Why help the rich? God be with the rich man, he's got
enough of his own! But the poor—do you know what Christ
said about the poor?'

Porfiry Vladimirych rose and kissed his mother's hand.

'Mother dear! Allow me to present to my brother two pounds
of tobacco.'

Arina Petrovna did not reply. She looked at him and thought:
can he really be such a bloodsucker that he would turn his own
brother into the street?

'Well, do as you think best! If he's to live in Golovlevo, so be it!' she said finally. 'You've got me fenced and fettered. To start it's "Just as you wish, Mother dear!" but at the finish you've got me dancing to your tune. Well, just you listen to me: he's a bugbear to me, all his life he's brought me torment and shame, and in the end he's even cast aside his parents' blessing—but be that as it may, if you should ever turn him out of doors or make him go abegging, you'll not have my blessing! No, never, never! Now, off the both of you go to see him! I expect his eyes are on stalks with looking for you!'

Her sons left, and Arina Petrovna stood by the window watching as, without speaking, they crossed the front yard to the office. Porfisha kept taking off his cap and crossing himself in the direction of the church gleaming white in the distance, the chapel, and the wooden post to which the alms-box was fixed. Pavlusha was evidently unable to take his eyes off his new boots, the toes of which glittered gaily in the rays of the sun.

'And who have I provided for, going short of sleep, going short of food? Who for?' the anguished cry broke from her breast.

The brothers left; the house at Golovlevo was again desolate. Arina Petrovna applied herself with added vigour to the concerns of the estate which had been interrupted; in the kitchen the clatter of the cooks' knives was stilled, but there was redoubled activity in the office and in the barns, store-houses, and cellars. Summer the provider was drawing to its close; bottling, pickling, preserving were in full swing; from every quarter provisions for the winter poured in, from every estate came carts bearing the peasant-women's dues in kind: dried mushrooms, berries, eggs, vegetables, and so on. All this was weighed up, checked in, and added to the stocks of former years. Not for nothing had the mistress of Golovlevo had a whole range of cellars, store-houses, and barns built; they were all packed full, and of the contents considerable quantities had gone bad and could not be approached because of the rotting smell. At the end of the summer all these supplies were sorted, and any that proved to be unsound were sent to the servants' hall.

'The cucumbers are still all right, a bit slimy on the outside, that's all, and they smell a bit—very well, they can be a treat for

the servants', Arina Petrovna would say, as she ordered this tub
or that to be retained.

Stepan Vladimirych settled to his new situation with a surprising ease. Every so often he was desperate to 'take a snort', 'dip
the beak', or, in general, 'have a binge' (as we shall see, he even
had money for this purpose), but he selflessly restrained himself,
as though he calculated that the 'right time' had not yet come.
He was constantly occupied, for he took a keen and solicitous
interest in the provisioning that was going on, disinterestedly
rejoicing and sorrowing at the successes and failures of the parsi-
monious Golovlevo economy. In a kind of fervour he would go
from the office to the cellars, bare-headed, clad in nothing but his
dressing-gown, and there, hiding from his mother behind the
trees or the assortment of coops and hutches that cluttered the
front yard (in fact, Arina Petrovna several times spotted him and
her maternal heart was strongly moved to put the Booby firmly in
his place, but on reflection she let it pass)—there, outside the
cellars, he would watch with feverish impatience as the carts
were unloaded and jars, casks, and tubs were carried from the
house before being sorted and finally disappearing into the yawning cavity of the cellars and store-houses. For the most part he
was satisfied.

'They brought mushrooms in from Dubrovino today—saffron
milk-caps, two loads of them—jolly good they are too, old boy!'
he would delightedly inform the clerk. 'And we thought we
wouldn't have any this winter! All thanks to Dubrovino! Good
lads! They've saved our bacon!'

Or:

'Mother told them to catch the carp in the pond today—fine
old fellows they are: over a foot long some of them! We should
be having carp every day this week!'

Sometimes, however, he lamented too:

'The cucumbers have done badly this year, old boy. Rough
and spotted they are—no proper cucumbers at all, and that's
that! We'll have to eat last year's—the new lot are only fit for
the servants.'

However, overall he disapproved of Arina Petrovna's domestic
management.

'The amount of stuff she's let go to rot—it's terrible! They were carting loads of it today: salt beef, fish, cucumbers—all of it she ordered to go to the servants! Does that make sense? Is that the way to run an economy? There's this mass of fresh provisions, yet she won't even touch it till she's finished off the stuff that's rotten!'

Arina Petrovna's certainty that it would be no trouble to get Booby Stepka to sign whatever document she wanted was fully borne out by events. He not only raised no objection to signing all the papers his mother sent him, but even bragged about it to the clerk in the evening:

'I've been signing papers all day today, old boy. Letters of renunciation, the lot of them—and now I'm skint! I haven't got a thing, not a bean—and no prospect I ever will! I've set the old girl's mind at rest!'

He parted with his brothers on good terms and was in ecstasy that he was now well stocked with tobacco. Of course, he could not resist calling Porfisha 'Bloodsucker' and 'Judas', but these expressions passed unnoticed in the stream of his banter, in which no single coherent thought was to be detected. On parting, the brothers in an access of generosity even handed him some money —Porfiry Vladimirych accompanying his gift with the following words:

'If you should need oil for the icon-lamp or want to offer a candle in church, you'll have money by! Oh yes, indeed! Just you live quiet and peaceful, then Mother will be pleased and you'll be at ease and we'll all be jolly and bright! Mother's a kindly soul, after all.'

'Oh, very kindly, very kindly indeed,' agreed Stepan Vladimirych, 'apart from making me eat rotten meat!'

'And whose fault is that? Who defiled his parents' blessing? It's your fault! It was you who squandered away your estate! And a good estate it was too—a nice tidy property, really profitable, really splendid! If you had but been more meek and mild, you would now be eating beef and veal and might even call for some gravy. And you would have plenty of everything: potatoes, cabbage, peas . . . Is it right what I am saying?'

If Arina Petrovna had heard this dialogue, she would probably not have desisted from saying: 'There he goes, oiling his tongue again!' But it was Booby Stepka's good fortune to have hearing which was, one might say, unretentive to the utterances of other people. Judas could talk as much as he liked and rest assured that not a word he spoke would find its mark.

In short, Stepan Vladimirych saw his brothers off amicably, and with some self-satisfaction showed Yakov the clerk the two twenty-five-rouble notes which he found in his hand after the farewells had been said.

'I'm set up now for a good long time, old boy,' he said. 'We've got tobacco and a stock of tea and sugar, all we haven't got is vodka and we can have that too if we want it! Still, for the time being I'll keep off it—no time now, I must get over to the cellar! If you don't keep a look-out, they'll filch the lot in no time! You know, the old witch saw me once going along by the wall of the servants' hall—she was at the window watching me and probably thinking I was the one if she found any cucumbers missing!'

It was now October at last; the rains set in and the roadway became black and impassable. There was no going out for Stepan Vladimirych, since on his feet he had nothing but his father's worn-out slippers and on his shoulders his father's old dressing-gown. Indoors all the time, he sat at the window of his room and gazed through the double panes at the peasants' houses in the village now sunk deep in the mud. These people—having survived the back-breaking toil of summer—moved nimbly around, black dots in the grey autumnal mist. The toiling had not ceased, it merely had now a new setting in which the jubilant tones of summer were replaced by autumn's unending dusk. The drying-barns were smoking into the small hours of the morning and the mournful drumming of the flails echoed through the neighbour-hood. Threshing was also going on in the barns of Golovlevo and they said in the office that they would hardly have all the estate corn threshed before Shrovetide. Everything had a dismal, somnolent look, everything bore the mark of oppression. The doors of the office were now not opened as they were in the summer, and in the room itself hung a blue-grey haze from the steaming wet sheepskin jackets.

It is hard to say what effect this picture of autumn labour in the country had upon Stepan Vladimirych or even whether he was actually conscious of the toil going ever on in this sea of mud and the ceaseless pouring rain; but fact it is that the grey, ever-weeping autumn sky depressed him. It seemed to hang right above his head, threatening to drown him in the muddy depths that yawned all around. He had no other occupation but to look out of the window and watch the ponderous masses of the clouds. At first light in the morning they filled the horizon; the clouds hung there as if fixed, held by some spell; an hour passed, two hours, three, and they still were there in the same place, with not the least perceptible change even in colour or contour. That cloud there that hung lower and blacker than the others: before, it had a broken shape (like a priest in his chasuble with arms outspread) and stood out clear against the whitish clouds higher up—now, at midday, it was still the same shape. True, the right arm was now shorter and the left grotesquely elongated, and the solid downpour of rain that came from it formed a darker, almost black streak against the already dark background of the sky. And that other cloud further off: it, too, had been earlier suspended like a great shaggy ball over the neighbouring village of Naglovka, threatening, it seemed, to smother it—and still it hung there in the same place, the same shaggy ball, though it now had paws stretched out beneath it, as if about to jump to the ground. Clouds, clouds, clouds, the whole day long. Around five in the afternoon, when dinner was over, a metamorphosis took place: everything around became gradually obscured in the growing murk until, at last, it was totally lost from sight. First, the clouds vanished, dissolving in a featureless black shroud; next, the wood and Naglovka disappeared; after Naglovka, the church, the chapel, the nearby village houses, the orchard all sank into the darkness, and only an eye that closely watched this mysterious disappearing process could still discern the manor-house that stood a few yards off. Inside his room it was already quite dark; in the office they eked out the twilight, not lighting the lamp; there was nothing else to do but walk on endlessly up and down, up and down the room. A morbid lassitude grips the mind; for all his inactivity, he feels his whole body seized by an unaccountable, inexpressible weariness; one thought revolves in his mind, nagging and oppressing him—and this was: coffin! coffin! coffin! Those dots out there seen just now bobbing against the dark background of the mud, by the village threshing-barns—they were not tormented by this thought, they would not perish beneath a burden of lassitude and dejection: they might not be exactly doing battle with the heavens, but at least they were struggling, fashioning something, making it secure and strong. Whether whatever they toiled day and night to create was worth securing and strengthening never occurred to him, but he knew well that even these nameless dots were immeasurably superior to him, that he could not even struggle, and he had nothing to make secure and strong.

He spent the evenings in the office, because Arina Petrovna, as before, would not allow him any candles. Several times he asked through the bailiff if he could have some boots and a sheepskin coat, but the reply came back that there were no boots for him, though when the frosts came he would be provided with felt overshoes. Evidently, Arina Petrovna intended to execute her scheme literally, i.e. to provide for the outcast merely enough to keep him from dying of starvation. At first, he cursed his mother, but he then seemed to forget about her; at first, he would recall things from the past, but then that too he stopped doing. He came to abominate even the light of the candles burning in the office, and closeted himself in his room to be alone in the darkness. Ahead there was only one resource, one which he still feared as yet, but which lured him on with irresistible power. This resource was: to drink himself into a stupor and forget. To forget entirely, without recall, to plunge so deep into the sea of oblivion that he could never emerge again. Everything pulled him in that direction: the roisterous habits of the past, the enforced idleness of the present, and his ailing body—the choking cough, the intolerable breathlessness that suddenly came over him, the ever increasing pains in his heart. In the end, he could hold out no longer.

'We must lay hold of a bottle tonight, old boy,' he said to the clerk one day with a note of ill-boding in his voice.

Today's bottle was followed by a regular succession of fresh bottles, and from then on, every night without fail, he drank. At nine o'clock, when the light in the office was doused and the servants went off to their dens, he set on the table the bottle of vodka procured for the occasion and a slice of black bread well sprinkled with salt. He did not start at once on the vodka, but approached it as if by stealth. The sleep of the dead was settling on all around; the only sounds were the scratching of the mice behind the paper hanging loose from the wall and the insistent ticking of the clock in the office. He took off his dressing-gown and, just in his shirt, paced hurriedly about the overheated room, stopping from time to time to go to the table and grope for the bottle in the darkness, before returning again to his pacing round the room. The first glasses he drained with some gabbled catch-phrase, luxuriating as he gulped the fiery liquid down; but gradually his heart beat more rapidly, his head burned, and his tongue began to mutter incoherently. His dulled imagination strove to form some clear images, his dimmed memory attempted to penetrate into the past, but the images were fragmented, mean-ingless, and the past offered in response not a single memory, bitter or blithe, as if between it and the present time a solid wall had risen up for ever. He had before him only the present in the form of his tight-locked prison, in which all idea of space or time had sunk without trace. The room, the stove, the three windows on the outside wall, the creaking wooden bedstead with its thin, flattened mattress, the table with the bottle on it—to no further horizons could his thoughts extend. But as the contents of the bottle diminished and his head grew more inflamed, so even this meagre awareness of the present became too much for him. His mutterings, which at the start had at least some coherence, became totally confused; the pupils of his eyes, straining to distinguish shapes in the darkness, dilated enormously; the dark-ness itself disappeared at last and was replaced by a space filled with phosphorescent brilliance. It was an endless void, dead, issuing no living sound, ominous in its radiance. It dogged his footsteps, followed his every turn. No walls, no windows, nothing existed, only the glaring void stretching on without end. He was filled with horror; he had to suppress his sense of reality so that even this void would disappear. A few more attempts—and his goal was achieved. On stumbling feet his insensate body staggered to and fro; from his breast there came no mutterings, just a wheezing sound; existence itself seemed at an end. There set in that peculiar state of torpor which, while bearing every mark of the absence of conscious life, gave also certain indication of the presence of some other separate life that carried on by itself, beyond the realm of circumstance. Groan after groan burst from his breast, without in the least disturbing his sleep; his constitutional ailment continued its work of destruction evidently without causing him physical pain.

In the morning, he awoke with the dawn and with him there awoke depression, revulsion, and hatred. Hatred, unprotesting and unreasoning, hatred for something without definition or form. His inflamed eyes settle senselessly first on one thing, then on another, gazing at them long and hard; his arms and legs shake; one moment his heart suddenly stops as if about to plummet to the depths, then it begins to pound so violently that his hand instinctively clutches to his chest. Not a single thought, not a single desire. His eyes meet the stove—and so engrossed is his mind with this object that it takes in no other impressions. The place of the stove is taken by the window . . . window, window, window . . . No need for anything, no need, no need, no need at all. His pipe is filled and lit mechanically and slips unsmoked from his hand; his tongue mutters something, but clearly only from habit. It is best to sit and say nothing, to say nothing and gaze into space. It would be good to have a drink now to clear the head, good to raise the body heat enough to have some brief sensation of the presence of life, but during the day vodka is not to be had for any price. He must wait till nightfall to achieve again those blissful moments when the earth disappears beneath his feet and instead of these four hateful walls there opens up before him the limitless, glaring void.

Arina Petrovna had no inkling of how Booby Stepka passed his time in the office. That chance spark of feeling which had flickered during her conversation with Bloodsucker Porfisha had died at once, without her even noticing. She was not even pursuing any systematic course of action, she simply forgot him. She completely lost sight of the fact that close by, in the office, there was a living being, bound to her by the ties of blood, a being who was, perhaps, languishing in longing for life. Having settled to a fixed pattern of life, she almost unthinkingly maintained it with the same content as before, and others, in her view, should act likewise. It never occurred to her that the very nature of what life contains varies according to a multitude of circumstances, and that in the end, while for some (herself included) the content of life was something agreeable and freely chosen, for others it was something hateful and imposed. So it was that although the bailiff several times reported that Stepan Vladimirych was 'poorly', his reports passed her by, making no impression on her mind. At most, she might make some stock reply:

'Never fear, he'll get over it and outlive the both of us! What's wrong with the great lanky lout? He's coughing! Why, some people cough for thirty years on end and think nothing of it!'

None the less, when one morning she was told that Stepan Vladimirych had during the night disappeared from Golovlevo, she suddenly came to. She immediately sent the whole household off to search for him and set about her own investigation, which began with an inspection of the room occupied by the outcast. The first thing which struck her was the bottle with some residue of liquid standing on the table, which in the commotion nobody had thought to clear away.

'And what's that?' she asked, as if failing to understand.

'Looks as if he was . . . at it,' answered the bailiff uneasily.

'Who got it for him?' she began, but stopped short and, concealing her anger, went on with her inspection.

The room was so dirty, black, and begrimed that even she, who neither had nor recognized any demands for comfort, was discomposed. The ceiling was black with smoke, the wallpaper had come apart and in many places hung down in shreds, the window-sills were covered with a thick black layer of tobacco ash, pillows lay scattered on the floor, which was coated with a layer of tacky grime, on the bed lay a crumpled sheet, grey with accumulated dirt. On one of the windows the winter frame had been removed —or rather, been ripped out—and the window itself had been left open: it was evidently by this route that the outcast had escaped. Arina Petrovna instinctively looked outside and was more than ever alarmed. It was by now early November, but the autumn had this year extended for an unusually long time and there had been as yet no frosts. The road and the fields were a sodden black morass. How had he got through it? Where had he gone? And then she remembered that all he had on was a dressing-gown and slippers (one of them was found beneath the window) and that by ill luck it had rained solidly all night.

'It's a good time since I last called in on you, my dears,' she said, as she inhaled, instead of air, the revolting mixture of cheap vodka, shag, and reeking sheepskins.

All day, while the servants scoured the woods, she stood at the window gazing stolidly into the bare distance. All this commotion on account of the Booby!—it was like some absurd dream. She had said at the time that he should have been packed off to the Vologda estate—but no, there was Judas, curse him, with his wheedling: 'Let him stay on, Mother dear, in Golovlevo'—and now you can have the joy of it! He could have lived there as he liked, out of my sight, and the Lord be with him! I would have done my part—one morsel squandered away, so I tossed him another, and if he had squandered that too, that's his look-out! The Lord himself can't fill the belly that always asks for more! And we would have lived in peace and quiet—but now see the dance he leads us! Goes and disappears in the woods! It'll be lucky if they bring him home alive—after all, a man in liquor is quite like to hang himself: a rope on a branch and round his neck and he's done for! His mother goes short of sleep and short of food, and then he goes and hangs himself! It would be different if he'd been hard done by, not been kept in food and drink or been overworked—but all he's ever done is traipse round his room all day like a man possessed, and eat and drink, eat and drink! Anybody else could never thank his mother enough for what I've done, but he goes and hangs himself—a fine obliging son he is!

But on this occasion Arina Petrovna's surmise that the Booby had come to a violent end was not borne out by events. Towards evening a kibitka* drawn by a pair of peasant horses came into view at Golovlevo and delivered the fugitive to the office. He was half-conscious, battered and cut, his face was blue and swollen. It appeared that during the night he had got as far as Dubrovino, which was twenty versts from Golovlevo.

He then slept for twenty-four hours and awoke on the following day. As usual, he began pacing the room, but did not touch his pipe, which he seemed to have forgotten, and, when questioned, uttered not a word. For her part, Arina Petrovna was so disturbed that she almost had him brought from the office into the manor-house, but then she recovered her composure and let him remain in the office, with orders that his room should be scrubbed and cleaned, the bed-linen changed, and blinds fitted to the windows, and so on. The next evening, when told that Stepan Vladimirych had woken up, she had him summoned into the house for tea and managed even to strike an affectionate note in her talk with him.

'Whatever did you mean going off like that from your mother?' she began. 'Don't you know how you worried me? A good thing Father didn't hear of it—what would it have done to him in his condition?'

But Stepan Vladimirych was apparently unmoved by his mother's show of affection and simply stared with fixed, glassy eyes at the tallow candle, as if observing the snuff that was gradually forming on the wick.

'Oh, what a silly boy!' Arina Petrovna continued, ever more affectionately. 'You should have thought what you might cause people to say about your mother—there are plenty who wish her ill and you never know what tales they might tell! They'll go and say I never fed or clothed you properly . . . ah, you silly, silly boy!'

The same silence, the same fixed gaze staring mindlessly into space.

'What was so bad about being here with your mother! You were well clothed, well fed. You had it all warm and cosy, so what more could you want! If you find it dull, too bad!—that's just country life. There's no balls and jollities here—we just sit in our corners and twiddle our thumbs. I'd be glad enough myself to go out singing and dancing, but one look outside and you're loath even to go to church in all that wet!'

Arina Petrovna stopped in expectation that the Booby would make at least some muttered reply; but the Booby seemed turned to stone. Arina Petrovna gradually began to simmer with anger, but still she controlled herself.

'And if anything wasn't to your liking—if you wanted more to eat or were short of linen, surely you could have spoken up and told your mother? You only had to say "Mother, be a dear, have them do me a bit of liver or a curd tart"—would your mother refuse you a bite to eat? Or vodka even—if ever you felt like a drink, why, bless you, a glass or two—would your mother begrudge you? But oh, no! You're not ashamed to ask it from a serf, but a word to your own mother is too much for you!'

But all these cajoling words were in vain: Stepan Vladimirych not only showed no emotion (Arina Petrovna had hoped that he might kiss her hand) or any sign of remorse, he seemed not even to hear what she said.

From then on he spoke not at all. For days on end he would walk about his room, frowning grimly, twitching his lips, and feeling no fatigue. Occasionally he stopped, as if wishing to say something, but was unable to find the word he wanted. He had evidently not lost the ability to think; but his mind had such a feeble grasp on things that impressions received were at once forgotten. Because of this, failing to find a requisite word did not even cause him to be impatient. For her part, Arina Petrovna was convinced he would set fire to the house.

'Never speaks a word all day long!' she said. 'He never speaks, but he's thinking something all the time. You mark my words and see if he doesn't burn the house down!'

But the Booby simply did not think at all. He seemed to be totally immersed in a dawnless darkness from which not only reality but even fantasy were excluded. His brain worked on something, but this 'something' had no relation to past, present, or future. It was as if he were enveloped from head to foot in a black cloud, at which he peered, ignoring all else; he watched its imagined fluctuations and occasionally shuddered and seemed to try and ward it off. The worlds of the flesh and of the mind were swallowed up for him in this mysterious cloud.

In December that year Porfiry Vladimirych received a letter from Arina Petrovna, the contents of which were as follows:

Yesterday morning we were afflicted by a fresh tribulation from the hand of the Lord: Stepan, my son and your brother, passed away. Only the evening before he had been quite well and had even eaten supper, but in the morning he was found dead in bed—such is this fleeting life! And most grievous of all to a mother's heart is that he should go just like that, with no word to commend him on his way as he departed from this vain world into the realm of the unknown.

And may this be a lesson to you all: whosoever scorns the bonds of family must ever expect to have such an end. Ill fortune in this life, an untimely death, and torment eternal in the life hereafter—all come from this. For however highminded or even grand we may be, if we honour not our parents, then all our highmindedness and grandness will be turned to naught. These are the rules which every man dwelling on this earth should learn, and serfs besides must honour their masters too.

This notwithstanding, however, all due respects were paid to the departed, as befitting for a son. The pall was ordered from Moscow and the interment was performed by the Father Archimandrite (who is known to you) with clergy in attendance. The forty-days prayers and remembrance for the dead are still being said according to Christian custom. I am sorry to lose a son, but venture not to complain, and counsel you, my children, to do likewise. For who can know?—while we complain here below, on high his spirit may be rejoicing!

KITH AND KIN

IT is noon on a hot July day. Around the manor-house at Dubrovino there is a deathly stillness. Not only those with time on their hands, but the workpeople too have drifted off to various nooks to lie down in the shade. The dogs lie sprawled beneath the canopy of the gigantic willow which stands in the middle of the front yard and their teeth can be heard snapping as, half-asleep, they try to catch flies. Even the trees stand wilting and motionless, as if exhausted. All the windows, both in the manor-house and in the servants' quarters, are wide open. The heat simply pours over you in a scorching wave; the ground with its covering of short, singed grass is blazing hot; an intolerable glare veils all around in a golden haze, making it hard to distinguish individual objects. The manor-house with its once grey paint now faded white, the small garden in front of the house, the birch-grove separated from the house by the highway, the pond, the village houses, and the rye-fields which start at once where the houses end—all are submerged in this gleaming haze. The air is thick with smells of every kind, from the scent of the flowering lime-trees to the miasma of the stock-yard. There is not a sound. Only from the kitchen comes the staccato chopping of the cooks' knives, presaging the invariable okroshka* and rissoles to be served for dinner.

Within the manor-house there is an atmosphere of hushed perturbation. The old mistress and two girls are seated in the dining-room and, not touching the stitchwork which lies tossed aside on the table, seem to be paralysed with expectation. In the maids' room two women are busy preparing mustard-plasters and lotions, and the rhythmic metallic beat of spoons, like the chirruping of a cricket, cuts through the general state of torpidity. In the passage young serving-girls move carefully about in bare feet as they scurry downstairs and back from the mezzanine to the maids' room. Occasionally a shout comes from upstairs: 'Where are those mustard-plasters! Have you gone to sleep? Eh?'—at which a serving-girl comes darting from the maids' room. At last, the creaking of heavy footsteps is heard on the stairs and into the dining-room comes the regimental doctor. The doctor is tall and broad-shouldered, with solid ruddy cheeks which are simply bursting with health. His voice is resonant, his step firm, his eyes bright and merry, his lips full and succulent, his look genial. Here is a *bon-viveur* in the fullest sense of the word, notwithstanding his fifty years—a *bon-viveur* who has not in the past held back and will not for a long while yet hold back from any occasion that presents itself to tipple or gormandize. He is wearing smart summer attire—a piqué tunic of uncommon whiteness with shiny crested buttons. He comes in smacking his lips and sucking at his tongue.

'Now, my dear, just bring us along some vodka and a bite to eat!' he orders, pausing at the doorway from the passage.

'Well? How is he?' the old mistress anxiously enquires.

'There's no end to God's mercies, Arina Petrovna!' replies the doctor.

'How can it be? Then he's . . .'

'That's how it is. He'll last another two or three days and then—curtains!'

The doctor makes an eloquent gesture with his hand and hums under his breath: 'Head-over, head-over-heels he'll go!'

'But how can it be so? All that treatment he had from the doctors, and then suddenly!'

'What doctors were they?'

'Our local one and another who came from the town.'

'Fine doctors!! If they'd done him a decent seton a month ago, he'd live on yet!'

'Is there really nothing that can be done?'

'As I said, there's no end to God's mercies, and I can't say more than that.'

'Perhaps it might work, though?'

'What might work?'

'What you're doing now . . . these mustard-plasters . . .'

'Possibly, ma'am.'

A woman in a black dress and black kerchief brings in a tray with a decanter of vodka and two plates, one of sausage and one of caviare. On her arrival there is a lull in the conversation. The doctor fills his glass, inspects it against the light, and clicks his tongue.

'Your health, ma'am,' he says, addressing the old mistress and swallowing the vodka.

'Good health to you, sir.'

'This is the stuff that's cutting off Pavel Vladimirych in his prime—vodka!' observes the doctor, screwing up his face with pleasure and spearing a round of sausage with his fork.

'Yes, it's the ruin of many.'

'It's not everybody who can stomach this fluid—that's the reason! But since we *can* stomach it, we'll have the same again. Your health, ma'am!'

'Drink, please do—it's no harm to you.'

'Not to me, no. Lungs, kidneys, liver, spleen—all in good order. Ah yes, I was going to ask,' he says, turning to the woman in black, who had paused at the door as if to eavesdrop on the mistress's conversation, 'What have you got for dinner today?'

'There's okroshka, and rissoles, and chicken for roast', the woman replies with a smile.

'And do you have a bit of pickled fish?'

'That we do, sir! There's sturgeon, sevryuga*. . . We'll find you some fish, as much as you please.'

'Then have them do a botvinya* with sturgeon for dinner, a good wedge of sturgeon, you know, nice and fat. What's your name? Ulitushka you're called, aren't you?'

'Yes, sir, Ulita is what they call me.'

'Well then, look lively, Ulita, look lively!'

Ulita goes out; for a minute there is an oppressive silence. Arina Petrovna gets up from her place and looks out of the door to make sure that Ulita has gone.

'And did you speak to him about the girls, Andrey Osipych?' she questions the doctor.

'Yes, ma'am, I did have a talk with him.'

'Well, and what did he say?'

'The same as ever. He says when he's better he'll be sure to make a will and draw up the bills of exchange.'

A still more oppressive silence falls on the room. The girls take up the embroidery canvas from the table and their hands visibly tremble as they make their stitches one by one; Arina Petrovna sighs with an air of hopelessness; the doctor paces the room, whistling 'Head-over, head-over-heels . . .'

'You should have told him straight, though!'

'What more could I have said! I told him he'd be a swine if he didn't provide for the orphans! You've been caught napping, ma'am, that's a fact! If you'd called me in a month ago, I could have fixed him a seton and tackled him about the will too. . . . But now it's Judas, as lawful heir, who'll get the lot . . . that's for sure!'

'Granny, whatever is going to happen!' says the elder of the girls plaintively, almost in tears. 'Why is Uncle treating us like this!'

'I don't know, dearie, I don't know. I don't even know about myself. I'm here today—and tomorrow I don't know where . . . Perhaps, by God's will, I'll be sleeping somewhere in a shed or putting up with one of the peasants.'

'Mercy, what a stupid uncle he is!' exclaims the younger of the girls.

'You, young miss, should hold your tongue!' observes the doctor, adding to Arina Petrovna: 'But what about you, ma'am, why don't you try to talk him round?'

'No, no, no! He won't have it! He'll not as much as see me! I looked in to see him a day or two ago and he says: "Come to perform the last rites, have you?" '

'I think Ulitushka's the main cause . . . it's she sets him against you.'

'Yes, it's her, she's the one! And she passes it all on to Bloodsucker Judas! They say he's got horses harnessed up all day in case his brother's time should come! And would you believe it—the other day she was making a list of everything: furniture, bedding, linen, crockery, in case anything should go missing, she said! The likes of her making out *us*—*us*!—to be thieves!'

'You ought to give it her military fashion . . . send her head-over-heels, you know . . .'

But the doctor had no time to elaborate, for into the room dashed one of the serving-girls, panting for breath, and cried in a frightened voice:

'Come to the master! He wants the doctor!'

The family which takes the stage in the present narrative is already known to us. The old mistress is none other than Arina Petrovna Golovleva; the dying owner of the Dubrovino estate is her son, Pavel Vladimirych; and lastly, the two girls are Anninka and Lyubinka, daughters of the late Anna Vladimirovna Ulanova, the same to whom once Arina Petrovna had 'tossed a morsel'. It is no more than ten years since we last saw them, but the situation of the *dramatis personae* has undergone such a change that no trace remains of those artificial bonds by virtue of which the Golovlev family had appeared to be an impregnable fortress. The family citadel, raised by the untiring hands of Arina Petrovna, has collapsed, but so imperceptibly has this come about that Arina Petrovna has herself unwittingly been a collaborator and even apparently the prime mover in this process of destruction, of which, needless to say, the real instigator was Bloodsucker Porfishka.

After being the absolute and fractious mistress of the Golovlev estates, Arina Petrovna is now a humble dependant in the household of her youngest son, a dependant with nothing to do and with no voice in the domestic management. Her head now droops, her back is bent, her eyes are lustreless, the spring in her step, the vigour of her movements have gone. With nothing to occupy her, she has in her old age learnt to knit, but even her knitting does not prosper, since her thoughts keep wandering—whither? —she cannot always say herself, but at any rate her mind is far from her knitting-needles. She sits and knits for a few minutes, then suddenly her hands involuntarily drop, her head falls against the back of her chair, and she begins recalling the past . . . She goes on raking up old memories until the drowsiness of old age takes full possession of her aged self. Or she gets up and goes wandering about the rooms of the house, all the time seeking something, looking here and there, like a woman who, having all her life held the keys, cannot now comprehend how and where she has lost them.

The first blow to the authority of Arina Petrovna was delivered not so much by the abolition of serfdom as by the preparations that preceded it. First there were just rumours, then the assemblies of the gentry with their declarations, then the provincial committees, then the editing commissions:* it was all wearing and upsetting. In her imagination—which was fertile enough anyway —Arina Petrovna entertained a multitude of trifling fancies. The question would suddenly present itself: what shall I call Agashka? Agafyushka, I suppose . . . but perhaps I'll have to call her Agafya Fedorovna!* Another time she would picture herself walking about the empty house, while the servants had taken themselves off to their own quarters and were stuffing their bellies. When tired of stuffing themselves, they would throw the food under the table! Then she fancied herself peeping into one of the cellars and seeing Yulka and Feshka there furiously cramming their faces with food, my word, how they crammed it in! She was all set to deliver them a reprimand, but the words stuck in her throat. 'How can you say anything to them! They're free now and beyond the law too, I dare say!'

However petty such fancies might be, they gradually create an entire fantastic reality that engulfs a man and totally paralyses his ability to act. So it was that Arina Petrovna suddenly allowed the reins of authority to slip from her hands and for two years all she did was to exclaim from morning to night:

'If there was only something for sure—all or nothing! Instead we've got "first convocation", "second convocation",* and it's neither one thing nor the other!'

It was at this time, when the various committees were in full swing, that Vladimir Mikhailych also died. He died reconciled and subdued, having renounced Barkov and all his works. His last words were:

'Thanks be to God that he did not permit that I should come before his presence on equal footing with my own serfs!'

These words made a deep impression on the sensitive soul of Arina Petrovna, and the death of her husband together with her own phantasmagoria of the future lent a certain tone of hopelessness to the whole way of life in Golovlevo. It was as if the old house of Golovlevo and all who dwelt in it had come simultaneously to the point of death.

With astonishing intuition Porfiry Vladimirych had, from

the few complaints expressed by Arina Petrovna in her letters, discerned the confused state of mind she was now in. Arina Petrovna in her letters no longer delivered reprimands or homilies, but for the most part spoke of trusting in God's help, 'which in these times of little faith does not forsake even the serfs, much less those who, according to their means, have been the trustiest support to the church and its adornment'. Judas instinctively grasped that if his dear mother was beginning to put her trust in God, then there was something amiss with her. And he worked on this failing with his characteristic cunning skill.

Just before the Emancipation took place he came quite unexpectedly to Golovlevo and found Arina Petrovna dejected and nearly prostrate with worry.

'What's the news? How does it look? What do they say in Petersburg?' were her first questions when the mutual greetings were concluded.

Porfisha dropped his eyes and sat saying nothing.

'Just think what it means to me!' Arina Petrovna went on, taking her son's silence as indication that no good was to be expected. 'I've got thirty of these hussies just in the maids' room —what am I supposed to do with them? If I'm still to give them their keep, what shall I feed them on? Now I've got cabbage, and potatoes, and corn—there's enough of everything and so we manage. If there's no potatoes, you can have them cook a bit of cabbage; if there's no cabbage, you can make do with cucumbers! But now when the time comes I'll be running myself to get everything from the market, paying for it all in cash, buying and spending all the time—how shall I ever provide for such a horde as that?'

Porfisha looked his dear mother in the eyes and smiled sorrowfully in token of his concern.

'Or will they let them go random free: off you run, my dears, with your eyes all agog!—I just don't know, I don't know, I don't know at all what will come of it!'

Porfisha grinned as if he found the prospect of 'what would come of it' highly amusing.

'No, my dear, don't you go laughing! It's a serious matter, that serious that if the Lord doesn't put more sense in them—well . . .

I'll but speak of myself: after all, I'm not a left-over, am I? I need to be looked after too. What's to be done about it? I ask you—what kind of upbringing did we have? They taught us to dance and sing and receive visitors. What shall I do without those hussies of mine? I can't serve or clear away or cook for myself—why, my dear, there's not a thing I can do!'

'God is merciful, Mother dear!'

'He was merciful, my dear, but that's all over now! He was merciful indeed, but there was a purpose: so long as we were good, our Father in Heaven rewarded us, but now we aren't—it's just too bad! I'm minded now to give it all up before the worst comes. Yes, I am. I'll build me a little house by Father's grave and live my days out there!'

Porfiry Vladimirych pricked up his ears; his lips watered.

'But who would manage the properties then?' he protested cautiously, as if casting a baited hook.

'Too bad! You'll have to manage them yourselves! God be praised, I've made provision! I can't go on for ever bearing all the burdens on my own . . .'

Arina Petrovna suddenly stopped short and raised her head. She was confronted by the grinning, slavering face of Judas, that seemed to be coated with oil and lit with some inner predatory gleam.

'You're all ready to bury me, aren't you!' she observed drily. 'A bit too soon, my dear! Don't you be mistaken!'

So, on the first occasion the matter came to nothing. But there are conversations which, once begun, do not come to an end. A few hours later Arina Petrovna returned to the topic of their interrupted talk.

'I'll go off to Trinity-Sergius Monastery,'* she mused. 'I'll divide the property; I'll buy a little house in the town there and settle down in peace!'

But this time Porfiry Vladimirych, the wiser for his recent experience, remained silent.

'Last year, when your dear departed father was still alive', Arina Petrovna mused on, 'I was sitting in my bedroom all alone and I suddenly heard like it was somebody whispering to me: "Go to the Miracle-Worker!* Go to the Miracle-Worker!"—a full three times, it was! So, well, I looked round, but there was nobody there. I thought, though: it's a vision been sent to me! Well, said I to myself, if my faith is found pleasing to God, then I'm ready to go! And no sooner had I said it than all of a sudden there was this fragrance in the room! Such fragrance! Of course, I had them pack straight away, and by evening I was on my way!'

There were actually tears in Arina Petrovna's eyes. Judas made the most of the situation by kissing his mother's hand, at the same time venturing to hug her round the waist.

'There, now you are being a good girl!' he said. 'Ah, dearest Mother, what a fine thing when you are at one with God! You turn to God with your prayers and God turns to you with his aid. Yes, Mother dear, oh yes indeed!'

'Hold now! I haven't finished yet. The next evening I come to the monastery and go straight to Saint Sergius. And in the church the Vigil Service was going on: the singing, the candles all alight, and such fragrance from the incense—I really couldn't tell if I was on earth or in heaven! After the service I went to Father Iona, and told his reverence how wonderful it was in the church that day, and he said to me "No wonder, ma'am! During the service Father Avvakum had a vision! Just as he was lifting his hands to pray he looked up and there in the very dome there was a light shining and a dove looking down at him!" Ever since then I've made up my mind that, come what may, I'll live out my last days at Trinity-Sergius.'

'But who will look after *us*? Who will take care of your children? Oh, Mother, Mother!'

'You're not little now, you can shift for yourselves! But I'll . . . take Anna's orphan girls with me and go and live there under the wing of the Miracle-Worker! And if so be that either of the girls should have a desire to serve the Lord, then there's Khotkov* just a stone's throw away! I'll buy a little house for myself and have a bit of garden, there'll be cabbage and potatoes, and I'll have ample for my needs.'

This idle conversation was carried on for several days; several times Arina Petrovna expressed the boldest of intentions, only to go back on them, then take them up once more—but in the end she had brought the matter to a point from which there was no

longer any retreat. Within six months of Judas's visit to her, the
position was this: Arina Petrovna had not gone off to Trinity-
Sergius Monastery, nor to a house by her husband's grave, but
she had divided the property, keeping only the cash capital for
herself. In the division it was Porfiry Vladimirych who got the
better share; Pavel Vladimirych did rather less well.

Arina Petrovna stayed on in Golovlevo as before, though not, of
course, without the enactment of a routine family comedy. Judas
wept and begged his dear mother to manage the estate with a free
hand, to receive the income from it and apply it at her own discretion, 'and with whatever you allow me from the income,
Mother dear, be it ever so small, I shall be well content.' Pavel,
on the other hand, was cool in his thanks ('like to bite me he
was'), immediately resigned his commission ('just like that! without his mother's blessing, cut loose and was off like a man
possessed!'), and settled in Dubrovino.
   From then on a state of obfuscation descended on Arina
Petrovna. That inward image of Porfishka the Bloodsucker which
she once had the rare perspicacity to discern in him was suddenly
as if veiled in mist. She seemed no longer to understand anything
except that, despite the division of the property and the freeing
of the serfs, she was living on as before in Golovlevo and was as
before accountable to no man. And there, nearby, was living her
other son—and what a difference! While Porfisha entrusted himself and his family entirely to the discretion of his mother, Pavel
not only never consulted her, but even, when they did meet,
treated her in a very tight-lipped manner.
   And the greater the obfuscation of her mind, the more was her
heart fired with concern for her affectionate son. Porfiry Vladimirych asked nothing of her—she herself anticipated his every
wish. She gradually began to find drawbacks in the conformation
of the Golovlevo holdings. In one place a corner of someone else's
land jutted into Golovlevo territory—it would be nice to buy it
up; in another place you could start up a separate farm, but for
there being too little meadow-land—there was, though, some
meadow adjoining up for sale, and good it was too! Arina
Petrovna was carried away, both as mother and as estate-manager,

in her anxiety to display to her affectionate son the full measure of her capabilities. But Porfiry Vladimirych seemed to have withdrawn into some impenetrable shell. In vain did Arina Petrovna attempt to beguile him with her proposals to purchase—to all her suggestions for acquiring a wood here or a meadow there he invariably answered: 'I'm well content as it is, Mother dear, with what you in the goodness of your heart have given me already.'

These replies merely galvanized Arina Petrovna. Absorbed on the one hand by the tasks of management, and on the other by certain polemical purposes relating to 'that scoundrel Pavlushka' who lived so close and chose to ignore her, she completely lost sight of her actual position with regard to Golovlevo. With new force the old passion for acquisition possessed her, only now it was acquisition not for herself, but for her favourite son. The Golovlevo estate expanded, filled out, and flourished.

And then suddenly, just when Arina Petrovna's own capital had diminished to a point where it was almost impossible for her to live independently on the interest, Judas sent her—enclosed with a most dutiful letter—a pile of book-keeping forms which were to be her guide in future when drawing up the annual accounts. Here, together with the principal items of the estate economy, there were entries for raspberries, gooseberries, mushrooms, etc. Each item had its separate account, roughly as follows:

Raspberry canes as at 18**			oo
To which add newly planted canes			oo
From which stock of canes fruit gathered to the amount of	oo *qu.*	oo *lb.*	oo *oz.*
Of this:			
Consumed by you, Mother dear	oo	oo	oo
Used to make preserves for the household of His Excellency Porfiry Vladimirych Golovlev*	oo	oo	oo
Given to the boy N. for good conduct		1*lb.*	
Sold to common folk for their indulgence	oo	oo	oo

| Gone to rot for lack of customers and other reasons | oo | oo | oo |

Etc., etc.

Note: In the event of the yield of the current year being less than the previous year's, explanation should here be given for his, e.g. drought, rain, hail, etc.

Arina Petrovna was taken aback. In the first place, she was astonished by Judas's niggardliness: never in her life had she known 'gooseberries' to figure as an item in accounts, yet he evidently regarded it as a matter of great moment; in the second place, she realized perfectly well that these forms were nothing more than a 'constitution' by which she was to be bound hand and foot.

The upshot was that after a lengthy and contentious correspondence Arina Petrovna, offended and indignant, moved to Dubrovino, following which Porfiry Vladimirych also retired from his post and settled in Golovlevo.

For the old woman there now began a succession of dreary days given up to enforced repose. Pavel Vladimirych, as a man bereft of deeds, was somehow particularly carping in his attitude towards his mother. He received her tolerably, that is, he undertook to provide board for her and his orphaned nieces, but on two conditions: first, that she should never enter his rooms in the mezzanine, and secondly, that she should never interfere in the running of his estate. The latter was particularly galling to Arina Petrovna. Pavel Vladimirych's affairs were managed entirely by two people—one was the housekeeper Ulitushka, a spiteful woman, who had been caught carrying on a secret correspondence with Bloodsucker Porfisha, the other was Kiryusha, his father's former valet, who knew absolutely nothing of farming and daily delivered obsequious homilies to Pavel Vladimirych. Both of them stole ruthlessly. How often was Arina Petrovna the anguished witness of the rampant plundering that went on! How often did she try to alert her son, to open his eyes to the loss of his tea, sugar, butter! Whole quantities of them disappeared, and more than once, before her very eyes, Ulitushka pocketed handfuls of sugar, quite unabashed by the old mistress's presence. Arina Petrovna saw all this and had to remain a silent witness of these depredations, for no sooner did she open her mouth to remark on anything than Pavel Vladimirych straightway checked her.

'Mother,' he would say, 'there can be only one person running the house. That's not what I say, it's what everybody does. I know the way I do things is silly—well, all right, it's silly. And the way you do things is sensible—well, all right, it's sensible. You are sensible, very sensible even, but still Judas put you out in the cold!'

On top of all else, Arina Petrovna was horrified to discover that Pavel Vladimirych drank. The craving took hold of him by stealth, as a result of his rural solitude, and finally made such fearful progress that it could have only one inevitable end. At first, when his mother came to live in his house, he still seemed to have some qualms of conscience and quite often came down from his mezzanine to chat with her. Observing how confused his speech was, Arina Petrovna for a long time put it down to his stupidity. She did not like his coming to chat and considered these conversations a great imposition on herself. Indeed, he was for ever making odd complaints: first, that there had been no rain for weeks and then it had suddenly come pelting down in torrents; then it was a plague of beetles that had stripped all the trees in the garden; then it was moles that had appeared and dug up all his meadows. All this provided an inexhaustible source of complaint. He would come down from the mezzanine, sit opposite his mother, and start:

'There are rain-clouds all around—and Golovlevo's no distance, is it? Yesterday the Bloodsucker had a downpour—but it never rains here! There are the clouds going round and round—but not a drop on our land!'

Or:

'Just look at that rain pouring down! The rye is just earing and it pours with rain! Half the hay has rotted already, and there it goes on bucketing down! And Golovlevo's no distance, is it? The Bloodsucker's got his hay in long ago—and we sit here waiting! Come winter, we'll be feeding the stock with rotten hay!'

Arina Petrovna remains silent as she listens to these stupidities, but from time to time she cannot contain herself and says:

'A fat lot you do to help it!'

But no sooner does she speak than Pavel Vladimirych flies off the handle:

'And what would you have me do then? Shift the rain to Golovlevo perhaps?'

'I'm not talking about the rain, just generally . . .'

'No, you just tell me what you think I am supposed to do—not "generally", but straight out . . . Perhaps you would like me to change the climate for you? There in Golovlevo, now, when they wanted rain, it rained, and when they don't want rain, it doesn't! So there everything grows . . . But here it's all the other way round! Let's see what you've got to say when there's nothing to eat!'

'Such, I suppose, will be God's will . . .'

'There you go on about it being God's will! Or else it's all "generally"—some explanation that is!'

Sometimes it came to a point where he found the estate itself an encumbrance.

'Why on earth did I get Dubrovino?' he would complain. 'What good is it?'

'There's nothing wrong with Dubrovino! It's got good land and everything in plenty. How can you have such a notion!'

'The notion I've got is that these days you're better off with no property at all! Money—that's all right! You take it, put it in your pocket, and clear off! But property . . .'

'And what's so special about these times that you shouldn't have property?'

'The times are such that evidently you don't read the papers, but I do. Nowadays there are lawyers everywhere*—and you know what that means! Once a lawyer gets wind of it that you've got property, he'll start hovering for the kill!'

'How can he do that, if you've got the rightful deeds?'

'He'll do it the way they all do. Or there's Bloodsucker Judas —he'll hire himself a lawyer and have him serve you writs without end!'

'What do you mean! There are laws in the land, aren't there?'

'That's why they'll serve me writs. If there weren't laws, they'd take my land without writs, but as it is they'll do it with writs.

Look at my old friend Gorlopyatov—his uncle died and he was fool enough to accept the inheritance. It turned out to be worth tuppence-ha'penny, with debts of a hundred thousand: promissory notes and every one of them a fake! They've had him in court for three years now: first, they relieved him of his uncle's property, then they auctioned off his own. That's property for you!'

'Is there really such a law?'

'If there wasn't a law, they wouldn't have sold him up. There's nothing the law won't cover. There's always a law for the man who's got no conscience, but never one for the man who has. Let him try and find one in the book!'

Arina Petrovna always gave way in these arguments. She was more than once moved to cry out: 'Out of my sight, you scoundrel!' but she would think better of it and hold her tongue. She might perhaps just murmur to herself:

'Lord above! Who do they take after, these monsters I brought into the world! One's a bloodsucker, the other's a simpleton! Who have I provided for? Gone short of sleep, gone short of food . . . for who?'

And the more Pavel Vladimirych succumbed to drink, the more fantastic and precipitate did his conversation become. In the end Arina Petrovna came to be aware that something was amiss. For instance, in the morning a whole decanter of vodka was put in the cabinet in the dining-room, but by evening there was not a drop left in it. Or she would sit in the drawing-room and hear a mysterious creaking coming from the dining-room in the proximity of the cherished cabinet. 'Who's that?' she would cry, and then hear footsteps as someone swiftly but cautiously retreated in the direction of the mezzanine.

'Merciful heavens! You don't mean to say he drinks!' she said to Ulitushka one day.

'He drinks all right,' answered Ulitushka, smiling caustically.

Once assured that his mother had found him out, Pavel Vladimirych abandoned all pretence. One fine morning the cabinet had vanished completely from the dining-room and in answer to Arina Petrovna's question as to its whereabouts Ulitushka replied:

'He's had it taken to the mezzanine. It'll be handier for him, drinking there.'

And indeed, into the mezzanine decanter followed decanter with amazing rapidity. In his solitary retreat Pavel Vladimirych abhorred the society of living people and created for himself a special fantastic reality of his own. It was a full-blown romantic extravaganza, complete with transformations, disappearances, and sudden acquisitions of fortune—a romance in which the principal characters were himself and Bloodsucker Porfishka. He had not fully realized himself the depth of his hatred for Porfishka. He hated him with his every thought, with every fibre of his being, hated him unceasingly, every moment of the day. As if alive, this loathsome image danced before his eyes, and his ears rang with the snivelling humbug of Judas's vacuous prattle— prattle which gave voice to an arid, almost detached malice towards any living thing that failed to conform to humbug's established code. Pavel Vladimirych drank and recalled the past. He recalled all the insults and humiliations he had suffered as a result of Judas's claims to the headship of the household. In particular, he recalled the division of the property, reckoned every kopek, compared every parcel of land—and hated. Flushed with wine, he created in his imagination whole dramas in which all these insults were avenged and in which it was he and not Judas who inflicted injury. He pictured himself having won two hundred thousand roubles and going to inform Porfishka (an entire scene with dialogue), whose face positively twisted with envy. Or their grandfather had died (another scene with dialogue, though in fact they had no grandfather), and he had left him a million, but to Bloodsucker Porfishka—not a bean. Or he had invented a means of making himself invisible and thus was able to play Porfishka such villainous tricks as had him groaning aloud. His capacity for devising these pranks was inexhaustible and his inane laughter rang long through the mezzanine—much to the pleasure of Ulitushka, who hastened to apprise brother Porfiry of what was going on.

He hated Judas and at the same time feared him. He knew that Judas's eyes exuded a bewitching venom, that his voice slithered like a serpent into a man's soul and paralysed his will.

Because of this, he flatly refused to have any meeting with him. The Bloodsucker occasionally visited Dubrovino in order to kiss his dear mother's hand (he had turned her out of his house, but never ceased to show respect)—and when he came, Pavel Vladimirych locked himself up in the mezzanine and stayed there while Judas and his mother chatted.

So the days went by until in the end Pavel Vladimirych found himself face to face with mortal illness.

The doctor stayed overnight 'for the sake of form' and early next morning drove back to the town. On leaving Dubrovino he bluntly declared that the sick man had not more than two days to live and that it was now too late to think of any 'arrangements', since he would be incapable even of signing his name properly.

'He'd scrawl whatever came into his head—and you might then be litigating for ever,' he added. 'Much as Judas respects his dear mother, he'd none the less bring an action for forgery, and if the law decided to dispatch his dear old Mum to Siberia all he'd do would be to have intercessions said "for those that travel"!'

The whole morning Arina Petrovna walked about in a kind of daze. She tried praying—to see if God might give some guidance—but the prayers did not come readily to mind and even her tongue was somehow uncompliant. She would begin 'Lord have mercy on me in thy great goodness' and then, without knowing why, suddenly switch to 'deliver us from evil'. 'Cleanse me! Cleanse me!' mechanically said her tongue, but her thoughts were far away: in her mind she would take a look upstairs, then visit the store-cellars ('The amount of stuff that was there in the autumn and now all of it pilfered!'), and then begin to recall some long-distant memory. It was a kind of all-pervading dusk, a dusk in which there were people, many people swarming, toiling, storing things away. 'Blessed is the man . . . Blessed is the man . . . as the incense . . . teach me . . . teach me. . . .' But now her tongue gradually slackens, her eyes stare unseeing at the icons, her mouth gapes, her hands rest folded on her waist, and she stands motionless, as if turned to stone.

At last, she sat down and wept. The tears poured from her lifeless eyes and down her aged, withered cheeks, lingering in the furrows of her wrinkles before dripping on to the greasy collar of her old cotton blouse. She wept from bitterness, total lack of hope, and impotent obstinacy. Old age, infirmities, the helplessness of her situation—everything, it seemed, was bidding her to death as the only solace, but at the same time the past, with all its power, prosperity, and freedom, had also its effect and the memories of this past clutched her tight and held her to the earth. 'I want to die,' she would think, but a moment later the one word gave way to the other: 'I want to live!' She remembered nothing of Judas or her dying son—both might have ceased to exist for her. She thought of no one, found fault with no one, censured no one: she even forgot if she had any capital or if it sufficed to provide for her old age. A mortal anguish had seized her whole being. Miserable, sick at heart!—only thus could she explain her tears. These tears stemmed from the distant past: they had accumulated drop by drop since tthe moment when she left Golovlevo and settled in Dubrovino. For all that now confronted her she had been prepared, it had all been expected and foreseen, but she had somehow never envisaged with such clarity that the expected and foreseen must have its end. And now that end had come, an end filled with anguish and hopeless solitude. All her life she had been scheming, spending herself to achieve something, and now it turned out that she had spent herself on an illusion. All her life the word 'family' had never been off her lips: in the name of the family she had punished some and rewarded others; in the name of the family she had deprived and tormented herself, marred her whole life—and suddenly it turned out that she *had* no family.

'Lord! And is it the same for everybody?' the thought kept coming to her.

She sat with her head resting on her hand and her tear-stained face turned to the rising sun, as if she were saying to it: 'See!' She uttered no groans or curses, only softly whimpered, choking, it seemed, with tears. And at the same time deep within her there was the agonizing thought:

'There's nobody, nobody! Nobody at all!'

But the tears dried up. She washed her face and went off aimlessly into the dining-room, where the girls beset her with fresh complaints which on this occasion she found particularly vexing.

'What is going to happen, Granny? Are we really going to be left with nothing at all?' lamented Anninka.

'What a silly uncle he is!' Lyubinka chimed in.

About midday Arina Petrovna resolved to make her way to her dying son. Cautiously, treading very lightly, she climbed the stairs and felt her way in the dark to the door which led to his rooms. A dusky gloom filled the mezzanine; the windows were hung with green blinds through which the light barely penetrated; the atmosphere in the long-unventilated rooms was imbued with a revolting mixture of assorted odours, constituents of which were berries, plasters, icon-lamp oil, and those particular miasmas the very presence of which is sure indication of sickness and death. There were only two rooms: in the first sat Ulitushka topping and tailing gooseberries and puffing furiously at the buzzing swarms of flies which circled round the piles of fruit and brazenly settled on her nose and lips. From the next room, through the half-open door, there came the unremitting sound of a short, dry cough, occasionally culminating in an agonizing expectoration. Arina Petrovna paused uncertainly, peering into the gloom and seeming to await Ulitushka's reaction to her arrival. But Ulitushka made not the slightest movement, as if only too well aware that any attempt to influence the sick man would be in vain. There was just a vicious flickering of her lips, and Arina Petrovna caught the whispered word 'Devil'.

'You can go downstairs, my dear,' said Arina Petrovna to Ulitushka.

'Oh, I can, can I? That's rich!' snapped the latter in reply.

'I have to talk to Pavel Vladimirych. Go along now!'

'Pardon me, ma'am, but how can I leave him? If anything should happen—there'd be nobody to lend a hand.'

'What's going on?' came a hollow voice from the bedroom.

'Tell Ulita to go away, my dear. I must have a talk with you.'

On this occasion Arina Petrovna's firm stand won the day. She crossed herself and entered the room. The sick-bed stood against the inner wall, away from the window. Pavel Vladimirych lay on his back, with a white blanket over him, and half-consciously puffed at a cigarette. Regardless of the tobacco smoke, the flies flew at him with such fury that he continually waved one arm or the other across his face. These arms were now so feeble and devoid of muscle that the outline of the bones was clearly visible and from wrist to shoulder they were of practically the same narrow width. His head clung hopelessly to the pillow, his face and the whole of his body burned with a dry fever. His great round eyes were sunken and gazed vacantly, as if looking for something; his nose was drawn and pointed, his mouth hung half-open. He did not cough but breathed so heavily that all his vital energy seemed to be concentrated in the working of his chest.

'Well now, how are you feeling today?' asked Arina Petrovna, lowering herself into the armchair by the foot of the bed.

'Not so bad . . . tomorrow . . . no, today . . . when was it the doctor came?'

'The doctor was here today.'

'Well then, tomorrow . . .'

The sick man tossed as if straining to think of the word.

'You'll be able to get up?' prompted Arina Petrovna. 'God grant you may, my dear, God grant you may!'

For a minute neither spoke. Arina Petrovna had something to say, but it could only be said in the course of conversation. Opening such a conversation was, though, the very thing she could never do when alone with Pavel Vladimirych.

'Judas . . . is he well?' the sick man asked at length.

'Why, whatever should ail him! He's fit as a fiddle!'

'He'll be thinking that once brother Pavel's dead, then by God's mercy he'll be coming into another property!'

'Well, we'll all of us die some time and then all our property will pass on to the . . . legal heirs . . .'

'Only not to the Bloodsucker! I'll throw it to the dogs rather than he should have it!'

It was an excellent opportunity: Pavel Vladimirych had himself broached the subject and Arina Petrovna did not let the chance slip by.

'You should give some thought to it, my dear,' she said casually, not looking at her son and inspecting her hands against the light as if for the moment they were her chief concern.

'What's "it"?'

'Well, for instance, if you don't want your brother to have your property ...'

The sick man was silent. Only his eyes dilated unnaturally and his face became redder and redder.

'You could bear it in mind that you've got two orphaned nieces—what capital have they got? And then there's your mother too ...' continued Arina Petrovna.

'You've let Judas have the lot, have you?'

'Be that as it may ... I know it's my own fault ... And it's no great sin, after all ... I had thought that his being my own son ... You might well not have brought that up against your mother.'

Silence.

'Well, what about it? Say something, whatever it is!'

'How soon is it you plan to bury me?'

'Nobody's planning to bury you, but all the same ... Other Christian folk ... Not everybody's going to die straight off, but still generally ...'

'There you go again with your "generally"! With you it's always "generally"! Do you think I can't see?'

'What is it you see, my dear?'

'What I see is that you take me for a fool! All right, suppose I am a fool, let me be a fool then! Why come and see a fool? So don't come! And stop your fretting!'

'I'm not fretting. I was just saying generally that every man's life has its span ...'

'Well, just you wait then!'

Arina Petrovna hung her head and pondered. She could well see that things were going badly, but the hopelessness of the future so tormented her that even the most patent signs could not persuade her of the futility of trying any further.

'I don't know why it is you hate me!' she said finally.

'I don't at all ... hate you ... not at all! I actually ... Really! You brought us up that way ... all alike ...'

He spoke in gasps; there was a kind of strained, but at the same time triumphant laughter in his voice; his eyes sparkled; his arms and legs jerked restlessly.

'If I *was* perhaps ever in any way at fault, then for mercy's sake forgive me.'

Arina Petrovna rose and bowed, touching her hand to the floor. Pavel Vladimirych closed his eyes and did not answer.

'As for the fixed property . . . It's true, in your present state there's no question of your arranging anything . . . Porfisha is legal heir—all right, so the fixed property goes to him . . . But what about the movable property? What about the capital?' said Arina Petrovna, now determined to speak her mind.

Pavel Vladimirych gave a start, but said nothing. Quite likely, on hearing the word 'capital', he paid no heed to the inference of what Arina Petrovna said, but simply thought to himself: yes, here we are in September, I should be getting the interest . . . 67,600 times five and divided by two—what does that come to?

'You may be thinking I want you to die—don't you believe it, my dear! You just go on living and I'll have a few worries in my old age! What can I want! Living with you, I keep warm, feed well, and should I fancy something lickerish—it's all there for me! All I'm saying is that it's Christian custom when you are preparing for the life to come . . .'

Arina Petrovna paused as if trying to find the appropriate word.

'To provide for your own,' she concluded, looking out of the window.

Pavel Vladimirych lay still, quietly coughing to clear his throat, with not a gesture to reveal if he was listening or not. He had evidently had enough of his mother's laments.

'Capital can be passed on in your lifetime,' Arina Petrovna said, as if mentioning the idea in passing, as she returned to the inspection of her hands against the light.

The sick man gave a faint start, but Arina Petrovna did not heed it and continued:

'Capital is allowed to change hands, my dear, even the law says so. Because it is something acquired: one day you have it, the next day you don't. And you don't have to account for it to anybody— you can give it to who you like.'

Pavel Vladimirych gave a sudden malicious laugh.

'You must be thinking about the Palochkin affair!' he hissed. 'There was a man who passed his capital to his wife—and she ran off with her lover!'

'I've got no lovers, my dear!'

'So you won't run off with a lover, you'll run off with the capital!'

'A pretty way to understand me that is!'

'I don't understand you at all . . . You've declared me for a fool—so be it then, I'm a fool! And let me go on being one! You and your clever schemes—hand the capital over to them! And what about me? Do you expect me to go and save my soul in a monastery and watch you having the run of my money?'

He delivered this speech in one breath and with such malice and vehemence that it left him totally spent. For at least a quarter of an hour he coughed violently—it was, in fact, surprising that this wretched human frame should still have so much strength in it. At last he regained his breath and closed his eyes.

Arina Petrovna looked round in dismay. Up to now she had still not really believed it, but she was now absolutely certain that any further effort to persuade the dying man could only advance the day of Judas's triumph. Judas kept appearing in her mind's eye. She pictured him following the coffin, then giving his brother a last Judas-kiss as a couple of shabby tears dripped from his eyes. Now they have lowered the coffin into the ground: 'Farewell, farewell, brother!' declares Judas, twitching his lips and rolling his eyes upwards as he strives to impart a melancholy ring to his voice—before half-turning to Ulitushka and saying: 'The kutya*—don't forget to take it back to the house. Put it out on a clean cloth . . . we shall honour his memory again at home!' Now the funeral repast too is over, during which Judas has talked unflaggingly to the priest about the virtues of the departed, his praises being fully endorsed by the priest. 'Oh, brother, brother! You wished no more to abide with us!' he exclaims, leaving the table and stretching out his hand palm upwards to receive the priest's blessing. Now at last, Lord be praised, they have had their fill of food and have even taken a nap after the funeral lunch. Judas walks as master through the various rooms of the house, checking items and entering them in the inventory, and every now and then casting a suspicious glance at his mother when some matter of doubt arises.

All these inevitable scenes from the future kept coming before Arina Petrovna's eyes. And in her ears there sounded, as if in reality, Judas's unctuously piercing voice saying to her:

'You remember, Mother dear, those little gold studs my brother had . . . pretty they were, he used to wear them on feast-days . . . I really can't think where those studs have got to!'

Arina Petrovna had not reached the bottom of the stairs when on the hill by the church at Dubrovino a carriage and four came into view. In the carriage rode Porfiry Golovlev, occupying the place of honour, crossing himself with cap removed as they passed the church, and opposite him his two sons, Petenka and Volodenka, Arina Petrovna's blood ran cold: 'So Brother Fox has got whiff of the carrion,' she thought; the girls' spirits sank too and they clung forlornly to their grandmother. The previously quiet house was suddenly in a state of commotion: doors banged, servants scurried hither and thither, there were shouts of 'The master's coming! The master's coming!'—and the whole population of the manor-house poured out as one on to the front steps. Some crossed themselves, others simply stood expectantly, but every one of them was clearly aware that what had gone on before in Dubrovino had been but a passing phase and that only now was the real proper business of life beginning, with a proper master to run things. Under the 'old' master many of the elderly house-serfs with long service had received a monthly allotment of provisions; many had fed their cows on the master's hay, had had vegetable plots, and had in general lived 'free and easy'—it was naturally of interest to them all whether the 'new' master would leave things as they were or change them for new, Golovlevo, ways.

Judas had meanwhile driven up to the house and concluded from the way he was received that matters in Dubrovino were drawing to their end. He stepped down without haste from the carriage, waved aside the servants who rushed forward to kiss the master's hand, then placed the palms of his hands together and slowly started up the steps, whispering a prayer as he went.

His face displayed at one and the same time grief and steadfast resignation. As a man he grieved, as a Christian he did not venture to complain. He prayed for the sending down of grace, but above all he trusted and submitted to the will of Providence. His sons walked side by side after him. Volodenka mimicked his father, putting his hands together, rolling his eyes upwards, and moving his lips, while Petenka relished his brother's performance. A silent procession of servants brought up the rear.

Judas kissed his mother on the hand, then on the lips, then once more on the hand, then patted the small of her back, and declared with a sad shake of his head:

'And still you distress yourself! It's not right, Mother dear, oh, not right at all! You have only to ask yourself: what will God say to this? He will say: here am I in my wisdom ordering all things for the best, and she complains! Oh, Mother, Mother dear!'

He then kissed his two nieces in turn and said in the same engagingly familiar tone:

'And you too, my dears—all in tears! I'll not have it! Come now, smile and be done with it!'

And he stamped his foot at them—or, rather, pretended to stamp, since it was really only good-hearted jest.

'Just look at me!' he went on. 'As a brother I grieve! More than once, maybe, I have wept . . . I sorrow for my brother, sorrow deeply, it moves me to tears . . . But you weep and then it comes back to you: what after all is God's purpose? Does God really not know the why and the wherefore better than we do? Think of it in that way and you take heart. And you should all do that! You, Mother dear, and you, my nieces, and you as well . . . all of you!' he declared, turning to the servants. 'Just look at me and see what a brave soldier I am!'

And in the same engaging manner he displayed what a brave soldier he was by drawing himself erect, setting one foot back, throwing out his chest and tossing back his head. They all smiled, albeit somewhat sourly, as if each was thinking to himself: Yes, there he goes, the spider spinning his web!

His performance in the hall ended, Judas went into the drawing-room and once again kissed his mother's hand.

'So that's the way it is, Mother dear!' he said, settling himself on the sofa. 'Now brother Pavel too . . .'

'Yes, Pavel too . . .' Arina Petrovna answered quietly.

'Yes, yes, indeed . . . It seems soon, too soon! I too, Mother dear, though I keep up my spirits . . . inside, I grieve very, very much for my brother! He has never cared for me, has my brother, never cared for me at all—perhaps that's why God now afflicts him!'

'That's a thing you might better forget at a time like this! Old quarrels are best put aside . . .'

'I *have* forgotten it, Mother dear, long ago! I was only saying by-the-way that my brother has never cared for me—why, I don't know! For myself, I've tried every way—this way and that, straight out and round about, fair and friendly—and all he does is shy away! And now God in his unseen way has ordained his end!'

'You're not to speak like that, I say! With the man at death's door!'

'Indeed, Mother dear, what a great mystery is death! "Ye know neither the day nor the hour"—what a mystery it is! There was he planning his plans and thinking he stood high, so high that no man's hand could reach him, yet God at a stroke, in a moment of time, has cast down all his dreams. He would be glad enough now, maybe, to cover up his sins—but there they are already written down in the book of life. And anything, Mother dear, that is written in that book is not soon struck out!'

'Repentance, though, is surely accepted.'

'I wish it to be so, with all my heart I wish it for my brother's sake. He never cared for me, but I wish it none the less. I wish all men well, those who hate me and those who do me wrong—everyone! He was unjust to me—and God has sent him this sickness—not I, mark you, but God! Does he suffer much, Mother dear?'

'Middling . . . not too much. The doctor came and actually said there was some hope,' Arina Petrovna lied.

'How splendid! Never mind, my dear! Don't distress yourself! Perhaps he'll recover after all! Here we are grieving over him, complaining even against our Lord Creator, while all the time he may be sitting quietly up there in his bed and thanking God for restoring him to health!'

So taken was Judas with the idea that he even gave a little chuckle.

'The fact is, Mother dear, I have come to stay with you for a while,' he went on, as if giving her a pleasant surprise. 'It's no good, my dear . . . We're kith and kin! Anything can happen—and, after all, as a brother . . . I can give comfort, counsel, help . . . You will allow me to stay, won't you?'

'Who am I to allow anything! I'm a visitor here myself!'

'Well then, Mother dear, seeing that today is Friday, if you would be so kind, perhaps you would have them do me a little lenten fare for dinner. Might there be a bit of salt fish, mushrooms, cabbage? It's little I want. In the meantime I'll go along upstairs and see brother Pavel—we're kith and kin, after all! I may yet be in time to do some good—if not for his body, for his soul. And in his condition I dare say the soul is the more important. The body we can repair with mixtures and poultices, but for the soul, Mother dear, a more basic remedy is needed.'

Arina Petrovna did not demur. So overwhelmed was she by the inevitability of the 'end' that she saw and heard what was happening around her in a kind of stupor. She saw Judas get up, wheezing, from the sofa, saw the way he stooped and shuffled off (he liked on occasion to make a show of infirmity: it gave him more dignity, he thought); she was well aware that the sudden appearance of the Bloodsucker in the mezzanine would deeply disturb the sick man, perhaps even hasten the outcome; but after the turmoils of the day she was overcome by such weariness that she seemed to be in a dream-world.

While all this was going on, Pavel Vladimirych was in a state of indescribable agitation. Lying all alone in the mezzanine, he could hear the unaccustomed activity going on in the house. Every door that banged, every footstep in the passage evoked a sense of mystery. For a time he called and shouted for all he was worth, but seeing that his cries had no effect, he summoned all his strength, raised himself up in his bed, and listened. After the general bustle and the babble of voices, a deathly silence suddenly set in. Something unknown and terrifying had him now beset from every side. A meagre daylight filtered through the lowered blinds and the icon-lamp flickering in the corner made the dusk that filled the room seem even darker and denser. It was on this mysterious corner that he had fixed his gaze, as if some object in this recess had struck him for the first time. The icon in its gilt frame, with the lamp's rays shining directly on it, stood out startlingly bright in the darkness like some living thing; on the ceiling a circle of light quivered, now brighter, now fainter, as the lamp's flame grew stronger and diminished. The lower part of the room was in half-light, a back-cloth against which quivering shadows moved. On the wall by the lamp-lit corner a dressing-gown was hanging and on it too there were shifting bands of light and shadow that made it seem to be moving. Pavel Vladimirych peered intently and fancied that there in the corner everything was suddenly astir. Solitude, helplessness, deathly silence—and now these shadows, this swarming mass of shadows. And the shadows seemed to be coming, coming, coming . . . In a state of indescribable terror, with eyes and mouth agape, he looked into the mysterious corner and did not cry out, but groaned. His groans were hollow and spasmodic, as though he were barking. He had not heard the creaking of the stairs or the cautious shuffling footsteps in the outer room—when suddenly at his bedside there loomed the hated figure of Judas. Pavel Vladimirych fancied that he had stepped out from that darkness which had just been stirring so mysteriously before his eyes; he fancied there were more of them there, and more, and more . . . shadows, shadows, unending shadows! Coming, coming . . .

'What do you want? How did you get here? Who let you in?' he cried instinctively, as he feebly sank back on the pillow.

Judas stood by the bed. He peered at the sick man and sorrowfully shook his head.

'Are you in pain?' he asked, putting into his voice all the unctuousness of which he was capable.

Pavel Vladimirych said nothing and stared at him with senseless eyes, as if striving to comprehend. Meanwhile, Judas went up to the icon, knelt down, with a show of pious emotion bowed three times to the ground, arose, and once again appeared at the bedside.

'Up you get now, brother! God sends you his mercy!' he said, sitting himself in the armchair, his cheerful tone suggesting that he actually carried this 'mercy' in his pocket.

Pavel Vladimirych realized at last that he was confronted not by a shadow, but by the Bloodsucker himself in the flesh. He suddenly shrank, as if gripped by a fit of shivering. Judas's eyes shone with brotherly feeling (they were kith and kin), but the sick man could see full well that in these eyes a 'snare' lay concealed, which at any moment would spring forth and grip him by the throat.

'Oh, brother, brother! What a scallywag you are!' Judas continued banteringly (as kith and kin). 'Come along now, just buck yourself up! On your feet and run gallopy-hop! Let Mother see what brave soldiers we are! Upon my word!'

'Get out, Bloodsucker!' the sick man cried in desperation.

'Oh! Brother, brother! Here am I bringing you comfort and care, and you . . . what a thing to say! Oh, it really is wicked!' How could your tongue ever utter such a word to your own brother! Shame on you, old chap, shame! Shame! Wait a minute now, and I'll straighten your pillow.'

Judas got up and poked the pillow with his finger.

'There you are!' he said. 'That's splendid! Now you can lie comfy—it won't need straightening again till morning!'

'Get . . . out!'

'Ah! How sadly this illness has affected you! Your very character seems to have gone all contrary! "Get out! Get out!"—now how could I possibly leave you? You might want a drink—I can give you some water; the lamp there might not burn properly —I can see to it, put in a drop of olive oil. You lie there and I'll sit here, all nice and peaceful, and we won't notice how the time slips by!'

'Get out . . . Bloodsucker!'

'You abuse me, but I shall pray for you. Of course, I know that it is not you, but your illness makes you speak like that. I am accustomed to forgiving, brother—I forgive everybody. Today, for instance, on my way to see you I met a peasant who said something to me. What of it! The Lord be with him!—he defiled his own tongue! As for me . . . I not only wasn't angry, I actually gave him the sign of the cross—truly I did!'

'You'd . . . robbed him?'

'Who? Me? No, no, dear fellow, I don't rob people. It's highwaymen who rob people. I go by the law. I caught his horse in my meadow—so I said to him: "Off with you to the arbiter,* my friend! If he says it's permitted to trample other people's fields, all well and good! But if he says it's not permitted—that's that, you pay the fine!" I go by the law, my friend, I go by the law!'

'Judas! You traitor! You beggared your own mother!'

'I'll say again: be angry or not, as you will, but what you're saying isn't true! And if I weren't a Christian, I might . . . hold it against you!'

'You did, you did! You sent your mother begging!'

'Stop it! Stop it, I say! I'll say a prayer—you might calm down a little . . .'

Despite Judas's efforts to contain himself, the execrations of the dying man had struck home with such effect that his lips twisted and blenched. None the less, hypocrisy was so much a requirement of his nature that he could not cut short a comedy once begun. As he spoke his last words, he knelt down and spent some fifteen minutes lifting up his hands and whispering. Having completed this ritual, he returned to the dying man's bed with a composed, almost serene look on his face.

'Actually, brother, I have come to talk to you on a serious matter,' he said, settling into the armchair. 'Here you are abusing me, and all the time I am thinking of your soul. Tell me, please, when was it you last received the comfort of the sacrament?'

'God in heaven! What is this? . . . Take him away! Ulitka! Agashka! Is anybody there?' the sick man groaned.

'Now, now! There, there! Calm down, brother dear. I know you don't care to talk about these things. Yes, brother, you always were a bad Christian and you are still one now. But it would be a good thing, oh, a very good thing, if at a moment like this you gave some thought to your soul! After all, the human soul—oh, how carefully we must treat it, dear chap! What is it the Church tells us to do? Bring your prayers and thanksgivings, it says . . . And then again: a Christian end to our life is painless, peaceful, and unashamed—that's what it says, brother dear! You would do well to send for the priest and sincerely, contritely . . . All right! All right! I'll say no more! I'll say no more! But all the same . . .'

Pavel Vladimirych lay there purple in the face, almost choking. If at that moment he had been capable of dashing out his own brains, he would actually have done so.

'Then, about your property—perhaps you have already made your arrangements?' Judas continued. 'It's a nice tidy little property you've got—that's a fact. The land is even better than in Golovlevo: loam and sand. And then there's your capital, though I know nothing of that. I only know you let the peasants buy themselves out,* but what you did and how was never any concern of mine. Today, for instance—as I was coming to see you, I thought to myself: brother Pavel must have some capital! Though, of course, I thought, if he does have any, he'll certainly have made his arrangements!'

The sick man turned away and gave a deep sigh.

'You haven't?—so much the better, brother dear! By the law it's actually fairer that way. After all, it won't go to strangers, but to your own near and dear. Take me now, frail as I am, with one foot in the grave, still I think: what need to go making arrangements when the law can arrange everything for me? And what a good thing it is too, dear brother: no squabbles, no grudges, no quibbles—simply the law!'

It was terrible. Pavel Vladimirych felt that he had been put alive into his coffin, that he lay there as if fettered in a lethargic sleep, incapable of stirring a single limb, and listened while the Bloodsucker made mock of his body.

'Get out . . . for God's sake . . . go away!' he finally pleaded with his tormentor.

'There, there, there! Calm down! I'll go! I know you have no love for me . . . a shameful thing it is, very shameful not to love your own brother! See how I love you! As I always say to my children: even though brother Pavel has wronged me, still I love him just the same! So, you've made no arrangements then—excellent, brother dear! Though it does sometimes happen that a man's capital is carried off even while he is still alive, especially if he's on his own, with no relations . . . well, I'll keep an eye on things . . . Eh? What? You've had enough of me? All right then, so be it, I'll go! Only just let me say a prayer.'

He got up, placed the palms of his hands together, and hastily whispered something.

'Goodbye, old chap! Don't fret! Rest well—God may yet be merciful! And Mother and I will talk things over—perhaps we will come up with something! I've asked them to do me a little lenten fare for dinner, brother—a bit of salt fish, mushrooms, and cabbage—so you must excuse me! What? Too much of me? Really, brother, really! . . . All right, I'm going, I'm going! The main thing, dear chap, don't worry, don't excite yourself—you sleep and rest! Zzz . . . zzz!' he teased jocularly by way of conclusion, deciding to go at last.

'Bloodsucker!'—such was the piercing cry that rang after him that he felt he was seared with fire.

While Porfiry Vladimirych is babbling away in the mezzanine, downstairs Arina Petrovna has gathered the young people round her (not without some intention of gleaning information) and talks with them.

'Well, how are you getting on?' she asks Petenka, her eldest grandson.

'All right, Granny. Next year I'll get my commission!'

'You will, will you? The number of years you've been promising that! Perhaps your examinations are too hard—Lord knows!'

'Granny, in the last exams he came a cropper in "Rudiments". The priest asked him "What is God?" and he said "God is a spirit . . . a spirit . . . and to the Holy Spirit"!'

'Ah, poor boy! How could you say such a thing? Why, the girls here—I expect they know that!'

'Of course we do! God is a spirit, invisible . . .' Anninka hastens to display her knowledge.

'Whom no man has seen in any place . . .' Lyubinka intervenes.

'All-knowing, all-merciful, all-powerful, ever-present,' Anninka goes on. 'Whither shall I go from thy spirit? or whither shall I flee from thy presence? If I ascend up into heaven, thou art there; if I make my bed in hell, behold thou art there . . .'

'There now, if you had answered like that, you would be wearing your epaulettes now. And you, Volodya, what are you thinking of doing?'

Volodya flushes crimson and says nothing.

' "To the Holy Spirit"—you're just the same, I see! Ah, children! children! You look bright as buttons, but book-learning is beyond you. It's not that your father's one to spoil you . . . How does he treat you these days?'

'Same as ever, Granny.'

'Does he beat you? I had heard, though, that he had stopped that?'

'Not so much now, but still . . . He's such a nuisance, that's the trouble!'

'I don't quite understand that. How can anybody's father be a nuisance?'

'He is, Granny, a great nuisance! If you want to go anywhere or have anything, you've got to ask him . . . He's really rotten!'

'So ask him! It's not as if your tongue will drop off!'

'No fear! If you so much as speak to him, he never lets you go! "Hold now, wait a minute! Easy does it, all in good time!" . . . Oh, Granny, it's so boring the way he talks!'

'Yes, Granny, and he listens to us outside the door. But Petenka caught him at it the other day . . .'

'Ah, you mischiefs! And what did he do?'

'Nothing. I said to him: "Father, it's not a good thing to listen at doors; if you're not careful, you'll get your nose squashed in!" And he said "There, there! It's all right. I go as a thief in the night, my boy!" '

'Granny, he found a fallen apple in the orchard the other day and put it in his cupboard, but I took it and ate it. And he looked everywhere for it and had all the servants in for questioning . . .'

'There's a thing! Has he got very mean then?'

'No, not exactly mean. It's just that he fusses all the time about little things. He's for ever hoarding scraps of paper, looking for fallen apples . . .'

'Every morning he has the offertory performed in his study and afterwards he gives each of us a piece of the bread . . . really stale it is! Only once we played a trick on him, we found out where the communion bread was, cut a hole in the bottom and took out the inside, then filled it up with butter!'

'Really! What scamps you are!'

'But imagine how surprised he was next day! Communion bread—and butter!'

'You'll have copped it for that!'

'Nothing much . . . He just went round all day in a huff and kept muttering "Scoundrels!" Of course, we made out he couldn't be meaning us. You know, though, Granny, he's afraid of you!'

'Why should he be afraid of me . . . I'm not a scarecrow, am I?'

'He's afraid of you all right: he thinks you're going to curse him. He's scared to death of curses!'

Arina Petrovna grows thoughtful. The first thought that comes to her is: yes, what if I really did . . . curse him? I could go and curse him just like that . . . 'I cu-u-urse you!' Next to mind comes another, more pressing thought: what is Judas up to? What monkey business is he engaged in now upstairs? Something sly and slippery, no doubt! She has then a bright idea.

'Volodya!' she says. 'You're light-toed, my dear! You might just slip quietly along and listen to what's going on *up there*!'

'Glad to, Granny.'

Volodenka tiptoes to the door and disappears through it.

'And what made you think of coming to see us today?' says Arina Petrovna, turning her enquiries to Petenka.

'We've meant to come for a long time, Granny, but today there was an urgent message from Ulitushka saying the doctor had been and that Uncle would be sure to be dead in a day or two.'

'And has there been any talk of the inheritance?'

'Granny, we talk of nothing else all day. He keeps on about how things were in the time before Grandfather . . . Why, Granny, he even harks back to Goryushkino. There now, he says, if Aunt Varvara Mikhailovna hadn't had any children, Goryushkino would have belonged to us! And heaven knows, he says, who their father was . . . but let us not judge our brethren! For we see the mote in our brother's eye, but not the beam in our own—oh, yes indeed!'

'What a man he is! Why, your great-aunt was married, and if anything was amiss, it was all covered up by her husband!'

'Yes, Granny. But whenever we go past Goryushkino, he always brings it up. And he says, Granny, that as Natalya Vladimirovna was married out of Goryushkino—by all rights it should be in the Golovlev family, but, he says, his dear departed father went and gave it away as dowry for his sister! And the melons that used to grow there! Twenty pounds they weighed, he says—oh, what melons they were!'

'Really, twenty pounds! I never heard that before! Well, and what are his thoughts about Dubrovino?'

'Same kind of thing. Melons, water-melons . . . piddling things like that! Lately, though, he's kept on saying: "What do you think, boys, has brother Pavel got much in the way of capital?" He's had it all worked out for a long time, Granny: how much compensation there was for the peasants,* when the estate was mortgaged, and how much of the debt has been paid off . . . We actually saw the paper he'd done the sums on—only we took it away, Granny! We nearly drove him crazy with that paper! He had put it in his desk, and we took it out and put it in the cupboard; then he locked it in the cupboard, but we got the key and tucked it in with the communion bread . . . Once he went to have a wash in the bath-house—and there was the paper on the shelf there!'

'A gay time you have there!'

Volodenka comes back; all eyes turn to him.

'Couldn't hear anything really!' he tells them in a whisper. 'All I could hear was Father saying something about "painless, peaceful and unashamed" and Uncle saying "Get out, Blood-sucker!"'

'And you heard nothing about any "arrangements"?'

'I think there was something, but I couldn't tell what it was . . . Father had shut the door very tight, Granny. I could just hear him droning on . . . and then suddenly Uncle crying "Get out!" So I made a dash and came back here!'

'If only the girls got something . . .' reflected Arina Petrovna longingly.

'If the property goes to Father, Granny, he won't give anything to anybody,' attests Petenka. 'I think he's going to cut even us off.'

'But he can't take it with him to the grave.'

'No, but he'll find a way. It's not for nothing he was talking to the priest the other day: he asked him if it would cost much to build another Tower of Babel!'

'Oh, that was just something to ask . . . out of curiosity, perhaps . . .'

'No, Granny, he's got some kind of plan. If it's not to build a Tower of Babel, he'll give it all to Athos,* and there won't be a bean for us!'

'Will Father have a large property, Granny, when Uncle dies?' enquires Volodenka.

'Why, God alone knows which of them will die first.'

'No, Granny. Father's reckoning on it for sure. Today when we got to Dubrovino dell, he actually took his cap off and crossed himself and said "God be praised, we'll now be on our own land!" '

'Granny, he's got it all planned. When he saw the wood: ah, he says, if it was properly looked after, that would be a nice little wood! Then he looked at the meadows: fine meadows, he says, look, look at all the hay-stooks! They used to raise horses there!'

'Yes, yes . . . the wood and the meadows—they'll all be yours, my dears!' sighs Arina Petrovna. 'Gracious! Was that the stair creaking?'

'Hush, Granny, hush! It's him . . . as a thief in the night . . . listening at the door.'

They fall silent; but it turns out to be a false alarm. Arina Petrovna sighs and mutters to herself 'Ah, children, children!' The young men eye the orphaned girls as if they would devour them; the girls are silent and envious.

'And you, cousin, did you ever see Mademoiselle Lotar?'* asks Petenka, to start the conversation.

Anninka and Lyubinka look blankly at each other as if to ask whether this was a history or geography question.

'In *La Belle Hélène** . . . at the theatre. She plays Helen.'

'Oh, yes . . . Helen . . . and Paris? "Being young and fair, he roused the goddesses' ardour" . . . Yes, yes, we know it!' cried Lyubinka with delight.

'Yes, that's it—that's the thing! The way she sings *"cas-ca-ader, ca-as-ca-der"* . . . it's simply marvellous!'

'When the doctor was here today he kept singing "Head-over heels".'

' "Head-over heels"—that was Lyadova,* alas, now dead—she was simply marvellous! When she died, two thousand people followed her coffin . . . they thought there was going to be a revolution!'

'Is it the theatre you're talking to them about?' intervenes Arina Petrovna. 'It's not to theatres they'll be going, my dear, but to the convent . . .'

'Granny, you're always wanting to bury us away in your convent!' complains Anninka.

'Don't you go to a convent, cousin! You hie away to Petersburg! We'll show you what's what!'

'It's not of pleasures they should be thinking, my dear, but of things divine,' Arina Petrovna continued improvingly.

'We'll give them a jaunt to the Sergius Hermitage,* Granny— that will be divine!'

The girls' eyes lit up and the tips of their noses turned pink at this suggestion.

'They say how marvellous the singing is there!' exclaims Anninka.

'You can be sure of that, cousin! You should hear their "Singing to the Trisagion"—Father himself couldn't do better. And then we'd take you for a spin down all three Podyachesky streets.'*

'We'd teach you all about everything, cousin! There are lots of girls like you in Petersburg: they walk along and make their heels go tap-tap.'

'And you're going to teach them that!' Arina Petrovna intervenes. 'For the Lord's sake, let them be . . . teachers! Going into teaching now, are you . . . book-learning, I suppose! No, when Pavel dies, I'll take the girls off with me to Khotkov . . . We'll settle down nicely there!'

'Still talking profanities!' a voice comes suddenly from the doorway.

In the course of their conversation no one has heard Judas creeping up—as a thief in the night! He stands there, tear-stained, with drooping head, pale face, hands placed together at his breast, and whispering lips. He casts his eyes around in search of the icon, locates it, and briefly elevates his spirit.

'He's poorly, oh, very poorly!' he declares at last, embracing dear Mother.

'Is he really that bad?'

'He's in a very bad way indeed, my dear . . . and do you recall what a fine fellow he used to be?'

'That he was ever a fine fellow I somehow don't remember!'

'Oh no, Mother, you mustn't say that! He was always . . . I remember him now when he left the cadet school: a fine upstanding fellow, broad shoulders, the very picture of health . . . Yes, indeed yes, Mother dear! We are all in the hands of God. Today we are strong and healthy, keen to live and enjoy ourselves and taste the fleshpots, but then tomorrow . . .'

He gestured with his hand and was moved with pious emotion.

'Did he at least say anything?'

'Little, Mother dear. All he said was: "Farewell, brother!" But he feels it, Mother, he feels that he's in a bad way!'

'You're bound to feel it when you're coughing out your lungs like that!'

'No, Mother, I don't mean that. I'm talking about that insight, which they say is given to man: a man who is going to die can always feel it before the time. Though sinners are not accorded this consolation.'

'What did he say though? Did he talk about any "arrangements"?'

'No, Mother dear. He was going to say something, but I stopped him. No, I said, there's no need to talk of any arrangements! Anything you might in your goodness leave to me, brother, I shall be content with, and if you leave me nothing at all—I'll pray for your soul's rest *gratis*! But oh, Mother, he still so wants to live, so very, very much!'

'Everybody wants to live!'

'No, Mother! Speaking for myself, should it please the Lord God to call me unto him, I should be ready even now!'

'Being called to God is all right, but what if it's to Satan?'

In this vein the conversation continues until dinner, during dinner, and after dinner. Arina Petrovna's impatience is such she can hardly sit still. The more Judas babbles on, the more often does the thought occur to her: what if I actually should . . . curse him? But Judas has no inkling of the veritable storm that is raging in his mother's heart, and his gaze is clear and bright as he leisurely continues the torment of dear Mother with his futile rigmarole.

'I'll curse him! I'll curse him! I'll curse him!' Arina Petrovna repeats to herself with ever-growing determination.

There is a smell of incense in the rooms, the droning sound of chant reverberates through the house, the doors stand open, and those wishing to pay their last respects to the dead come and go. When he was alive, nobody paid any attention to Pavel Vladimirych; now he was dead, everybody felt sorry. They recalled that he 'never did any harm', 'never spoke a harsh word', 'never gave a cross look' to anyone. All these qualities which had seemed before to be negative were now seen as something positive, and from the indistinct snatches of customary funeral small-talk Pavel Vladimirych emerged as an exemplar of 'the good master'. Many felt remorse, admitting that they had on occasion traded on the dead man's simplicity—but then, who could have known that this simplicity was so soon to be cut off? It was there, alive, and they thought it would last for ever, and then suddenly . . . Of course, if this simplicity were still alive, they would have plucked it just the same: Pluck away, boys! Fools were made for plucking! One peasant brought three roubles to Judas and said:

'I owed it to the late master. We didn't have anything in writing—so here it is.'

Judas took the money, commended the peasant, and said that he would use the three roubles to buy oil for a perpetual iconlamp.

'And you, my good fellow, will see and everyone will see, and the soul of the departed will rejoice. He might even procure you something by his prayers *up there*! When you're not expecting it, God will suddenly send you good fortune!'

It is very probable that in the world's assessment of the dead man's qualities comparison played some part. Judas was not liked. It was not that he could not be out-smarted, but he was a great pettifogger and would plague and pester a man. There were few who would even venture to rent land from him, because once he had leased a plot, for every inch that plough or scythe went beyond it, for every minute's delay in payment of the rent he would immediately start dragging the tenant through the courts. Many had he hounded with his litigations with no profit to himself (his propensity for cavilling lawsuits was so widely known that his claims were barely considered and regularly turned down), though bringing ruin on the peasants by the endless procedures and time lost from their work. 'Don't choose your house, choose your neighbour', says the proverb, and all knew well what sort of neighbour the master of Golovlevo was. No matter if the magistrate does find you in the right, *he* will torment you to death with his own satanic law. And since malice (not even malice, but moral induration), cloaked by hypocrisy, invariably inspires a certain superstitious dread, the new 'neighbours' ('my dear neighbours', as Judas called them affably) timorously bowed low as they filed past the Bloodsucker, who, all in black, stood by the coffin with palms pressed together and eyes lifted up to heaven.

While the dead man lay in the house, the servants went on tiptoe, cast glances into the dining-room (the coffin was there on the table), shook their heads, and conversed in whispers. Judas pretended to be barely alive; he shuffled down the passage, went in to see the 'dear departed', was piously moved, straightened the pall on the coffin, and exchanged whispered words with the police superintendent, who was drawing up inventories and fixing seals to the dead man's property. Petenka and Volodenka fussed around the coffin, placing and lighting candles, presenting the censer, and so forth. Anninka and Lyubinka wept and through their tears added their shrill voices to the requiems being sung by the chanters. The women-servants in black calico dresses wiped their noses, red from weeping, on their aprons.

As soon as the death of Pavel Vladimirych occurred, Arina Petrovna went to her own room and locked herself in. It was no time for tears, for she knew well that she must at once come to

a decision. There was no question of her staying on in Dubrovino
—'Not for anything!'—and consequently there was only one
thing to do: go to Pogorelka, the estate of her orphaned granddaughters, the property that had once been the 'morsel' she had
tossed to her disrespectful daughter, Anna Vladimirovna. Having
made this decision, she felt a sense of relief, as if Judas had suddenly and for ever lost all power over her. She calmly counted
the number of five per cent bonds (there proved to be fifteen
thousand roubles of her own capital and a similar amount—built
up by her—belonging to the girls) and calmly calculated the cost
of putting the Pogorelka house in order. She then straightaway
sent for the Pogorelka village elder, gave instructions for the
hiring of carpenters and dispatch of a cart to fetch her own and
the girls' belongings from Dubrovino, ordered her carriage to be
made ready (in Dubrovino she had her own carriage, and she
had *proof* that it was *hers*), and began packing. For Judas she felt
neither hatred nor affection: she simply found it repugnant to
have any further dealings with him. She even ate little and with
reluctance, because from that day on the food she ate was not
Pavel's, but Judas's. Several times Porfiry Vladimirych looked
into her room for a chat with dear Mother (he was perfectly aware
of her preparations to leave, but pretended not to notice), but
Arina Petrovna would not allow him to stay.

'Go along, my son, go along!' she would say, 'I'm too
busy.'

Three days later Arina Petrovna was fully prepared for her
departure. They had attended mass, held the burial service, and
committed Pavel Vladimirych to the grave. At the funeral everything took place exactly as Arina Petrovna had envisaged on the
morning of Judas's arrival in Dubrovino. Just as expected, when
the coffin was lowered into the grave Judas cried out 'Farewell,
brother!', and just as expected, he then turned to Ulitushka
and said hastily:

'The kutya—don't forget to take it back to the house; put it out
on a clean cloth . . . we shall honour his memory again at
home!'

The three priests (one of them the Archdeacon) and the deacon
were invited to dinner, which was served according to custom

as soon as they returned from the funeral. The chanters were provided with their own repast in the hallway. Arina Petrovna and the girls appeared dressed for the road, but again Judas pretended not to notice. Going up to the zakuski,* Porfiry Vladimirych requested the Archdeacon to bless the food and drink; he then poured a glass of vodka for himself and each of the reverend fathers, and, moved with pious emotion, declared:

'Everlasting memory to the newly departed! Ah, brother, brother! You have forsaken us! You, of all people, should have gone on living! It's too bad of you, brother, too bad!'

Saying which, he crossed himself and drank his vodka. He then proceeded to cross himself again as he swallowed a helping of caviare, and yet again as he partook of the sturgeon fillet.

'Do have something, Father!' he urged the Archdeacon. 'These are all from the store of my dear departed brother. How he loved his food! He ate well himself, but was happier still to be entertaining others! Ah, brother, brother, you have forsaken us! It's unkind of you, brother, quite too bad!'

In short, he was so carried away that he even forgot about dear Mother. He remembered her only just as he had scooped up a spoonful of mushrooms and was about to direct them into his mouth.

'Mother! Dear soul!' he exclaimed in consternation. 'Here am I like a noodle eating away—oh, how wicked of me! Mother dear! a little something! Some mushrooms, these saffron milk-caps! From Dubrovino they are, highly esteemed!'

But Arina Petrovna merely nodded in reply and did not move. She seemed to be listening to something with great interest. It was as though some new light was shed before her eyes, and the whole of this comedy, which she had seen rehearsed from her earliest years and in which she herself had always taken part, appeared to her suddenly as something entirely new, which she had never seen before.

Dinner began with a family wrangle. Judas insisted that dear Mother should sit at the head of the table; Arina Petrovna declined.

'No. You're master here—so you sit where you want to sit!' she said coldly.

'But you're the mistress! You, Mother dear, are mistress every-where! At Golovlevo, at Dubrovino—everywhere!' maintained Judas.

'That I'm not! Sit there! Where God ordains that I'm mistress I'll choose myself where I sit! But you're the master here—so sit down in your place!'

'Then this is what we shall do!' said Judas with a show of emotion. 'We'll leave the master's place empty! It will be like having Pavel here to share our repast unseen . . . he shall be the host and we shall be his guests!'

This they did. During the serving of the soup Judas selects a fitting topic and starts conversing with the priests, addressing himself chiefly, though, to the Archdeacon.

'Many people these days don't believe in the immortality of the soul . . . but I do!' he says.

'It will be certain desperate folk who don't,' replies the Arch-deacon.

'No, it's not just the desperate. There's a science which says so. They claim that man exists on his own account . . . He lives, then suddenly he's dead!'

'There's far too much of this science nowadays—there should be less of it! People believe in science, but they don't believe in God. Why even the peasants want to be scholars.'

'Yes, Father, very true. Most concerned they are to be scholars! Take my peasants at Naglovka: they've nothing to eat, but only the other day they declared they want to start a school . . . Scholars, indeed!'

'There's sciences for everything these days. If you don't want rain, there's a science for that, and if you want fine weather, there's a science for that too. In times gone by it was all very simple: you came to church, made your intercessions, and God would provide. If it was fine weather you wanted, he sent fine weather; and if you wanted rain, God could provide that too in good measure. All things are plentiful with God. But now since they've taken to living by science, it's suddenly come to a stop and everything is out of season. At sowing-time there's drought, and at mowing-time there's rain!'

'It's true, Father, true indeed! In times before, when people prayed more often, the earth gave better yields. Harvests were not what they are today—four-fold, five-fold: the earth yielded an hundredfold. I dare say Mother will remember that. Do you remember, Mother dear?' Judas turns to Arina Petrovna, intending to draw her into the conversation.

'I never heard of it in these parts. Perhaps it's the land of Canaan you've read about—it's said to have happened there,' Arina Petrovna responds drily.

'Yes, yes, yes,' says Judas, as if not hearing his mother's remark. 'They don't believe in God, they don't acknowledge the immortality of the soul . . . yet they expect to stuff their bellies!'

'To stuff themselves and drink—that's all they want to do!' concurs the Archdeacon, tucking back the sleeves of his cassock in order to place a slice of the funeral pie on his plate.

They begin on the soup; for a time nothing is heard but the clinking of spoons on plates and the priests snorting as they blow on the hot liquid.

'And then there's the Catholics,' continues Judas, stopping eating. 'Even though they don't deny the immortality of the soul, on the other hand they do say the soul doesn't go straight to Paradise, but for a certain time goes . . . somewhere in between.'

'No substance in that either.'

'How should I put it to you, Father . . .' Porfiry Vladimirych says pensively, 'talking from the point of view . . .'

'Talking of nonsense is a waste of time. What does the Holy Church sing? "In a place fertile and cool, where sorrow and sighing are no more" . . . How can there be any talk then of "somewhere in between"?'

Judas, however, does not entirely agree and is about to make some rejoinder. But Arina Petrovna, who is beginning to chafe at all this talk, cuts him short.

'Come on, eat up, eat up . . . you theologians! Your soup will be long gone cold!' she says and, to change the subject, she turns to the Archdeacon. 'How is your rye, Father? Gathered in?'

'Yes, ma'am, it's gathered in; good rye it is this year, but the spring corn is not so promising. And the oats hasn't filled properly, though already it's ripening: we can expect neither grain nor straw.'

'Everybody's complaining about the oats this year!' sighs Arina Petrovna, watching Judas closely as he spoons up the last of his soup.

Another course is served: ham and peas. Judas takes the opportunity to renew his interrupted conversation.

'Now this is something that Jews never eat.'

'The Jews are heathens,' the Archdeacon replies. 'That's why people taunt them with the pig's ear.'*

'But Tartars don't eat it either . . . There must be a reason for it . . .'

'The Tartars are heathens too—that's the reason.'

'We don't eat horse-meat and the Tartars don't touch pork. Now in Paris during the siege they say people ate rats.'

'Oh well, that's the French!'

The whole of dinner proceeds in this way. Carp in sour cream is served—and Judas comments:

'Do have some, Father! These are special carp: my dear departed brother was most fond of them.'

Asparagus is served—and Judas says:

'There's real asparagus for you! Asparagus like this would cost you a silver rouble in Petersburg. My dear departed brother tended it himself—just look how thick it is!'

Arina Petrovna is fuming inwardly: a whole hour has gone by and dinner is still only half-way through. Judas seems to be taking his time on purpose: he eats a little, then sets his knife and fork down, talks a little, eats again, and again talks. How often in times past Arina Petrovna had scolded him for doing this: 'Eat up, you little devil! (Lord, forgive that I should say so)'—but Judas has evidently forgotten his mother's injunctions. But perhaps he has not forgotten, and is doing it deliberately, taking his revenge. Or perhaps he is not even consciously taking revenge, but simply acting on the impulse of his spiteful nature. At last the roast was served, but just at the moment when everyone stood and the deacon intoned: 'The Blessed Repose . . .' there was a great commotion and shouting outside in the passage, which totally ruined the effect of the doxology of the prayer for the departed.

'What's all that row!' cried Porfiry Vladimirych. 'Is it a tavern we're in?'

'There's no need to raise your voice! It's my doing—they're moving my trunks,' Arina Petrovna responded, adding with a tinge of irony: 'Do you want to inspect them?'

Everyone fell silent. Even Judas was discomposed and turned pale. However, he was at once aware of the need to dispel the unpleasant atmosphere created by his mother and, turning to the Archdeacon, began:

'Now, black grouse, for instance . . . They are plentiful in Russia, but in other countries . . .'

'For the Lord's sake, eat up your dinner! We've got twenty-five versts to go and want to get there before dark,' Arina Petrovna interrupted him. 'Petenka! there's a dear, get them to hurry up and serve the pudding!'

There was silence lasting a few minutes. Porfiry Vladimirych rapidly finished his piece of grouse and sat pale, with quivering lips, tapping his foot on the floor.

'You hurt me, Mother dear! You hurt me deeply!' he says at length, not, however, looking at Arina Petrovna.

'Who'll ever hurt you! And how is it I've hurt you so deeply?'

'It's very hurtful . . . very hurtful indeed that you should at such a moment . . . go away! . . . You've been living here all this time . . . and then suddenly . . . And, finally, these trunks . . . and talk of inspection . . . I'm very much hurt!'

'Well, if you want the truth, I'll give it you. As long as my son Pavel was alive, I lived here; and now he's dead, I'm going away. And as for the trunks, Ulitka's long been spying on me—on your instructions. To my way of thinking, you'd be better telling your mother straight out she's under suspicion than hissing at her like a snake from behind someone else's back!'

'But Mother! . . . Mother dear! . . . You . . . I . . .' moaned Judas.

'That's enough!' Arina Petrovna cut him short. 'I've had my say.'

'But, Mother dear, how could I . . .'

'I tell you I've had my say—so let it be done with! For the Lord's sake, now let me go in peace. The carriage is ready, I think.'

Indeed, outside there was the sound of harness-bells and the carriage rattling up to the porch. Arina Petrovna got up first from the table, and was followed by the others.

'Right, let's just sit for a minute* and then we'll be off!' she said, making her way into the drawing-room.

They sat briefly in silence, and Judas meanwhile completely regained his composure.

'But why don't you stay on at Dubrovino, Mother dear . . . Just see how nice it is here,' he said, looking his mother in the eyes with the fawning affection of a dog which has misbehaved.

'That's quite enough, now I don't want to say anything disagreeable to you in parting . . . but I can't stay here! There's nothing for me here! Father, let us say a prayer.'

They all stood and prayed. Then Arina Petrovna exchanged kisses with everyone, gave them her blessing . . . as kith and kin, and with heavy steps made her way to the door. Porfiry Vladimirych, heading the entire household, escorted her to the front steps, where, though, on seeing the carriage, he was possessed by the demon of sophistry. The thought flashed in his mind: 'But that carriage—it belonged to my brother!'

'We'll be seeing each other, Mother dear!' he said, helping her into her seat and casting looks at the carriage out of the corner of his eye.

'If God so wills . . . there's no reason for us not to.'

'Oh, Mother, Mother dear! Really, what a mischief you are! Have them unharness the carriage and come on back to your old nest . . . I mean it!' Judas fawned.

Arina Petrovna did not answer; she was now settled in her seat and had even made the sign of the cross, but the orphan-girls were being rather slow.

Meanwhile Judas kept on casting looks at the carriage.

'What will you do about the carriage, Mother dear? Will you send it back or would you like to have it fetched?' he said at last, unable to restrain himself.

Arina Petrovna positively shook with indignation.

'The carriage is mine!' she cried with such anguish in her voice that everyone felt awkward and embarrassed. 'It's mine! Mine! It's my carriage! It's . . . I've got proof . . . there are witnesses! As for you . . . I'll . . . I'll just wait and see what next you come out with! Girls! How much longer?'

'Mother, please! It's not that I begrudge it you . . . even if it did belong to Dubrovino . . .'

'It's *my* carriage, *mine*! It does *not* belong to Dubrovino, it belongs to *me*! Don't you dare say otherwise . . . do you hear!'

'Just as you say, Mother . . . Now you won't go forgetting us, will you, dearest . . . Nothing formal, no frills: we'll come and see you, and you'll come and see us . . . as kith and kin!'

'You're in, girls, are you? Away then!' shouted Arina Petrovna, hardly controlling herself.

The carriage jerked into motion and set off along the road at a jog trot. Judas stood on the steps, waved his handkerchief, and, until the carriage disappeared completely from view, went on calling after it:

'As kith and kin! We'll come and see you, and you'll come and see us . . . as kith and kin!'

FAMILY SCORES

It had never occurred to Arina Petrovna that a time might come when she would herself be an 'extra mouth' in the household, but that time now crept up on her and came just when for the first time in her life she realized in fact that her moral and physical powers were sapped. Such moments come always suddenly: a person may long be enfeebled, but still he somehow struggles along, keeping to his feet—then out of the blue there suddenly comes the final blow. To anticipate this blow, to be aware of its coming is very difficult; you must simply and silently submit to it, for this is the blow which at once and without recall reduces a man, but lately hale and hearty, to a wreck.

It had been a difficult situation for Arina Petrovna when she broke with Judas and settled in Dubrovino, but then at least she knew that Pavel Vladimirych, though not caring for her intrusion, was still a man of substance for whom it was no great matter to provide an extra helping. Now, though, things had taken quite a different turn: in Pogorelka she was head of a household where every 'helping' counted. She knew well the cost of these 'helpings', since a lifetime spent in the country among ordinary peasant-folk had instilled in her the peasants' understanding of the loss inflicted by any 'extra mouth' on a household economy which was already skimped as it was.

Still, for a time after her removal to Pogorelka Arina Petrovna remained cheerful, busily settling into her new home, and clear-headed as ever in her grasp of estate administration. But managing affairs at Pogorelka was a bothersome, petty business that demanded constant personal attention, and though she rashly supposed at first that it required no great wit to keep account where it was a matter of turning farthings to ha'pence and ha'pence to pennies, she soon had to acknowledge that such a belief was wrong. It did not indeed require great wit, but she was lacking her old zest, her old strength. Besides that, it was autumn, with that bustle of household activity which rounded off the year, and the weather, too, was inclement and imposed a curb on Arina Petrovna's endeavours. The infirmities of old age beset her and kept her housebound, and the long, tedious autumn evenings set in, condemning her to resigned idleness. The old woman was perturbed and fretful, but there was nothing she could do.

She could not, however, fail to notice that something was amiss with her orphaned granddaughters. They had suddenly become moody and depressed. Vague plans for the future made them restless—plans in which the prospect of work alternated with the prospect of pleasures (naturally, of the most innocent kind). These ideas were prompted by recollections of their school-days and notions of a life of toil randomly picked up from books, and also the modest hope that through their school connections they might gain hold of some guide-string which would lead them into the bright realm of human life. All these vague yearnings were, though, dominated by the one nagging and very definite thought: that, come what may, they must leave this hateful Pogorelka. And so, one fine morning, Anninka and Lyubinka declared to their grandmother that they neither could nor would remain in Pogorelka any longer, that it was really too bad, that they never saw a soul apart from the priest—and he, for some reason, whenever he met them, invariably started talking about virgins who let their lamps go out, and that it was altogether 'impossible'. The girls spoke out tartly, for they feared their grandmother and the courage they affected was proportionate to their anticipation of an angry outburst and rebuff. But, to their surprise, Arina Petrovna listened to their complaints not only without anger, but also showing no inclination to deliver one of those sterile homilies which impotent old age so freely gives. Alas, this was no more the domineering woman who in days gone by would announce with total assurance: 'I shall go to Khotkov and take the grand-children with me.' And it was not just the impotence of old age that brought about this change, but also the realization of a better, juster way in life. Fate's most recent blows had not merely subdued her; they had also illuminated certain recesses of her understanding which evidently no thought of hers had hitherto penetrated. She realized that within the human heart lie certain strivings which may long remain dormant, but which—once awakened—draw a person irresistibly on to where the light of life shines through, that joyous light which the eye has long sought in the hopeless gloom of the present. And once Arina Petrovna had understood the legitimacy of such a striving she was powerless to stand against it. True, she tried to dissuade the girls from doing what they proposed, but she did so feebly, without conviction. She was concerned about the future that awaited them, especially because of her lack of connections in so-called 'society', but at the same time she felt that to part with the girls was something requisite and inevitable. What would become of them? —the nagging question was constantly in her mind. But neither this question, nor other still more fearful questions will ever hold back someone who is striving to be free. The girls meanwhile would talk of nothing but their need to get away from Pogorelka. And indeed, after some hesitations and postponements to please their grandmother, they went.

With the departure of the orphans the house at Pogorelka sank into a kind of hopeless stillness. However self-centred Arina Petrovna was by nature, still to have a breath of human life nearby had been a comfort to her. After seeing her granddaughters off she felt, perhaps for the first time, that something had been cut loose from her and that she had suddenly gained a limitless freedom, so limitless that she could now see nothing before her but empty space. To conceal this emptiness from herself she immediately gave instructions to board up the main rooms and the top storey where the girls had lived (it will save firewood too, she thought). For herself she kept only two rooms; one contained the large glass case with her icons, and the other served as bedroom, office, and dining-room. To economize she also dismissed the servants, keeping only Afimyushka, the old housekeeper, who could scarcely get about, and Markovna, a soldier's wife with one eye who cooked and did the washing. But all these precautions helped little: the feeling of emptiness soon penetrated into these two rooms in which she had hoped to find refuge from it. Helpless solitude and cheerless inactivity—these were the two enemies which now confronted her and with which she was henceforth obliged to while away her old age. The effect of physical and moral decay was also not slow to manifest itself, the more cruel for the slight resistance offered to it by a life of empty inactivity.

Day followed day with that depressing monotony with which life in the country is so richly endowed if it lacks the provision of comfort, affairs to be managed, and food for the mind. Apart from the practical reasons which prevented her taking any personal part in the management of the estate, Arina Petrovna also felt an inward revulsion for the penny-pinching which had overtaken her in her latter days. This revulsion she might perhaps have overcome if there had been some purpose to justify her efforts, but purpose was just what was lacking. Everybody was sick and tired of her, and she was sick and tired of everything and everybody. The feverish activity of the past suddenly gave way to torpid idleness, and this idleness gradually demoralized her, bringing in its train such propensities as Arina Petrovna would never have dreamt of a few months before. The tough, self-possessed woman, whom no one would ever have thought of calling old, had become a total wreck, for whom there existed neither past nor future, but only the minute which had next to be lived through.

During the day she mostly dozed. She would sit in her arm-chair by the table laid out with foul-smelling playing-cards and doze. Then she would give a start, wake up, look through the window and, without any conscious thought, gaze long into the endless distance before her. Pogorelka was a sad property. It was stuck out on its own without any grounds, shade, or the least sign of comfort. There was not even a garden at the front. The house with its one storey was squashed-looking, and completely black from time and weather; at the back were a few out-buildings in a similar state of decay; and all around were fields, fields without end, and no wood in sight even on the horizon. But since Arina Petrovna had from childhood lived almost continuously in the country, not only did she see nothing dismal in this sparse landscape—rather it appealed to her heart and stirred what remnant of feeling still glowed within her. The better part of her being lived in these bare, unending fields, and her eyes instinctively sought them at all times. She gazed into the distance of the fields, gazed at those sodden villages that dotted the horizon, gazed at the white churches standing in the village graveyards, gazed at the patchwork on the flat expanse of the fields drawn by the clouds as they drifted in the rays of the sun; gazed at that unknown peasant tramping between the furrows in the field who seemed fixed for ever in the same spot. But as she watched her mind was blank, or, rather, the thoughts she had were so disconnected that they could focus on nothing for any length of time. She just watched and watched until once more the drowsiness of age brought a humming to her ears and drew a veil over fields, churches, villages, and the distant trudging peasant.

Sometimes, evidently, she recalled memories of the past, but they were disconnected, fragmentary. Her mind could not concentrate and constantly switched from one distant recollection to another. Now and then, however, some particular thing struck her, no cheerful memory—her past had been cruelly short of cheerfulness, but some affront, bitter, insufferable. She then had a surge of feeling, her heart filled with anguish, and tears came to her eyes. She would begin to weep, she wept hard and sorely, wept as pitiful old age weeps when the tears flow, pressed forth as if by nightmare visions. But even as the tears flowed, her unconscious mind continued working and, unnoticed by Arina Petrovna, carried her thoughts on, away from the source of her sadness, so that in a few minutes she herself wondered in surprise what it was that had come over her.

She lived in general as if she had no personal involvement in life, but existed solely because within this wreck there remained still some forgotten strands which had to be gathered, reckoned, and accounted for. While these strands were still there, life followed its normal course, causing the wreck to fulfil all the outward functions necessary to prevent the total disintegration of its half-dormant existence.

But if the days passed in unconscious dozing, the nights were a positive agony. At night Arina Petrovna was *afraid*; she was afraid of burglars, ghosts, devils—in short, of all that arose out of her upbringing and way of life. And against these there was poor protection, for apart from the decrepit servants mentioned above the entire night staff of Pogorelka was embodied in a limping peasant called Fedoseyushka, who came from the village for two roubles a month to act as nightwatchman at the house and usually dozed in the porch, going out at appointed intervals to bang a few times on a sheet of iron. True, there were a few estate workers, men and women, who lived by the stock-yard, but their quarters were some fifty yards from the house and it was no easy matter to call anybody from there.

There is something wearisome and depressing about a sleepless night in the country. About nine o'clock, or ten at the latest, life seems to come to a stop and a fearful stillness descends. There is nothing to do, it is anyway a pity to waste the candles, so like it or not you go to bed. Once the samovar was taken away off the table Afimyushka, following her habit acquired in the old days of serfdom, would lay a felt mat across the doorway of her mistress's bedroom, then she would scratch herself and yawn, and, as soon as she stretched out on the floor, was dead to the world. Markovna pottered about the maids' room a while longer, all the time muttering something, berating somebody; but in the end she, too, fell silent and a minute later could be heard by turns snoring and rambling in her sleep. The watchman clanged a few times on the iron sheet to announce his presence and was then long silent. Arina Petrovna sits now before an unsnuffed tallow candle, attempting to ward off sleep by playing patience; but no sooner does she begin to lay out the cards than drowsiness begins to overcome her. 'If I don't look out, I'll fall asleep and start a fire,' she tells herself, and decides to get into bed. But she has hardly sunk into her feather-bed than there is fresh cause for concern— sleep which has been luring her, overpowering her the whole evening now suddenly forsakes her. The room is anyway over-heated, with heat simply pouring from the open stove-vent, and the feather-bed makes the atmosphere insufferable. Arina Petrovna tosses from side to side; she wants to call for somebody to come, but she knows that nobody will respond. A mysterious silence reigns, a silence in which the attentive ear can distinguish a multitude of different sounds. Something bangs, there is a sudden howl, somebody seems to go along the passage, there is a movement of air in the room—it actually touches your face. The lamp in front of the icon is lit and in its light objects take on a deceptive character so that you think they are not real objects but only their shapes. Besides this dubious light there is another that comes through the open door of the next room, where four or five lamps are lit before the icon-case. This light falls in a yellow rectangle on the floor, cutting its shape into the darkness of the room, not merging with it. Everywhere there are shadows, flickering, moving soundlessly. A mouse scratches behind the wallpaper, Arina Petrovna cries at it 'Shoo! . . . pest!' and again all is silent. Again shadows, again whispers coming you know not whence. The greater part of the night is passed in this uneasy, fitful dozing; only towards morning does sleep come properly into its own. And at six o'clock Arina Petrovna is already up again, worn out by the sleepless night.

Besides all these things, which indicate well enough the wretchedness of the life led by Arina Petrovna, there were two more: the sparseness of her diet and the discomfort of her rooms. She ate little and badly, probably thinking she might thus make good the loss caused to the household by the lack of adequate supervision. As for her accommodation, the house at Pogorelka was damp and decayed, and the room in which Arina Petrovna closeted herself was never aired and for weeks on end never cleaned. And in the midst of this utter helplessness and total lack of comfort and care the decrepitude of age advanced apace.

But the more decrepit she became, the more strongly did she feel the desire to live—or, rather, she felt not so much the desire to live as the desire for creature comforts, together with a disregard for any thought of death. Previously she had feared death; now she seemed to have forgotten it altogether. And since her ideals in life were little different from those of any peasant, the notion of the 'good life' with which she beguiled herself was of a fairly lowly kind. All that throughout life she had denied herself —decent food, peace and quiet, communion with living souls—all this was now her most persistent preoccupation. All the characteristics of a confirmed parasite—idle chatter, fawning for sops, voracity—developed in her with astonishing rapidity. At home she ate the same soup as the servants with stale salt beef—and, as she did so, had visions of the store-cupboards at Golovlevo, the carp in the Dubrovino fish-ponds, the mushrooms filling the Golovlevo woods, the poultry being fattened in the yard there.

'A dish of giblet soup now would be nice or some mushrooms in sour cream,' she would think to herself, and so vividly did she picture it that even the corners of her mouth drooped. At night she twisted and turned, petrified by every sound of rustling, and thought to herself of Golovlevo, where there were good bolts, and trusty watchmen who banged and clanged on the iron sheet without tire, and where you could sleep sound as in the bosom of the Lord. In the daytime she would go for hours with never a soul to talk to, and while this forced silence lasted she could not help thinking that in Golovlevo there were always people about, someone to open your heart to. In short, Golovlevo was constantly recalled and in the course of these recollections it became a kind of radiant point in which the 'good life' was centred.

And the more often her imagination was disturbed by thoughts of Golovlevo, the more her will was sapped and the more those recent mortal affronts receded in her memory. The Russian woman is too easily disposed by the manner of her upbringing and circumstances of life to reconcile herself to the role of household dependant, and therefore not even Arina Petrovna could avoid this fate, however much it seemed that all her past life would protect and preserve her from such bondage. If she had not 'then' made the mistake of dividing the property and trusting Judas, she would still now have been a querulous and exacting old woman calling the tune to her children. But since the mistake had been made beyond recall, it was only a matter of time before the carping domestic tyrant turned into the submissive, fawning dependant. While her powers retained some remnant of their former vigour, the change did not show outwardly, but the moment she saw she was condemned for good to helplessness and solitude all manner of cowardly impulses entered her heart and gradually brought about the final corruption of her already shattered spirit. Judas, who on his visits to Pogorelka had at first met with a cool reception, suddenly ceased to be odious. The old affronts were somehow lost sight of and it was Arina Petrovna who took the first step towards reconciliation.

It began with asking for things. Emissaries from Pogorelka came to Judas, at first only occasionally, but then more and more often. First it was because there were no mushrooms growing at Pogorelka, then because the cucumbers were spotted as a result of the rain, or because the turkeys—so typical in this present age of freedom—had all died, 'and perhaps, dearie, you would have them catch a few carp for me at Dubrovino, which Pavel, my departed son, never refused to his old mother!' Judas pulled a wry face, but hesitated to show his displeasure openly. He grudged the carp, but worse than anything he feared that his mother might curse him. He remembered how she had once said that she would come to Golovlevo, have the church unlocked, send for the priest, and cry out: 'I curse you!' and this memory had restrained him from many shabby deeds (of which he was such a masterly performer). But in carrying out his dear mother's wishes he intimated to those around that God gives every man some cross to bear and this was not for nothing, since a man with no cross to bear will forget himself and fall into evil ways. To his mother he wrote: 'I am sending what I can manage in the way of cucumbers, Mother dear; as for turkeys, apart from the breeding birds there are only cocks left and, since they are enormous and your table is small, they won't do. Would you not care to pay me a visit at Golovlevo and share a humble repast? We might have a roast of one of these parasitic creatures (parasites indeed, for they are most expertly caponized by my cook, Matvey), and you, Mother dear, and I could then indulge to our heart's content.'

After that Arina Petrovna became a regular visitor to Golovlevo. With Judas she sampled the turkeys and the duck; she slept to her heart's content at night and after dinner, and she unburdened herself in endless chit-chat, to which Judas was excessively prone by nature and she from old age. She did not cease her visits even when Judas, wearied of his long widower-hood, took to himself as housekeeper a young woman of clerical stock by name of Evpraksiya.* Far from it, on hearing the news she drove at once to Golovlevo and, before she was even out of the carriage, shouted to Judas with childlike impatience: 'Come on, come on, you old sinner! Let's see her, let's see your duchess!' The whole day was one of perfect content for her, since Evprak-seyushka herself served her at table and made up the bed for her after dinner, and in the evening she, Judas, and his duchess all played 'donkey'. Judas was well pleased with this outcome and, as a mark of filial gratitude, had a pound of caviare stowed in Arina Petrovna's carriage when she left for Pogorelka—the highest possible token of respect, for caviare was not home produce, but purchased. This so touched the old woman that she could not restrain herself and said:

'Well, thank you very much! God will love you, my dear, that you comfort your old mother and look after her. At least when I get back to Pogorelka it won't be so wearisome. I've always been fond of caviare—and now, thanks to your kindness, I can indulge my fancy!'

Some five years have passed since Arina Petrovna removed to Pogorelka. Judas, having installed himself in his native Golovlevo, never sets foot outside it. He has aged considerably, faded, and lost his spark, but he cheats, lies, and prattles more than ever, since he now has dear Mother more or less permanently on hand, who for the sake of a toothsome morsel in her old age has become a captive audience for his prattle.

It would be wrong to think that Judas was a hypocrite in the same mould as, say, Tartuffe or some present-day French *bourgeois* who waxes eloquent about the 'bases of society'. No, if he was a hypocrite at all, he was a hypocrite of the pure Russian type—that is, simply a man without any moral standard whatsoever and knowing no truth but that contained in copybook axioms. He was infinitely ignorant, a pettifogger, a liar, a prattler, and, on top of everything, he was afraid of the Devil. These are all negative qualities and, as such, provide no sound basis for genuine hypocrisy.

In France hypocrisy is a product of upbringing; it is, you might say, an attribute of 'good manners', and it almost always has some clear political or social colouring. People are hypocritical about religion, about the bases of society, about property, family, and state,* and recently people have taken to being hypocritical even about 'law and order'. If this type of hypocrisy cannot quite be termed a belief, it is at least a rallying point for those who consider it advantageous to play the hypocrite about one thing rather than another. They are consciously hypocritical in regard to their cause, that is, they know themselves that they are hypocrites and know, moreover, that other people are aware of it too. As the French *bourgeois* sees it, the universe is nothing but a vast stage where an endless theatrical performance is being presented, with one hypocrite giving the cue to another. Hypocrisy is an appeal for decency, decorum, appearances, and—what is most important of all: hypocrisy acts as a curb—not, of course, for the hypocrites themselves, who have their being in the loftier spheres of society, but for those who swarm unhypocritically at the bottom of the social cauldron. Hypocrisy restrains society from profligacy and makes the latter a privilege enjoyed only by a very restricted minority. As long as profligacy is confined to a small and closely organized corporation, it not only does no harm, but actually maintains and promotes the traditions of refinement. Refinement would perish, but for the existence of a certain number of *cabinets particuliers* where it can be cultivated in moments when one is free from the cult of official hypocrisy. But profligacy is positively harmful as soon as it becomes accessible to all and when everyone is allowed to make his demands and demonstrate their legitimacy and naturalness. New social strata then come into being, which strive, if not to oust the old strata altogether, at least considerably to limit their scope. The demand for *cabinets particuliers* increases to such an extent that in the end the question arises whether it would not in future be simpler to do without them altogether. It is from such undesirable developments and questions that the ruling classes in France are protected by that systematic hypocrisy which, not content with its status as custom, is assuming the status of legality, and from being a mere feature of social behaviour is taking on the character of a legal obligation.

This law of respect for hypocrisy provides the foundation for practically the whole of the present-day French theatre. The principal characters in the best French stage productions—that is, those which achieve most success precisely for their uncommonly authentic presentation of the sordidness of life, always find time towards the end to offer a corrective to this sordidness with a few fine phrases declaring the sanctity and delights of virtue. Adèle may have spent the first four acts doing all she could to defile the marital bed, but in the fifth she is bound to declare publicly that the only haven for the Frenchwoman who seeks happiness is—the family hearth. Should you wonder what would have happened to Adèle if the author had chosen to continue his play for another five acts, you can be certain that in the first four of them Adèle would again be defiling the marital bed and in the fifth would again make the same declaration to the audience. There is in fact no need to suppose, all you need do is to go to the *Théâtre Français*, to the *Gymnase*, and on to the *Vaudeville* or the *Variétés*, to see that everywhere Adèle defiles the marital bed and everywhere at the end declares this very bed to be the one and only altar at which an honest French-woman can perform her sacred rites. This is now such an accepted part of social morality that nobody even notices the asinine contradiction underlying it: that the truth of life and the truth of hypocrisy go here together hand in hand, so entangled that it is hard to say which truth has the greater claim to recognition.

We Russians have no strongly weighted systems of education. We are not drilled, we are not turned out to be future champions and propagandists of this or that set of social bases; we are simply left to grow on our own, like nettles by the wayside. As a result, there are among us very few hypocrites, but a great many liars, humbugs, and prattlers. We are not required to play the hypocrite for the sake of any bases of society, for such bases are unknown to us and not a single one of them affords us protection. We exist in total freedom—that is, we vegetate, lie, and prattle entirely of our own accord without any bases whatsoever.

Whether this is a matter for rejoicing or regret is not for me to judge. I do, however, think that while hypocrisy may fill one with indignation and horror, aimless lying can lead to tedium and revulsion. It is better, therefore, to avoid considering the relative advantages of conscious hypocrisy and unconscious hypocrisy, and to keep well clear both of hypocrites and of liars.

Judas is, therefore, not so much a hypocrite as a sneaking scoundrel, a liar, and a prattler. Having shut himself away in the country, he felt at once that he was free, for nowhere else, in no other sphere of life could his inclinations find such scope as here.

In Golovlevo he encountered no direct repulse, nor even the least indirect impingement from any quarter, which might have caused him to reflect: 'I'd be glad to play some sneaking trick, but must think what people would say.' Here he was undisturbed by anyone's judgement, undaunted by anyone's indelicate gaze—and consequently there was no need for any self-control. Total laxness became the dominant feature in his attitude towards himself. He had long felt the attraction of this absolute freedom from all moral restraints, and the reason why he had not sooner gone to live in the country was solely because he feared being idle. Having spent more than thirty years in the dim atmosphere of a government office, he had acquired all the habits and cherished aspirations of the confirmed bureaucrat who requires that every minute of his life should be filled with some futile activity. But on closer consideration he had come to realize that the world of bureaucratic futility is sufficiently mobile to be transferred without difficulty to any place you wish, into any chosen sphere. And indeed, no sooner had he settled in Golovlevo than he created for himself such a multitude of petty, trivial functions as to provide him with a constant routine which could never be exhausted. In the morning he sat down to his desk and set about his business: to start with, he checked the accounts of the dairywoman, the housekeeper, and the bailiff, first reckoning one way, then another; he then had a highly complicated way of making up the books (cash and stock), entering every kopek, every item in twenty different ledgers, adding it all up, first finding half a kopek too little, then a whole kopek too much. Finally, he took his pen and wrote off letters of complaint to the magistrates and to the arbiter. All this activity not only left him with never an idle moment, it had, too, all the appearance of painstaking, taxing work. It was not of idleness that Judas complained, but of the lack of time to get everything done, even though he spent the whole day in his dressing-gown poring over papers in the study. There were always piles of petty reports, carefully docketed but still not checked, lying about his desk, among them the complete annual accounts for Fekla, the dairywoman, whose activities had from the outset struck him as suspicious, but which none the less he never found a spare moment to go through.

Every link with the world outside was totally severed. He received no books, no newspapers, not even letters. One of his sons, Volodenka, had committed suicide; to the other, Petenka, he wrote brief letters and then only when he was sending money. Around him there prevailed a heavy atmosphere of ignorance, prejudice, and painstaking futility, and he felt not the slightest impulse to escape from it. Even the news that Napoleon III's reign had ended* he learnt only a year after his death from the local police superintendent, and even then showed no special emotion; he simply crossed himself, whispered 'God rest his soul' and said:

'How proud he was! Upon my word! This was wrong, that wasn't right! Emperors went to pay their respects to him, princes served at his door. Yet God in a moment cast down all his schemes!'

In fact, he did not even know what was going on in his own estate, even though from morning to night he did nothing but count and reckon. In this respect he possessed all the qualities of the inveterate bureaucrat in a government office. Imagine the head-clerk whose principal says to him in a lighthearted moment: 'My dear fellow, I'm doing some calculations and need to know how many potatoes Russia can produce in a year—do a detailed estimate, will you?' Would the head-clerk be stumped by such a question? Would he, at least, ponder the means to be employed in carrying out the task he was set? No, he would take a much simpler course: he would draw a map, divide it into exactly equal squares, calculate the number desyatinas* represented by each square, then go to a grocery shop, discover how many potatoes are sown to the desyatina and what the *average* yield is, and finally (with the aid of God and the first four rules of arithmetic) would arrive at the result that, *given favourable circumstances*, Russia could produce such and such a quantity of potatoes and, *given unfavourable circumstances*, such and such. And his work would not only give satisfaction to his principal, but very likely also be published in volume 102 of some learned 'Transactions'.

Even the housekeeper he had selected was exactly suited to the situation he had created. Evpraksiya was the daughter of a church servitor at St Nicholas's at Kapelki and in every respect a perfect treasure. She was not quick-witted or resourceful or even efficient, but against that she was hard-working, acquiescent, and made practically no demands on him. Even when their relationship became 'close', she only asked if it meant that she could now have cold kvass* whenever she wanted and without asking: even Judas was touched by this unmercenary attitude and immediately put at her disposal not only the kvass, but also two tubs of pickled apples, free of any requirement to keep account of either item. Her looks also had no special attraction for the connoisseur, but for a man who was not fussy and knew what he wanted they were satisfactory enough. She had a broad white face, narrow forehead framed by somewhat sparse, yellowish hair, large lacklustre eyes, nose completely straight, and a weak mouth with that enigmatic, fleeting smile one sees on portraits done by home-bred artists. In general, there was nothing outstanding about her, except perhaps her back, which was so broad and powerful that even the most indifferent of men would instinctively raise a hand to 'give the lass one' between the shoulder-blades. She was aware of this and never took offence, so that when Judas for the first time ran his fingers over the plump nape of her neck, all she did was to shake her shoulders.

In these dull surroundings the days passed by, one the same as the next, without change, without hope of anything fresh intruding. Only the visits of Arina Petrovna brought a little life into this existence and, if the truth be told, Porfiry Vladimirych, though at first he would pull a face at the sight of his mother's carriage in the distance, in time not only grew accustomed to her visits, but even liked it when she came. They satisfied his passion for idle prattle, for though he found it possible to prattle away to himself in isolation about his various reckonings and accounts, to prattle with dear Mother was much more to his liking. Once together, they would talk from morning to night and never be done. They talked about everything under the sun: how the harvests had been in the past and how they were now, how landowners had lived in the past and how they lived now, how, perhaps on account of the salt being better in the past, pickled cucumbers these days were not what they used to be.

The advantage of these conversations was that they flowed like water and were easily forgotten; in consequence they could be endlessly renewed with as much interest as if they were now being entered into for the first time. During these conversations Evprakseyushka was also present, Arina Petrovna having grown so fond of her that she never let her from her side. Sometimes, when they were tired of talking, the three of them sat down to cards and stayed up late into the night playing 'donkey'. They tried to teach Evprakseyushka how to play dummy-whist, but she could not grasp it. On such evenings the huge Golovlevo house seemed to come to life. In all the windows there were lights and fleeting shadows, and a passing traveller might have supposed that all manner of merriment was afoot. Samovars, coffee-pots, zakuski stood all day on the table. And Arina Petrovna was merry and light at heart and, instead of one day, she would stay on for three days or four. And as she departed for Pogorelka she was already thinking up some pretext for a speedy return to the blandishments of the 'good life' at Golovlevo.

It is late November. As far as the eye can see the ground is shrouded in white. Outside it is night, with driving snow. The cold, cutting wind furrows the fallen snow, in a moment piling it into drifts, it lashes everything in its path, and fills the whole vicinity with its wailing. Village, church, and nearby forest—all have vanished in the swirling snowy mist; there is a mighty din in the old garden of Golovlevo. But inside the manor-house it is light, warm, and cosy. In the dining-room stands the samovar, around which are gathered Arina Petrovna, Porfiry Vladimirych, and Evprakseyushka. To one side is a card-table with dog-eared cards scattered on it. Open doors lead on one side of the room into the oratory, which is filled with the light of the burning icon-lamps, and on the other side into the master's study, which also has a small lamp glowing before the icon. It is stuffy in the over-heated rooms, there is a smell of lamp-oil and fumes from the charcoal in the samovar. Evprakseyushka is ensconced opposite the samovar and is washing the cups and drying them on a cloth. The samovar is in full voice, one moment thrumming mightily, the next emitting a shrill wheeze as if going off to sleep. Clouds of steam billow from beneath the lid, enveloping in mist the tea-pot which for the last quarter of an hour has been on its stand on the top of the samovar. They sit chatting.

'How many times is it you've been "donkey" today then?'
Arina Petrovna asks Evprakseyushka.

'I wouldn't have been at all if I hadn't let it happen. I only
do it to please you,' replies Evprakseyushka.

'Go on with you! I saw how pleased *you* were when I played
those threes and fives to you just now. I'm not Porfiry Vladimirych, remember: he spoils you, keeps putting down only one
all the time. But there's no need for me to do that.'

'Oh yes, but you cheated!'

'Now that's a thing I never do!'

'And who did I catch just now? Who was trying to pass off
the seven of clubs and the eight of hearts as a pair? I saw it
myself, I caught you!'

Saying which, Evprakseyushka gets up to take the tea-pot off
the samovar and turns her back to Arina Petrovna.

'My word, bless you, what a back you've got!' Arina Petrovna
exclaims without thinking.

'Oh yes, she's got a back . . .' Judas responds automatically.

'How you keep on about my back . . . you are awful! What's
my back ever done to you?'

Evprakseyushka looks right and left and smiles. Her back was
her pride and joy. Not long ago even old Savelich the cook had
gawped at it and said: 'Lord love us, what a back! 'Tis like a stove-
top!'—and she had not made any complaint about him to Porfiry
Vladimirych.

The cups are filled with tea and the samovar begins to quieten
down. The blizzard meanwhile rages ever worse, one minute
battering the window-panes with a regular cloud-burst of snow,
the next wailing some inexpressible lament as it courses through
the flue-pipe of the stove.

'The storm's going full blast,' observes Arina Petrovna. 'Listen
to it howling and yowling!'

'Well, let it yowl. It can yowl away, and we'll just drink up our
tea—yes, Mother dear, yes indeed!' replies Porfiry Vladimirych.

'Dearie me! It's bad for anybody caught out in this by God's
good will.'

'Bad for some, but small sorrow to us. Some are out in the dark
and cold, but we're all cosy in the light and warm. Here we sit

drinking our tea, with a touch of sugar, spot of cream, bit of lemon. And with a dash of rum too, should we so fancy.'

'Why yes, like now did you mean . . .'

'If you don't mind, Mother dear. I was saying—it's a bad thing to be out in the country now. No road, no path—all covered in snow. Then there are wolves. But here it's all light and snug and we've nothing to fear. We can just sit back in peace and harmony. A hand of cards if we feel like cards, a sup of tea if we feel like tea. We'll not drink more than need be; so much as we need, so much will we drink. And why is this so? Why, so it is, Mother dear, because God's mercy does not forsake us. But for God, our heavenly King, why we too perhaps might be wandering lost out there even now, all in the dark and cold . . . Nothing but a poor jerkin, a tatty old belt, and bast-shoes . . .'*

'Bast-shoes, indeed! You're gentry-born, aren't you? Whatever they're like, it's still boots we wear!'

'And do you know why it is, Mother, that we are gentry-born? It's all because God had mercy on us. But for that, we'd be sitting now in some peasant hut, and there'd be no candle burning, just a rushlight, and as for tea or coffee, why we'd never dare think of it. There we'd sit. I'd be plaiting bast-shoes and you'd be cooking a bit of plain cabbage soup for supper. Evprakseyushka would be weaving . . . Then the constable might call us out on wagon-duty for the military . . .'

'Oh, go on! Not even the constable would order anybody out at a time like this!'

'You never know, Mother dear! Any moment the troops might be on the march! There might be war or rebellion—and the troops must be there in time. Why, only the other day the superintendent told me Napoleon III had passed on—so there's bound to be some monkey-business from the French. Of course, our men advance straightaway—and the peasant must provide his wagon! There may be frost and snow and the roads are all gone, but they make no allowance—the peasant must go if that's the order. But the likes of you and me they'll spare for the moment—no wagon-duty for us!'

'It goes without saying, great is God's mercy on us!'

'And what am I saying? God, Mother dear, is everything. It's he gives us wood to warm us and stores to feed us, it's all due to him. We think we provide everything ourselves, bought with our own money, but when we look and see and think about it—it's all God's work. And if he doesn't want us to, we won't have a thing. Like now, I'd love a few oranges. I'd have one for myself, and I'd give one to you, Mother dear, and there'd be one for everybody all round. And I've got the money to buy them too: I'll fetch it out and take the oranges, thank you . . . But, oh no! God says: "Whoa, there!"—and this little piggy has none!'

They all laugh.

'It's like you say,' replies Evprakseyushka. 'I had an uncle who was sexton at Holy Assumption church in Pesochnoe. Well, he was that pious, you'd think God might have looked after him, but he got caught out in a snowstorm—and froze to death just like anybody else!'

'The very thing I'm saying. If God so wishes, a man will freeze; if he doesn't, he'll stay alive. And then, you can say the same about prayers: there are those which are pleasing to God and those which aren't. One which is pleasing is answered, one which isn't might just as well never be said. Your uncle's prayer was perhaps not a pleasing one and so was never answered.'

'I remember going to Moscow back in 'twenty-four (I was carrying Pavel at the time)—it was in December, and there was I travelling . . .'

'If you don't mind, Mother dear. I'll just finish what I was saying about prayers. Man prays for everything, because he needs everything. Butter, cabbage, cucumbers—everything. In his human frailty, though, he'll sometimes pray for a thing that he doesn't need. But from his seat on high God knows better. You ask for butter, and he'll give you cabbage, onions maybe; you beg him for a spell of hot, dry weather, and he'll send you rain and hail. And this you must understand and not complain. Like this September, we kept pleading to God for frosts to save the winter corn from damp rot, but God sent no frost and so our corn rotted.'

'Yes, that it did!' commiserated Arina Petrovna. 'The peasants' winter corn at Novinki is all past saving. When winter's past they'll have to plough again and sow spring seed.'

'That's just it. Here are we, so clever and smart, scheming and planning, and then God at a stroke, in a moment turns all our projects and plots to dust. But, Mother dear, you were about to tell us what happened to you in 'twenty-four?'

'What was that? There now, I've gone and forgotten. To do with God's mercy it must have been, something of the sort. I can't remember, my dear, I can't remember.'

'Well, God grant, you'll remember it some other time. Now, Mother dear, with all that swirling and burling going on outside, why don't you have a nice taste of jam? This one is cherry—our own from Golovlevo. Evprakseyushka made it herself.'

'I'll have some. Cherries, I must say, are something I rarely get now. Time was, I used to have them often, but now . . . You've got good cherries at Golovlevo, juicy big ones. At Dubrovino, try as we might to train them, they always turn out sour. And you, Evprakseyushka, did you put some of that French vodka in the jam?'

'What else! I did it just the way you taught me to do. And there's something I wanted to ask you—when you pickle cucumbers, do you put in some cardamom?'

Arina Petrovna thinks for a time and, at a loss, makes a gesture of despair.

'I can't remember, my dear. Yes, I think I used to put in a bit of cardamom too. I don't now—but then, what pickling do I do these days! I used to put some in, though—yes, I can remember it well. When I get home I'll have a look through my recipes and see if I can find it. When I had my strength, I used to take note of everything and write it down. If there was something I liked anywhere, I would ask about it straight away, jot it down on a piece of paper, and try it out at home. Once I got a secret recipe. Such a secret it was that people offered a thousand roubles for it, but the person would never tell, and that was that! But I just slipped twenty-five kopeks to the housekeeper and she told me all about it, every jot and tittle!'

'Oh yes, Mother dear, but you in your time were a regular . . . minister of state!'

'Minister . . . Perhaps I was, perhaps I wasn't, still I can be thankful that I never squandered, but added to the store. Here am I now eating the fruits of my righteous labours, for I was the one who got the cherries to grow in Golovlevo!'

'And thanks be to you for that, Mother dear, many, many thanks! Everlasting thanks—from me and your descendants—oh, yes indeed!'

Judas stands, goes up to his mother, and kisses her hand.

'And thank you too for looking after your old mother. Yes, you've got a good stock of provisions, a very good stock.'

'What provisions do *we* have! Why you were the one for provisions! The number of cellars alone there were and nowhere a foot of space!'

'Yes, I used to keep good stocks. I'll not tell a lie, I was never a slack housekeeper. As for having a lot of cellars, why, in those days it was a big concern—ten times as many mouths to feed then as now! The number of servants alone—and every one had to be provided for and fed! Cucumber for one, kvass for another—a little bit here, a little bit there, but it all mounted up.'

'Yes, good times they were. There was plenty of everything then. Corn, fruit—all in abundance.'

'There was more manuring done then, that's what made things grow.'

'No, Mother dear, it wasn't that. It was God's blessing—that's what made things grow. I remember once dear Father brought an Oporto apple in from the garden. We could hardly believe it—it wouldn't even fit on a plate.'

'I don't remember that. I know we did have good apples, but I don't remember any as big as a plate. But they did catch a twenty-pound carp in Dubrovino pond at the time of the old Tsar's coronation*—that certainly happened.'

'Carp and fruit—they were all big in those days. I remember Ivan the gardener grew water-melons—this big!'

Judas extends his arms sideways, then bends them round to make a show of being unable to hold one in his grasp.

'Yes, there were water-melons too. With water-melons, my dear, it depends on the year. Some years there are plenty and they are good, but another year there'll be few about and no flavour to them, and then there'll be a year when there are none at all. And there's another thing—fruit will grow in one place, but not in another. Take Grigory Aleksandrych's—at Khlebnikovo —nothing would ever grow there, no berries, no fruit, no nothing. Only water-melons. But what melons they were!'

'So God's mercy was on his melons then.'

'Why, certainly. Without God's mercy you'll never get by, nor can you ever escape it.'

Arina Petrovna has already had two cups of tea and is beginning to cast glances at the card-table. Evprakseyushka is also dying to do battle in a hand of 'donkey'. But these plans are confounded by courtesy of Arina Petrovna herself, for she suddenly recalls something.

'Ah, I've got some news!' she declares. 'I had a letter from the girls yesterday.'

'Not a word from them all this time and now they write. Hard up, are they, and asking for money?'

'No, they're not. Here, take a look at it.'

Arina Petrovna takes a letter from her pocket and gives it to Judas. He reads:

Granny, don't send us any more turkeys or chickens. Don't send any money either, save it up to earn interest. We're not in Moscow, but Kharkov, we've gone onto the stage and in the summer we'll be touring round the fairs. I (Anninka) had my début in *La Périchole*, and Lyubinka in *Pansy*.* I had several curtain calls, especially after the scene where *la périchole* comes on tipsy and sings "I'm re-eady, I'm ready, I'm re-e-eady!" They loved Lyubinka too. The manager's fixed my wages at a hundred roubles a month with a benefit in Kharkov, Lyubinka's getting seventy-five a month and a benefit in the summer at one of the fairs. As well as that we get presents from admirers— officers and lawyers. Only the lawyers sometimes give us forged money,* so you have to be careful. You, Granny dear, make yourself at home in Pogorelka. We're never going to come back there and really can't understand how anybody could live there. Yesterday we had the first snow and went for a troika ride with two of the local lawyers. One of them is like Plevako*—he's awfully dishy! He put a glass of champagne on his head and danced the trepak—terrific fun! There's another who is not terribly good-looking, rather like Yazykov* in Petersburg. Just fancy, he's put his brains out of joint reading *Best Russian Songs and Romances*, and is so run-down he even has fainting fits in court. We spend most days either with the officers or the lawyers. We go for drives, have dinner and supper in the best restaurants, and never pay a thing. Granny, don't stint yourself at Pogorelka—all the produce: corn, chickens, mushrooms, have it for yourself. We'd be glad too if the capital . . .

Goodbye for now, our *beaux* have arrived—they want to take us on another troika ride. Sweetheart! My divine! Goodbye!

Anninka
—and from me, Lyubinka

'Pshaw!' Judas spits in disgust as he returns the letter.

Arina Petrovna sits deep in thought and for a time makes no reply.

'You've not answered them yet, Mother?'

'No, not yet. I only got the letter yesterday and I came on purpose to show you, but what with one thing and another I nearly forgot.'

'Don't answer at all. That's the best.'

'How can I not answer? I'm bound to give them an account of things. Pogorelka is theirs, after all.'

Judas also sets to thinking: some sinister plan is floating in his mind.

'What I'm concerned about is how those girls will ever keep themselves decent in that peep-show!' Arina Petrovna continues meanwhile. 'That's a matter where one false step—and there's a girl's honour gone for good! You can whistle in the wind for it!'

'Much they care about that!' snaps Judas.

'Never the less . . . For a girl—it's what you might say, the greatest treasure of all . . . Who would marry that sort of girl afterwards?'

'These days, Mother dear, women live with men whether they are married or not. These days people mock the precepts of religion. You find a bush, get married under it,* and that's all there is to it. Civil marriage, that's what they call it.'

Judas suddenly stops short, recalling that, after all, he is himself living in sin with an unmarried woman of clerical stock.

'Of course, sometimes in case of need', he corrects himself, 'if a man happens to be still in his prime and in widowed state . . . In case of need, even the law has its exceptions.'

'It goes without saying. In case of need a stint will sing like a nightingale. Even the saints sinned in case of need, much less sinners like us!'

'Precisely so. Now, if I were in your place, do you know what I would do?'

'What would you advise, my dear, you tell me.'

'I would have them make over to me full power of attorney for Pogorelka.'

Arina Petrovna looks at him apprehensively.

'But I've got full powers of management as it is,' she says.

'I don't mean management. I mean power to sell and mortgage and generally act at your own discretion . . .'

Arina Petrovna lowers her eyes to the floor and says nothing.

'Of course, a matter like this needs proper consideration. Just give it some thought, Mother,' Judas urges.

But Arina Petrovna remains silent. Although, because of old age, her wits are considerably less sharp than in the past, she still feels some unease at Judas's promptings. The fact is that she is afraid of him: she would miss the warmth and space and plenty which rule at Golovlevo, yet at the same time she senses that his talk of power of attorney is not without purpose and that he is again laying some fresh snare. Her situation becomes so tense that already she is inwardly upbraiding herself for showing him the letter. Luckily, Evprakseyushka comes to the rescue.

'What about it then? Are we going to play cards?' she asks.

'Yes, yes, let's!' Arina Petrovna hastens to reply, and promptly gets up from the tea-table. But as she moves to the card-table, a fresh thought strikes her.

'Do you know what day it is today?' she asks Porfiry Vladimirych.

'The twenty-third of November, Mother dear,' replies Judas, puzzled.

'The twenty-third, yes, the twenty-third. And do you remember what happened on the twenty-third of November? You've forgotten, I suppose, about the requiem?'

Porfiry Vladimirych blenches and crosses himself.

'Lord! What a terrible thing!' he exclaims. 'Is that right? Is it? Let's look in the calendar.'

In a few minutes he comes back with the calendar and searches till he finds an inserted sheet with the inscription:

'Twenty-third of November. Commemoration of my dear son, Vladimir.

'Rest, dear dust, until the joyful morn! and pray to God for your Papa, who on this day will never fail to have held for you a requiem and mass.'

'There you are!' declares Porfiry Vladimirych. 'Ah, Volodya, Volodya, you're not a good son to me! You're a bad fellow! You can't be praying to God for your Papa if he makes him so forgetful! Mother dear, what can we do?'

'It's not the end of the world. You can always have the service tomorrow. A requiem and mass—we'll have them both. It's all my fault, forgetful old woman that I am. I came on purpose to remind you, and it slipped my mind on the way.'

'Oh, what a terrible thing to do! It's a good thing the lamps in the oratory are lit. Really it was a heaven-sent thought I had. Today is not a feast-day or anything—it's just that the lamps have been lit since the Presentation of the Virgin,* and only yesterday Evprakseyushka came and asked if she shouldn't put out the side ones. And I don't know what prompted me—I gave it a moment's thought and said to her: "Leave them be. Bless them, let them go on burning." And then look what happens!'

'A good thing the lamps at least have been lit. It's a comfort. Where are you going to sit then? Do you intend playing after me again or are you going to pamper your duchess?'

'Oh, I really don't know, Mother, whether I ought . . .'

'Why shouldn't you? Sit you down! God will forgive you. It was not on purpose, not with intent, it was just forgetfulness. That happened even to the saints! And tomorrow we'll be up first thing, have a mass and requiem—do it all as is proper. And his soul will be glad that his parents and good folk have remembered him, and we shall be easy in mind knowing that we did our duty. Yes, yes, my dear. And don't you sorrow. It's what I always say: first, sorrowing won't bring the boy back to you, and second, it's a sin before God.'

Judas is persuaded by his mother's words and kisses her hand, saying:

'Oh, Mother, Mother dear, you've got a heart of gold, you really have. But for you, I don't know what I would have done just now. I would have been simply lost, all in a pickle, lost completely!'

Porfiry Vladimirych sees to the arrangements for the next day's ceremony, and the three of them sit down to cards. They have one hand, then another; Arina Petrovna gets cross, incensed with Judas for constantly playing single cards to Evprakseyushka. In between hands Judas gives way to memories of his dead son.

'What an affectionate boy he was!' he says. 'He would never take a thing without asking. If it was paper he wanted, he'd say: "Papa, please can I have some paper?" "Help yourself, my dear," I'd say. Or "Papa, would you please be so kind as to order carp in sour cream for lunch?" "Certainly, my dear." Oh, Volodya, Volodya! You were such a good boy, in all but one thing—that you went and left your Papa!'

A few more hands are played; and again memories.

'What suddenly came over him—I don't understand it at all! There he was living a nice quiet life, everything fine, and a joy to his father—what more could you want?—then suddenly "bang", he shoots himself! Just think of it: what a terrible thing to do! Just think, Mother dear, what it was that the boy raised his hand against—his own life, given him by his heavenly Father. And what for? Why? What did he lack? Money? I don't think I'm one to hold back anyone's allowance, am I? Not even my enemies would say that of me. Of course, if it seemed a bit short, that's too bad, my boy! Money doesn't grow on trees for Father either. If you're short of cash, you must know how to restrain yourself. It's not sweets all the time, life's not a bed of roses, you must take the rough with the smooth. Yes indeed, my boy. Look at your father—he was reckoning on some money the other day, but then the steward came and told him that the Terpenkovo peasants hadn't paid their quit-rent. There was nothing else for it, so I wrote off a petition to the arbiter . . . Oh, Volodya, Volodya! No, you're not a good boy, abandoning your father and leaving him all alone in the world!'

And as the game becomes more animated, so his memories become ever more lavish and sentimental.

'And how clever he was! I remember once when he had measles —he couldn't have been more than seven—Sasha, my late lamented, went up to him and he said to her "Mummy, mummy! It's true, isn't it, that only angels have wings?" And she said, "Yes, only angels." "Then why", said he, "did papa have wings when he came in just now?" '

The game in the end assumes Homeric proportions. Judas is left 'donkey' holding *eight* cards in his hand, including the ace, king, and queen of trumps. There is laughter and teasing, in which Judas joins, taking it all in good part. But in the midst of this general jollity Arina Petrovna suddenly falls silent and listens intently.

'Stop! Not so much noise! Somebody's coming!' she says.

Judas and Evprakseyushka also listen, but hear nothing.

'Somebody's coming, I tell you! There . . . hark! You could hear it just then on the wind. Listen! It is somebody. Nearby, too.'

They again strain to listen and hear, indeed, a distant sound of jingling, now louder, now fainter as it is carried by the wind. Five minutes pass, and the harness-bell is now clearly heard, followed by the sound of voices outside.

'It's the young master! Petr Porfirych has arrived' is heard from the hall.

Judas rose and stood rigid, pale as a sheet.

Petenka came rather languidly into the room, kissed his father's hand, performed the same ceremony in respect of his grand-mother, bowed to Evprakseyushka, and sat down. He was a fellow of about twenty-five, quite good-looking, in the travelling dress of an officer. That is as much as can be said about him, and Judas himself scarcely knew any more. The relations between father and son were such that they could not even be called strained: they virtually did not exist. Judas knew there was a person recorded as being his son, to whom he was required at certain times to send an allowance agreed upon (fixed by himself, that is) and from whom in return he had the right to demand respect and obedience. Petenka, for his part, was aware that he had a father, who could at any time impose on him. He quite enjoyed going back to Golovlevo, especially since he had gained his commission, not because he took any pleasure from talking to his father, but simply because anyone without a clear purpose in life has an instinctive hankering for a place *where he belongs*. But he evidently came now from necessity, by constraint, which meant that he showed none of those marks of joyful wonderment with which as a rule the prodigal gentry-son signalizes his return home.

Petenka showed no inclination to talk. To all his father's exclamations—'What a surprise!', 'So good of you to come, my boy!', 'There was I sitting and thinking: mercy, who can that be out and about by night, and all the time it was . . .', and so forth— he responded either with silence or with a forced smile. And to the question what had suddenly decided him to come he answered even rudely: 'I just thought I'd come, so I did.'

'Well, thank you, thank you! You remembered your father! Made him happy! And your old grandmother you remembered, too, no doubt!'

'Yes, Granny too I remembered.'

'Ha, and perhaps you had it in mind that today is the anniversary of your brother Volodya's death?'

'Yes, I had that in mind too.'

The conversation continued for about half an hour in this vein, so that it was impossible to tell whether Petenka was answering straight or simply prevaricating. Because of this, however, even Judas, resistant though he was to the indifference of his children, lost patience and said:

'There's no affection in you, is there, my boy? Nobody could say you were an affectionate son.'

If at this juncture Petenka had held his tongue, if he had meekly accepted his father's rebuke, or, better still, if he had kissed his hand and said 'Please forgive me, dear kind Father. It's just that I'm tired after the journey,' all would have been well. But Petenka behaved like a total ingrate.

'I am what I am,' he answered rudely, as if to say: 'Just do me a favour and leave me alone!'

At that Porfiry Vladimirych was so pained, so deeply pained, that he could no longer keep silent.

'Really! After the way I have cared for you!' he said. 'Even now I sit here wondering how to make things better, smoother, so that everybody can be fine and cosy with no sorrow or want . . . And you all shun me!'

'What do you mean, "you all"?'

'Well then, you alone . . . though your late brother (God rest his soul) was just the same . . .'

'All right then! I'm extremely grateful to you!'

'There's no gratitude from either of you! No gratitude, no affection, nothing!'

'I'm not affectionate by nature, that's all. And what do you keep on talking about the two of us for? One of us is dead . . .'

'Yes, dead. God punished him. God punishes unruly children. Yet still I remember him. He was an unruly boy, but I remember him just the same. So tomorrow we'll have a mass and requiem for him. He wronged me, but still I remember my duty. Good Lord in Heaven, what are the times coming to? A son comes home to his father and straightaway he's grumbling! It's not the way we behaved when I was young. You'd go home to Golovlevo and for the last thirty versts be repeating "Remember, Lord, King David and all his meekness!" There's Mother here as a living witness—she can tell you! But nowadays—I can't understand it, can't understand it at all.'

'Nor can I understand. I arrived here quietly, greeted you, kissed your hand, and now I'm sitting here, doing you no harm, drinking tea, and, if you give me any, I'll have supper too. What's all the fuss about?'

Arina Petrovna sits in her chair and listens to them. She feels she is hearing some long familiar tale that began way back, she cannot remember when. It was a tale that seemed to have ended, but now, once more, it is about to be reopened at the page where it had stopped. None the less, she realizes that no good is augured by an encounter such as this between father and son and so considers it her duty to intervene in the quarrel and say a conciliatory word.

'There, there, you turkey-cocks!' she says, trying to impart a jocular note to her admonition. 'No sooner do you see each other than you set to! The way you go for each other! You'll soon have the feathers flying! My, oh my—what a terrible thing! Now, why don't you young fellows just sit quiet and have a friendly chat, while this old woman listens and looks on? Petenka, you should give way. You should always give way to your father, dear, because he is your father. If you think he's hard on you sometimes, you must bear it willingly, humbly, respectfully, because you are his son. The bitter pill might suddenly turn sweet and then it's all for your good! And you, Porfiry Vladimirych—have a bit of lenience. He's your son, young and coddled, and he's just travelled seventy-five versts over bumpy, snowed-up roads: he's tired and chilled and ready for sleep. We've finished tea, so have them serve supper now, and then off we go to bed. Yes indeed, my dears. We'll each to our own room, say our prayers, and that'll put paid to our spleen. And any dark thoughts we had God will drive out from us by sleep. First thing in the morning we'll be up and say our prayers for the departed. We'll have the mass and requiem and when we get back we can have a talk. With a good night's rest, everybody can tell his tale in proper style. You, Petenka, can tell us all about Petersburg, and you, Porfiry, can tell about life here in the country. So now let's have supper, and then, God bless us, up the wooden ladder!'

This homily is effective, not because there is any real substance to it, but because Judas himself sees that he has gone too far, and that it would be better to end the day peaceably. He therefore gets up from his place, kisses dear Mother's hand, thanks her for 'the benefit of her wisdom', and orders supper to be served. Supper passes off grimly, in silence.

The dining-room is now deserted. Everyone has retired to their rooms. The house gradually falls silent and a deathly hush steals from room to room until finally it comes to the last refuge, in which, longer than in the other bolt-holes, the ritual life persists: that is, to the study of the master of Golovlevo. At long last Judas, too, after much time spent prostrating himself before the icons, has gone to bed.

Porfiry Vladimirych lies in bed, but cannot settle to sleep. He senses that his son's arrival forebodes something out of the ordinary and even now all manner of vacuous homilies are forming in his mind. These homilies have the merit that they can serve for any occasion and contain no coherent train of thought. Nor have they any need of grammatical or syntactic form. They accumulate in his mind as disjointed aphorisms and are delivered to the world simply as they come to his lips. Despite this, it needs only some unusual situation to arise for his head to be set in a turmoil by the flood of aphorisms which even sleep cannot still.

Judas cannot sleep: a multitude of trivialities swarm round the head of his bed and press down on him. In fact, the mysterious arrival of Petenka causes him no special concern, for, whatever the occasion, Judas is always prepared *for anything* in advance. He knows that *nothing* can catch him unawares, and that *nothing* can make him depart in any way from that web of empty, putrid aphorisms with which he has enveloped himself from head to toe. For him there exists neither sorrow nor joy, neither hatred nor love. The whole world in his eyes is a tomb, fit only to serve as pretext for his endless prattling. How much more grievous it was when Volodya committed suicide, but he had been proof even against that. That had been a very melancholy affair, which went on for two whole years. For two whole years Volodya had held out; at first, he showed pride and determination to do without his father's help; but then he weakened, began to implore, argue, threaten . . . And all he ever got in reply was some ready-made aphorism—the stone given to the hungry man. Whether or not Judas was aware that it was a stone and not bread is a moot point; but in any case he possessed nothing else and the stone he gave was all that he had to give. When Volodya shot himself, he held a requiem, entered in the calendar the day of his death, and promised that each year in the future on 23 November he would have a requiem with mass held for him. But when occasionally there rose even in him a dim voice, which murmured that to resolve a family quarrel by suicide was supect, to say the least, then he marshalled forth a whole succession of handy aphorisms, such as 'God punishes the unruly child', 'God stands against the proud', and so on—and again he felt at ease.

It is the same now. There is no doubt that some misfortune has overtaken Petenka, but, whatever has happened, he, Porfiry Golovlev, must be above such chance events. 'You got yourself into the mess, you get yourself out', 'As you make your bed, so you must lie on it', 'You must pay the price for your pleasures':

yes, just that—that is precisely what he will say next day, what-ever it is that his son may have to tell him. And what if, like Volodya, Petenka also refuses to accept the stone given in place of bread? What if he too . . . Judas banishes the idea in disgust, ascribing it to the workings of the Devil. He tosses from side to side, trying hard to get to sleep, but cannot. As soon as he becomes drowsy, suddenly: 'The sky is beyond the reach of man', or 'Cut your coat according to your cloth', 'That's my way, but you . . . oh, sharp you are, but you know the saying "Speed your need only for catching of fleas".' He is set about by trivialities, which creep and crawl and press down on him. And Judas lies sleepless, weighed down by the empty verbiage with which next day he hopes to assuage his soul.

Petenka cannot sleep either, although he is fairly worn out after his journey. He has business which can only be settled here, in Golovlevo, but it is of such a kind that there is no knowing how best to set about it. The truth is that Petenka understands per-fectly well that his case is hopeless, that his journey to Golovlevo will result in nothing but more unpleasantness, but the fact of the matter is that man has in him some instinct of self-preservation which overrides all consciousness and urges him simply to carry on trying to the end. So he has come; but instead of steeling him-self and being prepared to stomach anything, he has at the outset nearly had a row with his father. What will be the outcome of his journey? Will the miracle which is supposed to change stone to bread take place, or not?

Would it not be more straightforward to take a pistol, put it to his temple, and say: 'Gentlemen, I am unworthy to wear your uniform! I have embezzled the regimental funds! I therefore pro-nounce on myself this just and severe sentence! Bang!'—and it would be all over. 'Delete from muster-roll: Lieutenant Golovlev, deceased.' Yes, that would be decisive and fine. His comrades would say 'He was unlucky, he let himself go, but—he was an *honourable* fellow!' But instead of taking *this* course at once, he had let things go on until it became common knowledge what he had done, and now he had been given a fixed period of leave in which to make good the embezzled money without fail. And then—get out, leave the regiment! And it was for this purpose—

and with nothing more in prospect than a shameful end to his scarce-begun career—that he has come to Golovlevo, has come, knowing full well that in place of bread he will receive a stone!

But perhaps something will come of it? After all, it does happen ... The present Golovlevo might suddenly disappear and a new Golovlevo appear in its place with a new order of things, and he could ... Not that his father should ... die—why should he?—but just generally there would be a new 'order of things' ... There is Granny, too, she might—after all, she's got money! If she knows I'm in a jam, she'll fork out. There you are, she'll say, now off you go quick, before the time runs out! And away he goes, urging on the drivers, barely making it to the station—and returning to his regiment with just two hours to spare. 'Well done, Golovlev!' his comrades will say. 'Noble fellow! Give us your hand! And now let bygones be bygones!' And not only does he stay on in the regiment, but is promoted—to staff-captain, captain, then he is made regimental adjutant (paymaster he has already been!), and finally on the regiment's anniversary ...

Ah, if only this night would end! Tomorrow ... well, tomorrow, come what may! But what he will have to listen to—what an earful that will be! Tomorrow ... but why should it be tomorrow? He has still another whole day ahead of him ... After all, he had got himself two days so as to have time to talk round, rouse pity in his father ... Ha, dammit! a fat chance of talking round or rousing pity here! Not a hope ...

At this point his thoughts become totally confused and gradually, one by one, they are sunk in the mist of sleep. A quarter of an hour later the whole of Golovlevo has subsided into uneasy rest.

Early next morning the whole household is up. Everyone has gone to church (except Petenka, who has stayed home on the pretext of being tired after his journey). At last, the mass and requiem completed, they returned home. Petenka, as was his custom, went to kiss his father's hand, but Judas, as he proffered his hand, looked the other way, and everyone observed that he did not make the usual sign of the cross to bless his son. They drank their tea and ate kutya. Judas, looking grim, shuffled about the room, shunning conversation, sighing, continually putting his hands together in silent prayer, and never so much as glancing at his son. Petenka, too, was on edge and smoked cigarette after cigarette, saying nothing. The strained situation of the previous day had not only failed to improve overnight, it had now become so obviously acute that Arina Petrovna was seriously concerned and decided to find out from Evprakseyushka whether anything had occurred.

'What's happened?' she asked her. 'What are they looking daggers at each other for this morning?'

'How should I know? Am I party to their affairs?' snapped Evpraksiya.

'It's not on account of you, is it? Perhaps the boy has been hanging round you?'

'Hanging round me! All he did was to waylay me in the passage and Porfiry Vladimirych saw him.'

'So that's what it was!'

And, true, regardless of the extremity in which he found himself, Petenka made no effort to restrain his natural frivolity. He, too, had been carried away by the sight of Evprakseyushka's mighty back and resolved to tell her so. It was actually with this in mind that he had not gone to church, hoping that Evpraksiya, as housekeeper, would also be staying at home. Then, when the house was quiet, he had draped his greatcoat over his shoulders and hid in the passage. A minute went by, and another, then the door from the hall into the maids' room banged and Evpraksiya appeared at the end of the passage carrying a tray with a warm bun-loaf for the morning tea. But scarcely had Petenka given her a good whack between the shoulders, scarcely had he pronounced that hers 'was a right proper back!', when the door of the dining-room opened and his father appeared in the doorway.

'If you've come here, you scoundrel, to engage in depravity, I'll have you thrown out of the house,' Judas declared with measureless malice in his voice.

Of course, Petenka beat a hasty retreat.

He could not, however, fail to understand that this event of the morning was not one to benefit his prospects. He decided, there-fore, to say nothing and defer his explanation until the following day. At the same time, though, he not only did nothing to diminish his father's irritation—on the contrary, he behaved with the utmost imprudence and folly. He smoked non-stop, regardless of the fact that his father was vigorously fanning away the clouds of smoke with which he filled the room. Then every other minute he was making sheep's eyes at Evprakseyushka, causing her to smile in a sidelong way, which Judas also noted.

The day dragged by. Arina Petrovna tried a game of 'donkey' with Evprakseyushka, but it was no good. Nobody was in the mood for cards or for conversation, no trivialities even came to mind, although this was a commodity of which they all had a plentiful store. So it wore on until dinner-time, but dinner too was a silent affair. When it was over, Arina Petrovna made to leave for Pogorelka, but Judas was positively terrified that dear Mother should have any such thing in mind.

'Lord have mercy, Mother dearest!' he exclaimed. 'You don't mean to leave me alone with that . . . wicked son of mine? No, no, you mustn't think of it! I won't let you go!'

'Why, what's up? Has there been something between you? Tell me!' she asked him.

'No, there's been nothing so far, but you'll see . . . No, you really mustn't leave me! You must be here for it . . . It's not for nothing, oh no, not for nothing that he's turned up . . . So if anything does happen, you shall be a witness.'

Arina Petrovna shook her head and decided to stay.

After dinner Porfiry Vladimirych retired to sleep, having first sent Evprakseyushka off to the village to call on the priest. Arina Petrovna, with her departure for Pogorelka deferred, also went to her room and settled down to doze in her chair. Petenka reckoned this the best time to try his fortune with his grandmother and went to see her.

'What is it? Come for a game of "donkey" with your old granny?' Arina Petrovna said on seeing him.

'No, Granny, I've come to see you about something.'

'Well then, you tell me all about it.'

Petenka hesitated for a moment, then suddenly came out with it:

'Granny, I've gambled and lost the regimental funds.'

At this unexpected announcement it went black before Arina Petrovna's eyes.

'Was it much?' she asked in a horrified voice, her eyes fixed as she looked at him.

'Three thousand.'

There was a minute's silence. Arina Petrovna glanced from side to side as if looking for someone to come to her aid.

'You know you can end up in Siberia for a thing like that,' she said at last.

'Yes, I know.'

'Your poor boy, you poor boy!'

'Granny, I wanted to ask you if you would give me a loan . . . I'd pay you good interest.'

Arina Petrovna was now thoroughly frightened.

'What's that? What's that?' she said, in a flutter of agitation. 'I've no money left, only enough to pay for my coffin and prayers when I'm gone. I only have my keep through the charity of the girls and your father when I come here. No, no, no! Let me be, now! Let me be, there's a good boy. You know what—you should ask your father.'

'What's the good of that! From the iron priest you get stone bread. It was you I was depending on, Granny.'

'Really now! Of course, I'd gladly help, but what money do I have? Not that sort of money at all. But you ask your father, be nice to him, be respectful. You just tell him all about it, say you did wrong, put it down to your young years . . . Butter him up, kiss his hand, go on your knees, shed a few tears—your father likes that, and he'll unbutton his purse for his dear boy.'

'Yes, what about it! Maybe I should? But here, wait a minute—how would it be, Granny, if you told him that if he won't give me the money, you'll curse him! That's something he's always been afraid of.'

'Now, now, why should I curse him? You just ask him, without that. Ask him, my dear. Bow to your father once more or less, your head won't drop off, that's for sure: after all, he *is* your father. And he'll see it, too . . . you go on and do it!'

Petenka walks up and down with hands on his hips, as if turning it over in his mind. At last he stops and says:

'It's no good. He won't let me have it anyway. Whatever I do, I can bow till I cave my head in, but it won't make a scrap of difference—he still won't give it to me. But if you threatened to curse him . . . Oh, what on earth can I do, Granny?'

'I really don't know. Have a try—you might soften his heart. But whatever possessed you to do such a thing? It's no light matter gambling away official money. Did somebody put you up to it?'

'No, I just went and lost it. Well, all right, if you've got no money of your own, you can let me have some of the girls' money.'

'What! Have some sense! How can I give you the girls' money? Spare me, do! Don't talk of it, for mercy's sake!'

'You won't then? Pity. I'd pay you good interest. Would five per cent a month do you? No? Then how about double the capital back in a year?'

'Don't you try to tempt me,' Arina Petrovna cried, flapping her hands. 'For the Lord's sake, go away from me. Suppose your father should hear and say it was I put you up to it! Lord, oh, Lord! Here am I, an old woman, just going to have a rest, even dozed off I had, when he comes to see me about a thing like that!'

'All right, I'll go. So you won't do it then? Fine. The real kith and kin spirit! For three thousand roubles your grandson will go to Siberia. Don't forget the intercessions to speed me on the way!'

Petenka stalked off, banging the door behind him. One of his frivolous hopes had come to nothing—what should he do now? There was only one thing left—to tell the whole thing to his father. But perhaps . . . Perhaps something . . .

'I'll go and get it over with!' he told himself. 'Or no—no, why do it today? . . . Perhaps something . . . but then what "something" could there be? No, better tomorrow! That'll give me today at least . . . Yes, better tomorrow! I'll tell him, then go.'

And so he finally decided: that tomorrow would put an end to everything . . .

After the talk with his grandmother the evening dragged worse than ever. Even Arina Petrovna was subdued now that she knew the true reason for Petenka's visit.

Judas attempted to play up to his mother, but, seeing there was something on her mind, he lapsed into silence. Petenka, too, did nothing and just smoked. At supper Porfiry Vladimirych put the question to him:

'And are you finally going to say what it was you came for?'

'I'll tell you tomorrow,' replied Petenka sullenly.

Petenka rose early after an almost entirely sleepless night. He had been plagued by the persistent dichotomy—beginning with the hope: 'Perhaps, after all, he'll let me have it', and ending invariably with the question: 'Why did I come?' Perhaps he did not understand his father, but, as far as he knew, there was in him no feeling, no weakness which he could possibly seize on and exploit to his advantage. He felt only that in the presence of his father he was confronted by something inscrutable and incalculable. Not knowing what line to take or how to broach the subject aroused in him if not actual fear, at least concern. It had been like that ever since childhood. For as long as he could remember, it was always the case that it seemed better to abandon a thing altogether than make it dependent on the decision of his father. It was the same now. Where should he start? And *how* should he start? What should he say? . . . Ah, why on earth had he come!

He was filled with dejection. Still, he realized that he had only a few hours left and must do *something*. Putting on a brave front, he buttoned up his coat and, whispering something as he went, set off with quite firm step to his father's study.

Judas was praying. He was very pious and liked to devote several hours a day to prayer. But he prayed not because he loved God and hoped through prayer to have communion with him, but because he feared the Devil and hoped that God would deliver him from the Evil One. He knew a great many prayers and, in particular, had an excellent mastery of the technique of praying. That is, he knew when it was necessary to move his lips and to roll his eyes upwards, when it was proper to place his hands together and when to lift them up, when it was appropriate to be emotional, and when to be staid and cross himself with fitting moderation. At certain moments indicated by devotional practice his eyes and his nose turned red and moist. But prayer did not restore him, did not clarify his feelings, did not bring any light into the dimness of his existence. He could pray and perform all the requisite motions—and at the same time be looking out of the window to see if anyone was going to the cellar without permission, and such like. It was something separate, a way unto itself, which had its own self-sufficient existence independent of the common way of life.

When Petenka entered the study, Porfiry Vladimirych was kneeling with upraised hands. He did not alter his position, but simply agitated one hand in the air to betoken that it was not yet time. Petenka took himself to the dining-room, where the table was laid for morning tea, and began to wait. The half-hour he waited seemed an eternity—the more so as he was sure his father kept him waiting on purpose. The show of firmness he had put on gradually gave way to vexation. At first he sat quietly, then began to pace up and down the room, and finally started whistling some tune, as a result of which the door part opened and through it came the irritated voice of Judas:

'People who want to whistle can go and do it in the stables!'

Soon afterwards Porfiry Vladimirych emerged, clad entirely in black with fresh linen, as though prepared for some solemn rite. His face was bright and serene, exuding humility and joy, as if he had only that moment 'found favour' with God. He went up to his son, made the sign of the cross over him, and kissed him.

'Good morning, my son,' he said.

'Good morning.'

'And how did you sleep? Did they make you up a nice comfy bed? No bugs or fleas to bite you?'

'Thanks. I slept all right.'

'You did—then God be praised! Home's the place for the sweetest slumber. That I know from my own experience: however comfortable I was in Petersburg, I never slept as soundly as I did in Golovlevo. It's like rocking in a cradle. Well now, what are we going to do? Do we have tea first or did you want to say something now?'

'Yes, it's best to talk now. In six hours' time I've got to go and you might need time to think things over.'

'Very well. Only, my boy, I must tell you straight: I'm not one to think things over. My answer is always ready. If you ask for something that's right—then you shall have it. I never refuse anything which is right. It might be a bit difficult, more than we can manage, but if it's right, I can't refuse. It's the way I'm made. But if you ask for what isn't right—it's just too bad! Pity you as I might, I'll still refuse. There's nothing devious about me, my boy. Open as the day I am. Now come along, come along into the study. You have your say and I'll listen. Let's hear, let's just hear what it's all about.'

When they were both in the study, Porfiry Vladimirych left the door ajar. He did not sit down himself nor offer a chair to his son, but instead began pacing the room, as if sensing that the matter would be a delicate one and that it gave more scope to discuss such things if you were on the move. It made it simpler to conceal a facial expression, easier to cut short the conversation if it took too disagreeable a turn. And with the door left ajar it would also be possible to call in witnesses, for Mother and Evprakseyushka must surely soon be coming to the dining-room for their tea.

'Papa, I lost the regimental funds at gambling,' Petenka declared blankly and abruptly.

Judas said nothing. One could only detect a quivering of his lips. After which, as was his custom, he started to whisper.

'I lost three thousand,' explained Petenka, 'and if I don't return it by the day after tomorrow, there could be some very unpleasant consequences for me.'

'Well then, return it!' Porfiry Vladimirych said affably.

Father and son took a few turns round the room in silence. Petenka wanted to go on with their talk, but felt a block in his throat. At last he spoke:

'Where am I to get the money from?'

'My dear boy, I don't know what your resources are. You must pay it out of whatever resources you had in mind when you were gambling away the regimental money.'

'You know full well that in such cases a man never thinks of his resources.'

'I know nothing at all, dear boy. I have never in my life played cards—except maybe a hand of "donkey" with dear Mother in order to humour an old woman. Please don't involve me in these sordid affairs—let's go and have some tea instead. We can have tea, sit a while, perhaps have a talk—but, for mercy's sake, not on this matter!'

And Judas made for the door in order to dart into the dining-room. But Petenka stopped him.

'But, look here—' he said, 'I've got to get out of this somehow!'

Judas gave a smile and looked Petenka in the face.

'Yes, you have, dear boy.'

'Then help me!'

'Now that's quite another matter. You've got to get out of your situation somehow—that's a fact, what you say is true. But *how* you get out of it—that's no concern of mine!'

'But why won't you help?'

'First, because I've no money to cover up your squalid affairs, and second, because it is absolutely none of my business. You got yourself into this mess, you get yourself out. You must pay the price for your pleasures. Yes indeed, my son. As I was saying just now—if you ask for what's right . . .'

'I know, I know! With you it's all words . . .'

'Wait now! Not so much of your impertinence! Just let me finish. I'll soon prove to you it's not just words . . . So, as I was saying just now: if you ask for something right and reasonable—then certainly, my boy! I'm always ready to accommodate you. But if you come asking for something *un*reasonable, then I'm sorry! For squalid affairs I have no money, none whatsoever! And never will have, you can be sure of that. And don't you dare tell me that this is just "words", but understand that these words stand very close to deed!'

'But just think what will happen to me!'

'What happens will be as God wills,' replied Judas, uplifting his hands slightly and a glancing aside at the icon.

Father and son completed a few more turns round the room. Judas did so reluctantly, as if aggrieved at being kept captive by his son. Petenka, hands on hips, followed him, chewing his moustache and grinning nervously.

'I'm the only son you have now,' he said. 'Don't forget that!'

'From Job, my boy, God took everything, but Job did not repine.

He only said: "God hath given, God hath taken away, Thy will be done, oh Lord." Yes indeed, dear boy.'

'That was God taking away—you take away from yourself. Look at Volodya...'

'So! It's vulgar abuse now, it seems!'

'No, it's not abuse, it's the truth. Everybody knows that Volodya...'

'No! No! No! I'll not listen to your abuse! It's enough anyway. You've had your say, and I've told you my answer. Now we'll go and have tea. We'll sit a while, have a chat, a bite to eat, a drink for the road, and then God speed! See how merciful God is to you—the snow-storm's passed and the road will be that much smoother. Easy does it, all in good time, trit-trot, trit-trot, you'll be at the station before you know it.'

'Look! All right, then, I beg you! If you've got a scrap of feeling...'

'No! No! No! We're not going to talk about it! Come on into the dining-room. Why, poor Mother will be dying for her tea. We mustn't keep the old lady waiting.'

Judas turned sharply on heel and practically ran for the door.

'Go or stay, please yourself! But I'm not going to leave it at that!' Petenka shouted after him. 'It'll be worse talking in front of witnesses!'

Judas turned back and faced his son.

'Tell me what it is you want from me, you good-for-nothing!' he demanded in an agitated voice.

'I want you to pay the money I lost.'

'Never!'

'And that's your final word?'

'See that?' exclaimed Judas solemnly, pointing to the icon hanging in the corner. 'You see it? That was my father's blessing... And I say before it: never!!'

And he stalked out of the room.

'Murderer!' the cry came after him.

Arina Petrovna is already sitting down at the table, as Evprakseyushka makes the preparations for tea. The old woman is pensive, taciturn, and seems uneasy on account of Petenka. Judas, as usual, comes up to kiss her hand, and she, as usual too, automatically makes the sign of the cross over him. Then there are the usual enquiries as to whether everyone is well and did they sleep soundly, which receive the usual monosyllabic replies.

She was low-spirited the evening before. Now, since Petenka asked her for the money and recalled to her the idea of cursing Porfiry, she had fallen into a curious state of unease, and the thought kept coming to her: and what if I did curse him? Having learnt in the morning that the meeting in the study was under way, she called Evprakseyushka to her aid:

'You, miss, go and listen quietly at the door to see what they are saying.'

'They're just talking. Not much shouting going on!' she reported on her return.

Arina Petrovna, unable to contain herself, went personally to the dining-room, where the samovar had meanwhile been set in readiness. But the meeting was already near its end. All she could hear was Petenka raising his voice and Porfiry Vladimirych seeming to drone on endlessly in reply.

'Droning, yes, that's what he does,' the thought played in her mind. 'He droned on like that before! How did I fail to realize it then?'

Finally, both father and son appeared in the dining-room. Petenka was flushed and breathing heavily, with eyes gaping, hair ruffled, and fine beads of sweat on his brow. Judas, on the other hand, when he came in, was pale and rancorous; he wished to appear unmoved, but despite his efforts his lower lip quivered. He barely managed to utter his usual morning greeting to dear Mother.

All took their places round the table. Petenka sat somewhat apart, lay back in his chair with his legs crossed and, lighting a cigarette, cast ironic glances at his father.

'Well, Mother, the storm has eased off nicely for us,' Judas began. 'What a turmoil we had yesterday, and then suddenly it's all peace be still and God's holy will! Isn't that so, Mother dear?'

'I don't know. I've not been out of doors today.'

'It's timely we should be seeing off our dear visitor,' Judas continued. 'No sooner was I out of bed than I peeped through the window, and lo and behold outside all was peace and quiet, as if an angel of the Lord had passed over and in a moment's space calmed the uproar with his wing.'

But to these tender sentiments nobody responded. Evprakseyushka, blowing and snorting, noisily supped tea from her saucer; Arina Petrovna looked into her cup and was silent; Petenka rocked on his chair and continued to gaze at his father with a look of defiant irony which suggested that it cost him the greatest effort not to burst out laughing.

'Now, even if Petenka makes no great haste,' said Porfiry Vladimirych, starting up again, 'he'll still easily get to the station by evening. We've got our own horses, they're not hard used, fodder them for a couple of hours in Muravevo and they'll have you there in a trice. And then peep! peep! and off you chug in the train! Ah, Petenka, Petenka, you're a bad boy! You should stay on with us here, make a visit of it—indeed you should! It would cheer us up, and it would do you a power of good to have a week here, too!'

But Petenka continues rocking on his chair and gazing at his father.

'What do you keep looking at me for?' Judas says, exploding at last. 'To see pretty pictures, is it?'

'I'm just looking, wondering what you might yet come up with.'

'Look till you're blue in the face—you'll get nothing from me! It will be as I said. I won't budge from my word!'

There is silence for a minute, in the course of which is distinctly heard the whisper:

'Judas!'

Porfiry undoubtedly hears this apostrophe (he actually blenches), but pretends that it does not relate to himself.

'Ah, children, children!' he says. 'We pity you, want to treat you kind and gentle, but clearly there's nothing for it—it's not the will of Fate. You abandon your parents, you find your own friends who mean more to you than a mother and father. It can't be helped. When you think long and hard, you've got to accept it. You are young, and everybody knows young folk would rather have young company than a crabbed old man. So we humble ourselves and make no complaint; all we ask of our Heavenly Father is that Thy will be done, oh Lord!'

'Murderer!' Petenka whispers again, only this time so clearly that Arina Petrovna eyes him in terror. Suddenly a fleeting vision has passed before her eyes—was it the shade of Booby Stepka?

'To whom might you be referring?' asks Judas, shaking with emotion.

'Oh, someone I know.'

'So! Well, go on then, speak out! God alone knows what you're thinking of: perhaps your abuse is intended for one of the present company?'

They are all silent; the tea-glasses stand untouched. Judas, too, leans back in his chair and nervously rocks himself. Petenka, seeing all hope is lost, feels something like the despondency of the dying, which makes him ready to go to extremes. Father and son look each other in the eye, smiling inscrutably. However much Porfiry Vladimirych has drilled himself, the moment is near when even he will be incapable of further restraint.

'You had better go before there is any unpleasantness!' he declares at last. 'Yes!'

'I'm going anyway.'

'Why wait then? I can see you're spoiling for a quarrel, and I don't want to quarrel with anybody. We live here in peace and quiet, without quarrelling and squabbling—and with your old grandmother sitting there, you ought to be ashamed of yourself. What did you come here for?'

'I've told you what.'

'If that's all you came for, then you've wasted your time. You go, my boy. Hey! Whoever's there—have the kibitka harnessed up for the young master! And fetch out a roast chicken and some caviare, and anything else there—a few eggs, perhaps—wrap it all up in some paper. There, my boy, you can have a bite to eat at the post-station while they feed the horses. Now, off you go—and God speed!'

'No, I'm not going yet. I'm going over to the church first to order a requiem for God's servant Vladimir, who was killed.'

'Who killed himself, you mean.'

'No, who was killed.'

Father and son glare at each other. At any instant, it seems, they will leap to their feet. But Judas makes a superhuman effort to contain himself and turns his chair to face across the table.

'Amazing,' he says, his voice strained. 'A-maz-ing!'

'Yes, who was killed!' repeats Petenka with blunt persistence.

'And who was it killed him?' Judas enquires, evidently hoping even now that his son would control himself.

But Petenka is quite unabashed and retorts like a cannon-shot: 'You!!'

'Me!!'

Porfiry Vladimirych is overcome with astonishment. Hastily he gets up from his chair, turns to the icon, and begins to pray.

'You! You! You!' Petenka repeats.

'There now, thanks be to God, I'm feeling better after saying a prayer,' says Judas, sitting down again at the table. 'Hold now. Wait a minute. Though, as your father, I don't have to enter into the rights of things with you—still, let's do it. So you think it was I who killed Volodenka?'

'Yes, you!'

'Well, I think differently. I think he shot himself. I was here at the time in Golovlevo, and he was in Petersburg. So how could I be involved? How could I kill him, when he was seven hundred versts away?'

'As if you didn't understand!'

'Well, I don't understand . . . as God is my witness, I do not understand.'

'Who was it left Volodya penniless? Who was it cut off his allowance? Who?'

'Now, now, now! Why then did he marry against his father's wishes?'

'You gave your permission, didn't you?'

'Who? I? Bless you, I never gave permission! Never!'

'All right, you did what you usually do. Every word you say means ten different things—make what you can of it!'

'I never gave permission. He wrote to me at the time and said: "Father, I want to marry Lidochka." "I want", do you see? and not "I ask your permission." And so I answered him: "If you *want* to get married, get married. I cannot stand in your way!" That's all there was to it.'

'That's all there was to it!' Petenka mimics him. 'And wasn't that permission?'

'No, that's just the point. What did I say? All I said was that I couldn't stand in his way. But as for permitting or not permitting—that's another matter. He never asked for permission; he simply wrote and said he *wanted* to marry Lidochka—so I said nothing about permission either. If you *want* to get married, then bless you, go ahead and get married, my boy. Marry Lidochka, marry Lidochka's maiden aunt—I can't stand in your way!'

'No, you can just cut him off without a crust. You could easily have written to him and said: I don't like what you propose doing, and though I won't stand in your way, I must warn you not to reckon on any further financial support from me. That, at least, would have been clear!'

'Oh, no! That's something I would never allow myself to do. Use threats against a grown-up son? Never. I make it a rule never to stand in anybody's way. You want to get married—then get married, but don't blame me for the consequences! You should foresee them yourself—that's what God gives you brains for. I don't meddle in other people's affairs, my boy. And not only do I not meddle myself—I won't have other people meddling in my affairs either! I won't have it, I won't have it at all—indeed, I forbid it! Do you hear, you wicked, disrespectful boy—I for-bid it!'

'Go ahead and forbid it! But you won't shut everybody up.'

'If he had only repented! If he had only realized how he had offended his father! You do a base act—it's up to you to repent! Ask forgiveness! Father dear, please forgive me the pain I've caused you! But he—oh no!'

'But he wrote to you. He told you he had nothing to live on, that he couldn't go on . . .'

'You don't "tell" your father, you ask him for forgiveness—that's all there is to it.'

'But he did that too. He was that wretched he even asked forgiveness. He did everything, everything!'

'Even if he did ask, he was still in the wrong. If he asks once for forgiveness and sees his father doesn't give it, he should ask again!'

'Ha! You!'

After saying this, Petenka suddenly stops rocking on his chair, turns to the table, and puts his elbows on it.

'And now it's me . . .' he says, his voice scarcely audible.

Gradually his face becomes contorted.

'And now it's me . . .' he repeats, breaking into hysterical sobs.

'And who is to bla—'

But Judas did not manage to complete his homily, for at this very moment a totally unexpected event occurred. During the exchange of fire between father and son Arina Petrovna appeared forgotten. She was, though, far from being a detached observer of this family scene. On the contrary, one look at her was enough to make one aware that something out of the ordinary was taking place within her and that perhaps the moment had come when in her mind's eye she saw set out before her in all its starkness the sum total of her own life. Her face became animated, her eyes widened and shone, her lips moved as if purposing to utter some word which they could not form. And all at once, just as the dining-room was filled with the sound of Petenka's sobbing, she rose from her chair, stretched out her hand in front of her, and a wailing cry burst from her breast:

'I cu-u-urse you!'

THE NIECE

So Judas did not after all give Petenka the money, although at the moment of departure he did, as a good father, give instructions for chicken, veal, and a pie to be stowed in the kibitka. Then, despite the bitter cold and wind, he came in person on to the steps to see his son off, asked if he was comfortably seated and had his legs well wrapped up, after which, back in the house, he stood for a long time at the dining-room window making the sign of the cross and sending farewell injunctions after the kibitka that bore his son away. In short, he carried out the entire ritual in such a manner as befitted kith and kin.

'Ah, Petka, Petka!' he said, 'It's a bad son you are! Oh, bad indeed! Just think of the trouble you've caused: what a pickle you've got yourself in . . . oh dear, oh dear, oh dear! So you're not going to live a quiet, easy life in peace and harmony with your Father and your old Granny! Upon my word! You and your "We know what's what, we've wit to manage on our own!" Much good your wit did you! What a sorry pass!'

But as he spoke, not a muscle twitched on his wooden face and in his voice not a note was heard to suggest any kind of appeal to the prodigal son. But then, nobody actually heard what he said, for the only person in the room was Arina Petrovna and she, after the shock she had just undergone, was suddenly bereft of all vitality and sat by the samovar with gaping mouth, hearing nothing and staring blankly into space.

Life then went on as before, filled with idle bustle and endless prattle.

Contrary to Petenka's expectations, Porfiry Vladimirych took his mother's curse quite calmly and budged not the slightest from those decisions which were, so to speak, always at the ready in his mind. True, he did blench slightly and rush to his mother, crying:

'Mother! Dearest! Bless you! Calm yourself, my dear! God is merciful! Everything will be all right!'

But these words were rather an expression of concern for his mother than for himself. Arina Petrovna's move had been made so suddenly that Judas never even thought of feigning fright. Only the day before his mother had been kindly disposed to him, had joked and played 'donkey' with Evprakseyushka—so, clearly, it was just a momentary whim, not anything premeditated or 'really meant'. In fact, he feared his mother's curse very much, but he had always envisaged it quite differently. His idle fancy had created an elaborate setting for the event: icons, burning candles, and his mother standing in the middle of the room, awesome, with darkened face, as she pronounces her curse. Following which—thunder, the candles go out, the curtain rends, darkness covers the earth, and in the clouds on high is seen amid lightning-flashes the wrathful visage of Jehovah. But since none of this had happened, it could only have been a passing fancy of his mother, she had imagined something and that's all there was to it. And anyway there was no reason why she should wish to curse him 'properly', since latterly there had not been even any pretexts for discord between them. Since the occasion when he had expressed doubt as to his mother's ownership of the carriage (Judas inwardly conceded that *there* he was in the wrong and deserved to be cursed), much water had flowed under the bridge; Arina Petrovna was now subdued and Porfiry Vladimirych had no other thought but to soothe and comfort dear mother.

'The old lady's in a bad way, oh, a very bad way! She's started losing track of things!' he consoled himself. 'The old dear sits down for a game of "donkey", and all of a sudden there she is dozing!'

In fairness it must be said that Arina Petrovna's infirmity actually did perturb him. He was not yet prepared for this loss, he had not worked anything out, had not completed the necessary calculations: how much capital did his mother have on leaving Dubrovino? How much income might this capital produce per annum, how much of this income might she spend and how much set aside? In short, he had still to attend to a multitude of trivialities, which, as long as they remained undone, always made him feel that he was being caught napping.

'The old lady's well-off,' he would sometimes muse. 'She can't spend *all* of it—what could she spend it on! At the time she gave us our shares, she had a good capital. Might she, though, have parted with some of it to the girls?—no, she wouldn't give much even to them! Yes, she's got some money all right!'

But these thoughts had so far not been of any substance and passed readily out of mind. The mass of daily trivialities was already too great to have added to them other, new ones which were of no immediate concern. So, Porfiry Vladimirych had gone on putting things off until the sudden 'cursing' scene made him realize that the time for action had arrived.

The blow followed, however, sooner than he expected. The day after Petenka left, Arina Petrovna departed to Pogorelka and never returned again to Golovlevo. She spent a month or so in total isolation, never quitting her room and only very rarely allowing herself to exchange a word even with the servants. After rising in the morning, from habit she sat down at her desk, from habit began laying out the cards for patience, but she practically never finished and seemed to go rigid in her chair with her eyes fixed on the window. What her thoughts were or whether indeed she had any thoughts could not be fathomed by even the most percipient expert in the secret workings of the human heart. She seemed to want to remember something—perhaps, how she came to be there, within these walls?—but could not. Alarmed at her silence, Afimyushka would look into her room, straighten the cushions by which she was propped in her chair, and try to make conversation, but all she got in reply was impatient monosyllables. Once or twice during this time Porfiry Vladimirych came over to Pogorelka from Golovlevo and tried to fire her imagination by reminding her of the mushrooms, carp, and other blandishments of Golovlevo, but in response to his suggestions she only smiled enigmatically.

One morning she was going to get out of bed as usual, but could not do so. She felt no particular pain, made no complaint of anything wrong, but simply could not get up. She was not even perturbed by this, but took it as being in the normal course of things. The day before she had been sitting to table, able to walk about—and now here she was abed, infirm! She actually felt more at ease. But Afimyushka took alarm and, unbeknown to her mistress, sent a messenger to Porfiry Vladimirych.

Judas arrived early the next morning; by then Arina Petrovna was considerably worse. He made detailed enquiries among the servants as to what his mother had been eating, whether she might not have over-indulged herself, but received the answer that in the last month Arina Petrovna had scarcely eaten a thing and since the day before had refused food entirely. Judas grieved, flapped his hands, and, like a good son, before going in to his mother, warmed himself by the stove in the maids' room so as not to expose the invalid to any chill air. And to suit the occasion (he had a devilish nose for the scent of death), he at once set about making arrangements. He asked about the priest and if he was at home, so that he could be sent for immediately should need arise, he enquired as to the whereabouts of his mother's document-box and if it was locked, and then, having set his mind at rest on these essentials, he summoned the cook and gave orders for his dinner.

'It's little enough I need!' he said. 'Is there chicken?—well, make a little chicken broth! Perhaps there's salt beef?—then do a bit of salt beef! And a roast of some sort—for me that will suffice!'

Arina Petrovna lay in bed flat on her back with her mouth wide open, breathing heavily. Her eyes gaped; one hand had come out from beneath the hareskin coverlet and hung rigid in the air. She had clearly listened to the flutter of noise caused by her son's arrival, and Judas's commands had perhaps also reached her ears. With its blinds lowered, her room was sunk in the gloom of dusk. The wicks burned low in the bottom of the icon-lamps and could be heard sputtering as they came in contact with the water.* The air was heavy and fetid; it was unbearably stuffy from the over-heated stoves, the fumes of the icon-lamps, and the general stench. Porfiry Vladimirych, in high felt boots, glided like a snake to his mother's bed; his tall, gaunt figure swayed mysteriously in the dusk. Arina Petrovna followed him with her eyes in mingled fear and surprise and shrank beneath the coverlet.

'It's me, Mother dear,' he said. 'What's all this about being out of sorts today! Oh, dearie me! That's why I couldn't sleep last night! All night long I had the feeling that I must find out how our friends at Pogorelka were faring! So this morning up I got, ordered the kibitka and pair—and here I am!'

Porfiry Vladimirych tittered affably, but Arina Petrovna made no answer and shrank deeper beneath the coverlet.

'God is merciful, though, Mother dear!' Judas continued. 'Most important is not to let it get on top of you! Snap your fingers at sickness! Get out of bed, take a turn round the room, be a brave soldier! Like this!'

Porfiry Vladimirych got up from his chair and demonstrated how a brave soldier takes a turn round the room.

'Just a minute, though—let me just raise the blind and have a look at you. Why, you look fine, my dear! If you were just to rally, say your prayers, and dress yourself up—you'd be fit for a ball! Here now, I've brought you a drop of Epiphany water.* Come on, try some!'

Porfiry Vladimirych took from his pocket a phial, found a glass on the table, filled it, and brought it to the sick woman. Arina Petrovna made an effort to lift her head, but could not do it.

'Send for the girls . . .' she moaned.

'There, now you're wanting the girls to come! Oh, really, Mother dear! What's the matter with you all at once! Just a teeny bit out of sorts and there you are losing heart! Everything will be seen to—we'll send to the girls by express and we'll fetch Petka from Petersburg, everything in its own good time! But there's no hurry: there's life before us yet, and what a life it will be! Come the summer, we'll be off together to the woods picking mushrooms, and raspberries, and strawberries and blackcurrants! Or we'll drive over to Dubrovino and catch some carp. We'll hitch up the old dun roan in the dray, and then easy does it, all in good time, trit-trot, trit-trot, in we sit and off we go!'

'Send for the girls . . .' Arina Petrovna repeated forlornly.

'The girls will come right enough. Give us time—we'll have them all here, we'll all come. We'll come and sit round you—you can be mother hen and we'll be your chicks: cheep! cheep! cheep! But for all that to happen you've got to be a good girl. Now it's not being a good girl taking poorly like this. Getting up to such a thing, you mischief! . . . Oh, dearie me! Instead of setting an

example—just see what you do! It's too bad of you, Mother dear,
too, too bad!'

But for all Porfiry Vladimirych's attempts to rally his mother
with his jests and jingles, her strength ebbed with every passing
hour. A messenger was sent to fetch the doctor from the town,
and as the sick woman continued to pine and call for the girls,
Judas penned a letter in his own hand to Anninka and Lyubinka,
in which he compared their conduct with his own, referring to
himself as a Christian and to them as ingrates. The doctor came
during the night, but it was already too late. One day had, as they
say, 'seen off' Arina Petrovna. Some time after three in the morning the death-agony began, and at six o'clock Porfiry Vladimirych,
kneeling at his mother's beside, wailed:

'Mother! Mother dear! Your blessing!'

But Arina Petrovna did not hear. Her open eyes gazed dully
into space as if she were trying to understand something, but
could not.

Nor did Judas understand. He did not understand that the
grave that had opened now before his eyes was bearing away
his last link with the living world, the last living creature with
whom he could share the dust that filled his being. And that
henceforth this dust, finding no release, would accumulate within
him until finally it choked him.

With his customary fussiness he plunged into the welter of
petty details relating to the funeral rites. He had requiems sung,
bespoke the forty-days prayers for the dead, deliberated with the
priest, went shuffling about from room to room, peeped into the
dining-room where the departed lay, crossed himself, lifted up his
eyes to heaven, rose in the night, stole silently to the door to listen
to the lector's monotonous reading from the Psalter, and so forth.
He was, at the same time, agreeably surprised to find he would
not even be involved in any additional expense, since while still
alive Arina Petrovna had caused a sum to be put aside for her
funeral expenses, with very detailed instructions about how much
was to be spent on each item.

After burying his mother Porfiry Vladimirych began at once
to sort out her affairs. In going through her papers he found as
many as ten different wills (in one of them he was referred to as

'disrespectful'); but they had all been made when Arina Petrovna was the domineering mistress of her estates and they had remained as drafts, without legal form. This was much to Judas's satisfaction, since he would not even need to bend his conscience to declare himself sole legal heir to the property left by his mother. This property consisted of a capital sum of 15,000 roubles and a meagre assortment of effects—including the celebrated carriage which had nearly become an apple of discord between mother and son. Arina Petrovna had been scrupulous in keeping her own accounts separate from those of the orphans' trust, so it was possible to see at once what belonged to her and what to the girls. Judas promptly informed the appropriate authority that he was the heir, sealed up the documents relating to the trust, distributed his mother's scant wardrobe among the servants, sent to Golovlevo the carriage and two cows which were listed as 'mine' in Arina Petrovna's inventory, and then, after a final requiem, made his way home.

'Await your young mistresses,' he told the servants who had assembled in the hallway to see him off. 'If they come, good welcome to them; if they don't, that's their affair! I have done all that was required of me; I have made up the trust accounts, nothing hidden or concealed, everything open and above-board. The capital dear Mother left is mine by law; the carriage and the cows I have sent to Golovlevo are also mine by law. It may be that certain things remain *here* which are also mine in fact, but never mind—give to the orphans, as God commanded! I grieve for dear Mother! She was a good old soul, so kindly! See how concerned she was for you who served her—all her clothes she left to you! Oh, Mother, Mother dear! It was too bad of you to go away and leave us like orphans in the storm! Yet, if it so pleases God, then must we too submit to his holy will! As long as your soul is at ease, then we . . . we are of no concern!'

The first grave was soon followed by another.

The attitude taken by Porfiry Vladimirych to the affair of his son was rather enigmatic. He received no newspapers, conducted no correspondence, and there was consequenly no source from which information might reach him about Petenka's trial. Indeed, it was scarcely likely that he would even want to know anything about it. He was in general a man who avoided disturbance of any kind and was sunk to his ears in a morass of trivialities relating to his own shabby self-preservation, and whose existence, as a result, left nowhere any trace. There is a sufficiency of such people in the world; all of them live their lives apart, with neither capacity nor concern to form bonds with anything, never knowing what awaits them from one moment to the next, and in the end bursting as bubbles burst in a puddle of rain. They have no associations through friendship, because friendship requires the existence of some common interest; and they have no associations through work, because even in the dead world of officialdom they are isolated by their own unendurable deadness. For thirty years Porfiry Vladimirych was ever about in his government office; then one fine day he was gone—and nobody noticed it. Because of this he was the last to learn of his son's fate, when the news was already common knowledge among the servants. But even then he pretended to know nothing of it, so that when Evprakseyushka let slip some remark about Petka, Judas flapped his hands at her and said:

'No, no, no! I don't know, I've never heard, and I don't want to hear! I don't want to know about his sordid affairs!'

But in the end he was to know after all. A letter came from Petka announcing his coming departure for one of the more distant provinces and asking if his father would send him means to support himself in his new situation. After this Porfiry Vladimirych spent the whole day in a state of evident perplexity; he scurried from room to room, glanced into the oratory, crossed himself, and groaned. However, by evening he had collected himself and wrote:

Peter, my criminal son,

As a loyal subject who is bound to respect the laws I really should not reply to your letter. But as a father susceptible to the frailties of man I cannot, from compassion, refuse good advice to my child, who has by his own fault cast himself into the abyss of evil. Here then briefly is my opinion on the matter. The punishment to which you are now subjected is severe, but fully deserved by you—that is my first and foremost thought and one which you should henceforth always keep in mind in your new life. All other fancies and even remembrance of the same you must abandon, for in your situation these things can only provoke and stir you to complain. You have already tasted the bitter fruits of highmindedness, try now tasting also the fruits of humility, the more so since there is for you nothing else in prospect. Do not complain of your punishment, for the authorities are not punishing you, but only providing you with the means to amendment. To show yourself grateful for this and seek to expiate what you have done—that should be your constant preoccupation, not thoughts of luxurious living, which, incidentally, I (who am not a convicted felon) do not enjoy either. Follow this counsel of reason and be reborn for a fresh life, be fully reborn, content with what the authorities in their mercy deem fitting to provide for you. And I, for my part, will pray tirelessly to the Giver of all good things to bestow on you steadfastness and humility, and indeed this very day on which I write these lines I have been to church and offered heartfelt prayers on this account. I bless you as you set forth on your new path, and remain your

Outraged, but still loving father

Porfiry Golovlev

It is unknown if this letter ever reached Petenka; no more than a month after it was dispatched Porfiry Vladimirych received official notification that his son, before reaching his place of exile, had been admitted to hospital in one of the towns along the way and had died.

Judas found himself all alone, but still at first did not realize that with this new loss he was finally projected into the void and left face to face with his own empty prattle. This happened soon after Arina Petrovna's death, when he was totally absorbed in his accounts and calculations. He went through all his late mother's papers, accounted for every single half-kopek, and established the connection of this half-kopek to the half-kopeks belonging to the trust—not wishing, as he said, either to take what was not his own or to let go what was. In the midst of this confusion it never even occurred to him to ask himself why he was doing all this or who would enjoy the fruits of his fussing. From morning to night he slaved away at his desk, finding fault with the dispositions of the deceased and even indulging in wild speculations of his own—with the result that, caught up with these concerns, he gradually came to neglect his own estate accounts.

And the whole house was hushed. The servants, who had

before anyway preferred the retreat of their own quarters, practically abandoned the house altogether and, when they did come
into the master's rooms, went on tiptoe and spoke in whispers.
There was something moribund about the house and about this
man, something that inspired an involuntary and superstitious
fear. With every passing day the dusk which already enshrouded
Judas was destined to deepen ever more.

In Lent, when the theatrical performances stopped, Anninka
arrived in Golovlevo and announced that Lyubinka could not
come with her because she had already made a contract for the
whole of Lent and had therefore set off for Romny, Izyum,
Kremenchug,* and other places, where she was to give concerts
and sing the whole of the 'cascade' repertoire.

   In the course of her brief artistic career Anninka had considerably matured. She was no longer the naïve, anaemic, rather
languid girl who in Dubrovino and Pogorelka had drifted about
the house, softly humming and swaying awkwardly, as if not
knowing what to do with herself. No, this was a girl now fully
developed, forthright, even unceremonious in manner, who, one
could rightly tell at a glance, had a ready tongue. She had also
changed in outward appearance, and Porfiry Vladimirych was
quite agreeably struck by this. She appeared before him as a tall,
shapely woman with good looks, rosy cheeks, a high, well-rounded
bosom, prominent grey eyes, and a splendid braid of ash-blonde
hair hanging heavily down from the back of her head—a woman
who, evidently, was thoroughly conscious of being la belle Hélène
herself, for whom the officers were doomed to sigh. It was early
morning when she arrived in Golovlevo; she at once retired to a
separate room, from which she emerged for tea in the dining-room
wearing a magnificent silk dress with a rustling train which she
very skilfully steered between the chairs. Judas, though he loved
his God above all else, was not thereby prevented from having a
taste for handsome women, especially if they were buxom. He
began, therefore, by making the sign of the cross over Anninka
and then kissed her firmly on both cheeks, giving an odd sidelong
glance at her bosom as he did so, which evoked from Anninka the
flicker of a smile.

They sat down to tea. Anninka raised both arms above her head and stretched.

'Oh, Uncle! How boring it is here!' she began, with a slight yawn.

'There now! You're hardly here before you find it boring! You stay with us a while and then we'll see: it might even seem jolly to you!' replied Porfiry Vladimirych, his eyes suddenly filming with an unctuous glaze.

'No, it's dull! What is there here? Snow all round, and no neighbours . . . There's a garrison close by, isn't there?'

'Yes, we have a garrison, and neighbours too, though that, I confess, is of no concern to me. However, if . . .'

Porfiry Vladimirych glanced at her and, without finishing what he was saying, simply gave a croak. He may have stopped short on purpose so as not to excite her feminine curiosity; in any event, the former, scarcely perceptible smile flickered again on her lips. She leant her elbows on the table and looked quite hard at Evprakseyushka who, with flushed cheeks, was wiping the glasses and casting furtive glances at her too with her great lustreless eyes.

'That's my new housekeeper—a hard-working body she is!' said Porfiry Vladimirych.

Anninka gave a faint nod and purred softly 'Ah! ah! que j'aime . . . que j'aime . . . les mili—mili—militaires!' while her hips wriggled, seemingly of their own accord. Silence settled on them, during which Judas, with meekly downcast eyes, took small sips of tea from his glass.

'How boring!' said Anninka, yawning again.

'Boring! Boring! You keep harping on—but just you wait and see, when you've been here a while . . . We'll have the sledge harnessed up and you can go for rides to your heart's content.'

'Uncle, why didn't you join the hussars?'

'Because, my dear, every man has his place in life ordained by God. One goes into the hussars, another into the civil service, a third into trade, a fourth . . .'

'Oh, yes! the fourth, the fifth, and the sixth . . . I forgot! And it's all as God ordains . . . isn't that right?'

'Yes, indeed, God. It's not a thing to joke about, my dear. You know what the Scripture says? "Except it be the will of God . . ." '

'The bit about the hair?—I know all that too! The trouble is, though, that nowadays everybody wears *chignons*, and that was never provided for! By the way, do have a look at my marvellous plait, Uncle . . . Isn't it fine?'

Porfiry Vladimirych came closer (for some reason on tiptoe) and held the plait in his hands. Evprakseyushka also leant forward, without relinquishing her saucer of tea, and enquired through the chip of sugar clenched in her teeth:

'That'll be a "shine-on" too, will it?'

'No, it's not a *chignon*, it's my own. I'll let it out one day for you to see, Uncle.'

'Yes, it's a very fine plait of hair,' said Judas with approval, at the same time giving a rather wicked leer; then, however, suddenly recalling that one must scorn such blandishments, he added: 'Ah, you flibbertigibbet! You've nothing on your mind but plaits and skirts and don't think to ask even about what really matters.'

'Of course, Granny . . . She died, didn't she?'

'Yes, my dear, she has passed on. And how she met her end—so quiet and peaceful that no one even heard! She was indeed vouchsafed an "unashamed end" to her life. She remembered everybody, blessed us all, sent for the priest and took the sacrament . . . And suddenly such peace came upon her, such peace! She even said herself: "It's so nice all of a sudden!" And fancy— she had no sooner spoken than she began to sigh. She sighed once, then again, and a third time—then we saw that she was gone!'

Judas stood up, turned to the icon, placed his palms together, and prayed. Tears came into his eyes: so well had he lied! But Anninka was evidently not one for sentiment. True, she was pensive for a moment, but her thoughts were on quite a different matter.

'Uncle,' she said, 'do you remember when we were small, Lyubinka and me, she used to give us sour milk to drink? Not latterly—these last years she was splendid . . . but before, when she was still rich, do you remember?'

'Come now, why drag up what's past! She gave you sour milk,

but, mercy, see what a fine young woman it's made of you! Will you be paying a visit to her grave?'

'Yes, let's go.'

'You know, though—it would be a good thing to cleanse yourself first.'

'What do you mean: "cleanse" myself?'

'Well, after all . . . you *are* an actress . . . Do you suppose your Granny took lightly to that? So before you go to her grave, you would do right to attend mass and cleanse yourself. I'll arrange for a service first thing tomorrow and then, God speed, off you go!'

Despite the absurdity of Judas's proposal, Anninka was momentarily discomposed. But she then gave an angry frown and said tartly:

'No, I'll go as I am . . . I'll go now!'

'Do as you will then! But it's my advice that we go to mass in the morning, drink our tea, order the kibitka and pair, and drive over together. And you would be cleansed, and Granny's soul would be . . .'

'Uncle, really! How can you be so silly! Heaven knows what nonsense you're talking, yet still you go on!'

'What's that? You don't care for the idea? Well, no offence, but I'm a straightforward man! I can't abide untruth, but I'll speak the truth to anybody and listen to it myself! Galling and bitter though truth may be, you must still hear it out! You must hear it out, because it is—the truth! Oh, yes indeed, my dear! When you've lived a time here and got into our ways, you'll see for yourself that you're better off here than travelling round fairgrounds with a guitar!'

'Heaven knows what you're saying, Uncle! Really, with a guitar!'

'Well, if not a guitar, something like it. A mandolin, perhaps? Anyway, you were the first to offend, calling me silly, and besides at my age I've got every right to speak the truth to you!'

'All right, let it be the truth; but we won't talk about it. Can you tell me, please—did Granny leave anything?'

'Why, of course she did! The legal heir was, though, to hand.'

'You, that is . . . It's best that way. Is she buried here in Golovlevo?'

'No. In her own parish, St Nicholas's, just by Pogorelka. It's what she wanted.'

'I'll drive over then. Are there horses for hire here, Uncle?'

'Why should you hire horses? We've got our own. You're not a stranger, after all! You're my niece, my nice little niece!' fussed Porfiry Vladimirych, grinning at her in kinship. 'You can take the kibitka . . . and a pair of horses—praise God, things are not that run-down here! What about going together? We could go to the grave and then on to Pogorelka! We could call in there, look about, have a talk, and think things over . . . It's a very pretty little estate you've got there, you know, some good bits of land on it!'

'No, I'll go alone . . . Why should you? Oh, and Petenka's dead too, isn't he?'

'He is dead, my dear, Petenka too is dead. And I grieve for him so I could weep—on the one hand, but then, on the other, it was all his own fault! He was always disrespectful to his father—and God punished him for it! And if God in his wisdom so orders a thing, it's not for us to try and change it!'

'Of course, we won't change it. I was just thinking, though: how can you not find life terrible, Uncle?'

'What can hold any terror for me? Don't you see how surrounded I am by grace?' Judas made a sweeping gesture towards the icons. 'There's grace here, grace in my study, and in the oratory Paradise itself! Just see how many protectors I have!'

'Yes, but . . . All the time you're here alone . . . it's terrible!'

'If I feel any fear, I kneel down and say a prayer, and it's gone! What anyway is there to fear? By day it's light and by night I have the icon-lamps lit in every room. From outside, when it's dark, you would think a ball was going on! But what kind of a ball goes on here! For me God's saints and protectors are the only ball I want to know!'

'Did you know that Petenka wrote to us before he died?'

'Yes, well, as a relation . . . It's something that he had still at least some family feeling!'

'Yes, he wrote to us. It was after the trial and the verdict. He said he had lost 3,000 roubles gambling and that you wouldn't give it to him. You are rich, aren't you, Uncle?'

'It's easy counting money in another man's pocket, my dear.

Sometimes you think a man has got mountains of money, but when you come down to it, all he can afford is lamp-oil and a candle—and they're not for him anyway, but for God!'

'We must be richer than you, then. We put together ourselves and got our *beaux* to contribute—we raised 600 roubles and sent it to him.'

'Who are these "*beaux*"?'

'Oh, Uncle! We are . . . actresses! You were just saying yourself that I should "cleanse" myself!'

'I don't like to hear you talk that way!'

'I can't help it. Like it or not, what's done can't be undone. According to you, that will be God's will too, won't it?'

'No blasphemy! Spare me that at least! Say what you like, but blasphemy . . . I'll not allow! What place did you send the money to?'

'I don't remember. Some small town . . . he told us where.'

'That's odd. If there was any money, it should have come to me after he died! He wouldn't have spent it all at once. It's odd I never received anything. I suppose the warders and guards helped themselves to it.'

'But we don't want it back—I only just mentioned it. It's still terrible, though, Uncle, that for three thousand roubles a man should come to grief!'

'Ah, but it wasn't for the three thousand roubles, that's the point. We just think it was, and so we keep on about the three thousand. But God . . .'

Judas was about to expatiate and explain in detail that God . . . and Providence . . . by unseen ways . . . and so on, but Anninka unceremoniously yawned and said:

'Oh, Uncle! It's so boring here!'

This time Porfiry Vladimirych was seriously offended and fell silent. For a long time they walked up and down the dining-room side by side, with Anninka yawning and Porfiry Vladimirych crossing himself at every corner. At last the horses were reported to be ready and the usual comedy of familial leave-taking began. Golovlev put on his fur top-coat, went out on to the steps, exchanged kisses with Anninka, called to the servants: 'Tuck up her legs! Tuck them up warm!' and 'The kutya! Have you got some? Dearie me, you mustn't forget that!' at the same time making the sign of the cross in the air.

Anninka went to her grandmother's grave, asked the parish priest of Voplino to hold a requiem, and when the chanters dolefully began singing 'Eternal memory . . .' she shed a few tears. The setting for the ceremony was a dismal one. The church where Arina Petrovna was buried was of the poorer kind; the plaster had fallen away in places and exposed large patches of the brickwork beneath; the bell made a faint, muffled sound; the priest's chasuble was old and worn. Deep snow covered the cemetery and a pathway had to be dug in order to reach the grave; there was as yet no monument, only a plain white cross without even any inscription. The cemetery was isolated, remote from any habitation; close to the church was a cluster of black-weathered timber houses occupied by the priest and church servitors, but otherwise all around in every direction there stretched the desolate snowy plain with odd spikes of brushwood sticking out above its surface. A keen March wind swept across the cemetery, constantly tugging at the priest's chasuble and carrying away the sound of the chanters' singing.

'And who would think, ma'am, that by the side of our poor church and beneath this humble cross there should have found repose she who was once the wealthiest landowner in the district!' said the priest when the service was over.

Hearing these words, Anninka shed a few more tears. She remembered the line 'On the table that once groaned with food— there stands a coffin now' and the tears poured from her eyes. She then went into the priest's house, had tea, and chatted with his wife, recalled again 'and pallid death regards us all',* and again she wept long and copiously.

There was no forewarning of the mistress's arrival in Pogorelka, so even the living-rooms of the house had not been heated. Without taking off her fur coat, Anninka went through all the rooms, only stopping for a moment in her grandmother's room and in the oratory. In the former was her grandmother's bed, on which still lay a disorderly pile of greasy feather quilts and a few pillows without cases. On the desk were scattered scraps of paper; the floor had not been swept and every object was covered with a thick layer of dust. Anninka sat on the armchair where her grandmother used to sit and fell to thinking. First to mind came memories of the past, which then gave way to thoughts about the present. The memories were fleeting snatches that passed unlingeringly by; it was the thoughts of the present that obsessed her. Was it so long ago that she was yearning to be free, so long ago that Pogorelka had seemed hateful to her—and now suddenly she was filled with a pathological desire to stay on in this hateful place? It was quiet here, not homely or attractive, but quiet, so quiet indeed that all around seemed dead. There was air and space; and fields—she felt an urge to run. To run, looking neither forward nor back, just to breathe more deeply, to feel the burning ache in the breast. *There*, in that semi-vagabond society from which she had just escaped and to which she *must* return—what awaited her? And what had she gained from it? Memories of stinking hotels, of endless noise from the dining-saloon and billiard-room, of unkempt, unwashed waiters, of rehearsals on stage in gloomy light amid painted canvas backdrops too revolting to touch, in draughts and damp . . . That was all! And afterwards: the officers, lawyers, scurrilous talk, empty bottles, wine-stained table-cloths, clouds of tobacco smoke, and noise, everlasting noise! And the things they said to her! The shameless way they touched her! . . . Especially that one with whiskers, with his hoarse drunkard's voice, bloodshot eyes, and eternal stench of the stables . . . ah, the things he said! Thinking back to it, Anninka shuddered and screwed up her eyes. But she recovered herself, sighed, and went into the oratory. There were now only a few icons left in the icon-case—only those which had unquestionably belonged to her mother, while the others, which were her grandmother's, had been removed and taken off by Judas—the rightful heir—to Golovlevo. The spaces thus created stared like empty eye-sockets. There were no icon-lamps either— Judas had taken them all: only the end of a single yellow wax candle remained waif-like, forgotten, in its little tin holder.

'He wanted to take the icon-case too and kept on asking if it really had come with your mother's dowry,' Afimyushka reported.

'What matter. He could have taken it. Tell me, Afimyushka, did Granny suffer long before she died?'

'No, not so very long, just a day and a bit. She just seemed to fade away. She had no proper illness, nothing really. And she hardly said anything at all, only spoke a time or two about you and your sister.'

'It was Porfiry Vladimirych who took the icons, I suppose?'

'Yes, he took them. "They're Mother's own icons," he said. And he took the carriage as well and two of the cows; he must have got it from the mistress's papers that they weren't yours, but your granny's. He was going to take one of the horses too, but Fedulych wouldn't let him: it's our horse, he said, it belongs in Pogorelka and always has done—so he left it, he was afraid to take it.'

Anninka also walked round the yard, looked into the out-buildings, the threshing-barn, and stock-yard. There, standing in the midden, was her 'working capital': twenty or so lean cows and three horses. She had a loaf of bread brought ('I'll pay for it,' she said) and gave a piece to each of the cows. Then the dairy-woman asked the mistress into her house, where there was a table set with a pitcher of milk and in the corner by the stove a new-born calf huddled behind a board partition. Anninka had some milk and hastened across to see the calf; impulsively she kissed its muzzle, but immediately wiped her lips in disgust, complaining that it was all slimy and horrid. Finally, she drew from her purse three rouble notes which she gave to the old servants and then prepared to leave.

'What will you do?' she asked as she got into the kibitka, turning to old Fedulych who, as village elder, was following his mistress with his arms crossed over his chest.

'What can we do! We shall go on living!' Fedulych replied simply.

Anninka again felt sad: she sensed there was irony in what Fedulych said. She stood lingering, then sighed and said:

'Goodbye, then.'

'But we were thinking as how you might come back and live here along with us!' said Fedulych.

'Oh, no . . . really! You just . . . go on living . . . as before.'

And again the tears streamed from her eyes, whereupon every-one else wept too. It was strange: there was nothing in this place for her to miss or even remember, yet here she was weeping. And they too—nothing had been spoken of other than questions and answers about daily concerns, yet they all felt sad and 'sorry'. They helped her into the kibitka, tucked her in well, and all as one heaved a deep sigh.

'Good luck!' the cry followed her, as the conveyance moved off.

Passing the cemetery, she once more ordered the driver to stop and she went alone, without any clergy, along the cleared path to the grave. It was quite dark now and the lights were lit in the houses of the church servitors. She stood with one hand clutching the cross on the grave; she did not cry though, only swayed as she stood. She thought of nothing in particular, she could not bring her mind to bear on anything precisely; she was, though, miserable, totally and utterly miserable. The misery she felt was not on her grandmother's account, but on her own. Quite unaware, she stood there swaying and leaning on the cross for some fifteen minutes; then suddenly she thought of Lyubinka, who perhaps at that very moment was warbling to the revelling throng in Kremenchug or wherever:

> *Ah! Ah! que j'aime, que j'aime!*
> *Que j'aime les mili—mili—mili—taires!*

She almost collapsed. She went running back to the kibitka, got in, and gave the order to drive as quickly as possible to Golovlevo.

Anninka returned to her uncle's house listless and quiet. How-ever, this did not stop her feeling somewhat hungry (in the rush Uncle had failed even to supply a chicken for the journey) and she was very pleased to find the table ready laid for tea. Porfiry Vladimirych, needless to say, was not slow to open the conversation.

'You've been, then?'

'Yes, I've been.'

'And you prayed at the grave? And had a requiem?'

'Yes, that too.'

'The priest was at home, then?'

'Yes, of course. Who else could have taken the service!'

'Yes, indeed . . . And were both the chanters there? Did they sing the "Eternal memory"?'

'Yes, they did.'

'Ah, yes! Eternal memory! Eternal memory to our dear departed! A kindly old soul she was, fond of her family!'

Judas got up from his chair, turned to the icons and said a prayer.

'Well, and how did you find things in Pogorelka? Was all well there?'

'I really can't tell. Everything seems to be as it should.'

' "Seems"—there's the rub! It always "seems" to us, but once you look and see, there's something broken here, something rotten there . . . We form notions of other people's wealth in just the same way: "it seems"! Always "it seems"! It's a pretty little estate you have, though. Dear Mother set you up nicely there, in fact she put quite a lot of her own money into that estate . . . But there, helping the orphan is no sin!'

Hearing these words of praise, Anninka could not resist teasing her tender-hearted uncle.

'Why, though, did you take away those two cows from Pogorelka, Uncle?'

'Cows? What cows? Would that be Chernavka and Prive-denka? Why, my dear, they were Mother's property!'

'And you're her rightful heir? What does it matter—you keep them! Would you like me to have them send you the calf as well?'

'There you go, now, flying off the handle! Just say what it is you mean! Whose cows do you think they were?'

'How should I know? They were at Pogorelka, though!'

'Well, I know, and I can prove it, that the cows belonged to Mother. I found the register, written down in her own hand, and it says just that: "mine"!'

'Let's drop it! It's not worth talking about.'

'Then there's a horse at Pogorelka—the one with bare patches, but of that I can't say for sure. It might well have been Mother's, but I don't really know. And what I don't know I can't talk about!'

'Let's drop it, Uncle.'

'No, why should we drop it? I'm a straightforward man, my dear, and I like to have a thing out. After all, why shouldn't we talk about it? Everybody begrudges his own: I do, you do—so, all right, let's talk about it! And if we're to talk, I can tell you straight: I want nothing that's anyone else's, but I'm not going to give up what's my own. And so, even though you and Lyubinka are not strangers to me, all the same . . .'

'And you even took the icons!' said Anninka, again unable to restrain herself.

'Yes, and I took the icons, and I took everything that belonged to me as rightful heir!'

'The icon-case looks as if it's full of holes . . .'

'That can't be helped! Pray before it as it is! God needs your prayers, not an icon-case! If you come to him in sincerity of heart, then, however poor the icons, your prayers will be heard. But if all you do is gabble your prayers, gawp about, and drop curtseys, then even good icons won't save you!'

Nevertheless, Judas rose and gave thanks to God that his icons were indeed 'good'!

'If you don't like the old case, have a new one made. Or put some other icons in the gaps. It was dear Mother who got the old ones together and put them there—you must get some new ones yourself!'

Porfiry Vladimirych even tittered at the logic and simplicity of what he said.

'Uncle, please will you tell me what I should now do?' asked Anninka.

'Wait a while. For a start, have some rest, a little comfort, get some sleep. Then we'll talk and think things over, we'll weigh it all up—between us, perhaps, we'll come up with something.'

'We are of age, aren't we?'

'Oh, yes, indeed. You are of age and can conduct yourselves and your affairs just as you please.'

'Thank heavens for that, at least!'

'It's my honour to congratulate you!'

Porfiry Vladimirych got up and advanced towards her to kiss her.

'You're so odd, Uncle! You're for ever kissing!'

'And why should I not! You're not just anybody—you're my little niece! I kiss you, my dear, out of family feeling! For kith and kin I'll do anything. Be it only the third or fourth remove, I'll...'

'Better still, just tell me what I must do. Do I have to go into town? Do I have to see to anything?'

'We'll go into town, we'll see to everything—all in our own good time. But first—rest, stay a while! Praise God, you're not in a tavern, but in your very own uncle's house! A bite to eat, a sup of tea, a taste of jam—we've plenty of everything here. And should there be a dish you don't care for, ask for something different. Ask for it, order it! If you don't want cabbage soup, ask for broth! If you want cutlets, duck, sucking-pig—just get on to Evprakseyushka! . . . Evprakseyushka, by the way, I was just boasting about our sucking-pig, though I don't rightly know if we've got any.'

Evprakseyushka, who at this moment was holding a saucer full of hot tea to her lips, gave an affirmative sniff.

'There, you see! Sucking-pig too! So anything the heart desires, just ask for it! Yes, indeed!'

Judas again stretched across to Anninka and patted her—in kinship—on the knee, in the course of which his hand, unintentionally, of course, lingered briefly, causing Anninka to draw instinctively away.

'But I must be going,' she said.

'The very thing I'm talking about. First we'll discuss it, talk it over, and *then* we can go: in proper style, at steady pace by God's good grace, not just up and away! Haste trips on its own heels! Hurry to a house on fire, but—praise God—we've no fire here! Lyubinka now, she's got to be off to the fair, but there's no need for you to hurry! Another thing I was going to ask: do you propose living in Pogorelka now?'

'No. There's no reason for me to live there.'

'I was also going to say—you should settle down here with

me: we could then live happily ever after—and a fine life it would be!'

Saying which, Judas regarded Anninka with such unctuous eyes that she felt uncomfortable.

'No, Uncle, I'll not settle here either. It's too boring.'

'Silly, silly girl! How you keep on about boredom! It's boring! It's boring!—but you don't know *what* is boring! A person who has tasks to do and knows how to organize himself is never bored, my dear. Take me, for example—I just don't notice how the time flies. Week-days there's the estate business: this to look at, that to see to, a call to be made, a word here, a word there—and the day's gone! Stay on here, you'll find things to do, and if there's nothing to occupy you—you can always play a hand of "donkey" with Evprakseyushka or get the sledge harnessed up and go for a joy-ride! Then, come the summer, we'll go to the woods and pick mushrooms! And picnic on the grass!'

'No, Uncle, it's no good your suggesting it.'

'But you really should stay on!'

'No. Look, I'm tired after my journey. Do you mind if I go to bed?'

'Bye-byes? Of course. There's a bed all ready for you and everything to hand. If it's bye-byes you want—sleep well and the Lord be with you! But still, think it over—how much better it would be if you stayed on here with us in Golovlevo!'

Anninka spent a restless night. The nervous humour that had come over her at Pogorelka still persisted. There are times when a person who has hitherto only *existed* suddenly comes to realize that not only is he indeed *alive*, but that his life has within it a canker. Whence it came, how and when exactly it formed—in most cases he cannot properly tell and more often than not attributes the origin of the canker to quite other causes than those which were responsible for it in fact. But he actually has no need for analysis: it is sufficient that the canker exists. The effect of such a discovery, though equally painful for anyone, varies in its practical consequences according to the nature of the individual. Some are revitalized by the knowledge and inspired with a determination to start a new life on new foundations; by others the knowledge is felt only as a temporary pain which in the future will bring no improving change, but in the present causes even greater distress than when the conscience is stirred, for the latter, in its new resolve, can see at least some rays of light ahead.

Anninka was not one of those persons who are prompted by knowledge of their canker to make a fresh start in life, but none the less, being a not unintelligent girl, she fully realized the vast difference that existed between the vague dreams of earning her living which had caused her to quit Pogorelka for ever and her present position as a provincial actress. Instead of a quiet life of toil, she had embarked on a boisterous existence filled with unending revelry, shameless indecency, and a chaotic round of activity that led nowhere. Instead of the deprivation and hard conditions of life which she had once been ready to accept, she now knew relative prosperity and luxury—which, however, she could not recall without blushing. And this entire transformation had somehow taken place without her noticing—she had been on her way to some nice place but had gone through the wrong door. Her desires had been, in fact, very modest. How many times, sitting in the mezzanine at Pogorelka, had she pictured herself as a serious girl, working, thirsting for education, resolutely enduring want and privation for some idea of 'good' (true, the word 'good' had no very precise meaning); but as soon as she embarked on her own course in life, she found herself caught up in a manner of existence that shattered her dream completely. Serious work does not come of itself; it is the result of persistent endeavour and of training, which, even if inadequate, still serves as some support at least to the endeavour. But neither Anninka's nature nor her education measured up to these requirements. In her nature there was no real passion, merely a capacity to be easily excited; and the store of knowledge provided by the education with which she set out on her working life was so insubstantial that it could not possiblly serve as foundation for any serious profession. Her education had been a compound of school-learning and operetta, with operetta just about having the edge. It was a chaotic jumble of elements, which included the arithmetical problem of the flock of geese in flight, the *pas de châle*, the sermon of Peter of Picardy and the escapades of la belle

Hélène, the 'Ode to Felitsa',* and grateful sentiments to the principals and patrons of the young ladies' institute. In this muddled concoction (apart from which she could justifiably call herself a *tabula rasa*) it was difficult enough to get any bearings, much less find a point of departure. The training she received instilled in her not love of work, but a love of fashionable society, a desire to be the centre of attention, to listen to the pleasantries of suitors, and generally to sink herself in the din, dazzle, and whirl of what is called 'society life'.

If she had observed herself more closely, then even in Pogorelka, in those moments when her plans for a working life were still only forming and she saw in them something like the deliverance from captivity in Egypt—even then she might have perceived that she envisaged herself not so much working as being in the company of congenial people and whiling away the time in intelligent conversation. Of course, the people in her dreams were intelligent and their conversation serious and honest, but still it was the brighter side of life which predominated. Poverty was something clean and tidy, and want meant only the lack of excess. Consequently, when her dreams of earning her daily bread were actually realized by the offer of an engagement performing in operetta on the stage of a provincial theatre, despite the contrast, she did not hesitate for long. She hastily brushed up her school knowledge of Helen's relations with Menelaus, supplemented this with a few details from the life of the magnificent Prince of Tauris,* and reckoned this to be adequate preparation for performing *La Belle Hélène* and *Excerpts from La Grande-Duchesse de Gérolstein** in the major provincial towns and fairs. At the same time it salved her conscience to recall a student she had known in Moscow who used to exclaim at every turn: 'Sacred art!'—and she was the more ready to adopt these words as her motto in life because they gave her a respectable pretext and lent at least some outward decorum to her entry on that path which by instinct she was dying to follow.

The life of an actress threw her off balance. Alone, without any training to guide her or any conscious aim, with nothing but a temperament that thirsted for fame, glamour, and adulation, she found herself whirling in a chaotic world thronged with an endless multitude of randomly changing people. They were people of the most various characters and convictions, so that her reasons for associating with one or another could never be the same. None the less, each and every one of them was equally a member of her circle, from which one can only conclude that the question of 'reasons' never actually arose. It was clear enough that her life had become something in the nature of a highway inn, at the gate of which anyone was free to knock who knew himself to be gay, young, and possessed of certain material resources. Clearly, it was not at all a matter of *choosing* company that was congenial, but of attaching oneself to *any* company at all so as not to languish in solitude. In fact, 'sacred art' had landed her in a cesspool, but her head was at first in such a whirl that she did not notice it. The unwashed faces of the servants, the tatty, slimy scenery, the din, stench, and racket of the hotels and inns, the cynical advances of her admirers—none of this sobered her. She even failed to notice that she was continually alone in the company of men and that between herself and women occupying a *regular position* in society an insuperable barrier had now been raised . . .

She was sobered for a moment by her arrival in Golovlevo.

From the morning she arrived, the first minute almost, something disturbed her. As an impressionable girl, she was very quick to respond to new sensations and no less quick to adapt to any situation. So, on arriving in Golovlevo, she suddenly saw herself as the 'young mistress'. She recalled that she did have something to call her own: her own house, her own graves, and she had a sudden desire to see again her old haunts and to breathe again the air from which she had so recently fled without regret. But this feeling was to be shattered straightaway when she was confronted with the reality of Golovlevo. In this respect, she might be likened to a man who comes with a friendly look into a company of people he has not seen for a long time and suddenly notices that his friendliness is greeted rather enigmatically. Judas's wicked sidelong glance at her bosom had at once reminded her that she bore a burden of experience which she could not easily shed. And when, after the naïve questions of the Pogorelka servants, the admonitory sighs of the Voplino priest and his wife, and the fresh homilies of Judas; she was left alone, and when she reviewed at leisure the impressions of the day, she realized with full certainty that the former 'young mistress' was now dead for ever, that henceforth she was just an actress on the wretched provincial stage, and that the position of an actress in Russia was very little removed from that of a common prostitute.

Until now she had lived in a dream world. She had exposed herself in *La Belle Hélène*, appeared intoxicated in *Périchole*, sung all manner of indecencies in *Excerpts from La Grande-Duchesse de Gérolstein*, she had even regretted that it was not done to display on stage '*la chose*' and '*l'amour*', thinking how seductively she could wriggle her hips and with what *chic* she could swing the train of her dress. But it never occurred to her to think about what she was doing. Her only concern was to ensure that her performances were always 'nice' and had '*chic*'—and appealed to the officers of the garrison. But what the true nature of this activity was and what feelings her shaking body aroused in the officers—these were questions she never asked herself. The officers were the audience which counted in the town and she knew that it was on them that her success depended. They forced their way back-stage, unceremoniously knocked at her dressing-room door when she was only half-dressed, called her affectionate names —and all this she regarded as a mere formality, some inevitable circumstance of her profession, and all she ever asked herself was whether in this too she was carrying off her part 'nicely' or not. But she still did not yet consider either her body or her soul to be public property. And now, when for a moment she felt herself again to be the 'young mistress', she was suddenly seized with disgust. It was as if she had been stripped of her last garment and was paraded naked in public; it was as if all those vile exhalations that reeked of wine and the stables had enveloped her completely; it was as if she could feel all over her the touch of sweaty hands and slavering lips and the roaming gaze of glassy, lusting eyes, which slid senselessly over the contours of her naked body, as though demanding from it the answer to the question 'What is "*la chose*"?'

Where could she go? Where could she leave this burden weighing on her shoulders? The question revolved hopelessly in her mind—but it merely revolved, and neither found nor even sought an answer. For this too was a kind of dream: her former life had been a dream, and her present awakening—that also was a dream. She was upset and had given way to her feelings—that is all it was. It would pass. There are good moments and bad moments in life, it is in the way of things. But these moments, good or bad, are a mere gloss, they make no difference whatever to an established course of life. To give some new direction to the latter great efforts are required, and courage too, not only moral but also physical. It is almost like committing suicide. Although a man intending suicide curses his life, although he is sure that death for him means freedom, none the less the fatal weapon trembles in his hand, the knife slips on his throat, the pistol does not fire into the forehead but shoots low only to disfigure. It is the same in the present case, only even harder. Here, too, the task is to kill one's former life—but to do so and go on living. The 'nothingness' which in a proper suicide is attained in a moment by pressing the trigger is attained in this other form of suicide, the suicide of 'regeneration', only by a succession of severe, almost ascetic exertions. The end result is still a state of 'nothingness', for it is impossible to describe as 'normal' an existence which consists entirely of exertions, deprivations, and restraints. A person of enfeebled will, a person whose morale has been sapped by easy living finds his head swirling at the very prospect of such a 'regeneration'. And, turning away and screwing up his eyes, filled with shame and self-recrimination at his own pusillanimity, he will none the less instinctively set off again along the old beaten track.

Oh, it is a great thing—a life of toil! But it is only the strong and those condemned to it by some accursed original sin who can take to such a life. Only for these does it hold no fear: for the former because, knowing the purpose and prospects of toil, they can find in it enjoyment, and for the latter because toil to them is first an inborn obligation and then, too, a habit.

It never even occurred to Anninka to settle down in Pogorelka or Golovlevo and in this respect she was much assisted by the professional situation which circumstances had placed her in and which instinct restrained her from abandoning. She had been given leave of absence and she had already planned the time ahead and fixed the day for her departure from Golovlevo. For weak-natured people those outward confines with which life besets them do considerably ease the burden of life. When in difficulty, weak people instinctively hug to these confines and in them find excuses for themselves. Anninka did just that: she decided to leave Golovlevo as soon as possible and, if her uncle pressed her to stay, to take refuge in the necessity of being back at the appointed time.

On waking the next morning, she went through all the rooms of the enormous Golovlevo house. It was everywhere deserted, unhomely, a world apart, moribund. The idea of living indefinitely in this house completely terrified her. 'Not for anything!' she repeated frantically. 'Not for anything!'

The following day Porfiry Vladimirych again greeted her with his customary benevolence—from which it was impossible to tell whether he was going to be nice to you or suck your blood.

'Well, now, you will-o'-the-wisp, did you sleep well? And where is it you're hasting off to now?' he said jestingly.

'Uncle, I really do have to hurry. It's only holiday I've got, after all, and I must be back in time.'

'Back to your clowning again? I won't let you go!'

'Whether you do or not, I'll go just the same!'

Judas sadly shook his head.

'And what will your dear departed Granny say?' he asked in a tone of fond reproach.

'Granny knew about it when she was alive. And, Uncle, why do you speak like that? Yesterday you had me travelling round fairgrounds with a guitar, now today you talk of clowning. I don't want you to talk like that, do you hear!'

'Aha! So the truth hurts, does it? Well, I have a great love for the truth! In my view, truth . . .'

'No, no! I don't want to hear! I don't want to hear! I don't need your truth or your untruth! Do you hear? I don't want you to speak like that!'

'Now, now! Temper! Come along, my flibbertigibbet, let's go while we may and have some tea! The samovar will have been long since huffing and puffing on the table!'

Porfiry wished by his banter to dispel the impression created by his reference to 'clowning' and as a token of reconciliation he even reached out to put his arm round his niece's waist, but Anninka found the whole business so stupid, if not vile, that she disdainfully evaded his intended mark of affection.

'I tell you again, Uncle, really I have to hurry!' she said.

'Well, let's go first and have some tea, and after that we can have a talk!'

'But why has it got to be after tea? Why can't we talk before tea?'

'Why? Just because! Because we must always do things in their proper turn. First one thing, then the other; first we'll have some tea and a chat, and then we'll talk seriously. We'll have plenty of time.'

Faced with this irrepressible stream of prattle, there was nothing to do but submit. They started tea, during which Judas quite maliciously took his time, taking small sips from his glass, crossing himself, slapping his thigh, chatting about dear Mother, and so on.

'Well now, let's have our talk,' he said at length. 'Is it long you intend staying with me?'

'I can't stay more than a week. I've still got to go to Moscow.'

'A week is a long time, my dear. You can do a lot in a week or a little—it depends how you set about it.'

'The more we get done the better, Uncle.'

'The very thing I'm saying. You can do a lot or a little. Sometimes you mean to do a lot and it turns out to be a little, and sometimes you think you're doing a little and then you find that unbeknown, with God's aid, you've got everything finished. Here you go hurrying off, you're supposed to go to Moscow, but, if anyone asked why, you wouldn't rightly know yourself. I think you would do better spending time on your affairs here than going to Moscow.'

'I've got to go to Moscow: I want to see if we can get work in the theatres there. And as for my affairs, why you say yourself how much can be done in a week.'

'Depending on how you set about it, my dear. If you set about it properly, you'll find it goes smooth and easy; but if you don't set about it properly, you'll have nothing but snags and hitches!'

'Then you shall guide me, Uncle!'

'There you are! When you're in need, then it's "Guide me, Uncle", but when you're not, then it's "boring" at Uncle's and you can't wait to leave! Isn't that true?'

'Please just say what I have to do.'

'Hold now! Wait a minute! What I'm saying is this: when you need your uncle, then it's "dear Uncle", "darling Uncle", "sweet Uncle", but when you don't need him, you turn your back on him! You don't think of asking your uncle's permission: "Uncle darling", you might say, "Do you think I could go to Moscow?"'

'You really are odd, Uncle! I've simply got to go to Moscow, so what would happen if you said I couldn't?'

'If I said you couldn't, then you'd stay here! It's not just anybody—it's your uncle speaking: you might do as your uncle says. Ah, my dear, my dear! It's lucky you've got an uncle—there's someone at least to care about you, someone to restrain you. There are those who have nobody—nobody to care for them, nobody to restrain them, growing up all alone! And then they suffer . . . all manner of . . . eventualities, my dear!'

Anninka was about to answer back, but realizing that this would only be adding fuel to the fire, said nothing. She sat with her eyes fixed hopelessly on Porfiry Vladimirych, who was now in full spate.

'There's something I've wanted to say to you for a long time,' Judas meanwhile continued. 'I don't like it, I don't like it at all your touring round these . . . these fairs! Though you didn't approve my mentioning guitars, still, after all . . .'

'But saying you don't like it isn't enough! You've got to show me some way out!'

'Live here with me—that's a way out for you!'

'Well, no . . . that's . . . No, not for anything!'

'Why is that?'

'Because I would have nothing to do here. What is there here to do? Get up in the morning, go and have tea, at tea think about lunch, and at lunch think about dinner, and at dinner think it will soon be time again for tea. And then supper and go to bed . . . I should die here!'

'That's what everyone does, my dear. First they have tea, then lunch, for those accustomed to it—I personally don't have lunch, because I am not so accustomed; then they have dinner, then evening tea, and last of all they go to bed. Really! I see nothing ridiculous or reprehensible in that! Now if I were to . . .'

'Nothing reprehensible, no, but it's not my way.'

'Now if I were to wrong or censure or speak ill of anybody— why then, certainly, I might well reproach myself for it! But as for taking tea, having lunch, dinner . . . why, bless you, however sprightly you are, you can't survive without food!'

'That's all very well, Uncle, but it's still not my way.'

'Don't measure everything by your own yardstick—have a little thought for your elders "My way" and "Not my way"—is that a proper manner to talk? Now if you said "God's way" and "Not God's way", that would make sense, that would be proper! If here in Golovlevo we don't live in God's way, if we act contrary to God or complain or envy or do some other wickedness, then indeed we are guilty and worthy of reproach. But first you would have to prove that we *don't* live in God's way. But that you don't do, you just say it's not "your way"! Well, let me tell you something: there are plenty of things that don't suit *my* way! It does not suit my way to have you talking like this to me and turning your nose up at my hospitality—none the less, I sit and say nothing! I think to myself: perhaps by a mild response I shall convey this and she will come to her senses. Perhaps, if I answer your gibes with a jest and a smile, then your guardian angel will set you on the true path! It pains me—not for myself, but for your sake! Oh, my dear, it really is bad of you! If I had ever wronged you in word or deed, if I had ever given you cause for offence—it would have been all very well! God does command us to accept the admonitions of our elders, but still, if I had offended you, you could be angry with me—and welcome! As it is, though, I sit here all meek and mild, never uttering a word, wondering only how to make things better and cosier, to bring joy and comfort to all—and you, upon my word, you do nothing but complain! That's your response to all my loving care! Don't you, though, let your tongue run away with you, my dear—first think, pray, ask God to give you understanding! And then, if . . .'

Porfiry Vladimirych expatiated at great length, never pausing. The words streamed from him one after the other like so much viscous saliva. Anninka watched him horror-struck, wondering how he managed not to choke. However, Uncle did not after all tell her what it was she should do in connection with Arina Petrovna's death. At dinner she again tried to put this question to him, and yet again at evening tea, but each time Judas launched into some irrelevant rigmarole, which made Anninka regret that she had ever raised the matter and think only of one thing: when would it all end?

After dinner, when Porfiry Vladimirych had departed to bed, Anninka was left alone with Evprakseyushka and felt a sudden urge to engage her uncle's housekeeper in conversation. She wished to find out why it was not terrible for Evprakseyushka to live in Golovlevo and what gave her the strength to endure the streams of empty verbiage which from morning to night spewed forth from her uncle's lips.

'Do you find it boring in Golovlevo, Evprakseyushka?'

'What call is there to be bored, Miss? We're not gentry!'

'Still . . . you're always on your own . . . you've got no pleasures or pastimes . . . you've nothing at all!'

'What pleasures do we need? If I'm bored, I look out of the window. When I lived with Father at St Nicholas's, there wasn't that much fun either.'

'Still, it was nicer at home, I expect . . . You had your friends, you could visit each other, play games . . .'

'Yes, of course.'

'While with Uncle . . . He says such boring things all the time and seems to go on and on. Is he always like that?'

'Yes, always. He talks like that all day long.'

'And don't you find it boring?'

'What's it matter to me! I don't ever listen to him!'

'But you can't stop listening altogether. He might notice and take it amiss.'

'How's he to know! After all, I do look at him. While he talks, I look on and think to myself the while.'

'And what is it you think about?'

'All sorts of things. If it's cucumber-pickling time, I think about the cucumbers; if I've got to have something fetched out from town, I think about that. Of if there's anything needed about the house—all sorts of things I think about!'

'So really, though you live together, you're actually on your own?'

'Yes, I'm pretty well on my own. Sometimes, maybe, of an evening he'll feel like a hand of "donkey", so we have a game. Even then, though, he'll stop in the middle of it and put down his cards and start off talking. I just look on. When Arina Petrovna, God rest her soul, was alive, it was more cheery. When she was here, he was afraid of speaking out of turn and the old lady would stop him sometimes. But the way he lets himself go now— it's like nothing on earth!'

'Don't you see! That's what's terrible, Evprakseyushka! It's terrible when somebody talks and you don't even know why he's talking or what he's saying or if he'll ever stop. Don't you think that's terrible? Doesn't it bother you?'

Evprakseyushka looked at her, as if struck by some astonishing revelation.

'You're not the only one,' she said. 'Many folk here don't like him on that score.'

'There you are!'

'Yes. The menservants, for instance. There's not one can put up with it here for long; we change them nearly every month. The same with the stewards. And it's all on that account.'

'Does he get on their nerves?'

'He grinds them down. Those that drink stay on, because a drunkard don't hear. A drunkard's deaf as a post and wouldn't heed the last trump. But that's trouble again, because *he* don't like drunkards.'

'Oh, Evprakseyushka! And he's actually trying to persuade me to live in Golovlevo!'

'Why not, Miss! You really ought to live here with us! With you here he might know better!'

'Oh no, really! No thanks! I couldn't bear to look him in the face!'

'That's true, of course! You're gentry. You can please yourself.

But then, please yourself as you might, I suppose there's still times when you've got to dance to somebody else's tune!'

'All too often!'

'Just what I thought! Now, there's a thing I was going to ask you: is it nice being an actress?'

'It's nice to earn your own living.'

'And is it true what Porfiry Vladimirych told me about actresses having all kinds of strangers put their arms round them?'

Anninka flushed.

'Porfiry Vladimirych doesn't understand,' she replied irritably. 'That's why he talks such nonsense. He can't even tell the difference between acting on the stage and real life.'

'Oh, I don't know about that! Why, Porfiry Vladimirych himself . . . when he saw you, he gave you such a leery look. It was all "Dear niece this" and "Dear niece that", like a proper uncle should, but all the time he was goggling at you real shameless!'

'Evprakseyushka! Why do you say such silly things?'

'Me? It don't worry me! You stay here, you'll see for yourself! I'm not a bit bothered! If he dismisses me, I'll go home to Father. Anyway, it *is* boring here. It's true what you said.'

'It's useless for you even to think I could stay here. But that it's boring in Golovlevo—that's true. And the longer you stay, the more boring you'll find it.'

Evprakseyushka thought a little, then yawned and said:

'When I lived with Father I used to be thin as a rake. And look at me now—I'm as round as a barrel! Boredom must be good for you, I reckon.'

'All the same, you won't stand it long. Mark my words: you won't stand it long!'

With this the conversation ended. It was fortunate that it was not heard by Porfiry Vladimirych, who would have found in it a new and rewarding theme which would doubtless have given fresh impetus to the endless stream of his moralizing discourses.

For two more days Porfiry Vladimirych tormented Anninka. He kept on saying: 'Be patient and wait!' 'Easy does it, all in good time!' 'Go with a blessing and a prayer!' and so on. He wore her out completely. Finally, on the fifth day he did make ready to go into the town, though even then he found means to torture his niece. For a full hour she waited in the hall with her fur coat on, while he, as if on purpose, leisurely took his time. He got dressed, washed, slapped his thighs, crossed himself, walked around, sat down, gave instructions such as: 'That's the way then!' or 'Just see that everything's all right!' In general, he acted as if he were leaving Golovlevo not for a few hours, but for ever. Having thoroughly wearied all concerned—the servants and the horses which had been waiting an hour and a half at the door—in the end he felt dry in the throat from uttering all these trivialities and decided to set off.

In the town the entire business was concluded while the horses ate their oats at the inn. Porfiry Vladimirych presented his account, which showed that the orphaned girls' capital at the time of Arina Petrovna's death consisted of just under twenty thousand roubles in five per cent bonds. The application for the termination of their wardship together with an affidavit that the girls were of age was then submitted and an order was made forthwith to terminate the Board of Guardians' control and authorize the transfer of the property and capital to the owners. The same evening Anninka signed all the papers and inventories which Porfiry Vladimirych had drawn up—and breathed freely at last.

The remaining days Anninka spent in a state of high agitation. She wanted to leave Golovlevo at once, straightaway, but all her endeavours to leave were countered by her uncle with jests which, despite their genial tone, concealed a mulish obstinacy that no human strength could break.

'You said yourself you would stay a week—so stay you shall!' he said. 'What's the matter? You don't have to pay for your lodging—you're welcome without! And if you want some tea or a morsel to eat, whatever you fancy you shall have!'

'But, Uncle, I really have to go!' said Anninka beseechingly.

'You may be dying to go—but I shan't give you any horses!' Judas bantered. 'I shan't give you any horses, and you will be my prisoner! When the week's up, I'll not say a word! We'll go to mass, have something to eat for the road, a cup of tea, a little chat . . . when we've had enough of each other—then God speed, away you go! Here, though—why don't you pay another visit to the grave at Voplino? You could take leave of your Granny— and she might even give you good advice!'

'Yes, perhaps I will,' Anninka agreed.

'Then this is what we'll do: Wednesday first thing we'll go to mass here, have dinner before leaving, then my horses will take you as far as Pogorelka, and from there you can have your Pogorelka horses take you on to Dvoriki. You're a landowner too now, with horses of your own!'

She had to submit. Rank meanness has enormous power; it always takes the inexperienced man unawares and, while he still looks about him in astonishment, it has him swiftly enmeshed and in its clutches. Anyone passing a cesspit has probably had occasion not only to hold his nose, but also to try and stop breathing; a man should similarly steel himself when he enters the realm of prattle and meanness. He must dull his senses—sight, hearing, smell, taste; he must suppress all sensitivity, he must be as wood. Only then will he not be stifled by the miasmas of meanness. Anninka realized this, though too late; and she decided anyway to let the matter of her release from Golovlevo take its natural course. Judas had so vanquished her by the irresistible force of his prattle that she did not even venture to turn away when he embraced her and—as kith and kin—stroked her back and told her what a good girl she was now. She instinctively shuddered each time she felt his bony, tremulous hand creep up and down her spine, but any further expression of disgust on her part was restrained by the thought: 'Lord, as long as he lets me go when the week is up!' Fortunately for her, Judas was not a pernickety man and though he may have noticed her gestures of impatience, he kept quiet. He evidently held to that theory concerning relations between the sexes which finds expression in the saying 'Love me, love me not, only look on me.'

At last the eagerly awaited day of departure came. It was barely six o'clock when Anninka got up, but Judas still was up before her. He had completed his customary devotions and while awaiting the first stroke of the church bell he sauntered round the house in slippers and dressing-gown, peeping, eavesdropping, and so forth. He was obviously on edge and, meeting Anninka, he

looked at her in a rather sidelong way. It was already light outside, though the weather was foul. The sky was covered with
unbroken dark clouds, from which a sleety spring drizzle
descended; on the black roadway through the village there were
puddles, which meant that out on the open road there would be
water-filled hollows under the snow; a strong southerly wind was
blowing, which promised a clammy thaw; the trees were now
bare of snow and their stark, wet tops swayed in disarray this
way and that; the outbuildings of the manor were now black
and looked to be coated with slime. Porfiry Vladimirych took
Anninka to the window and pointed to this scene of spring's
regeneration.

'Do you really mean to travel?' he asked. 'Shouldn't you stay?'

'Oh no, no!' she cried in alarm. 'It . . . it will pass over!'

'Not likely. If you leave at one o'clock, you'll hardly reach
Pogorelka before seven. You can scarcely travel by night with
the roads in this state, so you'll have to spend the night in
Pogorelka anyway.'

'Oh no! I can travel through the night too, I'll leave straightaway . . . after all, I'm brave, Uncle! And why wait until one
o'clock? Uncle darling, let me go now.'

'And what will Granny say? She'll say: what a granddaughter
I've got! She came, gave a hop and a skip, and never so much
as came for my blessing!'

Porfiry Vladimirych stopped and was silent. For a while he
shifted his feet, in turns glancing at Anninka and dropping his
eyes. Evidently he wished to say something, but was in two
minds about doing so.

'Just a minute—I've something to show you,' he ventured at
last, and handed Anninka a folded sheet of writing-paper which
he took from his pocket. 'There—read that!'

Anninka read:

'Today I prayed and asked the good Lord to let my Anninka
stay with me. And the good Lord said "Put your arms round
Anninka's plump little waist and give her a big hug." '

'How about it?' he asked, turning a little pale.

'Really, Uncle! How revolting!' she replied, looking at him in
dismay.

Porfiry Vladimirych turned even paler and, grating through his teeth 'I see it's hussars we want,' he crossed himself and shuffled out of the room.

A quarter of an hour later, however, he was back again as if nothing had happened and even joking with Anninka.

'So what will you do?' he said. 'Will you drop in at Voplino? Are you going to say farewell to your old Granny? Do that, do that, my dear! It was a good work remembering your Granny as you did. We should never forget our relations, particularly those who have, you might say, striven body and soul to help us!'

They celebrated mass, with a requiem, ate kutya in the church, then, arriving home, had more kutya and sat down to tea. Porfiry Vladimirych, as if on purpose, was more than usually slow, sipping his tea and lingering tormentingly over his words as he held forth in the intervals between sips. By ten o'clock, however, tea was over, and Anninka implored him:

'Uncle, can I go now?'

'But you will eat, you will have some dinner for the road? You surely never thought your uncle would let you go off just like that? Not on your life, never think of it! That was never the Golovlevo way! Why, my dear departed Mother would never let me into her sight, if she knew I had sent my own niece off on a journey without sustenance! Never think it! Don't imagine such a thing!'

She had to submit again. However, an hour and a half went by and no attempt was made even to lay the table. Everyone had gone off somewhere; Evprakseyushka, rattling her keys, was occasionally to be seen outside between the store-house and the cellar; Porfiry Vladimirych was deliberating with the steward, wearying him with senseless orders, slapping himself on the thighs, and generally contriving to spin out time. Anninka, alone, paced up and down the dining-room, looking at the clock, counting her steps, and then the seconds: one, two, three ... From time to time she looked out into the roadway and observed that the puddles were growing bigger and bigger.

At last there was a clatter of spoons, knives, and plates; Stepan, the manservant, came into the dining-room and threw a cloth on the table. But it seemed that some portion of the dust which

filled Judas's soul had entered also into him. With painful slowness he arranged the plates, blew into the glasses, and looked at
them against the light. It was exactly one o'clock when they sat
down to table.

'So you are going!' Porfiry Vladimirych said, opening the conversation as befitted a farewell occasion.

Before him was his plate of soup, but he did not touch it and
looked so meltingly at Anninka that even the tip of his nose
flushed. Anninka hurriedly swallowed her soup one spoonful
after another. He also picked up his spoon and very nearly
immersed it in his soup, but at once set it down again on the
table.

'You must excuse an old man like me,' he harped on. 'You've
eaten up your soup post-haste, but I'm a slowcoach and still
eating. I don't like treating God's gifts neglectfully. Our bread
is given to us to sustain us in our existence, and we heedlessly
scatter it abroad—see how many crumbs you've made? In general,
I like to do a thing thoroughly and well considered—the result
is always the sounder. It may vex you that at table I don't go
jumping through hoops or whatever you say for it: well, what
of that!—be vexed if you want to! You'll be vexed a while, but
in the end you'll forgive me. You won't be young for ever, you
won't always be charging through hoops, you too will learn by
experience one day—and then you'll say "perhaps after all Uncle
was right." Oh yes, indeed! You may be listening to me now and
thinking: naughty Uncle! what an old groucher! But when you
are my age, it will be a different tune: nice Uncle! he taught me
what is good!'

Porfiry Vladimirych crossed himself and swallowed two spoonfuls of soup. After which he once more put down his spoon and
leant back in his chair to signal that further conversation was
to come.

'Bloodsucker'—it was on the tip of Anninka's tongue, but she
restrained herself, hastily poured a glass of water and drank it at
a draught. Judas seemed to sense what was going on inside her.

'So you don't like what I say! Well, you may not like it, but
you listen to your uncle none the less! I've long been meaning
to talk to you about this hastiness of yours, but I've been too

occupied. I do not like this hastiness in you, it smacks of levity, lack of consideration. You were heedless before, when you left your Granny—with no concern for the pain you caused her—and for what?'

'Oh, Uncle! Why bring that up? It's already done! It's really too bad of you!'

'Just a minute! What I'm saying is not if it's good or bad, I'm saying that a thing done can still be undone. It's not just we sinners: God himself changes what he does—one day he sends rain, the next day sunshine! Come on! There's nothing so very marvellous about the theatre, after all! Come on! Decide to give it up!'

'No, Uncle, don't talk of it! Please!'

'And I'll tell you something else. Your levity is bad enough, but I like even less the little heed you pay to what your elders say. Your uncle wants what's good for you, and you tell him not to talk about it. Your uncle offers you affection, hospitality, and you snap at him! And do you know, anyway, who gave you your uncle? Come on, tell me: who gave you your uncle?'

Anninka looked at him in bewilderment.

'God gave you your uncle—that's who! God! But for God, you would be on your own, you wouldn't know how to manage or what form of request to make where and what might come of it. You would be in a maze; you would be wronged here, deceived there, or else just simply laughed at. But because you've got an uncle, with God's help we had the whole thing settled in a day. We went into town, called at the Board of Guardians, made your request, and got a decision. *That's* what it means to have an uncle, my dear!'

'And I'm grateful to you, Uncle.'

'Well, if you are grateful to your uncle, don't snap at him, but do as he says. Your uncle wants what's good for you, even if you do sometimes think . . .'

Anninka could hardly control herself. There remained only one way of escape from her uncle's homilies: to pretend that she at least in principle accepted his proposal that she should stay on in Golovlevo.

'All right, Uncle,' she said. 'I'll think about it. I can see myself it's not really convenient to live alone, away from your relations . . . But I can't anyway make a decision now. I'll have to think about it.'

'There you are now, you've come to see it yourself! But what is there to think about? We'll have the horses unhitched, your bags taken out of the kibitka—and there's an end to your thinking!'

'No, Uncle, you're forgetting I've got a sister.'

There is no knowing if Porfiry Vladimirych was in fact persuaded by this argument or if the whole scene had been staged by him simply for the sake of form and he did not rightly know himself if he wanted Anninka to stay in Golovlevo or if it was a momentary whim and he did not really want her to at all. In any event, after this dinner proceeded at a more lively pace. Anninka agreed with everything and replied to all he said in such a way as to give him no opportunity to indulge in prattle. For all that, it was half-past two by the clock when dinner came to an end. Anninka leapt up from the table as if she had all the time been sitting in a steam-bath, and ran to bid her uncle goodbye.

Ten minutes later Judas in his fur top-coat and bearskin boots was seeing her out at the porch and personally supervising the seating of the young mistress in the sledge.

'Easy down hill, do you hear! And no spills on the slope at Senkino!' he ordered the driver.

Finally, Anninka was wrapped up and settled in and the apron of the kibitka fastened.

'You should stay though!' Judas cried to her once more, wishing to ensure that before the assembled domestics everything should pass off in proper style, as befitted kith and kin. 'At least you'll come and see me, won't you? Do say you'll come!'

But Anninka already felt herself free and had a sudden mischievous urge. Leaning out of the kibitka and clearly enunciating every word, she replied:

'No, Uncle, I shan't come! It's terrible being with you!'

Judas pretended not to hear, but his lips blenched.

Anninka was so overjoyed by her liberation from captivity in Golovlevo that she never once paused to think that behind her there remained incarcerated for life a man for whom her departure meant the severance of all contact with the world of the living. She thought only of herself—that she had escaped and that now all was well. This sense of freedom affected her so strongly that when she visited again the graveyard at Voplino there was not a trace of that nervous sensitivity which she had displayed when first visiting her grandmother's grave. She heard the requiem through with composure, shed no tears as she bowed to the grave, and accepted the priest's invitation to take a cup of tea in his house.

The living conditions of the priest of Voplino were very poor. In the only decent room in the house, where visitors were received, a dismal bareness prevailed; along the walls stood a dozen or so painted chairs with horsehair upholstery worn through in many places and a matching sofa, the rounded back of which protruded like the chest of a general of the pre-Reform school; between two of the windows was a plain table covered by a soiled cloth on which lay the parish registers in front of an ink-pot with a pen stuck in it; in the east corner hung an icon-case containing the parental marriage-blessing and a burning icon-lamp; under the icon-case stood two chests which contained the priest's wife's dowry and were covered with faded grey cloth. There was no wallpaper; in the middle of one wall hung a few faded daguerreotype portraits of bishops. There was an odd smell in the room, as though it had long served as a graveyard for cockroaches and flies. The priest, though still a young man, had himself markedly faded in these surroundings: his thinning, whitish hair hung down from his head in lank strands like the branches of a weeping-willow; there was a despondent look in his once blue eyes; his voice was tremulous and his beard sparse; his woollen cassock did not meet properly at the front and hung on him as though on a hanger. The priest's wife, also young, from yearly child-bearing seemed even more spent than her husband.

None the less, Anninka could not help noticing that even these poor, spent, downtrodden people regarded her not as a proper parishioner, but rather with compassion, as a lost sheep.

'You've been to your uncle's?' began the priest, carefully taking a cup of tea off the tray held by his wife.

'Yes, I've been there about a week.'

'Porfiry Vladimirych is now the biggest landowner in the whole district—there's none mightier than him. But he seems to have little luck in life. First the one boy dies, then the other, and now his mother too. I'm surprised he didn't persuade you to settle down in Golovlevo.'

'Uncle did suggest it, but I wouldn't stay.'

'Why was that?'

'Because it's better to live in freedom.'

'Freedom, ma'am, is no bad thing, of course, but it has its dangers too. And seeing as you are Porfiry Vladimirych's closest kin and so direct heir to all his estates, I deem you might accept some restraint to your freedom.'

'No, Father. It's better to earn your own living. Life is easier somehow when you don't feel obliged to anybody.'

The priest looked at her dimly, as if wishing to ask 'Do you know what "earning your living" means then?', but thought better of it and just modestly drew the skirts of his cassock together.

'And do you get good wages as an actress?' asked the priest's wife, joining in the conversation.

The priest was totally abashed and even gave his wife an admonitory wink. He fully expected that Anninka would take offence. But Anninka did not, and answered with a perfectly straight face:

'I get a hundred and fifty roubles a month now, and my sister a hundred. And we're given benefit performances too. In a year we'll get about six thousand roubles between us.'

'Why don't they give your sister so much? Isn't she reckoned to be so good?' enquired the priest's wife further.

'No, my sister plays different parts. I've got a good singing voice—that's what audiences like best, but my sister's voice is not so good and so she plays in vaudevilles.'

'It's the same there then, is it—with priests and deacons and lesser orders?'

'In fact we share it evenly; it's what we agreed at the start—that we'd go halves with the money.'

'As kith and kin? What better? And how much will that be, husband? Six thousand roubles if you divide it by the month, what does that come to?'

'It's five hundred roubles a month, and if you halve that, it's two hundred and fifty roubles each.'

'There's money for you! It's more than we could ever spend in a year! Another thing I wanted to ask you—is it true that they treat actresses not the way they do proper women?'

The priest was on the verge of panic and even let the skirts of his cassock fall apart; however, seeing that Anninka was barely disconcerted by the question, he thought to himself: 'Oho, she's a cool customer all right', and calmed down.

'What exactly do you mean by "proper women"?'

'Well, they say like as though men kiss and hug them . . . And even, like, when they don't want to, they still have to . . .'

'They don't kiss them, they just pretend to. And it's nothing to do with wanting or not wanting—it's all according to what's in the play: whatever the play says, that's what they do.'

'Still, even if it is in the play . . . some man comes pressing himself on you with his slobbering chops fit to turn your stomach, but still you've got to let him kiss you!'

Anninka blushed crimson, she could not help it: she had a momentary vision of the face of the gallant Captain Papkov, who did just that—'pressed himself' on her, and not even, alas, because it was 'in the play'!

'You really have no idea what it's like on the stage,' she said rather stiffly.

'Of course, we've never been in any theatres, still I expect there's a bit of all sorts goes on there. The reverend and me, we often talk about you, Miss; we feel sorry for you, really very sorry.

Anninka was silent. The priest sat plucking at his beard as though bringing himself to have his own say.

'It's a fact, though, ma'am, that every calling has its pleasant and unpleasant sides,' he declared finally, 'but in his frailty a man takes delight in the former and the latter he does his best to forget. Why does he want to forget? Because, ma'am, in so far as he can he doesn't want to have before him any reminder of his duty and the path of virtue.'

He then added with a sigh:

'But the main thing, ma'am, is to preserve your treasure!'

The priest gave an admonishing look at Anninka; his wife gloomily shook her head as if to say: 'Some chance of that!'

'And preserving this treasure is, I deem, an uncertain matter in the calling of an actress,' the priest went on.

Anninka did not know what answer to make. It was becoming apparent to her that what these simple-minded people were saying about her 'treasure' was exactly equivalent to what the officers of the local garrison had to say about '*la chose*'. In general, she came to see that here, as at her uncle's, people regarded her as something apart, a person they could treat with some indulgence, but at a distance so as not to be contaminated.

'Why is the church here so poor, Father?' she asked, in order to change the subject.

'There's nothing to make it rich, that's why it's poor. The gentry have all gone away to their employments, and the peasants have no way to better themselves. There are only two hundred or more souls in the parish anyway!'

'Our bell's in a very bad way,' sighed the priest's wife.

'The bell and everything else. The bell we've got, ma'am, weighs but fifteen poods,* and it's gone and cracked too, alas. It doesn't ring properly now, just makes a dinning noise—a disgrace it is, really. Arina Petrovna, now departed, did promise to have a new one put in, and if she was still alive, by now we would have had our bell, of course.'

'You should tell Uncle that Granny had promised.'

'I did tell him, ma'am, and, to tell the truth, he heard my plea quite favourably, only he couldn't give me a positive answer: he had never heard anything about it from his mother, you see. She had never spoken to him about it. Though, he said, if he had heard, he would have been sure to carry out her wishes!'

'How could he not have heard!' said the priest's wife. 'The whole district knows, but he's never heard!'

'That's how we live. Time was, we at least had hope, but now we're left with no hope at all. Sometimes we have nothing for the communion: no bread, no red wine. As to ourselves, we make no mention.'

Anninka wanted to get up and take her leave, but a fresh tray appeared on the table with two plates containing mushrooms and some morsels of caviare and a bottle of madeira.

'Sit a while. Please join us . . . Have something to eat!'

Anninka did as she was bid, hastily swallowed two of the mushrooms, but declined the madeira.

'There's another thing I was going to ask you about,' said the priest's wife meanwhile. 'There's a girl in the parish, daughter of Lyshchevsky who's a servant at the manor; now she was in service with an actress in Petersburg. It's a good life actresses have, she says, only they've got to get a ticket* every month . . . Is that right?'

Anninka gaped at her, failing to understand . . .

'Gives them exemption,' the priest explained. 'But I don't think it's true what she says. On the contrary, I've heard that many actresses even have state pensions granted them for their services.'

It was clear to Anninka that they were getting into deep water and she began finally to take her leave.

'But we were thinking you would stop being an actress now?' the priest's wife went persistently on.

'Why should I?'

'Well, after all! You're a lady. You've come of age now, you've got your own property—what more could you want?'

'And then, after your uncle's gone, you're the direct heir,' added the priest.

'No, I shan't live here.'

'But we so hoped you would! We kept saying to ourselves: the young mistresses are sure to come and live in Pogorelka! And it's really very nice here in the summer: you can go picking mushrooms in the woods,' said the priest's wife beguilingly.

'There are plenty of mushrooms here even in a dry summer,' the priest chimed in.

Finally, Anninka departed. On arriving at Pogorelka, the first words were: 'The horses! Please, quickly, the horses!' But in response to her request Fedulych merely shrugged his shoulders.

' "The horses" indeed!' he grumbled. 'They're not even foddered yet.'

'But why on earth not! My God! Are you all conspired against me?'

'Yes, we are. And how should we not be, when anybody can see that you can't travel by night in full thaw. Out on the open road you'll be going through the snow into water, so, as we see it, you're better off at home!'

Her grandmother's rooms had been heated. In the bedrooms the bed was already made for her and the samovar was puffing away on the desk. Afimyushka had scraped from the bottom of Arina Petrovna's ancient tea-caddy the tea that was left after her death. While the tea was brewing, Fedulych, with his arms crossed, stood at the door facing his mistress, flanked by the dairywoman and Markovna in postures which suggested a readiness at a sign to rush off at once to do her bidding.

Fedulych was the first to speak.

'It's your granny's tea still,' he said. 'There was some left in the bottom. Porfiry Vladimirych was going to take the caddy away too, but I wouldn't have it. The young mistresses might come, I said, and might want a dish of tea before they've got their own by. That was all right—he even made play and said I was an old rogue and would drink it myself, and he said I was to be sure to send the caddy on to Golovlevo afterwards. You see if he don't have it fetched tomorrow!'

'You should have let him have it then.'

'Why let him have it? He's got plenty of tea of his own. And at least now we can have a drink of what you leave. And there's this, ma'am: are you meaning to turn us over to Porfiry Vladimirych?'

'It's never entered my head.'

'That's as well, ma'am. For we were going to stand fast against you, if you did. We thought that if so be we're set under the master at Golovlevo, then we'd all ask to retire.'

'Why is that? Is Uncle really so terrible?'

'He's not so terrible, but he grinds you down. His tongue's too loose. Why, with his talk he can fester a man's soul!'

Anninka could not help smiling. It was precisely some kind

of pus that oozed forth in Judas's effusions. It was no ordinary prattle, it was a festering sore discharging a constant stream of pus.

'And have you decided what you will do with yourself, ma'am?' Fedulych asked further.

'And what is it that I'm supposed to be "deciding"?' Anninka asked in some embarrassment, sensing that here too she would have to endure discourses on the subject of her 'treasure'.

'Do you mean you're not going to stop being an actress?'

'No, I'm not . . . that is, I haven't yet thought about it . . . But what's wrong with my earning a living as best I can?'

'What's right with it! Travelling round fairs with a mandolin, entertaining drunks! After all—you're a lady!'

Anninka made no reply, only frowned. She was tormented by the question that pounded in her head: Lord! When shall I get away from here?

'Of course, you'll know best what you should do, but we were thinking as you would come back to us here. It's a warm house, plenty of space—room there to play "catch" if you so wanted. Your granny, now departed, she set it up handsome! And if you got bored, why, we could hitch up the sledge, or in summer you could go mushrooming in the woods.'

'There's all kinds of mushrooms here,' mumbled Afimyushka beguilingly. 'There's milk caps, white caps, sponge caps—tons of them!'

Anninka leant her elbows on the table and tried not to listen.

'There's a girl here, she was in service in Petersburg,' Fedulych went on mercilessly, 'and she said as how actresses have all got to have a ticket and show it every month at the police-station.'

Anninka was stung: the whole day long she had heard nothing but *this*!

'Fedulych!' she burst out. 'What have I done to you? Do you really take pleasure in insulting me?'

She had had enough. She felt she was choking and that one more word and she would break down.

ONE day, not long before the disastrous affair of Petenka, Arina Petrovna observed during one of her visits to Golovlevo that Evprakseyushka seemed to have filled out in figure. Trained as she was in the practical school of serfdom, when the pregnancies of servant-girls were the subject of close—and often diverting—enquiry and considered to be practically an item of income, Arina Petrovna had a sharp and infallible eye for such things, and she had only to let her glance rest for a moment on Evprakseyushka's waist for the latter to hide her deeply blushing face in full acknowledgement of her guilt, with never a word uttered.

'Come on, Miss, come on! Look at me! Expecting are you?' the wily old woman interrogated the peccant dove; but there was no reproach in her voice, on the contrary, her tone was jocular, almost cheery, as if she had caught a whiff of the good old times.

Evprakseyushka, both ashamed and pleased with herself, said nothing; only her cheeks blushed an ever deeper shade of scarlet beneath the inquisitorial gaze of Arina Petrovna.

'So that's it! I saw yesterday the way you were holding yourself in! Strutting about, putting on you're all you should be! But you can't fool me! I can tell what you young maids have been up to a mile away. Something the wind blew in, was it? How far are you gone? Own up now! Tell me all about it!'

There followed a detailed interrogation and a no less detailed account of the matter. When were the first signs? Had she fixed on a midwife? Did Porfiry know of the happy event in store for him? Was Evprakseyushka taking care of herself and not lifting heavy weights? And so on. It turned out that Evprakseyushka was in her fifth month; that she had not so far fixed on a midwife; that Porfiry Vladimirych, though he had been informed, had said nothing, but merely placed his hands palm to palm, whispered inaudibly, and looked up at the icon as a sign that all things come from God and that he, our Lord in Heaven, would himself make full provision; and that, finally, Evprakseyushka had indeed without thinking lifted up the samovar and felt a sudden pang inside her.

'Really, you must be out of your minds!' bemoaned Arina Petrovna on hearing these admissions. 'I can see I'll have to take a hand in it myself! Of all things—five months gone and not even fixed the midwife! Why, you stupid, you might at least have got Ulitka to have a look at you!'

'I was going to, but the master don't that much care for . . .'

'Poppycock, ma'am, poppycock! If Ulitka's in the master's bad books, that's neither here nor there. In *this* matter he's of no account. We're not going to go making up to her, are we? No, there's no question about it, I'll have to take a hand in this myself!'

Arina Petrovna was about to indulge in a fit of melancholy and take advantage of the situation to complain that even now, in her old age, she had still to bear all the burdens of family life; however, the subject of conversation was so much to her liking that she only smacked her lips and continued:

'Now, ma'am, you'll have to make a clean breast of it! You must pay the price for your pleasures. Just see how you like it! I've raised three sons and a daughter and buried five infants besides—I know what it means! These menfolk, they give you plenty to worry about up here!' she added, tapping her knuckles on the back of her head.

A thought suddenly dawned on her.

'Merciful heavens! Won't that have been on a fast-day eve? Hold on, wait a minute! I'll reckon it out.'

They began counting on their fingers; they counted once, twice, and a third time—and it did indeed come out precisely on the eve of a fast-day.

'Well, I never did! So much for his piety! Oh, you just wait, I'll tease him! Our man of prayer getting into a scrape like that! I'll tease him all right, you see if I don't!' the old woman jested.

And, indeed, that evening at tea Arina Petrovna chaffed Judas in the presence of Evprakseyushka.

'Now then, meek and mild, what's this you've been up to! Or has your duchess got something the wind blew in? I'm surprised at you!'

At first, Judas winced squeamishly at his mother's jokes, but, seeing that Arina Petrovna was speaking as 'kith and kin' and 'in good part', he gradually became merrier himself.

'Ah, Mother dear, what a one you are! You really are a mischief!' he responded, jesting in turn; but, as was his wont, evading the real subject of the family conversation.

'What do you mean, I'm a "mischief"! We've got to talk this over seriously! It's an important matter, this! It is a "mystery", that's a fact. Not in the proper way, maybe, but still . . . No, we must give it careful thought, *very* careful thought! What do you think? Will you have her confined here or take her into the town?'

'I don't know, Mother dear, I don't know a thing!' said Porfiry Vladimirych evasively. 'You are a mischief! You really are!'

'Just you wait then, Miss! You and I will talk this over in our own good time! How and what—we'll work it all out. As for these menfolk—well! all they want is to have their way with us, and we women are left to answer for them as best we can!'

Having made her discovery, Arina Petrovna was in her element: the whole evening through she talked to Evprakseyushka, unable to stop. There was even a flush in her cheeks and a youthful sparkle in her eyes.

'Well, Missy, and what do you think? It's God's work, that's what it is,' she persisted, 'for it's right, even if it isn't regular . . . But just you look out! If it really was the day before a fast, then Lord save you! I'll make such sport of you I'll see you to kingdom come!'

Ulitushka was also summoned to share in their deliberations. First, they discussed all the ins and outs of the matter in hand, whether an enema should be given or the stomach rubbed with soothing cream, but they then got back to their favourite topic and began reckoning on their fingers—and still it came out precisely on a fast-day! Evprakseyushka blushed scarlet as a poppy, but did not deny it, referring instead to her dependent situation.

'I can't help it!' she said. 'It's for me to do as the master wants! And if the master commands—how can the likes of me not do his bidding!'

'Come on now, you sly one! Don't give us that!' teased Arina Petrovna. 'I'm sure you . . .'

The women, in short, took to the matter with great relish. Arina Petrovna recalled a number of instances from her own past and, of course, did not fail to recount them. First she told them of her pregnancies: how she had suffered with Booby Stepka, how, when expecting Pavel Vladimirych, she had travelled by post-chaise to Moscow so as not to miss the auctioning of Dubrovino and had then very nearly expired as a result, and so on, and so on. All her confinements had been remarkable in some way: only one had been easy—and that was when Judas was born.

'I didn't feel the least bit burdened,' she said. 'I used to sit and think to myself: Lord, can I really be expecting? And when my time came, I just lay down on the bed for a minute, and how it came about I don't know, but all at once there I was—delivered! He was the easiest one I had—far and away the easiest!'

Then she went on to tales about the servant-girls: how many of them she had 'caught out' herself, how many she had detected with the aid of her trusted agents, chiefly Ulitushka. The old woman's mind retained these memories with astonishing clarity. In the whole of her grey past, totally absorbed as it had been with money-grubbing on the small scale and the large, the detection of concupiscent servant-girls was the one element of romance that had ever touched a living chord in her.

It was like the fiction section in some boring journal, in which the reader, expecting to encounter learned articles concerning dry fogs or the burial-place of Ovid, suddenly reads instead: 'See, the dashing troika speeds . . .'* The denouement of these artless romances of the maids' room was generally very harsh, even inhuman (the guilty maid was packed off to be married in some distant village—invariably to a widowed peasant with a large family; her guilty partner was reduced to the rank of herdsman or sent off to soldier as a conscript); but the memory of these denouements had somehow faded (with regard to their own past conduct the memory of the 'cultivated' class* is generally lenient), though the actual process by which an 'amorous intrigue' was detected came still vividly to mind. And well it might! In those days of yore this process was attended by the same gripping interest as we now experience reading a serial novel, in which the author, instead of consummating at once the mutual desires of hero and heroine, at the crucial moment puts a full-stop and writes: 'To be continued.'

'I had trouble with them, I can tell you!' Arina Petrovna recounted. 'Some would hold out right to the end, thinking they could hoodwink me. But you won't outsmart me, my sweetheart! I'm an old hand at this game!' she added almost sternly, as though actually addressing a threat to someone.

Finally, there were tales of pregnancies belonging to what might be termed the 'political' category, in which Arina Petrovna's role had been not that of chastiser, but of harbourer and accessory.

Her father, for instance, Petr Ivanych, a decrepit old man of seventy, had also had his 'lady', who was also suddenly in the family way, and higher considerations required that the old man should know nothing of this offspring. As ill luck would have it, Arina Petrovna at the time was at loggerheads with her brother, Petr Petrovich, and he, for some political reasons, was keeping an eye on the pregnancy and intended to open the old man's eyes concerning his 'lady'.

'And what do you think! We carried the whole thing off practically under his very nose! Father was asleep in the bedroom, and we were hard at it just next door! It was all whispers and tiptoes, I can tell you! With my own hands I covered her mouth to stop her crying out and with my own hands I cleared away the linen too, and her little boy—a pretty, lusty baby he was—I saw to him as well: hired a cab and took him off to the Foundlings' Home. The week after, when my brother heard of it, he was all agog at what that sister of his had done!'

There was another 'political' pregnancy that had to do with her sister-in-law, Varvara Mikhailovna. Her husband had gone off to fight the Turks, and she must go and be careless. So she rushed like a scalded cat to Golovlevo, begging Arina Petrovna to save her.

'Well, though we were on bad terms at the time, I made no show of it: I gave her good welcome, comforted her, calmed her down, and by making out she was just on a visit I carried it off so well that her husband went to his grave without ever knowing.'

Thus Arina Petrovna told her tales and, in truth, rarely has a story-teller had such attentive listeners. Evprakseyushka hung on every word, as if before her very eyes some wonderful fairy-tale was unfolding; as for Ulitushka, she, having been an accomplice in most of the events narrated, simply smacked her lips.

Ulitushka had also blossomed forth and was at ease. She had had a troubled life. From her early years she had been consumed by a servile ambition, had dreamed night and day of serving her masters and ruling her fellow-servants—but all to no avail. As soon as she got her foot on a higher rung of the ladder, some unseen force would displace her and push her back to the nether depths. She had to perfection all the qualities desired in a helpful servant: she was spiteful, back-biting, and ever ready to betray, but she suffered also from a too ready compliancy, which caused all her spite to be of no effect. In times gone by Arina Petrovna had readily made use of her when she had some secret investigation to carry out in the maids' room or, in general, any shady affair to bring off, but she never appreciated her services or allowed her any position of real consequence. As a result, Ulitka complained and vented her spite; but no heed was paid to her complaints, since everyone knew that Ulitka was an ill-tempered wench, who one moment would be damning you to eternity and the next, if you but beckoned her with a finger, would come running and fawning to do your bidding. And so she had gone on through life, all the time trying to advance herself, but never achieving anything, until the disappearance of serfdom had finally put an end to her servile ambitions.

In her youth there had even been an episode which gave her very serious hopes. During one of his stays in Golovlevo Porfiry Vladimirych entered into a liaison with her and, according to Golovlevo legend, had even had a child by her, which caused him for a long time to be in Arina Petrovna's bad books. Whether this liaison continued during Judas's subsequent visits to the paternal home is not known; in any case, when Porfiry Vladimirych came to live permanently in Golovlevo, Ulitushka's aspirations were shattered in the most galling way. As soon as Judas arrived, she rushed to him with a pack of gossip, in which Arina Petrovna was practically accused of swindling him; but, though the 'master' listened approvingly to the gossip, he looked at her coldly and did not in any way recall her past 'services'. Disappointed in her expectations and offended, Ulitushka switched her allegiance to Dubrovino, where Pavel Vladimirych in his hatred for brother Porfiry readily took her in and even made her his housekeeper. Here her stock seemed to recover. Pavel Vladimirych sat in the mezzanine drinking away, glass after glass, while she from morning till night briskly bustled about the stores and cellars, jingling her keys and cursing aloud, and even came to get at odds with Arina Petrovna, whom she nearly drove to the grave.

But Ulitushka was too fond of all kind of treachery to enjoy in tranquillity the good life that had befallen her. It was just at the time when Pavel Vladimirych was drinking so heavily that certain hopes could now be entertained regarding the outcome of his abandoned drunkenness. Porfiry Vladimirych realized that in this situation Ulitushka was an inestimable treasure—and once more with a finger he beckoned her. She was given instructions from Golovlevo not to leave the cherished victim's side, to contradict him in nothing, even in his hatred for brother Porfiry, and especially, by whatever means, to ward off any interference from Arina Petrovna. This was one of those villainies Judas performed as kith and kin, not so much after mature consideration as just without thinking, as a perfectly normal undertaking. Needless to say, Ulitushka fulfilled her commission punctiliously. Pavel Vladimirych did not cease to hate his brother, but the more he hated, the more he drank and the less he was capable of listening to anything Arina Petrovna had to say concerning his 'arrangements'. Every gesture, every word of the dying man was known at once in Golovlevo, so that Judas could, with full knowledge of how things stood, determine the moment when he should step from the wings and take the stage as true master of the situation which he himself had created. And of this he had taken advantage—by descending on Dubrovino at the precise moment when it fell, so to speak, of itself into his hands.

For this service Porfiry Vladimirych presented Ulitushka with a length of woollen material for a dress, but still kept her at a distance. Once more Ulitushka was cast down from the heights of grandeur into the nether depths, and this time it seemed that nobody would ever beckon her forth again.

As a special favour for 'having tended my brother in his last moments' Judas allotted her a corner in the cottage which served as a general haven for meritorious house-serfs who remained after the abolition of serfdom. There Ulitushka finally submitted to her lot—so that when Porfiry Vladimirych bestowed his favours on Evprakseyushka, she not only showed no sign of fractiousness, but was even the first to call and pay her respects to the 'master's lady' and kiss her on the shoulder.

Then suddenly, just when she saw herself that she was spurned and forgotten, fortune smiled on her again: Evprakseyushka became pregnant. It was remembered that somewhere in the servants' quarters there was 'just the person'—who was duly beckoned. True, it was not the 'master' himself who did the beckoning, but it was quite sufficient that he did not oppose it. Ulitushka marked her entry into the manor-house by relieving Evprakseyushka of the samovar and, with a slight jut of the hip, strutting with it into the dining-room, where Porfiry Vladimirych was just then sitting. And the 'master' said not a word. She thought he even smiled when, on another occasion, she met him in the passage while carrying the same samovar and shouted as she approached:

'Careful, master! Mind I don't scald you!'

Summoned by Arina Petrovna to the family council, Ulitushka for a time made a show of reluctance and would not sit down. But when Arina Petrovna cried sharply but amiably:

'Come on now, sit down, sit down! There's no call to carry on like that! The Tsar's made us all equal now—so sit you down!' —she did sit: subdued at first, but later giving free rein to her tongue.

This woman had her reminiscences too. Accumulated in her memory was a quantity of purulent matter relating to practices in the old days of serfdom. Apart from fulfilling delicate commissions to detect concupiscence among the maids, Ulitushka had played the part of apothecary and physician to the Golovlev household. The number of mustard-plasters, bleeding-bowls, and enemas she had applied in her lifetime—and especially enemas! She had given enemas to the old master, Vladimir Mikhailych, and to the old mistress, Arina Petrovna, and to each and every one of the young masters—and had thereof the most grateful memories. And now for these memories there was offered almost limitless scope . . .

The Golovlevo house came somehow mysteriously to life. Arina Petrovna would now and then come over from Pogorelka to visit her 'good son', and under her supervision preparations went actively ahead for the—as yet still unnamed event. After evening tea all three women retired to Evprakseyushka's room, where they indulged themselves with home-made jam, played 'donkey', and sat up till dawn recalling past memories, which on occasion caused the master's 'lady' to blush violently. Every slightest incident was a pretext for more and more stories. If Evprakseyushka served raspberry jam, Arina Petrovna would tell how, when she was expecting her daughter Sonya, she could not stand even the smell of raspberries.

'As soon as anybody brought some into the house I could smell them! And I'd holler out "Take those damnation raspberries out! Take them away!" Later though, when I was brought to bed, I was all right again and liked them well as ever.'

If Evprakseyushka brought out some caviare, Arina Petrovna would recall some incident concerning caviare too.

'I once had an experience with caviare—most odd it was! I was just a month or two married at the time, when suddenly I had this craving for caviare, I just had to have it. I'd sneak off to the pantry and eat and eat! I said, though, to my goodman "Why is it, Vladimir Mikhailych," I said, "that I keep on eating caviare?" And he just smiled and said "Why, my dear, you're expecting." And true enough—exactly nine months later I was brought to bed and had Booby Stepka!'

Meanwhile Porfiry Vladimirych continued to regard Evprakseyushka's pregnancy as enigmatically as ever and never once openly declared his own involvement in the matter. This quite naturally acted as a constraint on the womenfolk, curbing their effusions, and Judas, as a result, was almost totally ignored and sent packing whenever he dropped in at Evprakseyushka's room of an evening.

'Be off with you, be off, you young buck!' Arina Petrovna would say. 'You've done your bit, now it's women's work! It's our turn for the fun!'

Judas meekly retreated and, though he did not miss the chance to complain to dear Mother that she had turned against him, he was inwardly well content that they did not bother him and that Arina Petrovna was involving herself so keenly in this, for him, awkward situation. Had she not done so, heaven knows what he would have to have done in order to hush up this abominable business, the very thought of which caused him to wince and spit in disgust. But now, with Arina Petrovna's experience and Ulitushka's dexterity, he hoped that the 'disaster' would pass off without becoming common knowledge and that perhaps he himself might only learn of its outcome when all was over.

Porfiry Vladimirych's calculations, however, were not borne out by events. First, there was the disaster with Petenka, and not long after that there was the death of Arina Petrovna. He was left to pay the score himself, and without hope of working some shabby ploy to save himself. He could not dispatch Evprakseyushka back to her family 'for waywardness' because, owing to Arina Petrovna's involvement, the matter had gone too far and everyone knew of it. Nor was there much hope to be placed in the zeal of Ulitushka, since, smart wench though she was, trusting yourself to her could well land you in trouble with the investigating attorney. For the first time in his life Judas seriously and sincerely bemoaned his isolation, for the first time he had some inkling that the people around him were not simply pawns fit only to be exploited by him.

'What would it have cost her to wait a shade longer?' he thought reproachfully in private of his dear mother. 'She'd have arranged it all sensibly and quietly, and that would have been that, bless her! But her time came—it can't be helped! Grieve as we might for the old soul, if such be the will of God, then our tears and doctors and medicines and we ourselves are all powerless against it! She lived her life and enjoyed what it gave. She went through life as mistress of her property and left her children as masters. She lived her life—and that is that.'

And, as was usual, his niggling mind, which never cared to dwell on any matter posing practical difficulties, at once turned to a simpler topic, one on which he could prattle without hindrance and without end.

'And how well she died! Only to the righteous is such an end vouchsafed!' he lied to himself, though unaware in fact if it was lie or truth. 'No pain, no disquiet—just like that! She gave a sigh and then we saw that she was gone! Ah, Mother, Mother dear! She had a smile on her face and colour in her cheek! And her hand was held as if in blessing, then she closed her eyes . . . and adieu!'

And suddenly, in the full flow of his plaintive words, he feels again the stabbing pang . . . Again this abominable business . . . pshaw! pshaw! pshaw! After all, what would it have cost dear Mother to wait a shade longer! Another month, that was all, even less—and she had to go and die!

For a time he tried to fob off Ulitushka's questions in the same way he had those of his dear mother: 'I don't know! I don't know a thing!' But a woman as brazen as Ulitushka, and one, moreover, who had sensed the power she possessed, was not so lightly treated in this way.

'Am I the one who knows then? Am I the one who swelled her smock?'—thus at the outset she stopped him short and brought it home to him that his calculation of combining successfully the role of fornicator with that of independent observer of the fruits of his fornication was totally confounded.

The disaster loomed ever nearer, inescapable, palpable almost. It pursued him every minute of the day and, worst of all, paralysed his capacity for thinking empty thoughts. He strove every way to banish it from his mind, to drown it in a flood of empty words, but in this he was only partly successful. He sought to take refuge in the unquestionability of the laws of Divine Providence and, as was his custom, turned the subject into a skein which he went on endlessly unwinding, at the same time entwining with it the parable of the hair which falls not from a man's head and the story of the house built on sand; but just as his empty thoughts went cascading freely one after another to vanish into some mysterious abyss, just as the unwinding of the skein seemed set to go on for ever—suddenly from nowhere a single word irrupted to snap the thread in two! Alas! the word was 'fornication', signifying a deed which Judas would not admit even to himself.

And now, when, after these vain attempts to forget and expunge, it was at last becoming clear that he was caught, he was thrown into a state of melancholy. He took to pacing the room, thinking of nothing, feeling only the nagging ache and trepidation within him.

This was an entirely new, never before encountered curb to his thinking of empty thoughts. Until now, whatever course his vacuous fancy chose to follow, it always encountered an unbounded space in which all manner of expedients were ready to hand. Even the fate of Volodka and Petka, even the death of Arina Petrovna were no impediment to his empty thoughts. These events were everyday, acknowledged facts and there existed an acknowledged and long-established framework to take account of them. Requiems, forty-days prayers for the dead, funeral dinners, etc.—all this he had, according to custom, done as was fitting and he had thus, so to speak, justified himself in the eyes of the world and of Providence. But fornication . . . what was that? It was, after all, the denunciation of his whole life, the exposure of its inner falsehood! Even though, before, people had regarded him as a pettifogger, yes, even perhaps a 'bloodsucker', there was such slight juridical basis for this common gossip that he could confidently retort: 'Prove it!' But now, suddenly . . . fornicator! A proved and undoubted fornicator (he had not even taken any *measures*—thanks to Arina Petrovna (Ah! Mother! Mother!), had not even told any timely lies), and then too 'on the eve of a fast' . . . Pshaw! pshaw! pshaw!

In these inner dialogues with himself, confused though their content was, there was to be noted even something akin to the awakening of conscience. The question was, though: would Judas go further along this path or would, after all, the empty workings of his mind perform their usual service and provide him with some fresh loophole through which he might, as ever, escape unscathed?

While Judas was thus wilting beneath the burden of his empty heart, in Evprakseyushka a quite unexpected transformation was gradually taking place. Impending motherhood had evidently loosened the mental bonds which had constricted her. Until now she had been indifferent to everything and had regarded Porfiry Vladimirych as 'the master' to whom she was merely a subordinate. Now, for the first time, she had come to realize something: that she had in life some concern of her own, in which she was the mistress and in which nobody could put upon her with impunity. As a result, even in the expression of her face, which was normally dull and ungainly, there was now a spark of intelligence and light.

The death of Arina Petrovna was the first event in her dimly conscious life to have a sobering effect on her. However curious the attitude of the old mistress to Evprakseyushka's impending motherhood was, still there was evident in it some undoubted sympathy, and not just the vile squeamish evasiveness which she encountered in Judas. And so Evprakseyushka came to see in Arina Petrovna a kind of champion, as if she sensed that some attack was being prepared against her. This presentiment of attack dogged her the more persistently because it was not consciously envisaged, but simply felt, filling her whole being with a constant depressing unease. Mentally she had no clear understanding of whence the attack would come or what its nature would be; but so keenly were her senses alerted that at the sight of Judas she felt an unaccountable fear. Yes, it would come from there!—was the response that echoed deep inside her. It would come from there, from him—that coffinful of dust to whom she had hitherto been assigned as a simple hireling and who by some miracle had now become the father and lord of *her* child! The feeling evoked in her by this thought was something close to hatred, and hatred it would most certainly have become, if it had not been diverted by the concern shown her by Arina Petrovna, whose kindly chatter left her no time to be pensive.

But first Arina Petrovna removed to Pogorelka and then she passed away for ever. A feeling of dread came over Evprakseyushka.

The silence into which the house of Golovlevo had now sunk was broken only by the rustling which proclaimed that Judas, with the skirts of his dressing-gown gathered in his hand, was prowling about the passage and listening at doors. Occasionally one of the servants would come in from outside, bang the door of the maids' room, and silence would again come stealing in from every corner—a silence which filled one's being with a superstitious, agonizing melancholy. And since Evprakseyushka was now near her time, she did not even have the distraction of the domestic chores which in the past had left her so exhausted in body that by evening she was ready to drop. She tried being affectionate with Porfiry Vladimirych, but each time her attempts resulted in short but sharp scenes which even her primitive nature found painful. She therefore had to sit doing nothing and thinking—that is, feeling alarmed. And her cause for alarm grew with every passing day, for the death of Arina Petrovna had given Ulitushka a free hand and introduced into the house of Golovlevo a new element—gossip, which now became the sole living concern in which Judas's spirit found repose.

Ulitushka realized that Porfiry Vladimirych was being a coward and that in this empty-hearted, meretricious nature cowardice was very close to hatred. Besides which, she knew perfectly well that Porfiry Vladimirych was incapable not merely of affection, but even of simple pity for anyone; she knew that he kept Evprakseyushka solely because it was due to her that his domestic routine went smoothly, never departing from its appointed course. Armed with these basic facts, Ulitushka had every possibility to feed and foster the hatred that seethed in Judas's heart each time he was reminded of the 'disaster' to come.

Before long Evprakseyushka was thoroughly enmeshed in a whole net of gossip. Ulitushka would 'report' from time to time to the master. She would come for instance to complain of the reckless management of the household stores.

'A mighty quantity of goods seems to get used up here, master! I was down in the cellar recently to fetch some salt beef: it's not that long since a new tub was started, but when I looked there was only two or three pieces left in the bottom!'

'Really?' said Judas, fixing her with his gaze.

'If I hadn't seen it with my own eyes, I'd never have believed it! It's a wonder to me where it all goes! Butter, meal, cucumbers —everything! In other houses they give the servants goose-dripping with their kasha—and that's that!—but here it's always with butter, good dairy butter!'

'Really?' said Porfiry Vladimirych, almost in alarm.

Or she would come and suddenly report on the master's linen.

'You ought to put a stop to Evprakseyushka, master. Of course, she's but a young maid and there's a lot she don't know, but just take what she's done with the linen . . . A whole pile of it she's used up to make sheets and napkins, and all fine linen too!'

In response, Porfiry Vladimirych merely flashed his eyes, though at her words his empty heart sank within him.

'Naturally, she's concerned for the baby!' Ulitushka went on in her honeyed voice. 'She thinks it's something out of this world —as if she was giving birth to a baby prince! Though in *her* station in life you'd think the baby could sleep well enough on hemp sheets!'

Sometimes she simply baited Judas.

'I've been meaning to ask you, master,' she began, 'What do you intend doing with the baby? Are you going to make him your son or will you send him off like the others to the Foundlings' . . .'

But as Ulitushka began her question Porfiry Vladimirych gave her such a black look that she fell silent.

And thus, in the midst of this simmering hatred, the moment drew ever nearer when the appearance in the world of a tiny, wailing 'servant of God' would bring some resolution to the moral turmoil reigning in the house of Golovlevo and would add simultaneously yet one more to the number of all those other wailing 'servants of God' who people the Universe.

It is past six in the evening. Porfiry Vladimirych has already taken his after-dinner nap and is sitting in his study covering sheets of paper with arithmetical calculations. On this occasion, the question concerning him is how much money he would now have if Arina Petrovna had not herself appropriated the hundred roubles in assignats given to him at birth by grandfather Petr Ivanych, but instead invested it at interest on behalf of the infant Porfiry? It did not come to much, however: a mere eight hundred assignat roubles.

'It may not be a large sum,' Judas pursued his idle thoughts, 'but it would be good to know it was there for a rainy day. You could draw on it when it's wanted. No need to ask anybody, no need to supplicate—you could draw on what's yours, your very own, your grandfather's gift. Ah, Mother, Mother dear! Whatever possessed you to do such a reckless thing!'

Alas, Porfiry Vladimirych had recovered from the alarms which had so recently paralysed his capacity for idle thinking. Those odd glimmerings of conscience which had been aroused in him by the difficulties posed by Evprakseyushka's pregnancy and Arina Petrovna's untimely death had gradually died away. In this too his empty thinking had come, as usual, to the rescue, and by dint of prodigious effort Judas was able in the end to sink all thought of the 'disaster' in an abyss of empty words. It cannot be said that he came to any conscious decision, but the old favoured formula had somehow spontaneously come to mind: 'I know nothing, I permit nothing, I allow nothing!'—that formula to which in case of difficulty he always had recourse and which now promptly put an end to the inner turmoil that had temporarily disturbed him. He now regarded the impending birth as a matter which was no concern of his and tried therefore to look impassive and impervious. He virtually ignored Evprakseyushka and did not even refer to her by name—if he had occasion to ask about her, he would frame the question: 'And what about *her*? Is she still unwell?' In short, he so demonstrated his strength that even Ulitushka, who in the school of serfdom had acquired no small skill in the art of reading hearts, realized that there was no contending with a man who was so ready and so willing to adapt to any situation.

The house of Golovlevo is sunk in darkness; only in the master's study and in the distant side-room occupied by Evprakseyushka is there any glimmer of light. In Judas's apartments all is quiet, except for the clicking of the beads of the counting-frame and the scratching of the pencil with which Porfiry Vladimirych writes down his calculations. All at once the general silence in the study is broken by a distant, but still heart-rending groan. Judas shudders; his lips quiver for a moment; his pencil makes a false stroke.

'One hundred and twenty-one roubles and twelve roubles ten kopeks . . .' whispers Porfiry Vladimirych, struggling to overcome the unpleasant impression created by the groaning.

But the groans occur ever more frequently and become in the end disturbing. It is now so difficult to work that Judas leaves his desk. At first, he walks about the room, trying not to hear, but curiosity gradually gets the better of his empty heart. He quietly eases open the study door, pokes his head into the darkness of the next room, and, in expectant posture, listens.

'Oh dear! They seem to have forgotten to light the lamp before "Assuage my sorrows" ',* it suddenly strikes him.

But now there was the sound of hurrying, troubled footsteps in the passage. Porfiry Vladimirych immediately popped his head back inside the study, carefully closed the door, and scurried on tiptoe to the icon. A second later he was already in proper state, so that when the door burst open and Ulitushka came running into the room, she found him at prayer with his hands pressed together.

'Our Evprakseyushka—she's like to give up the ghost!' declared Ulitushka, caring nothing about disturbing Judas's devotions.

But Judas did not even turn round—he merely worked his lips more rapidly and, instead of replying, waved a hand in the air as if warding off some bothersome fly.

'What are you waving about like that for? Evprakseyushka—she's in a bad way, I tell you! She may well die!' Ulitushka bluntly persisted.

This time Judas did turn round, but his face bore such a tranquil, unctuous expression, as if he had just then, in contemplation of the divinity, set aside all earthly cares and could not at all understand why he should be disturbed.

'Sin though it is to give rebuke after praying, still, as a man, I cannot forbear to complain: how many times have I asked that

I should not be disturbed when I'm at prayer!' he said in a tone fitting to his devotional mood, though allowing himself a shake of the head by way of Christian reproach. 'Well, what else is it?'

'What else do you expect: Evprakseyushka—she's in agony, she can't produce the baby! As if you never knew . . . You! . . . At least you could go and see!'

'Why should I? Am I a doctor, then? Is there some advice I can give? I know nothing, nothing of your affairs! I know we have a sick woman in the house, but I confess that I've not been prompted to discover what her ailment is or how she came by it! If her case is serious, send for the priest—that is something I can recommend! You send for the priest, join with him in prayer, light up the icon-lamps . . . then afterwards the Father and I will take a glass of tea!'

Porfiry Vladimirych was highly satisfied that in this critical moment he had expressed himself so categorically. He looked at Ulitushka blithely, confidently, as if to say: There now, get the better of me if you can! Even Ulitushka was at a loss when confronted with such equability.

'You ought to come and see, though!' she repeated once more.

'I shan't come, because there's no reason for it. If there was any cause, I'd come without your asking. If there's need—for a cause —to go five miles, I'll go five miles; or if it's ten miles, I'll go ten! It might be freezing and snowing, but still I'll go! Because I know it's for a cause and you've got to go!'

It seemed to Ulitushka that she was asleep and that this was Satan himself expatiating to her in a dream.

'Now to send for the priest is a good thing. There's cause for it. Prayer—do you know what the Scripture says about prayer? "Prayer healeth the sick"—that's what it says! So you go and attend to it! Send for the priest, pray together . . . and I'll pray at the same time. You pray there in the oratory, and I'll be here in my study asking God to be merciful . . . We'll join strength— you there and me here—and in no time our prayers will be heard!'

The priest was sent for, but by the time he arrived Evprakse-yushka had after much agony and torment been delivered of her child. Porfiry Vladimirych could tell from the sudden scurrying and banging of doors that came from the direction of the maids' room that some decisive event had occurred. And, indeed, in a few minutes steps were again heard hurrying along the passage and Ulitushka came running full tilt into the study, bearing in her arms a tiny mortal wrapped in linen.

'There now! Just you look!' she pronounced triumphantly, lifting the baby right up to Porfiry Vladimirych's face.

Judas seemed for a moment uncertain, his body even leant forward and a spark glinted in his eyes. But it was only for a moment, for he then turned squeamishly away from the infant and flapped his hands at it.

'No! No! I'm afraid of them . . . I don't like them! Go away . . . go away!' he muttered, his face expressing utter aversion.

'You might ask at least if it's a boy or a girl,' Ulitushka chided him.

'No! No! . . . there's no need . . . it's no concern of mine! It's your affair, all this, and I don't know anything about it . . . I don't know and I don't need to know . . . For mercy's sake, leave me alone! Go away!'

Once again it was a dream, once again Satan . . . it was too much for Ulitushka.

'How would it be if I dropped him on your couch and left you to nurse him yourself!' she threatened.

But Judas was not a man to be rattled. While Ulitushka was uttering her threat, he had already turned to the icons and meekly lifted up his hands. Evidently he was beseeching God to forgive all men—those who sinned 'wittingly and unwittingly' and those who sinned 'by thought, word, and deed', and also giving thanks that he was not himself a thief or a usurer or a fornicator, and that God in his mercy had set him in the path of righteousness. Even his nose quivered with pious emotion—at which Ulitushka, who was watching him, spat in disgust and went.

'There, God has taken one Volodka from me—and given me another!' the untimely thought suddenly struck him, but he was immediately aware of this mental vagary and said inwardly: Pshaw! Pshaw! Pshaw!

The priest came, intoned, and censed. Judas, hearing the

chanter singing 'Zealous Intercessor', was moved to join in and took up the strain. Again Ulitushka came running, to shout in at the door:

'He's to be called Vladimir!'

The strange coincidence of this with his own recent mental aberration which had also recalled the dead Volodka touched Judas. He saw in it the will of God and this time did not spit in disgust, but said to himself:

'God be praised then! He has taken one Volodka and given me another! You lose a thing in one place and think it's gone forever, and then elsewhere God pays you back an hundredfold!'

Finally, it was announced that tea was served and the priest was awaiting him in the dining-room. Porfiry Vladimirych was now quite calm and filled with pious sentiment. Father Aleksandr was, indeed, already sitting in the dining-room waiting for Porfiry Vladimirych. The Golovlevo priest was a politic man who tried to maintain a worldly tone in his dealings with Judas; he knew full well though that each week and at all the main festivals a Vigil Service was held at the manor and that every first day of the month there were intercessions too—all of which brought to the parish a good hundred roubles in income each year. Apart from this, he was aware that the boundaries of the church land were still not properly defined and more than once, driving past the priest's glebe, Judas had remarked: 'A nice little meadow that!' For this reason the worldly manner of the priest contained no small element of 'fear of the Jews',* which found expression in his attempting, whenever he met Porfiry Vladimirych, to be bright and cheerful (however little cause there was for it), and when in conversation Porfiry Vladimirych ventured to propound certain heresies concerning the ways of Providence, the future life, and so forth, the priest, while not directly approving them, regarded them none the less not as sacrilege or blasphemy, but merely the natural audacity of mind to be expected from the gentry class.

When Judas came into the room, the priest hastily gave him his blessing and even more hastily drew back his hand, as if fearing the Bloodsucker might bite it. He was about to congratulate his spiritual son on the birth of Vladimir, but, uncertain yet what Judas's attitude to the event might be, he cautiously refrained.

'It's drizzling sleet outside,' the priest began. 'Popular belief (superstitious though it is in some measure) says such weather is a sign of thaw.'

'Or frost too, perhaps: there are we thinking it means thaw, but God may go and send us frost!' rejoined Judas, fussily and even almost cheerfully sitting down at the tea-table, where on this occasion the footman Prokhor was doing the honours.

'True it is that often man in his fancies seeks to attain the unattainable and to accede to the inaccessible: and finds for himself therein cause for regret or, indeed, affliction.'

'The very reason why we should concern ourselves less with signs and portents and be content with what God sends us. If God sends us warmth, we'll be glad of the warmth; if God sends us frost, we'll be happy with frost! We'll stoke the stoves up hotter, those who travel will wrap themselves up snugger—and we'll all be nice and warm!'

'Very true.'

'Many people these days like to cavil and quibble: this is wrong, that's not to their liking, something else should be done another way—well, I don't care for it. I don't read signs myself and I don't approve of it in others. It's highmindedness—that's what I think of it!'

'Also very true.'

'We are all here wayfarers: that's how I see myself. To have a sup of tea, a light repast . . . that we're allowed! For God has given us a body and other parts . . . Even the government doesn't forbid it: eat by all means—as long as you keep a bridle on your tongue!'

'Very true again,' grunted the priest as he jubilantly tapped his saucer with the bottom of his emptied tea-glass.

'I consider that man is given his mind not in order to probe the unknown, but in order to desist from sin. For instance, if I should feel some infirmity or temptation of the flesh and call upon my mind to show me how this infirmity might be overcome—then I act rightly. For on such occasions the mind can indeed give benefit.'

'Faith, though, still more,' said the priest, correcting him slightly.

'Faith and mind have their different functions. Faith points to the object, the mind seeks ways to attain it. It probes and prods, it strays this way and that and will make the while some beneficial discovery. Medicaments, for instance—herbs, plasters, decoctions —they are all discoveries and inventions of the mind. But it must all accord with faith and be for the benefit and not the harm of man.'

'That, too, is not to be denied.'

'I read a book once, Father, which said just that: the ministrations of the mind, if it be directed by faith, should in no wise be scorned, for a mindless man soon becomes a plaything of the passions. Indeed, I think that man's first fall occurred because the Devil in the shape of the serpent clouded man's reason.'

The priest did not dissent, but neither did he praise him, since he was still not clear in his mind what the drift of Judas's words was.

'Often we see people not only sinning in thought, but even committing crimes—all because they are lacking in mind. The flesh tempts a man, and if he has no mind to guide him, down he goes headlong into the abyss. People desire all that's sweet and merry and pleasant in life, womenfolk in particular, and how can they preserve themselves if they haven't got a mind to think with? But if I do have a mind, then I take a little camphor or oil, rub here, sprinkle there—and there's temptation banished in a trice!'

Judas fell silent, as if waiting to see what the priest would say in reply, but the latter was still unable to understand what Judas was getting at and therefore just grunted and said apropos of nothing:

'I've got chickens in my yard . . . they're all in a fluster because of the solstice: they rush and flap about all the time, just can't keep still . . .'

'That's all because birds and beasts and reptiles don't have minds. A bird—what is it? It knows neither sorrow nor care—it just flies around! Only the other day I looked out of the window and the sparrows were pecking in the mire—that's all they want! But man needs more than that!'

'And yet, even the Scriptures point to the birds of the air in certain cases!'

'In certain cases, yes. In cases where faith alone saves without the mind, there we should imitate the birds. But for praying, composing verses . . .'

Porfiry Vladimirych stopped. He was talkative by nature and was actually now itching to say something about the day's event. But evidently the form in which he could decently hold forth on that particular subject had not yet matured in his mind.

'Birds have no need of a mind,' he said at last, 'because they are free from temptations. Or rather, they do have temptations but nobody calls them to account for them. For the birds all is natural: they have no property to look after, they have no wedlock, and so they have no widowed state. They do not have to answer to God or to the authorities: their only superior is the cock!'

'The cock, yes, true indeed! Among the birds he's like the Sultan to the Turks!'

'But man has so ordered things that for him there are no natural ways, and he therefore needs the mind—and plenty of it too— to keep himself from sin and not lead others into temptation. Is that no so, Father?'

'Verily so. And the Scriptures counsel that the offending eye should be plucked out.'

'That is the literal sense, but it is possible, without plucking out the eye, to prevent it leading you into temptation. By praying more often, by quelling the malignancy of the flesh. Take me, for example: I'm a man in the prime of life and not to be called frail . . . Well, I have women-servants . . . What of it! You can't do without servants, that I know, so I have them! I've got menservants and women-servants—all sorts! You need womenservants about the house—to fetch things from the cellar, pour out the tea, see about something to eat . . . well, Lord bless them! They do their work and I do mine . . . and that's how we live!'

As he spoke, Judas tried to look the priest in the eyes and the priest tried also to look Judas in the eyes. But, as luck had it, a candle stood between them so that, look as they might, they could see nothing but the candle-flame.

'Apart from which, I also think that if you become familiar with the servants, they're sure to start ruling the house. There'll be wrangling and upheaval, squabbling and insolence—answering you back . . . I keep clear of such things.'

The priest's eyes were quite dazzled from staring at Judas. And for that reason, and feeling too that social decorum required him to contribute at least an occasional word to the conversation, he shook his head and said:

'Hm . . .'

'But if one acted in the way others do . . . like my neighbour, Anpetov, or my other neighbour, Utrobin* . . . then you're close at hand to sin. Just look at Utrobin—there are five or six of his sinful brood there grubbing about in the yard . . . I want none of that. I say that if God has taken away my guardian angel from me, it must be his holy will that I be a widower. And if, by the grace of God, a widower I'm to be, then I must live chastely in my widowed state and keep my bed undefiled. Is that not so, Father?'

'It's a hard thing, sir.'

'I know it's hard, but still I do it. People say it's hard, but I say—the harder the better, if only God gives strength. The sweet and easy path is not for all to follow—*somebody* has to labour for the Lord! Deny yourself *here*, and *there* you will reap your reward! What is called "toil" *here* is *there* called "merit"! Is it right what I say?'

'As right as could be!'

'There's this to be said about merits, too. They are not equal. One merit is great, another small. It stands to reason!'

'That is so, of course. A merit is either great or small.'

'So it's as I say: if a man comports himself properly—does not speak profanely, does not indulge in idle talk, does not condemn others, and if besides he has never distressed or deprived anybody . . . and has been circumspect with regard to these fleshly temptations, then he will always have a clear conscience. And nothing, no filth will ever stain his character. And should anyone condemn him behind his back, such aspersions ought not, in my view, be taken account of. A fig for them!'

'In such situations Christian precept commends forgiveness as the better course!'

'All right, or forgive them! It's just what I always do: if any man condemns me, I forgive him and I pray for him besides. It's good for him that he's prayed for, and it's good for me that I've prayed and all's forgotten!'

'True it is that nothing so relieves the soul as prayer. Afflictions, anger, even sickness—all flee before it, as the darkness of night before the sun!'

'Praise God! We should always so behave that our whole life may be viewed from any side, like the candle in a lanthorn . . . People will condemn us the less—for they will have no cause! Take us, for example: we've sat and talked and chatted—who can ever condemn us for that? And now we shall go and say our prayers and then off to bye-byes. And in the morning we'll be getting up again . . . Is that not so, Father?'

Judas stood up and noisily moved his chair back to indicate that the conversation was now at an end. The priest also rose and was about to raise his hand in blessing, but Porfiry Vladimirych as a mark of special favour on this occasion caught his hand and pressed it in both his own.

'So, Father, he's to be called Vladimir?' he said, sadly shaking his head in the direction of Evprakseyushka's room.

'Yes, sir, in honour of the saintly and apostolic Prince Vladimir.'*

'Praise God! She is a hard-working, loyal servant, but lacking when it comes to *mind*! That's how they come to lapse into . . . for-ni-ca-tion!'

The whole of the next day Porfiry Vladimirych stayed in his study and prayed, asking God for guidance. The day after that he appeared for morning tea not, as usual, wearing his dressing-gown, but festively attired in a frock-coat, as was always his practice when he purposed taking some decisive action. His face was pale, but bore an air of spiritual illumination; a blissful smile played on his lips; his eyes had a tender, it seemed all-forgiving look; the tip of his nose after his devotional exertions was tinged red. In silence he drank his customary three glasses of tea and after each mouthful he moved his lips, placed his hands together, and looked at the icon, as if still now, despite his devotional efforts of the previous day, he was expecting from it timely succour and protection. Finally, having swallowed the last of his tea, he summoned Ulitushka and stood before the icon in order once more to fortify himself by converse with God—and at the same time make it patently clear to Ulita that what was about to happen was not his doing, but God's. Ulitushka, however, as soon as she saw Judas's face, knew that deep down inside him some act of perfidy had been resolved on.

'There—I've been praying to God!' Porfiry Vladimirych began and, in token of his submission to his holy will, he bowed his head and spread his hands apart.

'A very fine thing too!' replied Ulitushka, but with a note of such unquestionable percipience in her voice that Judas instinctively raised his eyes at her.

She stood before him in her usual posture, with one hand placed across her chest and the other supporting her chin; but her face was positively glinting with laughter. Porfiry Vladimirych gave a slight shake of his head as a mark of Christian reproof.

'And God, no doubt, gave you grace?' Ulitushka continued, unabashed by Porfiry Vladimirych's admonitory gesture.

'You persist in blaspheming!' Judas burst out. 'How many times have I tried by quip and kindness to keep you from doing it, but still you go on! You've got a wicked . . . venomous tongue!'

'I just thought . . . It's usual—when you pray, God gives you grace!'

'You "just thought", indeed! Well, don't you go blabbing whatever you "just think"! You should know how to hold your tongue sometimes! I've got business to settle, and she goes on about what she "just thinks"!'

Instead of replying, Ulitushka merely shifted from foot to foot, as if to indicate that she had long since known perfectly well everything Porfiry Vladimirych was about to say to her.

'Now then, listen!' Judas began. 'I've been praying to God; I prayed yesterday and again today, and the answer is just the same: that one way or another we must find a place for young Volodka!'

'Of course, he must be found a place! He's not a puppy—you can't drown him in the ditch!'

'Hold now! Wait a minute! Let me speak . . . You're a viper, oh, a viper! Well then, this is what I say: one way or another we must find a place for Volodka. First, we must have concern for Evprakseyushka, and second, we must make a man of him.'

Porfiry Vladimirych glanced at Ulitushka, probably expecting she would now warm to the subject, but her response was very simple, cynical even:

'Shall I take him to the Foundlings' then?' she asked, looking him straight in the face.

'Ah! So it's already been decided . . . you blabbermouth!' interposed Judas. 'Ah! Ulitka, Ulitka! What a flitterbrain you are! You and your tongue just never keep still! And how do you know: perhaps I'm *not* thinking of the Foundlings' after all? Perhaps I've got something else in mind for Volodka?'

'All right, something else then . . . nothing wrong with that either.'

'This is what I say: though, on the one hand, one is sorry for Volodka, on the other, when you give it thought and consider, it's clear it wouldn't be right to keep him at home.'

'Of course not. What would people say? Where did that stray brat up at the Golovlevs come from?—that's what they'd be saying!'

'Yes, there is that, and then besides: it would not be good for him to be at home. His mother's young and she'd spoil him; I'm old—though, of course, it's none of my business—and for the sake of his mother's loyal service I'd likely do the same! Now and then you'd be sure to be soft. Suppose the boy's got to be thrashed for some mischief, there'd be the devil to pay, with women weeping and wailing—you'd just let it pass! Isn't that so?'

'You're right. It'd be a trial for you.'

'I want everything to be just right. That young Volodka should in due course become a proper man: a good servant of the Lord and loyal subject of the Tsar. And if God should grant he be a peasant, that he should know how to work the land . . . Reap and plough and hew wood—a bit of everything. And if Fate should have some other calling in store, like being a craftsman, or a scholar . . . Some of them, you know, leave there and become teachers!'

'From the Foundlings', you mean? Oh yes, from there they go straight on to be generals!'

'Well, I don't know about generals, but still . . . Volodka might one day be a famous man! They give them a splendid upbringing there! I know it for a fact! Nice clean little cots, good healthy wet-nurses, nice white little shirts for the babies, feeding-bottles, teats, napikins—all they need!'

'What could be better—for bastards!'

'And even if he should be fostered out to some country place—well, Lord bless him! He'll learn the ways of toil from childhood, and toil is, after all, another form of prayer! We, of course, pray in the real way: we stand before the icon and make the sign of the cross, and if our prayer is pleasing to God, he gives to us accordingly. But the peasant—he toils! Many would be glad enough to pray in the real way, but then they'd scarce have the time, even on a holy day. Still, though, God sees their toil—and for their toil God gives to them as he gives to us for our prayers. Not everybody can live in mansions and go hopping and skipping at balls—somebody's got to live in the humble hut and till and tend our good Mother Earth! As for happiness—it's a touchy thing: who knows where it lies? One man lives a pampered life in his mansion and weeps for all his riches, while another sleeps on straw and lives off bread and kvass, but is happy at heart! Is it right what I'm saying?'

'What better than being happy at heart!'

'So this, my dear, is what we'll do. You take this young scamp Volodka, wrap him up warm and cosy, and whisk him off sharp to Moscow. I'll have them provide you with the closed kibitka and a pair of horses; it's a smooth, even road we've got now, no bumps or ruts, and you can speed along regardless! But just see that everything's done proper—in my way, the Golovlev way, the way I like it! You must take a clean teat and bottle . . . and shirts, sheets, swaddling clothes, napikins, blankets—all in plenty! Take what's needed! Order it! If they won't give it to you, get on to me, come and complain to the old fellow! And when you get to Moscow, stop at an inn. Have them bring you victuals, a samovar, tea! Ah, Volodka, Volodka! What a terrible business! It's a shame to part with you, but it can't be helped, old chap! It's for your own good—you'll see for yourself later on and be grateful!'

Judas slightly lifted up his hands and muttered with his lips as a token of inward prayer; this did not prevent him, though, from stealing a glance at Ulitushka and observing the sardonic expression that played on her face.

'What is it? Have you got something to say?' he asked her.

'Ah, nothing. Of course, he'll be grateful—if he can but find his benefactors.'

'Ah, you're a stupid woman, that you are! As if we would hand him over without getting a docket for him! You see you get a docket! If we've got a docket, we can find him ourselves in a trice! When they've fed him and groomed him and taught him wisdom, we'll be there with the docket—give us back that lad of ours, we'll say, that scamp Volodka! If we've got a docket, we can fetch him up from the bottom of the sea . . . Is it right what I'm saying?'

But Ulitushka did not answer his question; the sardonic look playing on her face merely became more pronounced. Porfiry Vladimirych lost patience.

'You're a viper!' he said. 'You've got the devil in you . . . pshaw! pshaw! That will do, then. First thing tomorrow you'll take Volodka and off you go to Moscow, God speed—and get away quickly so Evprakseyushka doesn't hear. You know the Found-lings' Home?'

'I've been there,' Ulitushka replied tersely, as if alluding to some past event.

'Ah, if you've been there, then you know the ropes. All the ins and outs will be familiar to you . . . See you place him, and be humble when you ask those in charge to take him in—like this!'

Porfiry Vladimirych stood up and bowed, touching his hand to the floor.

'See that all's well with him there—not just anyhow, but all right and proper! And the docket, be sure to get the docket! Don't forget! If we've got a docket, we can seek him out later, no matter where he is. There'll be two twenty-five-rouble notes for your expenses. I know well what's required: you'll need to slip a bribe here, grease a palm there . . . Ah me! such sinful ways we have! We are all men, all human, we always want what's sweet and nice. Even our little Volodka! He's no size, just a little Tom Thumb, but just see the money he costs!'

Saying this, Judas crossed himself and bowed low to Ulitushka, silently commending to her unfailing care the scamp Volodka. The future of his illicit family had been settled in the simplest possible way.

The morning after this conversation, while the young mother was tossing in fever and delirium, Porfiry Vladimirych stood at the window of the dining-room, moving his lips silently as he made the sign of the cross through the window-pane. The bast-hooded kibitka carrying Volodka away was leaving the yard in front of the house. Now it reached the top of the hill, drew level with the church, turned to the left, and was lost to sight among the houses of the village. Judas made a final sign of the cross and sighed:

'There was the priest talking of thaw the other day,' he said to himself, 'but it's frost, not thaw that God has sent us! Frost, and a hard one too! That's the way it always is with us: we dream our dreams, build castles in the air, we have ideas and think we know better than God himself—and then God in a moment turns all our highmindedness to naught!'

LAST OF THE LINE

THE final agony of Judas began when the opportunities to engage in prattle, which till now he had so happily exploited, began noticeably to contract. All around him now were empty places: of those who had died and those who had departed. Even Anninka, despite the sorry prospect of her life as a strolling player, had not been tempted by the pleasures of living in Golovlevo. The only one left was Evprakseyushka, but she, apart from providing anyway very limited scope for his prattle, had also undergone a change for the worse, which speedily manifested itself and convinced Judas once and for all that the good days for him were now gone beyond recall.

Until now Evprakseyushka had been so utterly defenceless that Porfiry Vladimirych had been able to oppress her without the least misgivings. With her primitive mentality and supine nature, she had not even been aware of his oppression. While Judas uttered his profanities, she would gaze apathetically into his eyes and think of other things. But now all at once she had realized something, and the immediate result of this awakened understanding was a sudden, as yet unavowed, but malignant and insuperable revulsion.

Evidently the visit of the young mistress of Pogorelka to Golovlevo had had its effect on Evprakseyushka. Although she could not exactly say what manner of pain it was that her chance conversations with Anninka had evoked in her, she felt herself none the less in a state of inner turmoil. Previously it had never occurred to her to question why it was that whenever Porfiry Vladimirych met a living soul he began at once to ensnare him in a mesh of verbiage, which, though giving nothing to grasp on, yet depressed a man beyond endurance; she now saw that Judas did not in the strict sense converse, but tyrannized you with words and that it would be no bad thing therefore to 'put him down' and let him know that 'his day was done'. She began now listening attentively to his endless effusions and realized indeed that Judas only ever spoke in order to badger, pester, and annoy.

'The young mistress said he don't know himself what he talks for,' she thought to herself. 'But it isn't that. He does it from spite! He knows who can't stand up to him and makes sport with them as he will.'

This was, though, only a secondary matter. The main effect of Anninka's visit to Golovlevo was that it had roused in Evprakseyushka the instincts of her youth. So far, these instincts had only glowed dimly within her, but now they flared up with insistent ardour. Much of what she had previously viewed with total indifference she could now understand. For instance, why on earth had Anninka refused to stay on in Golovlevo and said straight out that it was 'terrible'? Why had she? Simply because she was young and 'wanted some life'. And she, Evprakseyushka, was young too . . . yes, young! It only seemed that her youth had run to fat and gone—no, it made itself felt keenly enough at times! It called and beckoned, dying down only to flare up again. She had thought that Judas would do well enough for her, but now suddenly . . . 'That mouldy old crock! How he got round me! How nice it would be to be living now with some true love—a real one, one who was young! We would cuddle up together, and my true love, he would kiss and caress me and whisper sweet nothings in my ear: "Oh, how white and soft you are!" he'd say. But that old bogey, curse him, some catch he is with his dry old bones! I bet the young mistress has got a sweetheart! She will have for sure. That's why she up and went. And I've got to sit here in these four walls and wait till it should take his old man's fancy . . .!'

Of course, Evprakseyushka did not declare her rebellion immediately, but once embarked on this course, she did not stop. She sought out pretexts to nag him, harked back to the past, and while Judas continued to have no inkling that within her some dark process was reaching its climax, she silently and increasingly with every passing minute worked herself up to a state of hatred. At first there were general complaints, such as 'My life's been ruined for me!'; then came comparisons: 'Palageyushka, now, who's housekeeper to the master at Mazulino—*she* sits about doing nothing and wears silk frocks. *She* never goes out to the stock-yard or the cellars—she sits in her own room, doing embroidery!' And this catalogue of grievances and protests ended always with the same general lament: 'Sick to death I am of you! You make me that spiteful, you really do!'

To this major cause of complaint there was now added another which was especially valuable as offering an excellent pretext for attack. This was the memory of her confinement and the disappearance of her son Volodka.

At the time of his disappearance Evprakseyushka reacted to the event blankly. Porfiry Vladimirych simply announced to her that the newborn infant had been put into good hands, and to console her had given her a new cashmere shawl. Then everything began again and went on as before. Evprakseyushka even more zealously than ever plunged herself into the morass of household chores, as if she wanted to work off on them her failed motherhood. But, whether it was maternal feeling that still lurked warm within her or just a fancy, the memory of Volodka suddenly came back to Evprakseyushka. And it came back back just at the moment when she felt herself aware of something new, free, and unconstrained, when she sensed that there was another life, quite different from the life she led within the walls of Golovlevo. Of course, it was too good a pretext to be ignored.

'What a thing to do!' she thought, goading herself to anger. 'Taking away my baby! Drowning him like a puppy in the ditch!'

Gradually, she came to be totally obsessed with this thought. She herself felt a passionate longing to be reunited with her child and the more insistent this longing became, the stronger grew her spite against Porfiry Vladimirych.

'At least now I'd have a bit of pleasure in life! Volodya! Volodyushka! My baby! Where is it you are? They packed you off to be mothered by some yokel in the country, I suppose! Oh, damn those cursed "gentry"! They bring babies into the world, then cast them away like a puppy in the ditch: and think they can get off scot-free! I'd have been better off to take a knife to my throat than let *him* misuse me, that wanton varmint!'

She felt hatred, a desire to plague him, to poison his life, to destroy him; and war commenced—that most intolerable of all wars : a war of nagging, taunts, and gibes. But this was precisely the one kind of war capable of vanquishing Porfiry Vladimirych.

One day at morning tea Porfiry Vladimirych had a very disagreeable surprise. Usually at this time he would be spouting forth quantities of his verbal pus, and Evprakseyushka, with saucer of tea in hand, would silently listen to him, clenching her teeth on a piece of sugar-loaf and giving an occasional snort. Now suddenly, no sooner had he begun to enlarge on the thought (there being warm, freshly baked bread served with their tea) that bread is of different kinds: the visible bread which we *eat* for the sustenance of our bodies, and the invisible, spiritual bread of which we *partake* for the preservation of our souls, than Evprakseyushka most unceremoniously interrupted his effusions.

'I hear tell that Palageyushka has a good life of it at Mazulino!' she began, sitting with her body turned full to the window and casually swinging her crossed legs.

Judas gave a slight start at the unexpectedness of this intervention, but on this first occasion paid no particular heed.

'And if for a long time we eat no visible bread,' he went on, 'we feel bodily hunger; likewise, too, if for any length of time we do not partake of the bread of the spirit . . .'

'I was saying, Palageyushka has a good life of it at Mazulino!' Evprakseyushka again interrupted him, and this time evidently with intent.

Porfiry Vladimirych gave her an astonished glance, but restrained himself from reproaching her, as if sensing trouble.

'Well, if Palageyushka has a good life, the Lord be with her!' he answered curtly.

'Her master, now,' Evprakseyushka rambled on, 'he don't put on her at all, never makes her work, *and* he dresses her up in silk frocks all the time!'

Porfiry Vladimirych listened with growing astonishment. Evprakseyushka's words were so totally incongruous that he was at a loss what to do in the circumstances.

'And she's got a different frock for every day,' Evprakseyushka maundered on, as if in a dream. 'One frock today and another tomorrow, and a best one for holy days. And they go to church

in a carriage and four, first her, then the master. And when he
sees the carriage coming the priest has the bells rung. And afterwards she sits in her own room. And if the master should want
her company, she receives him there in her room; and if he don't,
then she talks to her girl, the maid she's got, or else does
embroidery!'

'Well, and what of it?' inquired Porfiry Vladimirych, coming
at last to his senses.

'What I was saying was that Palageyushka has got a very good
life of it!'

'And you have such a bad life, I suppose? Oh, dear! Oh, dear!
There's no satisfying you!'

If at this point Evprakseyushka had held her tongue, Porfiry
Vladimirych would, of course, have let himself go and uttered
a spate of meaningless words in which all these stupid insinua-
tions of Evprakseyushka, which had disturbed the orderly flow
of his prattling, would have been sunk without trace. But it was
evident that Evprakseyushka had no intention of holding her
tongue.

'Oh, surely,' she snapped in reply, 'I don't have a bad time
at all! I don't wear coarse-cloth, praise God for that! Two cotton
frocks last year that cost you five roubles apiece—you lashed out
then, you did!'

'And the woollen dress: have you forgotten about that? And
who had a shawl bought for her not long ago? Oh, dear! Oh,
dear!'

Instead of answering, Evprakseyushka propped the elbow of
her saucer hand on the table and shot a sidelong glance at Judas
of such profound contempt that the very unfamiliarity of it quite
unnerved him.

'And do you know how God punishes the ungrateful?' he
muttered somewhat uncertainly, hoping at least that a reminder
of God would in some measure bring this inexplicably fractious
female to her senses. However, Evprakseyushka was not only unmoved by his reminder, she promptly cut him short.

'It's no good your trying to talk me round and bringing God
into it!' she said. 'I'm not a child! I've had enough! You're not
going to bully and put on me no more!'

Porfiry Vladimirych said nothing. His glass of tea, now almost cold, stood before him, but he did not touch it. His face had gone pale, his lips twitched slightly, as if vainly struggling to shape themselves into a smile.

'This will be Anyutka up to her tricks! She's the one, the viper, who put you up to this!' he declared at last, though not fully aware himself what he was saying.

'What tricks is that, then?'

'The way you're answering me back . . . It's her! She put you up to it! There's nobody else it can be!' Porfiry Vladimirych fumed. 'There you are—suddenly out of the blue wanting silk dresses! And do you know, you hussy, who it is of your sort that wears silk dresses?'

'You tell me, then I'll know!'

'It's only . . . only . . . wantons of the worst kind, that's who!'

But even this failed to shame Evprakseyushka to silence: on the contrary, she responded with a kind of brazen logic:

'I don't know why they're wantons . . . Of course, their masters make demands on them . . . If a gentleman persuades the likes of me to be his sweetheart . . . well, she . . . lives with him, don't she! It's not saying our prayers exactly, what we do, is it, but the same as what the master at Mazulino gets up to!'

'Ah . . . Pshaw! Pshaw! Pshaw!'

Porfiry Vladimirych's blood ran cold at this unexpected turn of events. He gaped at his unruly companion, and a host of idle words surged up in his breast. But for the first time in his life he had an inkling that there are occasions when a person is not to be slain with idle words.

'Well, my dear, I can see I shan't get anywhere with you today!' he said, rising from the table.

'No, not today, nor tomorrow . . . nor ever again! I've had enough! You'll put on me no more! I've listened to you all I'm going to; you listen now to what I've got to say!'

Porfiry Vladimirych hurled himself at her with clenched fists, but with such resolution did she thrust out her chest that he was at once confounded. He turned to the icon, lifted up his hands, moved his lips, and walked slowly off into his study.

The whole of this day he was perturbed. He had as yet no

definite fears for the future, but it was in itself disturbing that an event had occurred that did not in the least accord with his daily routine and that this event had gone unpunished. He did not emerge even for dinner, but, pretending to be ill, meekly begged, in an assumed feeble voice, that something should be brought to him in his study.

That evening, after tea—which for the first time ever was taken in total silence—he began, as usual, to pray; but in vain did his lips whisper the customary prayers for the ending of the day: his restive mind would not, even superficially, attend to the prayers. He was gripped by a niggling feeling of disquiet, and instinctively his ear listened to the fading echoes of the day that sounded still in the various corners of the house of Golovlevo. Finally, when the last desperate yawn was heard through the wall and all suddenly fell silent, as if sunk into some nethermost depth, he could contain himself no longer. He crept noiselessly along the passage and, reaching Evprakseyushka's room, put his ear to the door to listen. Evprakseyushka was alone and all that could be heard was her praying through her yawns: 'Oh, Lord, merciful Saviour! Our Lady of the Asstumption!' (at the same time giving herself a hearty scratch on the rump). Porfiry Vladimirych tried the door-handle, but the door was locked.

'Evprakseyushka! Are you there?' he called.

'Yes, I am, but not to you!' she snapped—so sharply that all Judas could do was beat a silent retreat to his study.

Next day there was a further conversation. As if on purpose, Evprakseyushka chose morning tea as the time to aggravate Porfiry Vladimirych. It was as though she knew instinctively that all his futile activities were arranged with such precision that a disturbed morning would cause trouble and pain to last him through the day.

'How I'd love to see the way some folks live! If only just a peep for the pleasure of it!' she began enigmatically.

Porfiry Vladimirych's heart missed a beat. 'It's starting,' he thought, but said nothing and waited to see what would come next.

'Yes, two of them together, she with her sweetheart—a *young* one too! I can picture them walking from room to room, the two of them, and eyes only for each other! He never says a cross word to her, nor she to him. "Darling" and "Dearest" is all they ever say! Nice that is! Superior!'

The topic was especially repugnant to Porfiry Vladimirych. Although he allowed fornication to be admissible within the bounds of strict necessity, he regarded amorous pastimes as a temptation of the Devil. However, on this occasion too he cravenly gave way—the more readily because he wanted his tea, which had for some minutes been stewing on the top of the samovar, and Evprakseyushka showed no inclination to pour it out.

'Of course, plenty of us women are stupid,' she continued, brazenly swaying back and forth on her chair and drumming her hand on the table. 'Some are that snared they'd do anything for a cotton frock, and others throw themselves away for nothing, just like that! . . . "You have all the kvass and cucumbers you want," he says—a fine way to get round a girl that is!'

'Is it then really only for gain . . .' Porfiry Vladimirych timidly ventured to observe, keeping an eye on the tea-pot, which was now belching forth steam.

'Who says it's only for gain? I'm supposed to be out for gain, am I!' said Evprakseyushka, suddenly changing tack. 'Now you're begrudging me a bite to eat! You hold that against me, do you?'

'I don't hold anything against you, I'm just saying—that it's not only for gain that people . . .'

'Oh, you're "just saying"! Well, say on, but don't you go too far! I serve you for gain, do I! Well, let me just ask you what gain it is I've had from you? Apart from kvass and cucumbers!'

'It's not only kvass and cucumbers, though . . .' expostulated Porfiry Vladimirych, likewise carried away.

'All right, you tell me then, tell me what else!'

'And who is it sends four sacks of flour to St Nicholas's every month?'

'All right, four sacks! And what else?'

'Meal, lenten oil . . . in fact, all sorts of things . . .'

'So, meal and oil . . . even that you begrudge my parents now! It's too bad!'

'I don't say I begrudge it, but you . . .'

'So I'm the one to blame! I don't get a bite to eat but I'm rebuked for it, and then I take the blame!'

Evprakseyushka broke down and burst into tears. And the tea meanwhile was stewing away on the top of the samovar, a matter of acute concern to Porfiry Vladimirych. He therefore mastered his feelings, sat down gently by Evprakseyushka, and patted her on the back.

'There, there, now . . . Just you pour the tea . . . What's all this snivelling for?'

But Evprakseyushka gave a few more sobs, pouted her lips, and stared dull-eyed into space.

'There you were just now talking about young people,' he continued, endeavouring to impart a caressing tone to his voice. 'Well, after all, we're not as old as all that ourselves, are we?'

'Ugh! Fine talk! Leave me alone!'

'Come on, now! Why, you know . . . when I was in the ministry, the director wanted me to marry his daughter!'

'She must have been well past it . . . some kind of freak!'

'No, she was all a girl should be . . . and how well she sang "Mother, sew not for me . . ."* Ah, how well she sang it!'

'So she might, but it was a poor partner she had to sing with!'

'Not at all, I . . .'

Porfiry Vladimirych was at a loss. He was ready even to stoop to showing her how he too could cut a figure at dancing. For which purpose he began incongruously swaying his body and even attempted to take Evprakseyushka by the waist, but she withdrew from his outstretched arms and shouted angrily:

'I mean it! Get away from me, you old bogey! Or you'll get boiling water over you! I don't want your tea! I don't want anything! What a thing to do—grudging me a morsel of food! I'll go away from here! I will, I swear it!'

And she went, slamming the door and leaving Porfiry Vladimirych alone in the dining-room.

Judas was thoroughly confounded. He tried to pour himself some tea, but his hands shook so that the assistance of the man-servant was required.

'No, this is impossible! We must settle it . . . determine what to do!' he whispered, as he walked agitatedly up and down the room.

But to 'settle' or 'determine' anything was precisely what he was incapable of doing. His mind was so accustomed to flitting unhindered from one thing to another that the simplest fact of everyday reality took him by surprise. No sooner did he begin to 'determine' a course of action than he was beset by a host of trivialities which blocked out all prospect of real life. He was seized by a kind of lethargy, a general mental and moral anaemia. He was drawn away from real life to the soft repose of a world peopled by his phantoms, which he could transpose from place to place, setting some aside, giving prominence to others, in short, disposing everything according to his will.

Once again he spent the day in total isolation, since Evprakse-yushka was not present either for dinner or evening tea, having gone off for the whole day to visit the priest in the village, whence she returned only late in the evening. He had nothing to occupy him, for even his trivial interests seemed temporarily to have forsaken him. He was tormented by the one hopeless thought: that he must, *must* somehow settle this! He was unable to engage in his futile calculations or say his prayers. He had the feeling that he was about to fall victim to some malady, as yet indeter-minable. Several times he stopped at the window, intending to fix his wandering thoughts on something, to find some distraction, but it was all to no avail. Outside spring was beginning, but the trees were bare, and there was no sign yet of any new grass. In the distance there were black fields, blotched here and there by the white of snow still lingering in the gullies and on lower-lying ground. The road was a sea of black mud with sparkling puddles. But all this was seen by him as through a veil. Around the sodden outbuildings there was no sign of life, though all the doors stood wide open; inside, too, there would be no answer if he called, even though he kept hearing sounds, as if of the distant banging of doors. It would be a good time to become invisible and listen to what these progeny of Ham had to say about him! Do the blackguards realize what bounty they enjoy from him or do they repay him for his goodness with tittle-tattle? These people, you can stuff them with food all day long, but they're never satisfied, it's like water off a duck's back. It was not that long since they had broached a fresh tub of cucumbers, and already . . . But no sooner did he lose himself in these thoughts, no sooner did he begin reckoning the number of cucumbers there would be in a tub and the maximum number of cucumbers to be allowed per head than the light of reality once again flashed in his mind and at once confounded all his calculations.

'Really! Going off like that without even asking!' he thought to himself, as his eyes scanned the distance, trying to pick out the priest's house, where, in all probability, Evprakseyushka was at this very minute giving free rein to her tongue.

And now dinner is served; Porfiry Vladimirych sits alone at the table and half-heartedly eats his plain soup (he cannot abide soup with nothing in it, but today *she* has ordered just such a soup on purpose).

'The priest will be sick to death with her for imposing on him like this!' he thinks. 'It will mean providing extra food, more cabbage soup and kasha . . . and perhaps for a visitor a roast as well . . .'

Again he is carried away by his imagination, again he begins to forget himself, as if transported into a dream world. How many extra spoonfuls of soup would it mean? How many spoonfuls of kasha? What would the priest and his wife have to say about Evprakseyushka's visit? And how they would curse her to themselves . . . All this—the food, what they would say—was clearly there, as if real, before his eyes.

'They'll likely all be eating from one bowl anyway! Going off like that! She doesn't know when she's well off! In all this mud and slush you could easily come to grief! You see, she'll be back with her feathers rumpled . . . Oh, you snake! Yes, snake! I must, *must* somehow . . .'

With these words his train of thought was invariably cut short. After dinner he lay down for his customary nap, but only wore himself out tossing and turning from side to side. Evprakseyushka did not come home till after dark and she crept so quietly to her room that he was not even aware of it. He had ordered the servants to inform him without fail when she returned, but they, as if by collusion, said nothing. He tried again to gain entry to her room, but once more he found the door locked.

On the morning of the third day, although Evprakseyushka appeared for tea, she began in a still more menacing and pointed manner.

'Wherever is my little Volodka now?' she said, with an assumed note of tearfulness in her voice.

Porfiry Vladimirych's blood ran cold at the question.

'If I could just have a peep to see how my baby's pining there! Though, of course, he might already be dead!'

Judas agitatedly moved his lips in whispered prayer.

'Nothing's done here like other people do it! When Palage-yushka had her baby girl by the master at Mazulino, they straightaway dressed her up in cambric and made her a nice little pink cot . . . And they gave the wet-nurse alone I don't know how many sarafans and kokoshniks!* But here . . . oh, honestly!'

Evprakseyushka abruptly turned her head to the window and heaved a very loud sigh.

'It's true when they say that all masters are damned! They bring children into the world and then they throw them in the ditch like puppies! And they don't care a bit! Nor do they answer for it—as if there was no God to punish them! Why, it's a thing not even a wolf would do!'

Porfiry Vladimirych heaved inwardly. For a long time he struggled to control himself, but in the end he gave way and grated through his teeth:

'You've taken on new ways, haven't you! Three days now I've listened to this backchat of yours!'

'New ways, is it? Call it that if you like! Why should you be the only one ever to speak? I suppose other people can put in a word! Indeed they can! You father a child, and what have you done with him! Packed him off to some peasant woman to rot in a hut without care or food or clothes . . . He'll be lying in filth, sucking a stinking rag-dummy!'

She shed a few tears and wiped her eyes with the corner of the kerchief round her neck.

'The young mistress from Pogorelka was right when she said living here with you was terrible. It is terrible! No pleasure nor joy, nothing but you and your shabby tricks . . . Convicts in gaol are better off. At least, if I had my baby with me, I'd have a bit of pleasure. But see what happened! I had my baby and he's been taken away!'

Porfiry Vladimirych sat in his place and shook his head in anguish, as if he was well and truly cornered. Even an occasional groan escaped from his breast.

'Ah, it's agony!' he said at last.

' "Agony", my eye! You've got only yourself to blame! I do believe I'll go to Moscow, just to have a peep at my Volodka! Volodka! Volodenka! My dear baby! Master—shall I? Shall I go to Moscow?'

'There's no point,' Porfiry Vladimirych replied in a flat voice.

'I'll go just the same! I shan't ask anybody's leave, and nobody can stop me going! Because I'm his mother!'

'What sort of mother are you! You're a harlot, that's what you are!' Porfiry Vladimirych burst out at last. 'Just tell me: what is it you want from me?'

Evprakseyushka was evidently unprepared for this question. She stared at Judas without speaking, as if trying to think what she did in fact want.

'There you go, calling me a harlot now!' she cried, bursting into a flood of tears.

'Yes, you're a harlot! A harlot! A harlot! Pshaw! Pshaw! Pshaw!'

Porfiry Vladimirych in temper leapt from his seat and practically ran out of the room.

This was the last outburst of energy he permitted himself. Almost at once he became limp, spiritless, faint-hearted—whereas there was no end in sight to the importunities of Evprakseyushka. She had at her command an enormous power: the stubbornness of the obtuse, and since this power was incessantly applied to a single object—to pester and poison his life, it at times took on a fearsome aspect. As time went on the arena of the dining-room became too limited for her: she would burst into his study and confront Judas there (where before she would never have thought of venturing when the master was 'busy'). She would go in and sit at the window, gaze heavy-eyed into space, scratch her shoulders against the window-jamb, and begin her ramblings. One topic she was particularly fond of was her threat to quit Golovlevo. In actual fact, she had never given the idea serious thought and would have even been much astonished if it had suddenly been suggested that she should indeed go back to her parents; but she had a feeling that Porfiry Vladimirych feared more than anything that she might go away. She always approached the subject gradually and in a roundabout way. She would sit saying nothing, scratch her ear, and then suddenly say, as if it had just come to mind:

'I expect they'll be making pancakes at St Nicholas's today!'

At this opening remark Porfiry Vladimirych turns livid with spite. He has just embarked on a highly complicated calculation about the price he could get for his milk if all the cows in the district died and only his were (by God's mercy) left unscathed and actually also produced twice their former yield of milk. However, in view of Evprakseyushka's arrival and her remark on the matter of pancakes, he abandons his labours and even attempts to force a smile.

'And why would they be making pancakes there today?' he asks, with an expansive grin. 'Why, merciful fathers, today is a Day of Remembrance!* What a scatterbrain I am, forgetting all about it! What a sin! We'll have nothing to commemorate dear Mother with!'

'I could eat some pancakes . . . like Mother makes!'

'Who's stopping you! See about it! Get on to Maryushka the cook! Or else Ulitushka! Oh, Ulitushka makes good pancakes!'

'Perhaps she gave satisfaction some other way too?' says Evprakseyushka sarcastically.

'No, it must be said, Ulitushka does make good, really good pancakes! Light, soft, a pleasure to eat!'

Porfiry Vladimirych tries jocularly to distract Evprakseyushka.

'I'd love to eat some pancackes, at home though, not in Golovlevo!' she persisted.

'There's nothing to stop you! Just get hold of Arkhipushka the coachman: have him hitch a pair of horses, and off you go!'

'No, what's the good! The bird's caught . . . and it's her own

silly fault; Who wants the likes of me? You said yourself the
other day I'm a harlot . . . What's the good!'

'Oh, dear, dear! Aren't you ashamed to slander me like that!
Do you know how God punishes the slanderer?'

'But you did! You called me a harlot, straight out like that!
Before the icon here, in the Lord's presence! Oh! I'm sick to death
of this place! I'll run away, yes, really I will!'

Saying this, Evprakseyushka deports herself without the least
constraint—rocking on her chair, picking her nose, and scratching herself. It is clear that she is putting on a show, baiting him.

'Oh, and Porfiry Vladimyrich, there was something I was going
to tell you,' she rambled on. 'I really must go back home.'

'Ah, you're thinking of staying a while with your father and
mother?'

'No, I shall go for good. I'll stay on at St Nicholas's.'

'Why is that? Has something upset you?'

'No, I'm not upset. It's just that . . . I'll have to go some
time . . . And anyway it's boring here . . . really terrible! The
whole place seems dead now! The servants do as they want—
they're always hiding away in the kitchens or in their own
quarters, and you're left to sit on your own in an empty house—
you might get your throat cut! And when you go to bed at night,
there's whispering noises all around!'

However, the days passed by and Evprakseyushka showed absolutely no intention of carrying out her threat. None the less,
the threat itself was very telling in its effect on Porfiry Vladimirych. He suddenly realized that, despite the fact that from
morning till night he exhausted himself at his so-called labours,
he did actually nothing at all, and it was possible for him to go
without dinner, clean linen, or decent clothes if there was not
someone's eye to see that the running of the household continued
without interruption. Up to now he had seemed to have no awareness of life, no understanding that it involved a framework which
did not come about by itself. His entire day followed an established routine; everything in the house was arranged around him
and for him personally; everything was done at its proper time;
every object was in its proper place: in short, there was overall
such immutable precision that he thought nothing of it. Due to

this order of things he was at perfect liberty to devote himself to his empty words and empty thoughts without any fear that he would ever be driven to face up to the realities of life. It was true that this whole artificial structure hung by a single thread; but it would never occur to a man so continually self-absorbed that this thread was a fine one that could easily snap. Life had seemed to him firmly established, for ever . . . And then suddenly it was all to collapse, collapse in a moment, all because of a few stupid words: 'No, what's the good! I shall go away!' What if she really did go away? he wondered. And he mentally began devising all manner of absurd schemes by which he might somehow keep her from going and even considered making concessions to Evprakse-yushka's rebellious youthful spirit which before would simply never have occurred to him.

'Pshaw! Pshaw! Pshaw!' he spat in disgust when the possibility of encounters with Arkhipushka the coachman or Ignat the clerk presented itself in all its offensive starkness.

He soon came to see, however, that his fear of Evprakseyushka's going away was largely unfounded and, after this, his existence entered suddenly a new and, for him, quite unexpected phase. Not only did Evprakseyushka not go away, she became also markedly less importunate. Instead, she entirely neglected Porfiry Vladimirych. May came, and with it fine days, and she was hardly to be seen in the house at all. Only from the continual banging of doors Judas assumed that she had come in to fetch something from her room—to disappear again at once. When he got up in the morning he did not find his clothes in their accustomed place and had to conduct lengthy negotiations to obtain any clean linen; tea and dinner were served either very early or else much too late, and the waiting at table was done by the tipsy footman Prokhor, who appeared in a stained frock-coat and everlastingly reeked of some repellent compound of fish and vodka.

Despite this, Porfiry Vladimirych was glad at least that Evprakseyushka left him in peace. He could even reconcile himself to the disorder as long as he knew that still there was someone in the house who had charge of it. What terrified him was not so much the confusion as the thought that he himself might become involved in the organization of daily life. With horror he envisaged that the time might come when he himself would be obliged to manage things, give orders, supervise. In apprehension of such a moment he made every effort to hold back his protests, to shut his eyes to the growing anarchy in the household, he kept in the background, made no comment. But in the meantime there were daily high-jinks at the manor. With the warm weather Golovlevo, previously staid and even grim, came to life. In the evening the entire servant population, supernumeraries and those currently in service, young and old alike, all poured out of doors. They sang songs, played accordions, laughed, shrieked, and ran about playing 'tag'. Ignat the clerk appeared in a bright red shirt and an incredibly tight jacket, which did not meet across his jauntily puffed-out chest. Arkhip the coachman had commandeered the smart silk shirt and sleeveless velveteen jacket intended for his wear on 'best' occasions and evidently vied with Ignat in having designs on the heart of Evprakseyushka. Evprakseyushka flitted between the two of them and like a mad thing threw herself first at one, then at the other. Porfiry Vladimirych was afraid to look out of the window for fear of witnessing some amorous scene; but he could not help hearing. From time to time there resounded in his ears the sound of a full-blooded slap—this was Arkhipushka the coachman giving Evprakseyushka an open-handed whack as he pursued her at 'tag' (and she not in the least annoyed, only giving slightly at the knees); occasionally a snatch of conversation would reach him:

'Evprakseya Nikitichna! Hey, Evprakseya Nikitichna!' the tipsy Prokhor called from the manor steps.

'What do you want?'

'The key for the tea-caddy! Master wants his tea!'

'He can wait ... the old bogey!'

In a short time Porfiry Vladimirych became totally withdrawn. The whole of his accustomed course of life was disturbed and distorted, but he no longer paid any attention to that. He wanted nothing from life but to be left alone and undisturbed in his last refuge—the study. Where before he had been carping and pestering to those around him, he now became in the same degree timorous and sullenly submissive. All contact with real life seemed to have ceased for him. To hear nothing, to see nobody— that was all he wished for. Evprakseyushka might not appear for whole days, the servants might idle and make free as they liked— he showed no concern, as if there was nothing amiss. Formerly, if the clerk was the least unpunctual in delivering his reports on the various branches of the estate administration, Porfiry Vladimirych would have plagued the life out of him with his homilies; now he had to go for weeks without reports, yet only occasionally did this trouble him—when he required a figure to support some fantastic calculation. All alone in his study, however, he felt himself the complete master, with opportunity to indulge to his heart's content in thinking empty thoughts. Just as his two brothers had died in the throes of drunkenness, he suffered from the same complaint. His drunkenness, though, was of another kind—it was the drunkenness of idle thinking. Closeting himself in his study, he sat at his desk from morning till night wearing himself out at his fantastic labours: he made all kinds of impossible projections, cast himself a role in them, held conversations with imaginary interlocutors, and created whole scenes in which the actors were any first person who came to mind.

In this vortex of fantastic images and events the principal element was a pathological lust for gain. Although Porfiry Vladimirych had always been petty and prone to litigiousness, nevertheless because of his practical ineptitude he never derived any actual benefit himself from these propensities. He harassed, tormented, and bullied (chiefly, the most defenceless of people— those who, so to speak, simply asked to be imposed on), but most often he was also himself the loser from his own ingenious schemes. These attributes were now transferred wholesale on to an abstract, fantastic plane, where there was no place for rebuttals and acquittals, where there were no strong and no weak, where there existed no police and no magistrates (or rather, they did exist, but solely for the protection of his, Judas's, interests), and where he was consequently free to enmesh the whole world in his net of pettifogging, persecution, and abuse.

He loved, in his thoughts, to extort, ruin, dispossess, suck blood. One by one he passed over in his mind all the branches of his estate economy: the woodland, stock-yard, corn, pasturage, and so on, and in respect of each constructed an elaborate edifice of fantastic impositions, together with intricate calculations concerning income from fines, usury, natural disasters, and the purchase of stocks and shares—in short, a whole tangled world embodying all the idle aspirations of a gentry landowner. And since it was all based on arbitrary assumptions about sums overpaid or underpaid, it meant that every single kopek paid over or under was a pretext for reconstructing the whole edifice, which thus became the subject of endless mutations. Then, when his wearied brain was no longer capable of following with due attention all the intricacies of his financial calculations, he would turn his fancy to a less constricting field of speculation. He recalled all the conflicts and disputes he had had with people, not only in the recent past, but long ago in his earliest years, and he so reshaped the course of those conflicts that out of every one he emerged victorious. Mentally he revenged himself on his former colleagues in the ministry who had been promoted ahead of him, so wounding his self-esteem that he abandoned his official career; he revenged himself on his school-fellows who had taken advantage of their physical strength to tease and bully him; he revenged himself on his neighbours who had resisted his claims and maintained their rights; he revenged himself on those servants who had ever spoken rudely to him or simply failed to show due deference; he revenged himself on Arina Petrovna, his dear mother, for having squandered so much money on improving Pogorelka—money which 'by rights' should have come to him; he revenged himself on Booby Stepka, his brother, for giving him the nickname 'Judas'; he revenged himself on Varvara Mikhailovna, his aunt, for having, contrary to all expectations, suddenly from who knows where produced a whole brood of children, which meant that the village of Goryushkino was now lost for ever to the Golovlev family. He revenged himself alike on the living and the dead.

In these fantastic flights he imperceptibly reached a state of intoxication; the ground vanished from beneath his feet, it was as if he had sprouted wings. His eyes gleamed, his lips trembled and frothed, his face went pale and took on a menacing look.

And as his fantasy grew, so the air around him became filled with phantoms, whom he engaged in imaginary conflict.

His existence came to have such fullness and independence that there was nothing left for him to desire. The whole world lay at his feet—that elementary world, of course, which came within his scant purview. On any theme of the simplest kind he could provide endless variations, time after time he could start again and develop any one of them in some fresh way. It was a form of ecstasy, of clairvoyance, akin to what happens at a spiritualistic *séance*. The unrestrained imagination creates an apparent reality which through constant mental stimulation is transformed into a concrete, almost tangible reality. This is not faith, not conviction, but mental dissipation, ecstasy. People become dehumanized, their faces contort, their eyes burn, their tongues make involuntary utterances, their bodies perform involuntary motions.

Porfiry Vladimirych was happy. He shut tight the windows and doors in order not to hear, he pulled down the blinds in order not to see. All the ordinary functions of life which had no direct link with his fantasy world he carried out perfunctorily, practically with revulsion. When the tipsy Prokhor knocked at the door of his room to announce that dinner was served, he impatiently rushed into the dining-room, contrary to all his old ways hurriedly bolted his three courses, and again disappeared into his study. When he encountered living people, even in his manner there was something both timid and fatuously mocking, as if he was at the same time both afraid and defiant. In the morning he hastened to rise as early as possible in order to set at once to work. He reduced the time he spent praying, and when he prayed he repeated the words apathetically, with no regard to their meaning; the ritual of crossing himself and lifting up his hands he performed mechanically, without precision. Even his vision of Hell and its torments (a special one for every sin) seemed to have abandoned him.

Evprakseyushka, in the meantime, was wallowing in the delights of fleshly concupiscence. Blatantly dividing her attentions between Ignat the clerk and Arkhipushka the coachman (and at the same time making eyes at Ilyusha the red-faced carpenter, who had come with his gang to line the master's store-cellar), she noticed nothing of what was going on in the manor. She supposed the master was acting out some new comedy, and there was no lack of jests on this score among the servants, who were now feeling their freedom. But once when she chanced to go into the dining-room as Judas was gobbling down a remnant of roast goose, she had a nasty shock.

Porfiry Vladimirych was sitting in a greasy dressing-gown, the padding of which was coming out in places; he was pale, unkempt, with a growth of stubble on his face in place of a beard.

'Why, Master! What's up? What's happened?' she rushed to him in alarm.

But to her exclamation Porfiry Vladimirych only responded with a silly caustic smile, as if to say 'All right, go ahead, just you try to get at me now!'

'Master! What is it? Tell me what's happened!' she repeated.

He stood up, fixed her with a look of utter hatred and said, slowly and deliberately:

'If you, you harlot, ever again . . . enter my study . . . I'll kill you!'

As a result of this chance occurrence, Porfiry Vladimirych's existence in outward terms changed for the better. Free of all material constraints, he abandoned himself to his isolation and did not even notice the passing of summer. It was now late August; the days were shorter; out of doors there was a constant drizzle; the ground was wet; the trees stood dejectedly, shedding their yellow leaves on the ground. An imperturbable quiet reigned in the yard and around the servants' quarters; the house-servants had taken refuge in their various nooks, partly because of the gloomy weather and partly because they guessed that something was amiss with the master. Evprakseyushka came to her senses, forgot all about silk frocks and sweethearts, and sat for hours on the chest in the maids' room not knowing what she should do or undertake. The tipsy Prokhor teased her, saying that she had done for the master, that she had poisoned him and would be sure to end up on the Vladimir road* on account of it.

And Judas meanwhile sits locked up in his study and daydreams. The fresher weather suits him all the better; the rain pattering on the windows of his study induces a slumbrous state in which his fancy can develop still more freely and expansively. He imagines himself invisible and, in his mind, he invisibly inspects his properties, accompanied by old Ilya, who was village elder back in his father's time and lies long since buried in the graveyard.

'A clever fellow is Ilya! One of the old kind of servant. They're dying out today, his sort. These days it's all blather and bluff, and then when it comes to work there's nobody,' Porfiry Vladimirych thinks to himself, much pleased at Ilya's resurrection from the dead.

Walking along at steady pace, by God's good grace, and unseen by anybody, they make their way through fields and gullies, valleys and meadows to Ukhovshchina, an outlying patch of waste-land, and for a time are unable to believe their eyes. Before them stands a great wall of solid forest with only the soughing of the tree-tops to be heard high overhead. The trees are all magnificent—pines, some of them two or even three arm-spans round; their trunks are straight and bare, their tops mighty and bushy with growth: so many a year yet will this forest stand!

'There's forest for you, my friend!' Judas exclaims delightedly.

'It's protected wood,'* old Ilya explains. 'They had a procession with icons round it way back in your grandfather Mikhail Vasilych's time—just look at how it's grown!'

'How many desyatinas would you think there are?'

'Well, in those days it was measured out to be seventy desyatinas exactly, but today, well . . . that was the old desyatina* then, half as much again as the one today.'

'And what do you think—how many trees would there be roughly to a desyatina?'

'Who knows! God keeps the score!'

'Well, I would say there'll be six or seven hundred to the desyatina—not the old desyatina, the present one. Hold now! Wait a minute! If it's six hundred—well, let's say six-fifty—how many trees will there be on a hundred and five desyatinas?'

Porfiry Vladimirych takes a piece of paper and multiplies 105 by 650: the answer is 68,250 trees.

'Now, if I sold off the whole forest . . . in lots . . . do you think I could get ten roubles a tree?'

Old Ilya shakes his head.

'Not enough!' he says. 'Why, that timber there—from every tree you'd get two mill-shafts, and a beam length fit for any building, then your 15- and 20-foot runs, and the trimmings besides . . . What do you reckon the cost of a mill-shaft?'

Porfiry Vladimirych pretends that he does not know, though he has long had it worked out and determined down to the last kopek.

'Round here a mill-shaft costs ten roubles, but for a shaft like this you'd get a fortune in Moscow. This is really what you call a shaft! Why, a three-horse team would barely cart it! And then there'd be the other shaft, not so thick, and the beam, and the timber runs, and the firewood, and the trimmings . . . A whole tree would fetch twenty roubles at the very least.'

Porfiry Vladimirych listens to Ilya's words in rapture. What a wise, loyal fellow Ilya is! Altogether, he had by God's grace been singularly lucky with his staff. Ilya's assistant is old Vavilo (also long in his grave)—there's a real stalwart for you! The clerk is his mother's scribe Filipp 'Switch' (he had been 'switched' from the Vologda estate to Golovlevo some sixty years before); the foresters are all seasoned, untiring men; the dogs guarding the barns are fierce! For their master's property men and dogs alike are ready to tear out the throat of the Devil himself.

'Now, let's just work out what it would bring if we sold it all off in lots.'

Porfiry Vladimirych once more reckons in his head the price of a big shaft, the price of a smaller one, the price of a house-beam, timber runs, firewood, and trimmings. Then he adds, multiplies, drops a fraction here, adds one there. The sheet of paper becomes covered with columns of figures.

'There, friend, see what it all comes to!' Judas shows the phantasmal Ilya some wildly extravagant figure which causes even Ilya, who is not himself averse to seeing his master's property increase, to wince slightly.

'Looks a bit on the high side,' he says, shifting his shoulders as he considers it.

But Porfiry Vladimirych has already cast all doubts aside and merely giggles merrily.

'You're a funny fellow! It's not me, it's what the figures say . . . A branch of science there is, my friend, what they call arithmetic . . . and that can never lie! All right, now we've done with Ukhovshchina, let's go over to Fox-Holes—it's a long time since I've been there. And I have a fancy the peasants there are playing up, dear me yes, playing up! And Garanka the keeper . . . Oh yes, I know, I know! He's a good man, Garanka, thorough, reliable, you can't say he's not! But still, he seems to be slipping a bit!'

They walk on unheard and unseen, hardly making their way through the birch thicket; then suddenly, with bated breath, they halt. Right there on the road a peasant's cart is lying on its side and the peasant stands by, lamenting as he regards the broken axle. Finishing his lamentations, he roundly curses the axle (and himself to boot), and gives a lick of the whip to the horse's back ('You would, you great rook!')—but something has to be done, he cannot stay there till tomorrow! The thieving peasant looks round, listens to see if anyone is coming, then selects a suitable birch-tree, and gets out his axe . . . And Judas still stands there, not moving a muscle . . . The birch shudders, sways, and then suddenly, like a swath of corn, falls to the ground. The peasant is about to lop from the lower trunk the length he needs for his axle, but Judas has already decided that the moment has come. He creeps stealthily up to the peasant and in a flash snatches the axe from his hand.

'Ah!' is all the surprised thief has time to gasp.

'Ah!' Porfiry Vladimirych mimics him. 'Is it permitted to steal other people's wood? "Ah!"—and whose birch tree have you just chopped down? Yours was it?'

'Forgive me, master!'

'Friend, personally I've long forgiven everybody. I have sinned myself before God and don't make bold to condemn others. I don't condemn, the law does. That axle you've chopped down there— bring it along to the manor, and while you're about it bring along the rouble fine too. In the meantime the axe can stay with me—it will be well looked after, never fear!'

Pleased to have been able to demonstrate to Ilya the justice of his opinion of Garanka, Porfiry Vladimirych mentally proceeds from the scene of the crime to the forester's cottage, where he delivers an appropriate admonition. Then he sets off for home and on the way catches three peasant chickens in his oat-field. Back in his study, he again sets to work and an entire novel system of estate economy takes shape in his mind. Everything that grows and springs forth upon his land, sown or unsown, is converted into cash at retail prices, with fines added in. All the peasants have suddenly taken to stealing his wood and letting their livestock run loose on his land, but Judas is not only not aggrieved by this—on the contrary, he actually rubs his hands in glee.

'Go ahead, dear sirs—thieve and trespass!* All the better for me!' he repeats, totally content.

And now he takes a fresh sheet of paper and starts doing various sums and calculations.

How much oats grows on a desyatina and what money might this oats bring in if it was trampled by the peasants' chickens and a fine was paid according to the quantity trampled?

'And then, even if it's trampled, the oats will recover again with a shower of rain!' Judas adds mentally.

How many birches are there in Fox-Holes and how much money can he get if the peasants fell them unlawfully and pay a fine for every tree felled?

'And even if they are felled, the birches can still go to heat the house, and that will save the expense of cutting firewood myself!' Porfiry Vladimirych adds mentally once again.

Enormous columns of figures cover the paper: first roubles, then tens, hundreds, thousands . . . Judas becomes so tired and—more particularly—so agitated by his work that he gets up from his desk bathed in sweat and lies down on his couch to rest. Even now, however, his turbulent imagination does not stop working, it merely selects a different, less taxing subject.

'She was a clever woman was dear Mother, Arina Petrovna,' Porfiry Vladimirych takes off again. 'She knew how to be demanding and how to be nice to people—that's why they were all so pleased to serve her! But she had her faults too! Oh my, yes, quite a few blemishes she had, the dear departed!'

No sooner does Judas make reference to Arina Petrovna than she is actually there; as if sensing that she must account for herself, she has come from the grave to appear before her dear son.

'I really don't know, my dear, what wrong I ever did you!' she says morosely. 'I think . . .'

'Tush, tush, now, Mother dear! It's no good pretending!' Judas rebukes her unceremoniously. 'If it comes down to it, I'll put it to you straight now. Why was it, for instance, that you didn't stop Aunt Varvara Mikhailovna?'

'How could I stop her? She was of age and had the right to do as she pleased!'

'That's not the case, pardon me! What was her husband? An old man and a drinker . . . the last person to beget children! And in the meantime she produces four of them . . . I ask you, where did they come from, those children?'

'Why, my dear, how strange you talk! As if I was responsible!'

'Responsible or not, just the same you could have influenced her! If you had humoured her, said a few kind words, she would soon have seen the error of her ways! But you did it all contrariwise! You had to get on your high horse—calling her a hussy and a baggage, making out she was mistress to practically the whole neighbourhood! So she got on her high horse too! The pity of it—Goryushkino would have now been ours!'

'You've got Goryushkino on the brain!' says Arina Petrovna, evidently nonplussed by her son's indictment.

'What do I care about Goryushkino! There's nothing I want: if I've enough to buy a candle and some oil for the icon-lamp, I'm quite content! But, after all, in all fairness . . . I'd be glad indeed, Mother, to keep silent, but I can't help saying it: you have a great sin on your conscience, a really very great sin!'

Arina Petrovna makes no further reply, but, distressed or perplexed, she simply spreads her hands apart.

'Or there's another matter we might raise,' Judas meanwhile goes on, gratified by his mother's confusion. 'Why did you buy brother Stepan that house in Moscow?'

'I had to, my dear. I had to toss a morsel even to him!' Arina Petrovna says in excuse.

'And he went and squandered it away! It would have been all

right if you hadn't known him for what he was—rowdy, foul-mouthed, and disrespectful, but oh no! And you wanted to give him Father's Vologda estate besides! And what an estate that is too! All compact, no neighbours, no scattered plots, a nice little wood, a good lake . . . a plum of an estate, God bless it! A good thing I was at hand to put a stop to it . . . Ah, Mother, Mother, wasn't that wicked of you!'

'But he was my son . . . you must understand . . . my son!'

'That I know and understand perfectly well! But still there was no need for it, you shouldn't have done it! Twelve thousand silver roubles was paid for that house, and where are they now? Twelve thousand roubles down the drain there, and then there's Goryushkino belonging to Aunt Varvara Mikhailovna (worth fifteen thousand at the very least): it's a tidy sum put together!'

'There now, that'll do! Stop it! For mercy's sake, don't you be angry!'

'I'm not angry, Mother dear, I'm only saying what's fair . . . the truth's the truth, falsehood I can't abide! With truth I was born, with truth I have lived, and with truth I shall die! God loves the truth and commands that we should love it too. As concerns Pogorelka, for instance, I shall always say it: you spent a lot, a *great* lot of money on improving it.'

'But then, I lived in it . . .'

On his mother's face Judas can clearly read the words 'You bloodsucking loon'—but he pretends not to notice.

'Never mind that you lived there, all the same . . . There's the icon-case that's still at Pogorelka—and who does that belong to? And there's that little horse, and the tea-caddy . . . I saw it with my own eyes in Golovlevo when Father was alive! A pretty little caddy it is too!'

'Really, what does it matter!'

'No, Mother, don't say that! Of course, you don't see it at once, but still, a rouble here, a half-rouble there, a quarter there . . . When you come to size it all up . . . The best thing is for me to set it down in figures straightaway! Figures are sacred, they never lie!'

Porfiry Vladimirych again heads for the desk in order to make it absolutely clear just what losses have been inflicted on him by his dear mother. He clicks his counting-frame beads, writes out columns of figures—in short, prepares all that is needed for the exposure of Arina Petrovna. But, fortunately for her, his faltering mind cannot concentrate for long on the same object. Imperceptibly for himself, the idea of a fresh kind of acquisition steals into his mind and this, as if by magic, turns his thoughts in an entirely different direction. Arina Petrovna, who a moment before had appeared so vividly before him, is now suddenly gone, sunk in the depths of oblivion. His figures go all awry . . .

Porfiry Vladimirych has long intended to work out what return his field-crops might bring, and this is just the moment for it. He knows that the peasant is always needy, always wants a loan, and always pays back faithfully with interest. The peasant is particularly unstinting with regard to his labour, which 'costs nothing' and on that account in any calculation is taken for granted, as a gesture of good will. Many are the needy folk in Mother Russia, many indeed! Many are they who cannot tell today what awaits them tomorrow, many are they who, wherever they turn their yearning eyes, see nothing but the same hopeless void, hear nothing but the same repeated words: Pay up! Pay up! And it is round these hopeless souls, these destitute poor that Judas spins his endless web, transported at times into a frenzied feast of fantasy.

It is April and the peasant, as is usual, has now nothing to eat. 'Eaten everything have you, my sweethearts! Living it up all winter, then comes the spring and you feel the pinch!' Porfiry Vladimirych muses, having himself, as if on purpose, only just completed his accounts for last year's crops. In February the last stacks of corn were threshed, in March the grain lay binned in the granary, and now in the last few days the entire store has been entered up in the appropriate columns of his account-books. Judas stands on watch by the window. Away in the distance, on the bridge, the peasant Foka comes into view driving his cart. At the Golovlevo turning he gives a hasty tug at the reins and, lacking a whip, bucks up the barely plodding horse with a smack of his hand.

'He's coming here!' Judas whispers. 'Just look at his horse! On her last legs! But feed her up for a month or two and she'd be all right! She would fetch twenty-five roubles, even thirty maybe.'

In the meantime Foka has driven up to the servants' quarters, hitched his horse to the fence, tossed her an armful of sparse hay, and a minute later he is already shifting uneasily from foot to foot in the maids' room, where Porfiry Vladimirych is accustomed to receiving such visitors.

'Well, my friend, what have you got to say?' Porfiry Vladimirych begins.

'Fact is, sir, I need a bit of rye . . .'

'How's that? Eaten all your own, have you? Ah me, such wickedness! Now, if you were to drink less vodka and do more work and say your prayers, the land would be the better for it. Where you have one grain of corn today, you'd then have two or three! And you wouldn't need to borrow!'

Foka, instead of replying, smiles uncertainly.

'You think that God is far away and so doesn't see?' Porfiry Vladimirych continues to moralize. 'But God is right here. He's here and there, he's with us now while we talk, he's everywhere! And he sees everything, hears everything, and only pretends not to notice. Let people go their own way, he says, and we'll see if they remember me! And we take advantage and instead of sparing something from our makings to offer God a candle in church, we're for ever going off to the tavern! And that's the reason God provides no rye—isn't that so, my friend?'

'That's a fact, there's no denying!'

'There—you see it yourself now. And why do you see it? Because God turned his mercy away from you. But once you get a crop of rye, you'll again go your own contrary way, and then God . . .'

'That's true, and if we . . .'

'Hold now! Let me finish! It always happens, my friend, that God gives reminder of himself to those who forget him. And of that we must not complain, but realize that it's all for our good. If we remembered God, he would not forget us. He would provide us with everything—rye, oats, potatoes—eat your fill! And he would take care of your livestock too—just look at that horse of yours! More dead than alive! And if you've got any poultry, he'd set them too in the proper way!'

'All what you say is true, Porfiry Vladimirych.'

'First of all, respect God, then respect your betters—people the tsars have marked for distinction: landowners, for instance.'

'But, Porfiry Vladimirych, I think we do . . .'

'You "think" so, but if you think a bit harder, you might find it's not the case. Now, when you come asking me for rye, you are—I must say—very nice and respectful; but the year before last, you'll recall, when I wanted some women reapers and came asking you peasants to help me out, what was your answer? I was told I could do my own reaping! It's not the old times now, you said, it's not for us to work for the masters, we've got our freedom now! Yes, you've got your freedom all right—but no rye!'

Porfiry Vladimirych looks edifyingly at Foka; but Foka stands stock still, as if turned to stone.

'Very proud you are—and that's the cause of your misfortune! Take me, now: I've had the blessing of God and the bounty of the Tsar—but I'm not proud! What am I? A worm! An insect! Pshaw! And it was for this, my humility, that God has given me his blessing! He favoured me himself with his mercy and inclined the Tsar too to reward me.'

'To my way of thinking, Porfiry Vladimirych, it was far better before when there was masters and serfs!' Foka says ingratiatingly.

'Yes, my friend, you had a fine time of it then! You lived the good life and had everything in plenty—rye, hay, potatoes! Ah well, why recall what's past! I bear no grudge. I forgot about the reapers long ago—it just came to mind, that's all. So, you say you need some rye?'

'That's it, some rye . . .'

'Is it a purchase you're thinking of?'

'Oh no, I couldn't buy any! I thought, if you could lend me some till the new crop.'

'Dear, oh dear! Rye, my friend, is mighty dear just now. I really don't know what we can manage . . .'

Porfiry Vladimirych ponders for a minute, as if he genuinely does not know what to do: anxious as he is to help a body, still with rye so dear . . .

'Yes, I can do it, my friend, I can lend you some rye,' he says at last. 'To tell the truth, I haven't got any rye for sale: trafficking in God's gifts is a thing I cannot abide! But as a loan—that's all right, I'll do it with pleasure. I don't forget that though today I am lending to you, tomorrow it's I who might be the borrower. Today I've got plenty—have a loan by all means! A quarter do you want?—a quarter it is! A half-quarter you need?—measure out a half-quarter! For tomorrow it might be my turn to come knocking at *your* window and asking my good friend Foka to lend me half a quarter as I've nothing to eat.'

'Never! As though you, sir, would ever come asking me!'

'True, I wouldn't, but as an example . . . There are stranger upsets in the world than that! See what they say in the papers: Napoleon, power that he was, even he's made mistakes and come to grief. Yes, indeed, my friend! How much rye were you wanting?'

'I'd like a quarter, if you'd be so good.'

'Yes, you can have a quarter. But I must tell you in advance: rye is mighty dear just now, mighty dear indeed! So what we'll do is this: I'll have them measure you out six bushels, and then in eight months' time you can pay me back two extra bushels to round it up to a quarter exact! I'm not charging interest, just a bit of rye from your surplus . . .'

Judas's proposition takes Foka's breath away; for some time he says nothing, only shifts his shoulders.

'Ain't that rather much, sir?' he asks finally, clearly unsure of himself.

'If it's too much, then try somewhere else! I'm not forcing you, it's just a friendly offer. I didn't send for you, you sought me out yourself. That's the way it is, my friend!'

'It is, sir, but the extra seems a lot, don't it?'

'Oh dear, dear, dear! And there was I thinking you a fair-minded, sensible man! What about me though, what am I supposed to live on? How am I going to cover my expenses? Have you a notion of the expenses I have? There's just no end to them, my friend! All the time it's pay out, settle up, cash down to somebody or other! Everybody wants cash, everybody badgers Porfiry Vladimirych, and it's Porfiry Vladimirych who foots the bill for all! And another thing: if I sold my rye to the chandler, I'd have the money paid on the spot. Money, my friend, is a sacred thing.

With money I could buy securities, tuck them away in a safe place, and live off the interest. No fuss, no worry—just tear off the slip and collect your cash! But with rye it's everlasting care and trouble and effort! How much will dry out, how much will be spilt, how much the mice will eat! No, my friend, money— that's the thing! I should have had more sense long ago and put everything into cash and gone away from you all here!'

'No, Porfiry Vladimirych, you stay on with us.'

'I'd like to, my friend, but I haven't the strength. If I had my old strength still, of course I'd stay and battle on. But no, it's time, time for repose! I'll go away, go to Trinity Monastery* and shelter under the wing of St Sergius—and then I'll be heard no more. How splendid it will be for me: peace, sanctity, quiet, no clamour, no quarrels, no noise—just like heaven!'

In short, for all Foka's prevarications, the deal is settled on Porfiry Vladimirych's terms. But as if that is not enough, just when Foka has agreed to the conditions of the loan, the small matter of Shelepikha comes up. It's nothing, just a poor patch of land with perhaps a desyatina of meadow, if that . . . so how would it be . . .

'I'm doing you a favour—you could do me one in return,' says Porfiry Vladimirych. 'Not to pay off interest, just as a favour. God helps us all and we help each other. If you could just take your scythe over this bit of meadow, I'll bear it in mind. For I'm a simple man, my friend! You do me a rouble's worth of work, and I'll . . .'

Porfiry Vladimirych gets up and as a sign that the business is concluded turns towards the church and prays. Foka, following his example, also crosses himself.

Foka has now vanished; Porfiry Vladimirych takes a sheet of paper, arms himself with his counting-frame, and the beads positively leap to the touch of his nimble fingers . . . Gradually a whole orgy of figures gets under way. The entire world is now veiled from Judas's eyes, as if by a mist: in feverish haste he turns from beads to paper, from paper to beads. The figures go on mounting up and up . . .

THE RECKONING

IT is mid-December. Outside, all around is silent and still, enveloped in the blanket of snow that stretches as far as the eye can see; on the road there are so many drifts from the overnight snow that the peasants' horses flounder as they struggle to pull forth the empty sledges. To the Golovlev estate there is hardly a track. Porfiry Vladimirych is now so unaccustomed to visitors that with the onset of autumn he had the main gate and the front entrance boarded up, leaving the servants to communicate with the world at large by way of the maids' room entrance and the side gate.

It is morning; eleven o'clock is striking. Judas, in his dressing-gown, stands by the window gazing aimlessly out. From crack of dawn he was pacing up and down his study, thinking all the time of something and reckoning up his imaginary income, till finally he lost count and grew weary. The fruitful garden that stretches before the main façade of the manor-house and the village that nestles beyond it—all is submerged in the drifted snow. It is a frosty morning after yesterday's blizzard and in the sun the snow shroud glistens with a million sparkling lights, at which Porfiry Vladimirych instinctively screws up his eyes. The yard is empty and still; there is no sign of life at all in the servants' quarters or in the stock-yard; even the village is hushed, as though dead. Only above the priest's house there is a curl of blue-grey smoke which takes Judas's notice.

'That was eleven o'clock striking and the priest's wife is still at her cooking,' he thinks. 'Forever stuffing themselves, these priests.'

With this as his starting point, he proceeds to calculate whether today is an ordinary day or holy day, a day of fasting or of normal fare, and what the priest's wife might therefore be cooking, but suddenly his attention is diverted. On the hill out of Naglovka village a black dot appears, which gradually approaches and grows bigger. Porfiry Vladimirych studies it and, needless to say, his first concern is to pose a multitude of idle questions. Who is this wayfarer? Is it a peasant or somebody else? There is nobody else it can be, so it must be a peasant. Yes, it is. What is he up to? If it's firewood he's after, there's the Naglovka wood on the other side of the village . . . no doubt, the rapscallion is off to steal his master's wood. If he's bound for the mill, he would have to turn right out of the village . . . Perhaps he's going to fetch the priest? Someone may be dying or already dead? Or is it a birth, perhaps? Which of the women could that be then? In the autumn Nenila was expecting, but it's early for her yet . . . If it's a boy, he'll be put in the tax-register later on—how many souls were there in Naglovka at the last census? And if it's a girl, they don't put girls in the register, and anyway . . . But then, you can't do without womenfolk . . . Pshaw!

Judas spits in disgust and looks to the icon, as if seeking there protection against the Evil One.

Most likely he would have rambled on for some time in this manner, if the black dot that had come into view by Naglovka had, as was usual, appeared only briefly and then passed out of sight; but it continued to grow bigger and bigger and finally turned on to the causeway leading to the church. Judas now saw quite clearly that it was a small covered kibitka drawn by a pair of horses harnessed head to tail. He watched it climb the rise and draw level with the church ('Perhaps it's the Archdeacon?' the thought struck him, 'That'll be why they're still cooking at the priest's!'), and then he saw it turn to the right and head straight for the manor: 'So it *is* coming here after all!' Porfiry Vladimirych instinctively drew the skirts of his dressing-gown together and started back from the window, as if afraid he might be seen by the traveller.

He was right: the conveyance drove up to the house and stopped at the side gate. A young woman hastily leapt out. Her dress was totally unsuited to the season—she had on a quilted town coat trimmed with lambswool (more for appearance than for warmth) and was obviously chilled to the bone. Being met by nobody, she flitted up the steps to the maids' room entrance and a few seconds later the door of the maids' room banged, then another door, after which in all the rooms on that side of the house there was the sound of footsteps, banging, and bustling.

Porfiry Vladimirych stood at the study door and listened. It was so long since he had seen anyone apart from his own domestics and he was in general now so unused to human society that he was thrown into consternation. About a quarter of an hour passed; the footsteps and banging of doors went on, but still nobody came to announce the visitor. This was even more disturbing. Clearly, the new arrival belonged to that category of persons who, as 'near and dear', gave no cause to doubt their right to hospitality. Who were his near and dear? He tried to recall them, but his memory was dull and slow. He had had a son Volodka, and another son Petka, and there had been dear Mother, Arina Petrovna . . . but that was long ago, ah, long ago! Then there was Nadka Galkina, daughter of his late Aunt Varvara Mikhailovna, who had come last autumn to live at Goryushkino —could it be her? No, never: she had tried once to intrude into the sanctum of Golovlevo and gone off with a flea in her ear. 'She'll not dare, she'll never dare!' Judas repeated to himself, roused to indignation by the very thought of Galkina coming. But who else could it be?

As he was thus trying to recall, Evprakseyushka came cautiously to the door and announced:

'The young mistress from Pogorelka, Anna Semenovna, has come.'

It was indeed Anninka. But so changed was she now as to be hardly recognizable. She arrived this time in Golovlevo not as she was when she came after Arina Petrovna's death—a handsome girl, brimming with youth and vitality, with ruddy cheeks, prominent grey eyes, high bosom, and heavy plait of ash-blond hair; she was now a frail, weakly creature with sunken chest, hollow cheeks, and sickly flush, languid in her movements, and stooping, almost hunched. Even her magnificent plait looked somehow scant, only her eyes looked larger than ever in her gaunt face and burned with a feverish brightness. Evprakseyushka peered at her for a long time, as if she were a stranger, before finally recognizing her.

'Miss! Is it you?' she cried, clapping together her upraised hands.

'Yes, it's me. Why?'

As she said this, Anninka gave a quiet laugh, as though wishing to add: 'Yes, here I am! See how the world has done for me!'

'Is Uncle well?' she asked.

'Your uncle, he's not too bad . . . He's still alive, I allow, though we scarce ever see him!'

'What's the matter with him?'

'Oh, nothing special—it's all from being bored, I suppose.'

'Do you mean he's actually stopped talking his nonsense?'

'He keeps quiet these days, Miss. He used to talk all the time, but then he suddenly shut up. We hear him sometimes in the study talking by himself, he sort of laughs even, but when he comes out he goes quiet again. They say it was the same with his brother who died—Stepan Vladimirych: always bright and cheerful, then suddenly he shut up. And what about you, Miss, are you still well?'

Anninka merely made a gesture of despair.

'And your sister, is she well?'

'She's been dead and buried a month since. By the roadside at Krechetov.'

'Goodness, Lord preserve us! And by the roadside too?'

'It's how they bury suicides, you know.'

'Lordie me! And her a young lady, going and laying hands on herself . . . How could it happen?'

'Yes, she was a "young lady" to start with, and then she poisoned herself—that's all there is to it. But I funked it. I wanted to live! So I've come here to you. But don't worry, it's not for long—I'll soon be dead.'

Evprakseyushka gaped at her as if failing to understand.

'Why do you look at me? A pretty sight, is it? Well, it's what I am . . . But that can wait . . . till later . . . Now have the driver paid his fare and tell Uncle I'm here.'

Saying this, she drew from her pocket a purse that had seen better days and took out two yellow rouble-notes.

'That's all my worldly goods,' she went on, pointing to her meagre travelling-bag. 'All my property is there, inherited and acquired! I'm so cold, Evprakseyushka, I'm chilled right through! Here am I all aches and pains, with not a bone in my body that doesn't hurt, and then here it's so bitterly cold . . . On the way I could think of nothing but getting to Golovlevo where at least I could die in the warm! I could do with some vodka—is there any?'

'Oh, but, Miss, tea would be better for you. The samovar will be ready in just a minute.'

'No. I'll have tea later. I want vodka now . . . But don't go telling Uncle about that for the moment . . . It will all come out later.'

While they were laying the table for tea in the dining-room Porfiry Vladimirych appeared. On meeting him, it was Anninka's turn to be astonished at seeing how thin, seedy, and aloof he had become. His manner towards Anninka was odd: not exactly cold, but offhand, as if she were of no concern to him. He said little and spoke in a constrained manner, like an actor who struggles to recall lines from parts played long ago. He was in general preoccupied: it was as though some other, portentous matter was exercising his mind and he was vexed at being distracted from it to attend to these trivial concerns.

'So you've arrived,' he said at last. 'What would you like? Some tea? Coffee? Just say what you want!'

In earlier days, on the occasions of family meetings, Judas would be the one to wax sentimental, but this time it was Anninka who gave way to her feelings and this she did in real earnest. She must have sunk indeed to the very depths of misery, for she fell on Porfiry Vladimirych's breast and hugged him tight.

'Uncle!' she cried, 'I've come to you!' and suddenly dissolved into tears.

'Very well, then! You're welcome! I've rooms enough—stay!'

'I'm ill, Uncle. Very, very ill!'

'If you're ill, you must pray to God! That's what I do when I'm ill—I cure myself by prayer.'

'It's to die I've come, Uncle!'

Porfiry Vladimirych gave her a searching look, and a barely perceptible sneer passed fleetingly over his lips.

'So, the show is over?' he said, hardly audibly, as if speaking to himself.

'Yes, the show's over. It's over for Lyubinka—she's dead. And for me too, but I'm . . . still alive!'

At the news of Lyubinka's death Judas piously crossed himself and whispered a prayer. Anninka meanwhile sat down, put her elbows on the table, and, looking out towards the church, continued to weep bitterly.

'Why, it's a sin to weep and despair!' Porfiry Vladimirych observed edifyingly. 'You know the Christian way, don't you: not to weep, but be resigned and trust in the Lord—that's the Christian way!'

But Anninka leant back in her chair and, disconsolately drooping her arms, repeated:

'Oh, I don't know, I don't know, I don't know!'

'If you're grieving like this on account of your sister, why that's a sin too!' Judas continued to admonish her. 'Because, commendable though it is to love your sisters and brothers, still, if it be God's will to call one or more of them . . .'

'Oh, don't, don't! Uncle, you—are you a good man? Are you a good man? Tell me!'

Anninka once more rushed to him and embraced him.

'Of course, of course, a good man. Now just you say if there's anything you want. Something to eat? Some tea or coffee? Just ask! Say what you want!'

And it suddenly came back to Anninka how on her first visit to Golovlevo her uncle had asked her if she would care for a little veal? or sucking-pig? or a few nice potatoes?—and she realized now that here she would find no other consolation.

'No thank you, Uncle,' she said, sitting again at the table. 'There's nothing I specially want. I'm sure I shall be well content with everything.'

'If you're content, that's splendid! Will you be going on to Pogorelka?'

'No, Uncle. I'll stay here with you for the time being. You won't mind that, will you?'

'Lord bless you! You stay! If I happened to ask about Pogorelka, that's only because if you were going, we'd have to make arrangements: order the kibitka, horses . . .'

'No. I'll go later, later!'

'Splendid! You go some time later on, but for now you'll stay here with us. You can help run the house—after all, I'm all alone, you know. The duchess here'—Judas with something near hatred pointed to Evprakseyushka as she poured the tea—'she's out roving all the time in the servants' quarters, and you can't always get anybody to come when you call—the whole house is empty! Well, I'll bid you farewell for now. I'm going to my room. I'll say my prayers, then see to some business, then pray again . . . yes, indeed, my dear. Is it long since Lyubinka passed away?'

'About a month, Uncle.'

'We'll go early to mass then in the morning and we'll have a requiem too for Lyubov, God's servant now departed . . . So, farewell for now! Do have some tea, and if you feel like a bite of something after your journey, well have them bring you a bite. We'll meet again at dinner. We'll talk and have a chat then; if there's need of anything, we'll see to it, and if there's no need, then we'll just sit!'

Such was this first family meeting. With its conclusion Anninka started on a new life in that hateful Golovlevo from which twice already in her short life she had been desperate to escape.

Anninka had gone rapidly downhill. The awareness that had been prompted by her visit to Golovlevo after the death of Arina Petrovna—that she was a 'lady', that she had her own home and her own family graves, that there was something else in her life besides the stench and racket of hotels and taverns, that there was a last refuge beyond the reach of her admirers with their foul breath reeking of vodka and stables, which could not be invaded by that whiskered one with the hoarse drunkard's voice and bloodshot eyes (oh, the things he had said to her! the gestures he had made in her presence!)—this awareness had vanished almost at once as Golovlevo passed out of sight.

Anninka had then gone from Golovlevo straight to Moscow and set about trying to get Lyubinka and herself taken on by one of the state theatres. With this in mind she approached, among others, *Maman*, the headmistress of the institute she had attended, and some of her former school-friends. But she met everywhere with an odd reception. *Maman* was at first perfectly cordial to her, but no sooner did she discover that Anninka was an actress in the provincial theatre than her benign expression suddenly changed and became grave and stern, while her school-friends, most of whom were married women, regarded her with such insolent amazement that she lost her nerve completely. Only one of them, better-natured than the rest, in order to show some concern, asked her:

'Do tell me, dear, is it true that when you actresses are changing in your dressing-rooms you have officers to tighten your stays?'

In short, her attempts to become established in Moscow never got any further. It must, though, be said in truth that she did not in fact possess any of the prerequisites for success on the stage in the capital. Both she and Lyubinka belonged to that category of spirited, but not specially gifted actresses who play the same part all their lives. Anninka was a success in *La Périchole*, Lyubinka in *Pansy* and *An Old-Time Colonel*.* And after that, whatever they did always came out as yet another *Périchole* or *Pansy*—or in most cases perhaps as nothing at all. Anninka also had occasion to play Hélène in *La Belle Hélène* (often even, according to the requirements of her job); for this she put on a flame-coloured wig over her ash-blond hair and wore a tunic with a cleavage that plunged to the waist—but still the effect was mediocre, lifeless, not even salacious. From playing in *Hélène* she went on to *Excerpts from La Grande-Duchesse de Gérolstein*, and since in this case her own lacklustre playing was combined with a quite absurd production, the result was something ludicrous indeed. Finally, she took on the role of Clairette in *La Fille de Madame Angot*, but her efforts to win the audience caused her so to overact that even the undemanding provincial theatre-goers gained the impression that the creature disporting herself on the stage was not an actress wishing to 'please', but just a wanton baggage. In general, Anninka acquired a reputation for being an adept actress with a reasonable voice and, since she was also good-looking, she might attract full houses in a provincial theatre. But no more than that. She could never make a name for herself and had no particular stamp of her own. Even among provincial audiences her following consisted entirely of servitors in the various branches of the military, whose main ambition was to have an *entrée* backstage. A career in the capital would have been possible only if she were foisted on a theatre by some powerful patron, and even then audiences would doubtless have dubbed her with some unflattering name, such as 'Good-time Girl'.

She had to go back to the provinces. While in Moscow, Anninka received a letter from Lyubinka telling her that their company was moving on from Krechetov to Samovarnov, the chief town of the province, which she (Lyubinka) was very glad of, because she was friendly with a member of the Samovarnov zemstvo,* who was so keen on her that he seemed 'ready to steal the zemstvo funds' in order to gratify her every whim. And indeed, when Anninka arrived in Samovarnov, she found her sister living in relative luxury and having frivolously decided to abandon the stage. Lyubinka's 'friend', the zemstvo official Gavrilo Stepanych Lyulkin, was present when Anninka arrived. He was a retired captain of hussars, until recently a *bel homme*, but now somewhat overweight. He had a noble visage, noble manners, and a noble cast of mind, all of which together none the less inspired the conviction that here was a man who would not be disposed to run a mile's distance if confronted with the zemstvo cash-box. Lyubinka welcomed her sister with open arms and announced that a room was prepared for her in her apartment.

But Anninka, influenced by her recent visit to her 'own home', got angry. There was a heated argument between the sisters and then a split. At the time Anninka could not help recalling what the priest at Voplino had said about the difficulty in the acting profession of keeping one's 'treasure' intact.

Anninka took a room in the hotel and severed all relations with her sister. Easter passed; the following week performances began again and Anninka learned that in place of her sister a Miss Nalimova was being brought from Kazan, who, though an indifferent actress, deported herself on stage with total lack of inhibition. As usual, Anninka appeared in *La Périchole* and enraptured the residents of Samovarnov. When she got back to her hotel, she found in her room a packet containing a hundred-rouble note and a short missive which read: 'In the event of anything, the same again. Kukishev, Purveyor of High-Class Drapery.' Anninka was furious and went to complain to the hotel proprietor, but he declared that Kukishev had this customary way of welcoming all new actresses on their arrival, and that he was anyway a quiet-living sort of fellow and there was really no need to take offence. Anninka accepted this advice. She sealed the note and money in an envelope and next day, after returning it whence it came, felt calm again.

But Kukishev turned out to be more persistent than the hotel-keeper had made out. He reckoned himself to be one of Lyulkin's set and was on friendly terms with Lyubinka. He was a man of means and he was also, like Lyulkin, as a member of the Town Council, very well placed with regard to the municipal cash-box. Besides which, again like Lyulkin, he was totally fearless. He was—by the standards of the market-halls—ravishingly handsome. He recalled, that is, the 'beetle' found by Masha in the song when she went gathering berries in the fields:

> A beetle black with whiskers,
> A curly head had he
> And eyebrows dark and shady—
> The very one for me!

Possessed of these good looks, he thought himself entitled to venture his luck also on account of Lyubinka's declared promise of assistance.

Lyubinka had, it seemed, in general burnt her boats once and for all, and there were rumours about her which were extremely disagreeable for her sister's self-respect. It was said that every evening a band of revellers gathered in her apartment and supped from midnight to morning; also that Lyubinka presided over this company and did a 'gipsy' turn in which, half-clad (Lyulkin crying to his drunken companions 'Look at that! There's breast-work for you!') and with her hair loose, she would sing, guitar in hand:

> Oh, what bliss it was to know
> That nice man with the whiskers!

Anninka listened to these tales and was disturbed. But what caused her most astonishment was that Lyubinka should be singing the 'Whiskers' song in the 'gipsy' style, as though she were the celebrated Moscow Matresha. Anninka had always given full credit to Lyubinka and if anyone had told her, for instance, that Lyubinka's rendering of the couplets from *An Old-Time Colonel* was 'inimitable', of course she would have thought it entirely natural and readily believed them. It was impossible to do otherwise, for audiences in Kursk, Tambov, and Penza still remembered the inimitable innocence with which Lyubinka had declared in her little-girl's voice how she would love to serve *under* the colonel ... But as for Lyubinka being able to sing in the gipsy style, like Matresha, that—begging your pardon—was just untrue! Now she, Anninka, *could* sing in that style, of that there was no question. It was her speciality, her role, and the whole of Kursk which had seen her in *Russian Romances on Stage** would readily testify to the fact that she *could*.

And Anninka picked up her guitar, looped the striped sling over her shoulder, and, sitting on a chair and crossing her legs, she began: 'Ee-eh! Ee-ah!'—and indeed it really did sound just like the gipsy Matresha.

Whatever else, it was certain that Lyubinka was living in the lap of luxury, and Lyulkin, not wishing to becloud the scenes of inebriated bliss by any kind of refusal, had evidently begun helping himself to loans from the zemstvo cash-box. Apart from the large quantities of champagne which were nightly drunk and slopped on the floor of Lyubinka's apartment, she herself became daily more capricious and demanding. First there were orders to Moscow for dresses from Madame Minangois, then for diamonds from Fulda.* Lyubinka was prudent and did not scorn valuables. The drunken life was one thing, but gold and jewels and especially prize bonds were another matter altogether. This, at any rate, was the life she led, not exactly gay, but wild and abandoned, with one state of drunken oblivion following another. There was only one disagreeable aspect: it proved to be necessary for her to get herself in the good books of the Chief of Police who, though one of Lyulkin's friends, none the less liked occasionally to let it be known that he was, in a sense, the law. Lyubinka could always tell when he was displeased with her hospitality, because on these occasions she invariably had a visit next morning from the local Superintendent wanting to see her passport. And she succumbed: in the morning she would serve the Superintendent vodka and zakuski and in the evening personally prepare for the Chief of Police a certain 'Swedish' punch of which he was particularly fond.

Kukishev witnessed this revelry and burned with envy. At whatever cost, he wanted to keep just such a free house and have just such a 'duchess' himself. There would be then a bit more variety in life: one night they could go to Lyulkin's 'duchess', the next to his, Kukishev's. This was his cherished ambition, the ambition of a stupid man—who, the stupider he is, the more doggedly he pursues the attainment of his ends. And the most appropriate person to provide the realization of Kukishev's ambition was—Anninka.

Anninka, however, did not give in. So far there had been no stirring of passion in her, though she had many admirers and was unrestrained in her behaviour towards them. There was a moment when she thought she could fall in love with the local tragic actor Miloslavsky Xth,* who was, it seemed, consumed by a similar passion for her. But Miloslavsky Xth was so stupid and, besides, so persistently unsober that he never declared himself, but simply gawped and hiccuped absurdly whenever she passed by. So this love withered in the very bud. All her other admirers Anninka regarded as part of the inevitable milieu to which a provincial actress is condemned by the terms of her profession. She submitted to these terms, enjoyed the small privileges they offered (applause, bouquets, troika rides, picnics, etc.), but in respect of what might be called 'overt' dissipation that was as far as she went.

She behaved in the same way now. All through the summer she kept firmly to the path of virtue, zealously guarding her 'treasure', as if wishing also thereby to demonstrate to the Voplino priest that even among actresses individuals exist who are capable of heroism. At one point she even decided to complain about Kukishev to the head of the district,* who gave her a sympathetic hearing and praised her for her heroism, recommending her to continue likewise in the future. But at the same time, taking her complaint to be nothing but a blind for an indirect attack upon himself, the head of the district was graciously pleased to add that, having expended all his strength in the conflict with internal enemies,* he had no strong reason to suppose he could be of any possible assistance in the matter of her request. On hearing which, Anninka blushed and left.

Kukishev in the meantime had had the wit to enlist the support of the theatre public in his importunings. Somehow the public suddenly came to see that Kukishev was right and that Miss Pogorelsky Ist (thus she was billed) was nothing all that fantastic to be playing the innocent touch-me-not. A party was formed which undertook to bring this fractious upstart to book. It began with the backstage *habitués* ceasing to frequent her dressing-room and instead making themselves at home next door in the dressing-room of Miss Nalimova. Then, though avoiding any show of outright hostility, they began to greet Miss Pogorelsky's entrances with such killing reserve that she might have been not the leading lady coming on stage but some dummy *ingénue*. Finally, they pressed the manager into taking away some of Anninka's roles and giving them to Nalimova. Stranger still was the fact that the most active part in this underhand intrigue was played by Lyubinka, with Nalimova acting as her *confidante*.

By the autumn Anninka found to her astonishment that she was now required to play Orestes in *La Belle Hélène* and that of her former leading roles she was left only with Périchole, and then only because Miss Nalimova could not bring herself to compete with her in this particular part. On top of this, the manager informed her that in view of the decline in her popularity her salary was to be reduced to seventy-five roubles a month with half-share in a benefit once a year.

Anninka took fright, since with such a salary she would have to leave the hotel and move into the inn. She wrote offering her services to two or three other managers, but from each she received the same reply—that Péricholes were at present ten a penny, and, since she was known on good authority to be 'difficult', her hopes of success were even less likely of fulfilment.

Anninka was coming to the end of her reserves of money.

Another week and there would be no escaping the inn, where she would be on the same footing as Miss Khoroshavina, who played the part of Parthénis and was the protégée of the local police-inspector. A feeling akin to despair descended on her, particularly since every day a mysterious hand left surreptitious notes for her, always with the same message: 'Pericoal! Yield! Your own Kukishev'. And it was at this difficult moment that Lyubinka quite unexpectedly burst in on her.

'For heaven's sake, what prince is it you're saving up your treasure for?' she demanded bluntly.

Anninka was taken aback. What struck her most of all was that the priest at Voplino and Lyubinka should make the very same use of the word 'treasure'. The only difference was that while the priest saw this treasure as a 'foundation', for Lyubinka it was a trifle—capable, none the less, of driving men, 'those swine', out of their minds.

And she could not help thinking to herself: what, after all, is this treasure? Is it really a treasure and is it worth preserving?— and, alas, she found to this question no satisfactory answer. On the one hand, to part with this treasure seemed wrong, on the other hand ... in heaven's name, can the whole point and purpose of life be to spend every minute fighting to defend it?

'In six months I've got thirty prize bonds,' Lyubinka went on. 'And so many clothes—just look at this dress I've got on.'

Lyubinka turned completely round, straightening her dress at the front, then at the back, and presented herself for inspection. The dress was indeed both expensive and wonderfully made: straight from Minangois in Moscow.

'Kukishev is nice,' Lyubinka started once more. 'He'll dress you up like a doll, and give you money too. You can chuck up the theatre ... Enough's enough!'

'Never!' cried Anninka with passion, still not having forgotten about 'sacred art'.

'You can keep it up if you want to ... You'd get your old salary again and be billed above Nalimova.'

Anninka said nothing.

'Well, goodbye for now! Our crowd is downstairs waiting. Kukishev's there too. Won't you come?'

But Anninka still said nothing.

'Well, think it over, if there's anything to think over ... When you've done your thinking, come round! Goodbye!'

On 17 September, Lyubinka's name-day, the posters of the Samovarnov theatres announced a *special* performance. Anninka was once more appearing as la belle Hélène and the same evening 'for this peformance only' Miss Pogorelsky IInd (Lyubinka, that is) was playing Orestes. To crown the occasion (and also 'for this performance only') they put Miss Nalimova in tights and a cut-away coat, daubed her face with soot, and sent her on stage with a piece of iron sheeting as Cleon, the smith. With all this in store, the audience was also in exalted mood. As soon as Anninka emerged from the wings, there was such a tumult of applause that she, unused as she now was to ovations, felt sobs rising in her throat. And when in Act III, in the waking scene at night, she rose practically naked from her couch, there went up from the audience quite literally a groan. Such indeed was the effect that one overwrought member of the audience, when Menelaus appeared in the doorway, cried out: 'Clear off, you old pest!' For his part, Kukishev, wearing tails, white tie, and white gloves, made a worthy show of his triumph and in the intervals dispensed champagne to all and sundry. Finally, the theatre manager too came full of jubilation to Anninka's dressing-room and fell on his knees, saying:

'Now my young lady's being a good girl! From this evening you're back on the top rate again and benefit shows according.'

In short, everyone praised her, congratulated her, and declared their support, so that she, after initially feeling diffident and desperately miserable, came quite unexpectedly to believe that she had ... fulfilled her mission in life!

After the performance they all went to Lyubinka's and there were still more congratulations. There was such a throng and the place at once became so clouded with tobacco smoke that it was hard to breathe. Straightaway they sat down to supper, and the champagne flowed. Kukishev never left Anninka's side, and, though she was obviously rather embarrassed, she no longer found his attentions irksome. To her it seemed rather comic, but flattering too, that with so little effort she had acquired for herself this sturdy, strong-armed merchant who could with the greatest of ease bend and straighten a horse-shoe, and whom she could now command and do with as she pleased. At supper there was general merry-making of that drunken, disorderly kind that engages neither the heart nor mind, and which leaves you next day with a throbbing head and nausea. Only one of the company, the tragic actor Miloslavsky Xth, wore a doleful look and, declining the champagne, he downed glass after glass of plain vodka. As for Anninka, she for a time restrained herself from 'inebriety', but Kukishev was so insistent and implored her so movingly on his knees: 'Anna Semenovna! You're in my dewbit (*debit*!)! I beg you kindly to drink to our happiness! To our love and concord! Be so kind!'—that though she was vexed at the sight of his stupid figure and the stupid things he said, she still could not refuse and, before she knew where she was, her head was awhirl. As for Lyubinka, she was magnanimous enough to suggest personally that Anninka should sing 'Oh, what bliss it was to know that nice man with the whiskers!'—which Anninka did to such perfection that all declared that she had it to a 't', 'just like Matresha!' Lyubinka responded with a masterly rendering of the couplets about wanting to serve *under* the colonel and straightaway convinced everyone that this was her true genre in which she was as unrivalled as Anninka was in songs with a gipsy flavour. The evening concluded with Miloslavsky Xth and Miss Nalimova performing a 'masquerade-sketch', in which Miloslavsky declaimed extracts from *Ugolino* (tragedy in five acts by N. Polevoy) and Nalimova responded with lines from an unpublished tragedy by Barkov.* So startling was the result that Nalimova came very near to eclipsing the Misses Pogorelsky and becoming the star of the evening.

It was almost daylight when Kukishev left the name-day celebrant and handed Anninka into his carriage. Pious townsfolk on their way home from matins, seeing Miss Pogorelsky Ist in all her finery and unsteady on her feet, muttered darkly:

'Here are folk coming out of church and they're still swilling vodka . . . scandalous it is!'

From her sister's Anninka went this time not to the hotel, but to her *own* apartment, which was small, but cosy and very nicely appointed. Kukishev followed her in.

The whole winter passed by in an uprecedented frantic whirl. Anninka's head was now completely turned and if occasionally she did think back to her 'treasure', it was only to say to herself at once: 'Really, what a fool I was!' Kukishev, proud to know that his notion of possessing a 'duchess' of the same quality as Lyulkin's had been realized, not only did not stint his cash, but, spurred by rivalry, invariably ordered two dresses when Lyulkin ordered only one and laid on two dozen of champagne when Lyulkin laid on one. Even Lyubinka began to feel some envy for her sister, since in the course of the winter Anninka acquired forty prize bonds as well as a fair number of gold trinkets, with stones or without. However, they were now good friends again and decided to pool their store of acquisitions. At the same time, Anninka still had dreams of something different and in a heart-to-heart talk with her sister said:

'When *all this* is over, we'll go back to Pogorelka. We'll have money and we can look after the estate.'

To which Lyubinka very cynically retorted:

'Do you really suppose that *all this* will ever be over . . . you fool!'

It was Anninka's ill luck that Kukishev had a fresh 'notion', which he began to pursue with his customary obstinacy. Uncultivated and indubitably unintelligent as he was, he thought it would be the height of bliss if his 'duchess' would 'keep him company', that is, drink vodka with him.

'Let's have a snort! The two of us! If you please, ma'am,' he kept badgering her (to Anninka he always adopted a formal mode of address, first in recognition of her gentry status, and secondly to show that he had not for nothing served his time as a counter-boy in the market-halls).

For a time Anninka refused, pointing out that Lyulkin had never tried to make Lyubinka drink vodka.

'But still for love of Mr Lyulkin the lady does partake,' protested Kukishev. 'If I may say so, duchess: why should the Lyulkins be an example for us? They're the Lyulkins, and we're the Kukishevs! So we'll take a snort in our way, the Kukishev way!'

In short, Kukishev prevailed. One day Anninka took from her lover's hand a glass filled with the green liquid and tipped it straight down her throat. Of course, she was knocked backwards, spluttered, coughed, and reeled on her feet—to the ecstatic delight of Kukishev.

'If I may say so, duchess: that's not the way to partake at all! You were too quick!' he informed her, when she had somewhat recovered. 'You should take the "gobble-it" (as he called the wine-glass) into your hands like this! You then lift it to your lips so and, nice and steady—one-two-three—God-bless-me!'

And he calmly and solemnly tipped the glass down his throat as if he were pouring its contents into a tub. He did not even blink; all he did was to take a tiny morsel of black bread from the plate, dip it in the salt-cellar, and munch it.

Thus Kukishev realized the second of his 'notions' and he set to pondering what new one he could think up so as to give the Lyulkins one in the eye. And, needless to say, he succeeded.

'D'you know what?' he suddenly announced. 'Later on, in the summer, let's all go down to my mill—the Lyulkins can come along, and we'll take a travelling-bag (his name for a hamper of wine and zakuski) and we'll go bathing in the river, all done by mutual consent!'

'That we shall never do!' protested Anninka indignantly.

'Why not then? First, we'll go bathing, then have a little snort and a bit of *dormez-vous*, and after that another bathe! We'll have a fine old time!'

Whether or not this latest 'notion' of Kukishev was ever put into effect is not known, but certain it is that this drunken oblivion went on for a whole year, in which time neither the municipal council nor the zemstvo equivalent showed the least disquiet concerning Messrs Kukishev and Lyulkin. Lyulkin did, though, for appearances' sake, make a trip to Moscow and say on his return that he had sold off his forest for timber. When reminded that he had already sold his forest four years earlier, when he was living with Domashka the gipsy, he replied that what he had disposed of then was his wood at Drygalovo and now it was an outlying piece of woodland called 'Dashka's Shame'. And to lend more weight to his story he went on to say that the wood he had now sold got its name because once, in the days of serfdom, a peasant-girl called Dashka had been 'caught at it' in the wood and been given a flogging for it on the spot. As for Kukishev, he by way of cover put it about that he had smuggled through a parcel of lace in a consignment of pencils from abroad and had made a fat profit out of the operation.

However, the following September the Chief of Police asked Kukishev if he might have a thousand roubles by way of a loan and Kukishev was imprudent enough to refuse. The Chief of Police began then having whispered discussions about some matter with the Deputy Prosecutor ('And the pair of them were every evening knocking back my champagne!' Kukishev later testified in court). And then, on 17 September, the anniversary of Kukishev's love-match, when he and the rest were once more celebrating Lyubinka's name-day, one of the municipal councillors came running to tell him that a meeting was being convened in the council office and that a formal report was being drawn up.

'They've found the "dewbit", I suppose?' exclaimed Kukishev quite jauntily, and without more ado he followed the messenger to the council chambers and from there straight on to the gaol.

Next day there was commotion in the zemstvo offices too. The members assembled, had the cash-box fetched out of the treasury, counted, counted again, but for all the clicking of their counting-frames it finally transpired that here too there was a 'dewbit'. Lyulkin attended the audit, pale and grim, but . . . noble! When the 'dewbit' was palpably revealed and each member was privately considering what Drygalovo wood he would himself be forced to sell to make good the sum embezzled, Lyulkin walked to the window, drew a revolver from his pocket, and there and then put a bullet in his temple.

This event gave rise to a great deal of talk in the town. People judged and compared. They felt sorry for Lyulkin and said of him that at least he had come to a noble end. As for Kukishev, the view was that he was nothing but a shop-keeper and that is all he would ever be. Of Anninka and Lyubinka, however, it was plainly stated that 'they were the ones' and it was 'all because of them' and it would be no bad thing to put them in gaol too as a warning to suchlike baggages in the future.

The investigating attorney did not, however, put them in gaol; he did, though, so thoroughly frighten them that they totally lost their grip. Of course, there were people at hand to give them friendly advice to conceal their more valuable possessions, but they listened without taking it in. In consequence, the plaintiffs' lawyer (both councils had engaged the same man), a very spirited fellow, in order to secure restitution for his clients turned up at the sisters' apartments with a bailiff in attendance, inventoried and sealed all that he found there, leaving at their disposal only their clothes and such items of gold and silver as, to judge by the inscriptions on them, were presentations made by their delighted public. Lyubinka did, though, in the course of this manage to snatch up a wad of notes given to her only the evening before and secrete it in her corset. The wad contained a thousand roubles—this for some indefinite time was all the sisters had to exist on.

In expectation of the trial they were detained in Samovarnov for some four months. The trial then began and for them, especially Anninka, it was a harrowing experience. Kukishev was abominably coarse; there was simply no need for all the details he recounted, but he was evidently keen to cut a figure before the ladies of Samovarnov and revealed absolutely everything. The prosecutor and the councils' lawyer, who were young men and anxious to give pleasure to the ladies of Samovarnov, made all they could of this in order to lend the trial some spice—in which, of course, they were entirely successful. Several times Anninka fainted, but the councils' lawyer, concerned only with winning his case, paid not the slightest heed and went on putting question after question. At last the enquiry ended and the parties concerned were given the opportunity to make statements. Late that night the jury pronounced Kukishev guilty, though with extenuating circumstances, in consequence of which he was promptly sentenced to exile without imprisonment in Western Siberia, 'in the less remote parts'.*

When the case was over, the sisters were able to leave Samovarnov. It was time too, for the thousand roubles they had concealed were by now running out. Besides which, the manager of the theatre in Krechetov, with whom they had a provisional agreement, insisted that they came to Krechetov at once, threatening otherwise to break off negotiations. Of their money, trinkets, and securities that had been placed under seal by the plaintiffs' lawyer there was neither sight nor sound.

Such were the consequences of failing to look after one's 'treasure'. Exhausted, harrowed, and dispirited by the general contempt, the sisters lost all faith in their own abilities and all hope of better things to come. They grew thin, gave way, lost heart. And on top of all this, Anninka, trained in the school of Kukishev, had taken to drinking.

Things got even worse. In Krechetov the sisters were scarcely out of the train before they were taken over. Captain Papkov of the cavalry got Lyubinka and the merchant Zabvenny Anninka. But it was not the old free and easy life. Papkov and Zabvenny were uncouth and pugnacious, though very moderate in their spending (as Zabvenny put it, 'It all depends on the merchandise'), and after three or four months their ardour had considerably cooled. To crown it all, the sisters' moderate fortunes in love were matched by their distinctly moderate fortunes on the stage: the manager who had engaged them in hopes of capitalizing on the scandal they had caused in Samovarnov had made a totally unforeseen miscalculation. At the very first performance, when both Misses Pogorelsky were on stage together, somebody from the gallery shouted: 'Yah! Gaolbirds!'—a sobriquet which stuck and at a stroke determined their theatrical fate.

It was a blank, lacklustre life they now led, devoid of the least mental interest. The audiences were unresponsive, the manager sulked, and their protectors did nothing to protect them. Zabvenny, like Kukishev, had visions of how he would 'press' his duchess to take a drink with him, how she would first be coy and then gradually give way—and he was much put out to discover that she was already thoroughly schooled and he was left only with the pleasure of gathering his friends to watch his Anyutka 'knocking back the vodka'. Papkov was also discontented, finding that Lyubinka had grown thin—or become, as he put it, 'nothing but a bag of bones'.

'You used to have a bit of flesh on you. Where's it all gone to?' he would demand.

And because of this he was not only unmannerly in his treatment of her, but even on occasion beat her when in his cups.

By the end of the winter the sisters had no 'proper' protectors
and no 'regular situation'. They still had a tenuous connection
with the theatre, but it was no longer a question of *Péricholes* or
Old-Time Colonels. Lyubinka was now, in fact, looking somewhat
brighter, but Anninka, who was the more highly strung, had
given way completely, seemingly oblivious of the past and unconscious of the present. Apart from which, she started coughing
suspiciously—an augury, evidently, of some mysterious ailment...

The following summer was terrible. It gradually came to the
point where the sisters were conveyed from one hotel to another
for the entertainment of travelling gentlemen, with a moderate
price attached to them. There was an endless succession of scan-
dals and brawls, but the sisters had tenacity—and, like cats, they
clung on, still wanting to live. They were reminiscent of those
pitiful dogs which, though scalded, battered, and broken-limbed,
still come back, yelping, to their wonted place. It was inconvenient
to have such persons about the theatre.

In the course of this dismal year only once did a ray of light
break into Anninka's existence. It came in the form of a letter
sent from Samovarnov by the tragic actor Miloslavsky Xth with
an offer of his hand and heart. Anninka read the letter and burst
into tears. All night long she tossed and turned, was (as they say)
'quite beside herself', but next morning she sent a brief reply: 'For
what? To drink vodka together?' And the darkness closed in
blacker than before and the unending drunken oblivion began
in all its squalor all over again.

Lyubinka was the first to see the light or, rather, she not so
much saw the light as felt instinctively that life had gone on long
enough. There was no longer any prospect of work: youth,
beauty, the promise of talent—all had suddenly vanished. Never
once did she recall that there was for them a haven in Pogorelka.
Pogorelka was something remote, vague, totally forgotten. If in
the past they had felt no inclination to return to Pogorelka, still
less did they now. Yes, now, when they were on the verge of
starvation, now least of all were they drawn to go back. What sort

of face would she return with? One on which the drunken breath
of all and sundry had burned the brand-mark 'Slut'. This accursed
breath, it was all over her, she sensed it everywhere, on every part
of her body. And terrible above all was that she and Anninka
were now both so inured to this breath that they had heedlessly
made it into an inseparable part of their existence. They were not
disgusted by the tavern stenches, the clamour of inns, or the
coarse drunken talk, and indeed if they did go back to Pogorelka,
they would most likely miss it all. Besides, even in Pogorelka
you needed something to live on. All these years they had been
roaming the world, but they never seemed to hear a word of any
income from Pogorelka. Was Pogorelka not a myth? Had not
everybody there died? All those witnesses of their long-lost,
never-to-be-forgotten childhood, when Granny, Arina Petrovna,
had brought them up as orphans on sour milk and stale salt-
beef . . . Ah, what a childhood that had been! And what a life this
was now . . . life altogether, in fact! Yes, life, life, life itself!

It was clear, they had to die. Once this idea comes to a person,
it is not to be dispelled. Quite often the sisters had moments of
awakening from their drunken oblivion, but for Anninka these
awakenings were a time for hysterics, sobbing, and tears, and
were the sooner over for that. Lyubinka, on the other hand, was
less emotional by nature and she did not weep or curse, but just
kept remembering that she was a 'slut'. And Lyubinka was,
besides, a rational creature and she saw quite clearly that there
was in fact no point in going on living. There was no prospect of
anything ahead but scorn, poverty, and the gutter. Scorn—that
was a matter of habit, that she could bear, but poverty—never!
Better put an end to everything, once and for all!

'We've got to die!' she said to Anninka one day in the same
coldly rational tone as she had used two years before when she
asked her for whom she was saving up her 'treasure'.

'Why?' said Anninka in fright.

'I mean it—we've got to die!' Lyubinka repeated. 'Look at us!
Have some sense! Come on!'

'All right, then . . . let's die!' Anninka agreed, scarcely though
aware of the grim significance of the decision.

The same day Lyubinka broke the heads off some phosphorus

matches and prepared an infusion in two glasses. She drank one herself, the other she gave to her sister. But immediately Anninka's courage failed her and she refused to drink.

'Drink it, you slut!' Lyubinka shouted at her. 'Sister! Dearest! Darling! Drink it!'

Anninka, terrified out of her wits, rushed screaming about the room. Instinctively she grasped her throat with her hands, as if trying to choke herself.

'Drink! Drink it ... you slut!'

The theatrical career of the Misses Pogorelsky was at an end. That evening Lyubinka's corpse was taken outside the town and buried. Anninka remained alive.

Within a very short time of her arrival in Golovlevo Anninka had introduced an atmosphere of vagrant slovenliness into Judas's old nest. She got up late; then, undressed and unkempt, with heavy head she would drift about the house until dinner-time, coughing so desperately that every time she did so Porfiry Vladimirych, sitting in his study, started in alarm. Her room was never tidied; her bed was left unmade; body-linen and articles of clothing lay scattered about on chairs and on the floor. At first, she saw her uncle only at dinner and over tea in the evening. Then the lord of Golovlevo would emerge from his study dressed all in black, say little and, as ever, eat with excruciating slowness. He was evidently sizing something up and from the oblique glances he directed at Anninka she surmised that the object of this sizing-up was herself.

After dinner the early dusk of December set in and there began the dreary procession back and forth through the long range of principal rooms. Anninka liked to watch the glimmering light of the grey winter day gradually fade, the world outside grow dim, and the rooms fill with shadows, after which the entire house would suddenly sink into impenetrable gloom. She was more at ease in the midst of this darkness and hardly ever lit the candles. Only at the end of the long hall a cheap palm-oil candle crackled and guttered, forming with its flame a small, bright circle of light. For a time the house stirred with the usual after-dinner activity—the clatter of crockery being washed, the

bump of drawers being opened and shut, but there soon came
the sound of retreating footsteps, after which there was a deathly
hush. Porfiry Vladimirych went to take his after-dinner nap;
Evprakseyushka snuggled beneath her feather-quilt; Prokhor
went off to the servants' quarters; and Anninka was left entirely
alone. She walked up and down, singing under her breath, trying
to tire herself and, above all, trying to stop herself thinking. As
she went towards the hall she fixed her eyes on the bright circle
of candle-flame; as she walked back she tried hard to pick out
some object in the gathering gloom. But, in spite of her efforts,
the memories came flooding in on her. There was her dressing-
room with the cheap wallpaper on the board partition, with the
inevitable cheval-glass and the equally inevitable bouquet from
Second-Lieutenant Papkov IInd; there was the stage with its
scenery, begrimed with smoke and the touch of hands, slimy with
damp; and there was she cavorting on the stage, yes, cavorting,
simply that, and pretending to herself it was acting; and there
was the auditorium that seemed from the stage to be so elegant,
if not splendid, but which was in reality mean and dark with its
miscellaneous furnishings and boxes upholstered in shabby crimson plush. And then to conclude there were the unending captains, lieutenants, second-lieutenants. And after that, the hotel
with the stinking corridor dimly lit by a smoking paraffin lamp;
the room to which she dashed to change after the performance
before proceeding to further triumphs, the room with the bed
unmade since morning, the hand-basin full of dirty water, the
rumpled sheet lying on the floor, and the drawers draped forgotten on the chair-back; then the hotel saloon with the kitchen
fumes and the table in the middle laid for supper; cutlets and peas,
tobacco-smoke, din, jostling, drunkenness, revelry . . . And again
captains, lieutenants, second-lieutenants . . .

Such were the memories of that time which once she had called
the time of her success, triumphs, and happiness . . .

After these came a new sequence of memories. Prominent
among them was an inn that really stank, with walls that froze
through in winter, rickety floors, and wooden partitions where
the glinting bellies of bed-bugs peeped from the cracks. Drunken,
brawling nights; travelling landowners who hurriedly drew out

a three-rouble note from their slim wallets; brash merchants egging on the 'hactresses' practically with whip in hand. And next morning the throbbing head, sickness, and depression, never-ending depression. And at the end of it all—Golovlevo.

Golovlevo—that was death itself, malign, empty-hearted; it was death, ever watchful for some fresh victim. There two uncles had died; there two cousins had suffered those 'grievous' injuries that resulted in death; and now, finally, Lyubinka too . . . Though it might appear that she had died in Krechetov or wherever 'on her own account', it was none the less here, in Golovlevo, that the 'grievous' injuries afflicting her were initiated. Deaths, blighted lives, cankers—they all originated here. It was here that they had been fed on stale salt beef, it was here there first fell on the orphans' ears the words 'wretches', 'beggars', 'parasites', 'greedy guts' and so on; here they got away with nothing, nothing escaped the penetrating eye of that crabbed, cranky old woman: the extra bite of food, the broken penny-doll, the torn rag-frock, the worn shoe. Every infringement was promptly redeemed by a chiding or a slap. So it was that, when they gained the freedom to live their own lives and realized that they could escape from this squalid misery, they did escape—to *there*! And no one stopped them in their flight, and no one could have stopped them, for there was nothing worse or more hateful than Golovlevo that they could possibly foresee.

Ah, if only all that could be forgotten! If only it were possible, even in fancy, to create something else, some magic world that would shut out past and present! But alas! the reality she had experienced was possessed of such iron vitality that every spark of imagination was automatically extinguished beneath its crushing power. In vain did her fancy strive to conjure forth visions of angels with silver wings—for over the angels' shoulders relentlessly reared the heads of the Kukishevs, Lyulkins, Zabvennys, Papkovs . . . Lord, is all really lost? Has even the capacity to lie and deceive oneself been sunk as well in those nocturnal orgies, in drink and debauchery? Somehow, still, she had to kill this past, to stop it poisoning her blood and rending her heart asunder! Some massy weight must fall on it, crush it and destroy it, utterly, absolutely!

How curiously and cruelly it had all worked out! It was impossible to imagine even in one's wildest dreams that there was any future, that there was any door by which to escape, that anything at all could happen. Nothing could ever happen. And hardest of all to bear was the thought that she was in fact already dead, though the outward signs of life persisted. She should have put an end to it *then*, with Lyubinka, but for some reason she had stayed alive. How had she failed to be crushed by the massive shame that bore in on her then from every side? And what sort of miserable worm did she have to be to have crept out then from beneath the heap of stones that had showered on her?

She groaned aloud at these questions. She ran, twisting and turning, about the drawing-room in an attempt to quell these agitated memories. But the visions kept coming: the Grande-Duchesse de Gérolstein swinging her hussar's *pelisse*, Clairette Angot in a wedding-dress slit down the front to the waist, and la belle Hélène with slits back, front, and everywhere . . . Nothing but wantonness and nudity . . . that had been her life! Had it really all happened?

At about seven o'clock the house began to waken once more. Preparations for the forthcoming tea could be heard and at length came the sound of Porfiry Vladimirych's voice. Uncle and niece took their places at the tea-table and exchanged observations on the passing day, but the content of the day being sparse, so too was the conversation. When they had drunk their tea and carried out the ritual of family goodnight kissing, Judas crept away to his lair, while Anninka went to Evprakseyushka's room for a hand of cards.

At eleven o'clock the revelry started. After making sure that all was quiet in Porfiry Vladimirych's room, Evprakseyushka set on the table various home-cured edibles and a decanter of vodka. Senseless, shameless songs were remembered, the guitar strummed, and between the songs and the loose talk Anninka drank. At first she drank in the Kukishev style, cool-headed and 'God-bless-me!', but then gradually she lapsed into more sombre mood and started to groan and curse . . .

Evprakseyushka looked on and pitied her.

'Miss, when I look at you,' she said, 'I feel that sorry for you! I really do!'

'You drink up with me—you won't feel sorry then!' Anninka retorted.

'Oh no, how could I! I was nearly took off the clergy register* as it is on account of your uncle, and if on top of that . . .'

'All right then, no point in talking about it. I'll sing you the "Whiskers" song instead.'

Again there was strumming of the guitar, again the whooping 'Ee-eh! Ee-ah!' Long past midnight, sleep, like a falling stone, would descend on Anninka. For a few hours this welcome stone obliterated her past and even brought some relief to her affliction. But the next day, shattered, half-demented, she crept once more from under it and began once more to live.

And then, on one of these sordid nights, as Anninka was giving Evprakseyushka a spirited rendering of one of her stock of sordid songs, suddenly in the doorway appeared the haggard, deathly pale figure of Judas. His lips quivered; his eyes were sunken and in the glimmer of the palm-oil candle seemed to be empty, unseeing sockets; the palms of his hands were pressed inwards together. For a few seconds he stood before the dumbstruck women, then, slowly turning, walked away.

There are families over which hangs a seemingly ineluctable destiny. It is something particularly evident among those ranks of the lower gentry who, with no practical concerns, no involvement in life at large, and no significance as a directing force, at first, scattered over the face of the Russian land, found shelter in serfdom, but who now, with no shelter whatsoever, live out their lives in decaying manor-houses. In the lives of these pitiful families success and failure are all, it seems, a matter of blind chance, occurring without rhyme or reason.

Occasionally such a family seems to have a sudden run of luck. Some impoverished cornet (retired) and his lady, who are quietly degenerating in their rural backwater, will suddenly produce a whole clutch of youngsters who are tough, trim, and sharp and with remarkable rapidity master the essentials of life—they are, in a word, 'bright sparks'. And all of them are the same, both boys and girls. The boys pass out from their institutes with top marks and while still in the schoolroom fix themselves up with connections and patronage. They know when appropriately to appear unassuming ('*J'aime cette modestie!*' their superiors declare) and also when appropriately to appear self-reliant ('*J'aime cette indépendance!*'); they have an untutive sense for every trend of the time and never abandon one trend for another without retaining in the former some sure foothold. They thus secure for themselves throughout life the possibility of decently and at any time shedding an old skin and donning a new one—and also, in case of need, of putting the old one back on again. In short, these are the real 'doers' of the present age, who always begin by thrusting themselves to the fore and *nearly always* end by stabbing someone else in the back. As for the girls, they too within their own sphere of competence contribute to the renaissance of the family—that is, they make good marriages and are then so discreet in the disposition of their allures that they have no difficulty in gaining prominence in what is termed 'society'.

As a result of these chance circumstances, success comes pouring in on the impoverished family. The first successful offspring—having blithely prevailed—raise up then themselves a new trim generation for whom life is that much easier, since now the main paths are not only marked, but also well-trodden. More generations then grow up until at last the family joins, as a matter of course, the ranks of those who, without any initial exertion at all, simply assume that they possess an inborn right to life-long junketing.

In recent times, because of the demand that has arisen for so-called 'fresh people'* (a demand created by the gradual extinction of the 'unfresh' category), examples of such successful families have started to appear with some frequency. In the past, too, some 'comet' would occasionally rise on the horizon, but it happened rarely: first, because in the wall around that happy land whose gate bears the inscription 'Here there's always filling to the pie', there was then hardly a crack, and, secondly, because to gain entrance to that happy land even a 'comet' was required to have some solid quality within. But now there are many more cracks in the wall and gaining entrance is simpler too, since no solid qualities are expected of the newcomer: 'freshness' is all that is required, nothing more.

But besides these successful families there is a great multitude of other families on whose members the household penates bestow from the cradle up nothing but endless misfortune. Adversity or vice will suddenly, like an infestation of lice, seize on a family and consume it. It spreads through the whole organism, worms itself to the very core, and goes on gnawing away generation after generation. There follows an assortment of weaklings, drunkards, petty roués, witless idlers, and failures in general. And as time goes on, the more they degenerate, until in the end there appear on the stage puny feeblings such as the young Golovlevs I once described,† who in their first encounter with life give way and go under.

It was just such an ill-starred fate that hung over the Golovlevs. For several generations three characteristic features had run through the history of the family: idleness, incapacity for any activity whatsoever, and hard drinking. The first two had as their corollary empty tongues, empty minds, and empty hearts, while the third was by way of being an inevitable conclusion to the general shambles of their lives. Porfiry Vladimirych had himself witnessed the extinction of several victims of this fate, and, besides these, there were legends of grandfathers and great-grandfathers who had gone the same way. They had all been roguish, frivolous, drunken good-for-nothings, and the Golovlev family would, no doubt, have run utterly to seed if amid this drunken shambles Arina Petrovna had not, like a chance meteor, suddenly shone forth. This woman by her own personal energy had raised the family fortunes to their highest point, but all her labour was none the less in vain, for she never passed on her qualities to any of her children, and indeed she herself died caught up in the toils of idleness, empty words, and empty-heartedness.

Porfiry Vladimirych, however, had so far held out. Perhaps he was consciously wary of drinking in view of past examples, but perhaps he had so far derived sufficient satisfaction from the drunkenness of his empty thinking. Be that as it may, it was not for nothing that local rumour foretold that Judas would succumb

† See 'Family Scores' [Saltykov's note].

to the real thing, the drunkenness of the drinker. At times he himself had a feeling that something was lacking in his existence, a feeling that the pursuit of empty thoughts, though giving much, did not give everything. What was needed was something overpowering, something keen, which would obliterate utterly all awareness of life and cast him once and for all into the void.

And now of its own accord this longed-for moment came. For a long time, ever since Anninka's arrival, Porfiry Vladimirych, closeted in his study, had listened to the vague noises coming from the other end of the house; for a long time he had conjectured and wondered . . . And at last he had found out.

The next day Anninka expected there would be remonstrations, but none came. As was his custom, Porfiry Vladimirych sat the whole morning closeted in his study, but when he emerged for dinner, instead of one glass of vodka (for himself) he poured out two and, with a sheepish grin, silently motioned towards one of them—a tacit invitation to which Anninka responded.

'So, Lyubinka's dead, you say?' Judas suddenly said half-way through dinner.

'Yes, Uncle, she's dead.'

'Well, God rest her soul! It's a sin to repine, but it's right to remember her memory. Shall we drink to it?'

'Yes, Uncle, let's.'

They each drank another glass, after which Judas fell silent: evidently he had not fully recovered from his long seclusion. But after dinner, when Anninka, observing the family ritual, came up to thank her uncle with a kiss on the cheek, he responded by patting her cheek and saying:

'What a girl you are!'

That evening during tea, which on this occasion went on longer than usual, Porfiry Vladimirych regarded Anninka for a time with an enigmatic smile on his face, before finally suggesting:

'Shall I have some zakuski put out?'

'Yes, all right . . .'

'It really is better doing it where Uncle can see rather than on the sly . . . Uncle, at least . . .'

Judas did not finish the sentence. Most likely, he was going on to say that Uncle, at least, would 'restrain' her, but somehow the words failed to come.

After that, each evening zakuski appeared in the dining-room. The outside shutters were closed, the servants went off to bed, and niece and uncle remained *tête à tête*. At first, Judas seemed to lag behind, but with a little practice he fully kept pace with Anninka. The two of them sat drinking without haste and, between glasses, they would recall and talk over the past. The conversations were inconsequential and listless at the start, but as their heads grew hotter, they became ever more animated and invariably ended as confused quarrels whose main theme was provided by memories of the various deaths and injuries that had taken place in Golovlevo.

The instigator of these quarrels was always Anninka. With merciless persistence she dug into the records of Golovlevo and took special delight in baiting Judas with the fact that he it was who, with her late grandmother, had been chiefly responsible for all the injuries inflicted there. At the same time her every word was imbued with such cynical hatred that it was hard to conceive how there could still be so much fire in this wasted, half-defunct organism. Her taunts were infinitely painful to Judas, but he protested only feebly, and for the most part got angry and, when Anninka's mischievous baiting went too far, he would shout and curse aloud.

Such scenes were repeated unchangingly day after day. Though all the details of the sorrowful family *synodicon** were very soon gone through, still the *synodicon* loomed so persistently before these desolated creatures that it absorbed all capacity for thought. Each episode, each memory of the past re-opened some old sore and each sore in its turn recalled a new sequence of Golovlev injuries. There was a bitter vindictive pleasure to be had in exposing these baleful deeds, in assessing, even in exaggerating them. Neither in the past, nor in the present was there a single moral support to cling to. There was nothing but wretched money-grubbing on the one hand, and insensible empty-heartedness on the other. In place of bread there was a stone, in place of instruction a buffet on the ear. Or by way of variation, a vile reminder of parasitism, good food wasted, beggary, and pilfered scraps.

Such was the response given to the young heart seeking sympathy, warmth, and affection. And yet, by some bitter irony of fate the consequence of this harsh schooling had not been an austere approach to life but a passionate desire to enjoy its poisonous offerings to the full. Youth performed a miracle of oblivion; it did not permit the heart to harden, did not permit the seeds of hate to flourish there at once, but intoxicated it instead with a thirst for life. Hence the reckless drunken oblivion which for a few years suspended consciousness and pushed far from mind all that concerned Golovlevo. Only now, as she sensed that the end was near, did the agonizing pain strike at her heart, only now did Anninka understand her past aright and begin aright to hate it.

These drunken conversations went on deep into the night and had they not been moderated by the very drunken incoherence of their thoughts and speech they might at the very outset have ended direly. Fortunately, however, though the vodka opened up inexhaustible sources of pain in their tormented hearts, it also brought them peace. As the night wore on, the more incoherent did their talk become, the more impotent the hatred that possessed them. By the end, not only was there no feeling of pain, but their entire present surroundings vanished from sight and were replaced by a glittering void. Tongues slurred, eyes drooped, movements became sluggish. Then uncle and niece would heave themselves up from their seats and go staggering off to their lairs.

Naturally, these nocturnal activities could not remain a secret in the house. On the contrary, their character was so clear from the outset that it struck nobody as out of place when one of the domestics said of them: 'Criminal goings-on!' The Golovlevo mansion was now completely still; even in the mornings there was no sign of life. The gentlefolk woke late and from then until dinner-time the house rang from end to end with Anninka's heart-rending cough and the stream of curses that accompanied it. Judas listened to these harrowing sounds in terror and sensed that for him too some disaster loomed that would crush him once and for all.

On every side, from every corner of this hateful house, it seemed, the dead came creeping forth. Whichever way you went or turned, everywhere grey phantoms stirred. There was father, Vladimir Mikhailych, in his white night-cap, poking out his tongue and quoting Barkov; there was brother Booby Stepka and brother Pashka Slyboots by his side; there was Lyubinka, and those last scions of the Golovlev line, Volodka and Petka ... And all of them drunken, depraved, tormented, bleeding . . . And hovering over these phantoms was a living phantom, and this living phantom was none other than he himself, Porfiry Vladimirych Golovlev, the last of this dying breed . . .

The constant reminders of these old deaths were bound in the end to have their effect. The past was now so clearly perceived that the least contact with it was painful. The natural result of this was a condition which was either fright or the stirring of conscience, and in fact the latter rather than the former. Surprisingly, conscience was still not totally absent; it had merely been suppressed and as though forgotten. It had thus lost that active sensitivity which inevitably reminds a person of its existence.

The stirrings of a neglected conscience are uncommonly painful. Unnurtured, untutored, seeing no light ahead, conscience brings no reconciliation, offers no hope of new life: it provides only endless, pointless torment. A man sees himself shut in a stone cell, mercilessly abandoned to the agony of remorse, to the sheer plain agony, with no hope of a return to life. And there is no other way for him to assuage this pointless, all-consuming pain than, in a moment of grim resolve, to dash out his brains against the stones of his cell . . .

Judas in the course of his long and empty-hearted life had never even mentally conceded that there, alongside his own existence, the infliction of deathly injuries was taking place. He lived his quiet, 'easy-does-it' life, at steady pace, by God's good grace, and never for a moment did he suppose that this itself could be the cause of some injury, more or less serious. Still less, in consequence, could he admit that for these same injuries he was himself to blame.

And suddenly that awful truth dawned on his conscience, but it did so too late and to no effect, when already he was confronted by the bare fact, irrevocable and irremediable. He was old now, cut off from life, with one foot in the grave, and there was not a single being in the world who might feel for him, pity him. Why was he alone? Why all around did he find not just indifference, but even hatred? Why had all that had ever had contact with him perished? Yes, here in this same Golovlevo there had once been a nest of humanity—how was it that of this nest not a feather now remained? Of all the fledglings raised here there was only his niece left, and she had come back only to abuse him and see him to the grave. Even Evprakseyushka, simpleminded as she was, she too hated him. She lived on in Golovlevo because her father, the sexton, was supplied every month with provisions, but she did so, doubtless, with hatred in her heart. He, Judas, had done her too a terrible injury, he had taken from her the light of her life, had taken away her son and cast him into some nameless pit. What had his life achieved? Why had he lied and prattled and bullied and hoarded? Even from the material viewpoint—that of his 'heritage'—who would benefit from the results of his life? Who?

I repeat, his conscience awoke, but all to no purpose. Judas groaned, raged, rampaged, and with feverish malignance waited for evening to arrive not only to make himself bestially drunk, but also in vodka to drown his conscience. He hated that 'wanton hussy' who with such cool impudence rubbed open his old sores and to whom at the same time he felt himself irresistibly drawn, as if there were things yet unsaid between them and more sores yet left to be opened up again. Every evening he made Anninka repeat her account of Lyubinka's death, and every evening his mind dwelt more and more seriously on the idea of selfdestruction. It came to him first as a chance thought, but as he realized more clearly the cause of those deaths, it insinuated itself ever deeper into his mind until at last it was the one bright spot in the darkness of the future.

As well as this, his physical health had sharply deteriorated. He was coughing now in earnest and at times had bouts of breathlessness which, his moral torments apart, were sufficient to make his life an unrelieved agony. All the outward signs of that special Golovlev bane were there, and already his ears rang with the groans of brother Pavlushka Slyboots, who had died gasping for breath in the mezzanine of the house at Dubrovino. Yet, this thin, sunken chest that seemed ready to burst at any moment proved surprisingly resilient. With each passing day it contained within itself an ever-increasing mass of physical torment, yet still it held, did not give way. It was as though his very organism by its tenacity was exacting vengeance for those old deaths. 'This surely must be the end,' said Judas hopefully each time he felt the onset of an attack; but still the end did not come. Evidently, some act of force was required to expedite it.

In short, however you looked at it, all scores with life were settled. Life was a torment and unneeded; the greatest need was to die; the trouble was that death would not come. There was something perfidiously mean about this wanton delay in the process of dying, when one's whole soul cried out for death and all it did was lure and tease ...

It was near the end of March and Holy Week was drawing to its close. However lax he had become in recent years, Porfiry Vladimirych was still affected by a sense of the sanctity of these days that went back to his childhood. The mind turned to serious things; the heart had no other desire but for absolute peace. In keeping with this mood, the evenings ceased to be occasions for ugly drunken scenes and were passed silently, in melancholy abstinence.

Judas and Anninka were sitting alone in the dining-room. It was only an hour since the Vigil Service with the twelve Gospel readings had ended and a strong smell of incense still hung in the room. The clock struck ten, the domestics had gone off to their various corners, and a deep, intense silence fell on the house. Anninka sat leaning on the table with her head clasped in her hands, sunk in thought; Porfiry Vladimirych sat facing her, silent and sad.

The effect of this service on Anninka was always deeply upsetting. Even as a child, when the priest said: 'And having woven a crown of thorns, they put it on his head and a reed in his right hand', she had wept bitterly and with her little treble voice had joined, sobbing, in the chanter's response: 'Glory to Thy long suffering, oh Lord! Glory be to Thee!' And when the service was ended, she would run in her distress to the maids' room and there in the gathering dusk (Arina Petrovna only allowed candles in the maids' room when there was work to be done) she recounted to the slave-women the Passion of our Lord. And the slave-women's quiet tears flowed and their deep sighs sounded. These slave-women sensed in their hearts the presence of their Lord and Redeemer, they believed that he would rise again, would truly rise again. And Anninka sensed and believed the same. Beyond the deep night of torments, vile taunts, and rebukes, for all these poor in spirit there was the vision of a realm of light and liberty. At this season even the old mistress, Arina Petrovna, usually so stern, became mild, she did not grouse, did not reproach Anninka for being an orphan, but instead stroked her head and told her not to be upset. But even in bed Anninka could not calm down and for a long time she would tremble and toss and turn and several times in the night she would start up and talk to herself.

After that came the years of learning and then the years of wandering. The former were devoid of content, the latter painful and sordid. But even in the midst of her sordid life as a strolling player Anninka had always conscientiously set apart these 'holy days' and on them managed to find in her heart some echoes of the past which helped her to feel spiritually at ease and sigh again as a child. But now, when life was exposed in all its detail, when the past was cursed of itself, when the future held no prospect of repentance or forgiveness, now, when the source of her spiritual feeling was dried up, and with it too her tears—the effect created by the story of the Road to Calvary which she had just heard was crushing indeed. Then, too, in childhood the deep of night had oppressed her, but then beyond the darkness she had felt there was light. Now she felt that ahead there was nothing, no prospect: there was night, everlasting, unchanging night—and nothing more. Anninka did not sigh, was not distressed, she seemed not even to think of anything, but merely sank into a profound torpor.

Porfiry Vladimirych too had from his early days been no less scrupulous in his reverence for the 'holy days', but, true idolator that he was, he revered them purely in their ritual aspect. Each year on the eve of Good Friday he summoned the priest, listened to the Gospel narrative, sighed, lifted up his hands, beat his head on the ground, marked off the Gospel readings on the candle with pellets of wax—but understood nothing. Only now, after Anninka had stirred him to awareness of the deaths and injuries of Golovlevo, did he comprehend for the first time that this was the story of an unparalleled injustice, by which bloody judgement had been executed on Truth . . .

It would, of course, be too much to say that this revelation caused him to see any correspondences in his own life, but his soul was now undoubtedly in turmoil, a turmoil that all but bordered on despair. The agony of it was the greater in so far as the past, which was its cause, had been lived by him without conscious awareness. In this past there was something terrible, but what it was he could not recall in the general mass of all that had gone before. Nor though could he forget it. It was something monstrous that so far had been static, concealed behind some impenetrable veil; only now had it begun to advance on him, every minute threatening to crush him. If it really did crush him, that would be best of all; but then he was resilient—he might still crawl out from under it. No, it was too uncertain a business to await resolution from the natural order of things; he must provide his own resolution in order to put an end to this unendurable turmoil. There was such a resolution, there was indeed. For a month or more he had been considering it and now, it seemed, he would not let it slip. 'On Saturday we shall take Communion— I must go to Mother's grave and ask forgiveness!' he thought suddenly.

'Shall we go then?' he said to Anninka, when he had told her of his intention.

'All right, we'll drive over . . .'

'No, not drive, we'll . . .' Porfiry Vladimirych began, but stopped short, as if realizing that Anninka might hinder him.

'It was I who drove dear Mother to death . . . I was to blame . . . I!' was the thought that floated meantime in his mind, and the yearning to beg forgiveness burned every minute stronger in his heart. He wished to beg forgiveness, though, not in the ordinary way, but to fall on her grave and lie there wailing in mortal agony.

'So you say Lyubinka took her own life?' he suddenly asked, evidently to give himself courage.

At first, Anninka seemed not to hear her uncle's question, but evidently she did, for after a minute or two she herself felt an overwhelming urge to revert to this death and lacerate herself with the memory.

'And she said "Drink it . . . you slut"?' he questioned her again, when she had repeated the story in full.

'Yes . . . that's what she said.'

'And you stayed alive? You didn't drink it?'

'Yes . . . here I am, still alive . . .'

He stood up and in a state of evident agitation paced several times up and down the room. In the end, he went up to Anninka and stroked her head.

'Poor girl! My poor girl!' he said quietly.

At his touch an unexpected thing happened to her. At first she showed astonishment, but then gradually her face twisted, more and more, and suddenly she burst out in a spate of terrible hysterical sobs.

'Uncle! Are you a good man? Tell me—are you?' she almost shouted.

With breaking voice, amid tears and sobs, she repeated her question, the same question which she had put to him on that day when finally, after her 'years of wandering', she had returned to take up residence in Golovlevo, and to which then he had made such futile reply.

'Are you a good man? Tell me! Answer me! Are you a good man?'

'Did you hear what they read at the Vigil Service?' he asked, when at last she was calmer. 'Ah! What sufferings they were! And only by such sufferings can we . . . And he forgave! Forgave everyone, for all time!'

Again he began to pace the room, taking large steps, in an agony of grief and suffering, unconscious that beads of perspiration were now covering his face.

'He forgave everyone!' he said, speaking aloud to himself. 'Not only those who *then* gave him vinegar and gall to drink, but all those too who later—now, and in time to come, throughout eternity—will put to his lips vinegar mingled with gall . . . It's terrible! Terrible!'

And suddenly, stopping before her, he asked:

'And you . . . Have you forgiven?'

Instead of answering, she rushed to him and held him tightly in her arms.

'You must forgive me!' he went on. 'For all . . . for yourself . . . and for those who are gone . . . What is it? What's happened?' he cried, near to distraction, as he looked round. 'Where are . . . *they all?*'

Shattered and exhausted, they went to their rooms. But Porfiry Vladimirych could not sleep. He turned in his bed from side to side, trying to recall the obligation that still lay upon him. And suddenly there came back to him quite distinctly the words that had chanced into his mind an hour or two before. 'I must go to Mother's grave and ask forgiveness' . . . As he remembered, he was seized by a terrible agony of disquiet.

In the end he could stand it no more: he rose from his bed and put on his dressing-gown. Outside it was dark and not a sound to be heard. For a time Porfiry Vladimirych paced the room, stopping before the icon of the Redeemer in his crown of thorns and gazing at it intently in the light of the icon-lamp. At last he decided. To what extent he was consciously aware of his decision is hard to say, but a few minutes later he had stealthily crept into the hallway and unclicked the latch that fastened the outer door.

Outside there was a swirling blizzard of wet March snow and a howling wind that filled his eyes with the driven sleet. But Porfiry Vladimirych walked on along the road, stepping through the puddles, feeling nothing of snow or wind, and only by instinct drawing about him the skirts of his dressing-gown.

Early next morning a horseman came galloping in from the village that lay nearest to the cemetery where Arina Petrovna was buried: he brought the news that a few yards off the road they had found the stiffened corpse of the master of Golovlevo.

They rushed to Anninka, but she was in bed unconscious, with all the symptoms of a fever. A fresh messenger was then mounted and dispatched to 'cousin' Nadezhda Ivanovna Galkina (daughter of Aunt Varvara Mikhailovna), who ever since the autumn had been keeping a close eye on events in Golovlevo.

NOTES

1 *quit-rent due from her peasants living there on permit*: not all Russian peasants were engaged in agriculture. In the days of serfdom some were licensed by their owners to work regularly or seasonally as craftsmen, cab-drivers, etc., in towns away from their native villages. From their earnings they paid dues (*obrok*, 'quit-rent') in cash to their owners in the same way as their agricultural counterparts. In the country quit-rent was payable in cash or kind and was generally regarded as preferable to the alternative form of due exacted by landowners from their peasants—*barshchina*, the obligation to spend part of their time working on their master's land.

2 *that the institution of serfdom had collapsed*: serfdom was abolished in 1861, some four or five years after the time in which the opening chapter of *The Golovlevs* is set.

3 *pack him . . . off to the recruiting station*: recruitment to the Russian army was chiefly by conscription, and there were regular levies. In the time of serfdom it was a matter for the serf-owner to decide which of his peasants would be conscripted —it was thus within his power to 'sentence' recalcitrants to military service effectively for life, since the period of service then was *twenty-five* years.

4 *Barkov*: I. S. Barkov (1732–?68), poet and translator, Russia's most celebrated writer of bawdy.

5 *Board of Guardians*: the Boards of Guardians were institutions responsible for the welfare of widows and orphans of members of the gentry; they also made loans to needy gentry on the security of landed or other property, which, if the loan was not repaid, was sold off at auction.

7 *one hundred roubles in assignats*: 'assignats' were a form of paper currency, introduced in Russia in 1769 and discontinued about 1840, by which time the value of the assignat rouble was less than a third of the silver rouble.

8 *the militia then being levied*: during the Crimean War a militia force was raised, drawn from all classes of society. The well-to-do could release themselves from service by paying someone to take

their place. The end of Stepan's career as a stand-in soldier came with the conclusion of peace in March 1856, when he was (at Kharkov) still some four hundred miles short of Sevastopol.

9 *village of thirty souls*: the size and value of an estate was commonly expressed in terms of the number of serfs ('souls') attached to it.

16 *the German Club*: the German Club, originally for foreigners, existed in Moscow from the early years of the nineteenth century.

17 *the Suzdal monastery*: the Monastery of the Saviour and St Euthemius in the ancient city of Suzdal, east of Moscow, besides being a monastery, was also a place of confinement for offenders against ecclesiastical law and—evidently by repute—for recalcitrants in general.

18 *Rogozhskaya Bar*: Rogozhskaya Bar (in the sense of gate, that is) on the eastern outskirts of Moscow was a centre of coaching and cabbying activities. It is mentioned again later as Arina Petrovna's point of arrival in Moscow from Golovlevo (p. 38).

19 *versts*: a pre-metrication measure of distance used in Russia, equivalent to about two-thirds of a mile.

20 *Zhukov's*: at the time a well-known brand of tobacco.

Serpukhov: Serpukhov, the 'two-gallon' stage on Stepan's march to the Crimea, is a mere sixty miles south of Moscow.

21 *liquor-contractors . . . receivers of stores*: the 'liquor-contractors' (*otkupshchiki*) were the private concessionaries for the state-controlled liquor trade. Profiteering by government contractors was rife during the Crimean War: this and other abuses had come under fire in a journalistic campaign in the late 1850s to which Saltykov had contributed.

exemption warrant: exemption, that is, from conscription. In ordinary circumstances such a warrant might be issued, for instance, if a place on the military strength intended to be filled by a conscript was taken by a volunteer. Such a warrant was negotiable and commanded a good price from a peasant threatened with conscription. As stated, the government compensated serf-owners with an exemption warrant for each of their serfs killed while serving in the militia.

23 *"And comes the morn—where art thou, man?"*: a line from the ode 'On the Death of Prince Meshchersky' (1779) by Russia's best eighteenth-century poet, G. R. Derzhavin (1743–1816).

23   *Archbishop Smaragd*: in the 1850s Smaragd was successively Archbishop of Orel and of Ryazan and Zaraisk—on the route, therefore, of military columns bound for the Crimea. Kromy and Oboyan are towns well on the way to Kharkov from Moscow, lying respectively south of Orel and of Kursk.

25   *kasha*: any dish of boiled meal or grain, variously eaten, sweet or savoury.

29   *house-serfs*: i.e. serfs employed as servants in the master's house.

38   *Rogozhskaya Bar*: see note to p. 18.

     Solyanka: a street in central Moscow where the building of the Board of Guardians was. Arina Petrovna's purpose was to attend the sales held there of estates surrendered by defaulting debtors.

     Iverskaya chapel: formerly at Voskresensky Gate in the centre of Moscow; the chapel housed the 'Iberian' (*Iverskaya*) icon of the Virgin, which was much venerated.

54   *kibitka*: a small covered sledge or conveyance.

58   *okroshka*: a cold soup made with kvass (see note to p. 120).

60   *sevryuga*: a fish of the sturgeon family.

     botvinya: a cold soup made with white wine and vegetables to which fish and and shellfish are added.

63   *assemblies of the gentry . . . editing commissions*: the emancipation of the serfs in 1861 was preceded by a considerable period of planning and consultation (from 1857). First, the assemblies of the gentry in each province were invited to register their support in principle by making a declaration in favour of forming a provincial committee to draw up a scheme for carrying out the reform. These schemes were then considered by the Editing Commission, which began work in 1859.

     Agashka . . . Agafya Fedorovna: Arina Petrovna's dilemma over the status of her liberated serfs is summed up in the question of how she should in future address her servant Agafya—Agashka is the most demeaning mutation of the name, Agafyushka is more accommodating, while the unmodified name with patronymic (Agafya Fedorovna) suggests treating her on equal terms.

     "first convocation", "second convocation": in 1859–60 two convocations of deputies from the various provincial committees were summoned by the Editing Commission to make representations and discuss details of the plans for emancipation.

65 *Trinity-Sergius Monastery*: one of the great monasteries of
    Orthodox Russia, some fifty miles north of Moscow in what is
    now the town of Zagorsk. The monastery dates from the four-
    teenth century and contains the shrine of its founder, St Sergius
    of Radonezh, which was (and is) a popular place of pilgrimage.

    'Go to the Miracle-Worker!': i.e. to St Sergius.

66 *Khotkov*: the convent at Khotkovo, less than ten miles from the
    Trinity-Sergius Monastery.

68 *His Excellency Porfiry Vladimirych Golovlev*: the title 'excel-
    lency' was accorded to officials who had reached the fourth
    grade in the 'Table of Ranks' (which divided the official hierarchy
    into fourteen grades). Later remarks about Porfiry Vladimirych's
    service career (see p. 251) are not convincingly compatible with
    his having reached this eminence, so he may be here simply
    using the title as a courtesy to himself.

71 *lawyers everywhere*: lawyers, in the Western sense, appeared
    in Russia only after the legal reforms introducing open court
    proceedings in 1865. They early gained a dubious reputation
    for their presumption and parasitism. For literary examples, see
    Tolstoy's *Anna Karenina* and Dostoevsky's *Brothers Karamazov*,
    both written at about the same time as *The Golovlevs*.

80 *kutya*: a mixture of boiled grain and honey which is eaten after
    Orthodox services for the dead (funerals, requiems). The in-
    gredients are regarded as symbolic—the grain of regeneration,
    the honey of the sweetness of the after-life.

87 *the arbiter*: arbiters of the peace were landowners officially
    appointed to deal with disputes arising between landowners and
    peasants and to judge minor offences in the period following the
    emancipation.

88 *you let the peasants buy themselves out*: at the time of the
    emancipation landowners had the option of voluntarily agreeing
    terms on which their peasants could acquire their freedom and
    an allotment of land. The landowners then received a capital sum
    provided by the government, which the peasants were required
    to pay off on a long-term instalment basis.

92 *compensation . . . for the peasants*: the redemption payment
    received by landowners for their liberated serfs and surrendered
    land. See previous note.

93 *Athos*: the celebrated centre of Orthodox monasticism in Greece.

93 *Mademoiselle Lotar*: an operetta-singer who performed in St Petersburg in the 1860s and 1870s.

   La Belle Hélène: Offenbach's operetta, first performed in 1864.

94 *Lyadova*: V. A. Lyadova, a popular star of operetta in St Petersburg, who died prematurely in 1870.

   Sergius Hermitage: a monastery near St Petersburg.

   all three Podyachesky streets: the suggestion of showing off the three (Great, Middle, Little) Podyachesky streets is jocular. The streets, which still exist under that name, are in an unprepossessing area of St Petersburg/Leningrad—in fact, in Dostoevsky territory: local lore places the house of the pawnbroker murdered by Raskolnikov in *Crime and Punishment* in one of them.

99 *zakuski*: the Russian word *zakuski*, sometimes inadequately rendered as 'hors d'œuvre', well deserves adoption into English. Zakuski are (the word is a plural) the essential accompaniment to vodka and may be anything from a simple piece of black bread to the finest caviare. Typically, zakuski might include caviare, fish, meats, sausage, gherkins, mushrooms, salads.

102 *'That's why people taunt them with the pig's ear'*: for this form of Jew-baiting, cf. the following passage in Pushkin's *History of the Village of Goryukhino*: 'Twisting the hems of their garments into trumpet-shapes they made mock of the Jewish driver, derisively crying out: "Yid! Yid! Eat a pig's ear!" '

104 *'. . . let's just sit for a minute . . .'*: it is Russian custom for a traveller before setting out on a journey to sit in silence for a short time with those from whom he is taking leave.

114 *of clerical stock*: Evpraksiya is not the daughter of a priest, but of a minor church servitor, who would though rate as belonging to the 'clergy' estate, one of the official social categories in pre-Revolutionary Russia (gentry, clergy, merchants, townspeople, peasants).

115 *property, family, and state*: the same three 'bases of society' the falseness of which Saltykov set out to decry in *Well-Intentioned Speeches*, the cycle of sketches in which the first several chapters of *The Golovlevs* originally appeared.

119 *Napoleon III's reign had ended*: Napoleon III died in January 1873. Saltykov had a low view of him and the Second Empire: in *In Foreign Parts* (1880–1) he referred to Napoleon as 'the most despicable bandit ever to burden the earth with the shame of his weight'.

119 *desyatinas*: the *desyatina* was the pre-metric Russian square measure, equivalent to 2.7 acres.

120 *kvass*: a kind of weak, sweetish beer, much drunk in Russia.

123 *bast-shoes*: peasant footwear made out of plaited strips of bast (inner bark of the lime-tree).

126 *the old Tsar's coronation*: i.e. the coronation in 1826 of Nicholas I, predecessor of Alexander II (Tsar 1855–81). It is in the latter's reign that the action of the novel principally takes place.

127 *La Périchole . . . Pansy*: *La Périchole*, an operetta by Offenbach, first performed in 1868; *Pansy* (*Anyutiny glazki*), a Russian adaptation of an original French operetta, popular from the 1840s.

   lawyers sometimes give us forged money: another stab at lawyers! See note to p. 71.

   Plevako . . . Yazykov: F. N. Plevako and A. I. Yazykov were real-life lawyers who were in the public eye at the time Saltykov was writing. The references to reading and fainting in the case of the second lawyer acquaintance are specific to Yazykov: he was a dabbler in poetry and published occasional verses and in another work of the time Saltykov makes mention of Yazykov fainting in court.

128 *You find a bush, get married under it*: the reference to common-law marriage as being married 'under a bush' seems to originate in popular lore, cf. the following from a *bylina* (folk epic song):

   > They were wedded in the open field,
   > They were married round the willow bush.

130 *Presentation of the Virgin*: the Feast of the Presentation of the Virgin Mary in the Temple is celebrated on 21 November.

157 *icon-lamps . . . sputtering . . . in contact with the water*: the best explanation of this odd reference seems to be that Arina Petrovna resorted to an economy practised by poorer people: to get full benefit from the oil in an icon-lamp the oil was floated on a layer of water.

158 *Epiphany water*: in the Orthodox Church there is a blessing of water at Epiphany, and water then blessed is particularly cherished, being reckoned to retain its purity through the whole of the following year.

163 *Romny, Izyum, Kremenchug*: lesser towns in the Ukraine, within a 100–200 mile radius of Kharkov.

169 *'On the table that once groaned with food . . .'* . . . *'and pallid
death regards us all'*: further lines from Derzhavin's poem 'On
the Death of Prince Meshchersky' (see note to p. 23).

178 *Peter of Picardy* . . . *'Ode to Felitsa'*: Anninka's insubstantial
education touches superficially on history (Peter the Hermit who
preached the First Crusade), Greek mythology as interpreted by
Offenbach, and literature (Derzhavin's light-hearted 'Felitsa'
addressed to Catherine the Great, a well-known anthology poem).

Prince of Tauris: i.e. Prince Potemkin, the most celebrated of
Catherine the Great's favourites. She accorded him the title of
Prince of Tauris for the annexation of the Crimea (Tauris) which
took place in 1783 during his appointment as Governor of New
Russia. A book of anecdotes about Potemkin by S. N. Shubinsky,
published in 1867, was doubtless the source to which Anninka
had recourse.

La Grande-duchesse de Gérolstein: another of Offenbach's successful operettas, first performed in 1867.

199 *fifteen poods*: the pood was a pre-metric measurement of weight
used in Russia, equivalent to about 36 lb.

200 *ticket*: the 'ticket' to which the priest's wife naïvely refers is the
'yellow ticket', a document issued by the police to prostitutes in
nineteenth-century Russia.

206 *'See, the dashing troika speeds . . .'*: a line from a poem (known
also in a song variant) by F. N. Glinka.

'cultivated' class: Saltykov used this term (*kulturnye lydi*, lit.
'cultured people') frequently in his writings from the late 1860s
to designate the idly ineffectual landowning class now in post-
emancipation decline.

219 *'Assuage my sorrows'*: the name of a well-known icon of the
Virgin.

222 *'fear of the Jews'*: by which the actions of the disciples and
Joseph of Arimathaea were guided after the Crucifixion (John
19:38, 20:19): it is one of Saltykov's favourite biblical phrases.

226 *Anpetov . . . Utrobin*: these neighbours of the Golovlevs, mentioned here incidentally, appear elsewhere in *Well-Intentioned
Speeches*: Utrobin is a reactionary old-style landowner (here,
characteristically, siring offspring by his peasants), while
Anpetov is a 'progressive' (though here also, by implication, of
lax morals).

227 *saintly and apostolic Prince Vladimir*: St Vladimir, Prince of Kiev, who brought about the Christianization of Russia in 988 and was revered as 'equal to the apostles'.

241 *'Mother, sew not for me'*: a song by Varlamov.

244 *sarafans and kokoshniks*: sarafan: a long sleeveless dress; kokoshnik: an elaborate women's head-dress. Both would be worn by peasant-women as 'best' on festive occasions.

246 *Day of Remembrance*: one of a number of Saturdays observed annually by the Orthodox Church as days of remembrance for the dead.

253 *the Vladimir road*: the road east from Moscow to Vladimir, the first stage of the route followed by convict-convoys on their way to Siberia.

254 *protected wood*: here a specific term used of forest reserved by the state for growing timber (for ships, etc.); or, generally, of any forest intended for the production of high-quality timber.

  old desyatina: the *desyatina* (see note to p. 119) was variously measured at different times, the distinction here being between 'old' and 'new' variants, respectively of 3,600 and 2,400 square *sazhens* (*sazhen*=approximately 7 ft).

257 *thieve and trespass*: with the emancipation the peasants lost a number of rights—wood-gathering, grazing, etc.—which they had previously enjoyed on their masters' land. If they continued their old practices in the new times they were liable to pay fines for their impingements.

264 *Trinity Monastery*: see the note on Trinity-Sergius Monastery, p. 65.

272 *An Old-Time Colonel . . . La Fille de Madame Angot*: the first a popular vaudeville of the time, the second an operetta by A.-C. Lecocq, first performed in 1872.

273 *zemstvo*: the zemstvos were elected organs of local government instituted in 1864 with responsibilities at district and provincial level for schools, highways, public health, etc. Though hailed by the liberals as a significant first step towards representative government, the zemstvos were regarded by hard-headed contemporaries as ineffectual and little more than a talking-shop. Saltykov was generally unsympathetic towards them, as was Tolstoy (cf. Vronsky's enthusiasm and Levin's scepticism about zemstvo activities in *Anna Karenina*).

275 *Russian Romances on Stage*: a vaudeville by N. Kulikov (1877) based on songs by different composers.

 Minangois . . . Fulda: well-known establishments on Kuznetsky Most, the 'Bond Street' of pre-Revolutionary Moscow.

276 *Miloslavsky Xth*: the name of Anninka's admirer seems to have been inspired by the contemporary actor N. K. Miloslavsky (1811–82).

 head of the district: though Saltykov does not name him as such, the 'head of the district' is clearly the governor of the province. This indirect statement may be seen as one of Saltykov's 'aesopisms', the tactical device he cultivated in his writings to avoid trouble with the censors.

277 *the conflict with internal enemies*: i.e. the conflict with revolutionaries. Saltykov wrote this chapter in 1880 when the Russian government was struggling against radical agitation and terrorist activity (a year later Alexander II was assassinated). Provincial governors were closely involved in anti-revolutionary activity and at different times were accorded special powers by the government to combat it.

280 *Ugolino . . . Barkov*: Ugolino was a historical tragedy by N. A. Polevoy (1796–1846), historian, journalist, novelist, and playwright, a prominent literary figure in the 1830s. For Barkov, see note to p. 4: it can be safely assumed that his 'unpublished tragedy' is invented.

284 *'the less remote parts'*: the phrase is that used in the Russian Penal Code in respect of the relatively less severe form of exile— to the remoter provinces of European Russia or to western Siberia, as distinct from the 'remote parts', which meant eastern Siberia. Exile was a common form of punishment for all kinds of criminals; it could be with or without confinement in a penal institution.

292 *took off the clergy register*: i.e. on account of her illicit union with Porfiry deprived of the status and privileges of the clerical 'estate' to which she belonged as the daughter of a church functionary (see note to p. 114).

293 *'fresh people'*: an echo of the times when *The Golovlevs* was written. The reforms of the 1860s had thrown up a new generation of administrators, and many of Saltykov's sketches of the late 1860s and 1870s depicted these new men as cynical, self-seeking careerists, more notable for their suitable rhetoric

than any positive achievements. This whole section can be read as a summary of Saltykov's opinions on these new pillars of the official establishment.

296   *synodicon*: a family 'remembrance' book listing the names of dead (and living) kin and other dear ones. This list of names is customarily read at requiems and certain other services.